DUBLIN – THE DEPOSED CAPITAL

Sackville Street from the top of Nelson's Pillar 1911. (Irish Architectural Archive)

DUBLIN

THE DEPOSED CAPITAL

A Social and Economic History

1860 - 1914

MARY E. DALY

CORK UNIVERSITY PRESS
1985

For P.J.

First published 1984
This edition 1985
Cork University Press, Cork, Ireland

© Cork Univeristy Press

Daly, Mary E.
  Dublin: the deposed capital, a social
  and economic history, 1860-1914.
  1. Dublin (Ireland) — History
  1. Title
  941.8'35   DA995.D75

ISBN 0-902561-33-2

Printed by Reprint Ltd., Dublin.

TABLE OF CONTENTS

ABBREVIATIONS

CSO/RP.	Chief Secretary's Office, Registered Papers
Dly. Exp.	*Daily Express*
Dub. Build.	*Dublin Builder*
Dub. mun. co.	Dublin municipal council
E. Tel.	*Evening Telegraph*
F.J.	*Freeman's Journal*
Ir. Build.	*Irish Builder*
I.T.	*Irish Times*
M.H.	Mansion House
P.R.O.I.	Public Record Office of Ireland
Stat. Soc. Irl. jnl.	*Statistical and social inquiry society of Ireland*

ILLUSTRATIONS

Reproductions by courtesy of: —
    The National Library of Ireland
    The Royal Society of Antiquaries of Ireland
    The Irish Architectural Archive
    Arthur Guinness Son and Co.

Quotations from *Dublin made me* are reproduced courtesy of the author, Dr. C.S. Andrews.

ACKNOWLEDGEMENTS

My initial interest in the history of Dublin was prompted by coming to live in the city as an undergraduate. The mass of large Victorian houses in areas such as Rathmines raised questions as to their original inhabitants and this curiosity led me to embark on the study of post-famine Dublin as the topic of an M.A. thesis. This material lay dormant for some years until I was happily invited by Prof. David Harkness to contribute a paper on Dublin to the Irish conference of historians under the theme *The town in Ireland*. This current work, though incorporating much of my earlier research, reflects this re vived interest in the topic.

In the course of my research I have drawn on the assistance of a wide range of individuals to whom I now make somewhat belated acknowledgement. In particular I wish to thank Michael Bannon, Brenda Collins, the late Prof. K.H. Connell, W.H. Crawford, Prof. L.M. Cullen, David Dickson, Prof. R. Dudley Edwards, Max Hartwell, A.C. Hepburn, Colm Lincoln, Prof. Donal McCartney, R.A. McCarthy, Aidan Mulkeen, Cormac O Grada, Prof. K.B. Nowlan, Peter Walsh and Prof. T.D. Williams. Students who took my final year honours class, the Irish Victorian city acted as unwitting guinea pigs for much of this material and I am grateful for the stimulation they provided.

I owe an immense gratitude to the staff of various libraries and institutions which afforded access to essential source materials; the Public Record Office of Ireland, especially Ken Hannigan, and David Craig; State Paper Office Dublin Castle; material from both these archives is reproduced by kind permission of the Deputy-keeper of State Papers; Dublin Corporation archives, transformed beyond all recognition by the work of Mary Clark; Dublin Port and Docks Board; Pembroke estate office; registrar of births, marriages and deaths; National Library of Ireland and the library of University College Dublin.

The research for my M.A. was financed by a scholarship from Monaghan Co. Council to whom I make a very belated acknowledgement. Cork University Press generously agreed to publish the history of a larger, rival city. My thanks to the committee, and in particular to Prof. Joseph Lee and to Donal Counihan, secretary to the Press. The final debt is to my family. My children Paul and Elizabeth have coped admirably with my teaching and research commitments, while P.J. has sustained me through innumerable crises. I hope that the book's dedication in part repays my debt.

University College Dublin

Brady's Cottages off Francis Street. (Darkest Dublin Collection, Royal Society of Antiquaries of Ireland)

Chapter I

THE CAPITAL OF IRELAND

A recent writer on Edwardian Belfast debated whether that city should be regarded as British or Irish.[1] This seems an unlikely question to raise in the case of Dublin. Yet in some senses nineteenth century Dublin can be seen as having a somewhat confused position: the capital of Ireland, the centre of British rule for centuries, the entrepot for British trade and commercial influence and presumably the main centre for the diffusion of British culture in Ireland. During the nineteenth century the focus of power in Dublin shifted from the Protestant ascendancy as Catholics gradually took control of local politics, and to a lesser degree of the city's businesses and professions. Yet strong residues of the colonial capital remained, particularly in suburbs such as Rathmines and Pembroke, while the new Catholic middle class was frequently accused of having betrayed its origins, dismissed by phrases such as 'Castle Catholic', or D.P. Moran's vituperative 'West Briton'.[2]

Perhaps it is because of this ambiguity that the history of the city from the union to independence has received little attention, with the exception of an outburst of interest focussed on the 1913 lock-out and the 1916 rising; events which can be readily fitted into the nationalist canon. For a similar reason, late eighteenth century Dublin, the city of Grattan's parliament has always evoked some interest. Its nineteenth century successor, the deposed capital, a city bereft of its parliament, a backwater in Irish politics, has been relatively ignored. The identification in the Gaelic revival of Irishness with peasant culture also served to confuse attitudes towards the city. Urbanization and urban

1

problems fitted uneasily with the strongly rural ethos of the newly-independent Ireland.

The fact that nineteenth century Dublin lost out relative to other European cities may also be important. Stories of failure are less interesting than those of success. At the time of the union Dublin was easily the second largest city in the British Isles and among the ten largest cities in Europe. By 1860 she was merely fifth in the U.K. rankings and by the end of the century was to suffer the ultimate indignity of being overtaken by upstart Belfast as Ireland's largest city.[3] Estimates of Dublin's population suggest a figure of perhaps 62,000 in 1706 reaching 140,000 by 1760 and 182,000 for the year 1800. The annual percentage growth appears to have been substantially higher in the first half of the eighteenth century. After 1800, with the exception of the 1840s — the famine decade — the slowdown intensified. Annual population growth in the combined city and suburban area never returned to the levels of the early eighteenth century, though the early twentieth century figures suggest a demographic revival in advance of self-government.

In registering a population increase in the second half of the nineteenth century, if only on a low level, Dublin contrasted with Ireland as a whole, which experienced steady population decline. Its general demographic indicators differed from rural Ireland. Emigration from Dublin city and county was extremely low. In the decade 1881-91, 24,856 of a national emigrant total of 768,105 came from Dublin city and county, and a mere 9,487 Dubliners emigrated from a national total of 430,993 in the following decade.[4] The Dublin marriage and birth rates were considerably above the national levels; the higher birth rate reflecting both the higher marriage rate, and in later years, the greater fertility per married woman. In common with most nineteenth century cities, Dublin had a death-rate significantly above the rural level. In this respect the city was very unhealthy indeed, with a much higher death-rate than the worst English or Scottish cities.

Despite these divergences, Dublin was thoroughly integrated into the Irish economic and political system. The city filled a composite role as an administrative and professional centre, a port and commercial city with some

2

Table I Dublin Population, 1685-1911[5]

	City	%	Suburbs	%	Total	% (annual rate)
1685	45,000					
1706	62,000	1.79				
1725	92,000	2.1				
1744	112,000	1.0				
1760	140,000	1.4				
1778	154,000	0.5				
1800	182,000	0.8				
1821	224,000	1.0				
1831	232,362	0.37	32,954		265,316	
1841	232,726	0.01	48,480		281,206	
1851	258,369	1.1	59,468	2.27	317,837	1.42
1861	254,808	-0.14	70,323	1.78	325,131	0.25
1871	246,326	-0.33	83,410	1.86	329,736	0.14
1881	249,602	0.13	95,450	1.45	345,052	0.35
1891	245,001	-0.19	102.911	0.78	347,912	0.08
1901old	260,035	0.63				
1901 new*	290,638	0.82	90,854	0.86	381,492	0.87
1911	304,802	0.49	99,690	0.97	404,492	0.61

* The city boundaries changed in the year 1900.

Table II Marriage Rate per thousand, 1871-1911[6]

	Dublin North	Dublin South	Ireland
1871-80	7.2	8.1	4.5
1881-90	6.9	7.4	4.0
1891-1900	6.8	7.5	4.8
1901-11	7.0	7.2	5.1

Table III Birth rate per thousand, 1871-1911

	Dublin City	Suburbs	Reg. District[7]	Ireland
1871-81	31	24.5	29.5	26.2
1881-91	30.3	21.5	28.5	22.8
1891-1901	32.7	20.4	29.2	22.1
1901-11	31.5	18.5	28.6	22.4

Table IV Fertility per thousand married women, 15-44

	Dublin	Ireland
1870-2	267.4	307
1880-2	281.0	284
1890-2	296	287
1900-2	304	292
1910-2	315	305

Table V Birthplace population Dublin city

	Dublin City or Co.	%	Elsewhere	%
1841	170,142	73.11	62,584	26.89
1851	156,811	60.69	101,558	39.31
1861	168,691	66.20	86,117	33.80
1871	155,861	63.28	90,465	36.72
1881	153,332	61,44	96,228	38.56
1891	164,813	67.28	80,162	32.72
1901	193,451	66.57	97,145	33.43
1911	214,364	70.33	90,415	29.67

important manufacturing industries. A comparison of the city's spread of occupations, derived from the population censuses reveals a city much closer to London in the variety of its activities than to any English or Irish provincial city.[8] Like London, Dublin contained a high proportion of servants and professional residents, suggesting that despite the loss of her parliament she retained many of the functions of a capital city. The Irish administration was centred in Dublin, and despite the Union many functions were carried out there, rather than in Whitehall. The expansion of government activity, the emergence of new institutions, such as the Local Government Board, or the Department of Agriculture, meant a steady rise in the numbers employed in government administration. By 1911, 3,526 persons were employed in central and local government, more than ten times the number in 1841. Dublin was also a traditional legal and medical centre, though law was not among the expanding occupations in the late nineteenth century. In medicine the city was dominated by a mass of small hospitals established to cater for various religious and charitable groups, and there was a similar profusion of medical schools. Doctor-patient ratios were considerably more generous than in English hospitals, while hospital beds were plentiful.[9] These hospitals catered not simply for local residents, but for a large number of rural patients, many from a considerable distance.

By the mid-nineteenth century Dublin University was one of the largest universities in the British Isles, with a total of 1,500 students, compared to 1,300 at Oxford.[10] There was no significant expansion for the remainder of the century, largely due to sectarian tensions which deterred the expanding Catholic middle-class from attending, but other university institutions emerged, such as the Catholic University and the Royal, with its related colleges. All these institutions catered for a national demand.

In matters of business and commerce Dublin remained the Irish capital, though Belfast became an increasingly autonomous centre serving the province of Ulster. Dublin was the largest centre of Irish banking, provided the Irish headquarters for British insurance companies and a comparatively active stock exchange plus the headquarters of major Irish railway companies, though in all cases links with London were prominent.

The overall trends in the city's occupational structure in the years 1841-1911, are broadly similar to those for the Irish economy as a whole. Charles Booth, in a examination of Irish occupational patterns in the late nineteenth century, noted the decline in manufacturing employment and the expansion of non-productive sectors such as transport, dealing, domestic service and general labouring.[11] Broadly speaking, these trends are also found in Dublin. The decline in manufacturing employment from 33.4% of the male workforce in 1841 to 20.4% in 1911 and its changing composition will be examined in some detail in the following chapter, but the overall coincidence of national and local trends suggests that many of the factors responsible pertain to the Irish economy as a whole, rather than to the city alone.

The establishment in the early nineteenth century of a free trade area between Britain and Ireland, combined with the emergence of a steamship and railways served to open the Irish economy to a substantial measure of competition. It also apparently led to a considerable increase in resources

5

devoted to transport. Only 2.97% of Dublin male workers were employed in transport in 1841 compared with 15.4% by 1911 and it seems probable that many of the city's general labourers were also attached, if only on a part-time basis, to the transport sector. Dublin was a major centre for both internal and external transport activities. Given the dependence on Britain as a source of imports and major destination for exports, Dublin, as an east-coast port, directly facing Liverpool, was ideally located for this role. The fact that the major Irish railway lines, with the exception of the Ulster lines, radiated from the city, reinforced this function.

The port of Dublin was of long-standing importance and was a key factor in the founding of the city. However its share of national tonnage invoiced fell from over half the Irish total for most of the eighteenth century, to 40% by the closing decade.[12] The early decades of the nineteenth century also showed a slow growth rate and a declining share of the national trade.[13] This may have reflected the city's lack of involvement in the expanding provision trade, or defects in port facilities. The depth of channel was relatively poor, and berths were situated mainly on the southern banks of the river. Berths on the northern banks, though in strong demand, were in short supply until 1821 when St. George's Docks were opened.[14]

The subsequent trade of the port was boosted by the steamship. In 1816 the first steamships were introduced.[15] By 1860 the overwhelming majority of cross-channel shipping was carried by steam, though both coal and overseas cargo was still carried by sail. The first steam colliers did not appear until 1880, while a majority of overseas shipping was not carried by steam until 1883.[16]

The Irish shipping fleet has been weak throughout the eighteenth century and much of the country's trade was carried by outsiders.[17] By 1851 Dublin registered shipping amounted to a mere 377 ships with a total tonnage of 34,407. The majority of vessels were sailing colliers. By the early twentieth century the number of ships has fallen but their average size had increased and several Irish-owned steamship companies had emerged. The largest of these, the City of Dublin Co. owner of eight steamers and four mail boats operated the mail contract across the Irish Sea.[18]

6

The dominant activity in the port was cross-channel shipping, reinforcing the links with the British economy. In 1860 overseas shipping accounted for only 12.6% of registered tonnage using Dublin port, though by 1910 this had risen to 23%, mostly consisting of bulk cargoes such as grain and timber.[19] Some of the city's commercial elements resented the dominance of the cross-channel trade. In 1855 the Dublin Chamber of Commerce stated that[20]

> the true interest of the merchant of Dublin is direct trade . . . . . . the first consideration should be the extent of the capabilities and conveniences of the port which at present were quite unequal to the essential requirements of improved foreign trade.

Further provisions for deep-sea berths were made by the Dublin Port and Docks Board which took over control of the port in 1867.[21] A substantial proportion of the North Wall extension undertaken in the 1870s was allocated for overseas use, while the early twentieth century brought the beginnings of another new deep-water dock at Alexandra Basin.[22] Despite these investments Dublin singularly failed to develop a significant deep-sea trade and the return on capital invested in berths and quay space for overseas shipping was low.[23] Part of the relative failure may be attributed to the dominance of the cross-channel steamship interests on the Board. They were exceptionally hostile to a proposed deep-water oil terminal in the port. However the failure to develop an extensive overseas trade, as in Liverpool or Southampton also reflects the changing scale of the international shipping industry — a scale with which both the port of Dublin, and the Irish economy were unable to cope. One grain trader complained in 1914 that[24]

> the whole tendency of trade seems to be in favour of large steamers and we are continually receiving offers of steamers . . . . . . In several cases we have had to arrange for large steamers to come to Dublin with only half cargo; we have been unable to purchase these vessels as whole cargo.

Goodbody's, the Clara jute processing firm had imported jute directly from India when ships' cargoes had amounted to 2-3,000 bales. When average cargoes increased to 40,000 bales the quantity proved beyond their capacity and they

7

were forced to take partial shipments from London or Dundee.[25] The tendency to tranship certain goods meant a loss of profit to Dublin commercial interests. By the early twentieth century imported fruit such as oranges was sent to the West of Ireland directly from Liverpool without any handling by Dublin merchants.[26] The integration of rail and shipping services was central to the success of cross-channel interests, and the building of connecting links between port and rail was one of the key commercial problems of the 1860s and 1870s. By 1855 Dublin was in direct rail communication with Belfast, Cork and Galway and the city contained five major railway stations. These were located on the periphery of the city, without any interstation connections. Transfer of goods from rail to port involved costly cartage through the city streets. This problem persisted for some decades. In 1867, W.T. Mulvany, the Ruhr mining entrepreneur remarked[27]

> of the railway systems which come into Dublin none of them go down to the harbour, they approach it, but they are not connected with the harbour or the shipping. The Midland Railway within the last two years has done what was proposed to be done very nearly eighteen years ago, to connect itself with the harbour and that is the only exception, the difficulty of passing from one system to another still remains.

The question was inextricably bound up with shipping rivalry on the Irish Sea, in particular with competition for the mail contract, and for control of the lucrative cattle export trade. Since 1850 the mail contract had been held by the City of Dublin Steam Packet Co. who operated services between Holyhead and Kingstown,[28] but the London and North Western Railway who operated from Holyhead to Dublin's North Wall were anxious competitors.[29] Cattle were the most rapidly expanding sector of Irish agriculture and proved to be a key cargo for both shipping and railway companies. The powerful London and North Western Co. who controlled cross-channel steamships in addition to the railway line from Holyhead to London tried to secure a virtual monopoly of cattle exports by proposing to build a cattle market at the North Wall. This scheme however was thwarted by the joint action of Dublin corporation and the city's cattle masters.[30]

8

The Irish-controlled City of Dublin Co. remained the dominant cattle shipper with nine cattle boats in 1875 compared with the Dublin and Glasgow Co.'s five, London and North West, four, and two owned by the shipping and coal importing firm of Tedcastle's. On average seven cattle ships left Dublin daily for Holyhead, Liverpool, and Glasgow with extra sailings during the peak months from September to March.[31]

In 1864 the Dublin Trunk Connecting Line, whose directors included William Thomas Mulvany received parliamentary approval for their proposed railway link. This provided for a line from the Dublin Kingstown route, running under the Liffey, to the east of the city, connecting with Amiens St. station and the Midland Great Western Railway's line. They also proposed to build an abbattoir at the docks. This scheme collapsed during the 1867 financial crisis, when it was discovered that 'not one-half of the shares were held by solvent or bona fide persons'.[32] However the Midland and Great Western Railway built a link from their railway to the port which served to consolidate their strong dominance in the cattle export trade.

The debacle of the Trunk Connecting Line led to the emergence of a new series of proposals. The elaborate and highly destructive plans for a line running through the centre of the city, first mooted and dismissed in the early 'sixties re-emerged. The original scheme, the Dublin Metropolitan Railway had proposed an overland line from Westland Row, terminus of the Dublin Kingstown line, to Kingsbridge station headquarters of the Great Southern and Western Railway Co. requiring the building of 33 bridges over major city streets, the displacement of 5,619 persons, the disfigurement of the grounds of Trinity College and a central station beside the old Parliament house in College Green.[33] Vociferous opposition, some of it in verse, killed this proposal, but variants re-appeared in the financial euphoria of the early 'seventies. The London and North Western Co. attempted to gain control by offering a bonus rent of £20,000 in addition to normal commercial tolls.[34] Opponents of this proposal included Liverpool businessmen who feared that it might channel trade to Holyhead. Leading Dublin businessmen such as Messrs. Pim and Roe and Dublin

9

corporation, united to favour the new proposal of Mr. Barry, the genius behind the abortive Dublin Metropolitan line.[35] The revised plans involved removing the central railway station to a more elaborate location — across the bed of the river Liffey. As the station alone was estimated to cost £600,000, its ultimate failure was not surprising.[36]

The connecting railways which were ultimately built were more modest and less destructive schemes running through the northern and western outskirts of the city. The London and North Western Railway, and the Great Southern and Western Railway developed a line which linked all major stations, except the south-side stations of Westland Row and Harcourt St. with the North Wall docks.[37] The final link between Westland Row and the other lines, though first mooted in 1878 was not actually built until the 1890s.[38]

The coming of the railways led to a major expansion of Dublin port. In 1841 inward and outward tonnage was 592,938 tons; by 1850 this had reached 749,000 tons and had risen to over 900,000 tons by 1856. In 1860 the figure of one million tons was surpassed and by 1878 tonnage had passed the two million level. Dublin's growth outstripped other Irish ports in the immediate post-famine decades, in contrast to her performance in the late eighteenth and early nineteenth century. From the mid 'fifties to the mid 'seventies, Dublin outstripped not only Cork and Belfast in its percentage growth, but also the major British ports of Glasgow and Liverpool-Birkenhead. By 1875 Dublin was not only Ireland's largest port, but the fifth largest in the U.K..[39] Much of this expansion reflects the buoyancy of the Irish economy in the post-famine decades and the growth of trade and imports resulting from the railways. However it seems probable that Dublin's favoured location as major railway terminal and port for the main cross-channel shipping lines, resulted in some diversion of trade in her favour.

It is considerably more difficult to interpret the shipping trends in the closing decades of the nineteenth century, as a complicated series of stratagems by the cross-channel steamship companies resulted in recalculations of net tonnage at a lower level.[40] In other words, reduced levels of net tonnage in the 1880s may indicate a declining volume of trade, or they may simply disguise what was in fact an increase. The best indications are that the volume of port business fell in the recession of the late 1870s and early 1880s, and that subsequent growth was at a much lower rate, though there was undoubted expansion around the turn of the century. The records of the Port and Docks Board reveal considerable complaints of overcrowding and demands for more space by the shipping companies in the mid 1870s.[41] Yet, despite the total cessation of port extension schemes after 1880, there are no complaints of crowding, and no evidence of pressure on berths until 1910. The closing decades of the nineteenth century are marked by a decline in Dublin's relative ranking as a port. By 1889 Belfast had grown decisively to become Ireland's largest port.[42] By 1907 Dublin was the twelfth port in the U.K., Belfast was ranked ninth and Dublin's growth rate had been exceeded by both Belfast and Cork.[43] The major commodities handled by the port of Dublin were agricultural. Cattle, sheep, pigs and porter constituted the major exports; coal, and flour and wheat the most readily identifiable imports. The figures suggest that Dublin controlled an increasing share of the major agricultural exports of the country,[44] while as early as the first decade of the nineteenth century Dublin exported over 90% of Irish beer. This picture of apparently poor growth in the final quarter of the nineteenth century, coupled with rising shares of exports, suggests that the slower growth of the port was due, not to factors under its direct control, but to the performance of Dublin's industry and of Irish agriculture. The expansion of the port of Belfast reflected its comparative independence from the fortunes of Irish agriculture and the strength of its industrial hinterland.

Irish agriculture failed to act as a stimulus for long-term growth in the non-agricultural economy. Agricultural output grew most rapidly in the decades immediately following the famine when cattle farming, in particular, expanded under the stimulus of steadily rising prices. From the late 1870s the growth of total output was slow, though as the labour force contracted output was maintained and even rose slightly, so that output per head increased. A falling labour force, even if compensated by rising productivity per worker did not imply a buoyant consumer market. The shift from tillage to cattle farming marked a transition to a type of agriculture which required few inputs in the form of fertiliser, or machinery, while the final product tended to be exported live from Ireland, generating little employment with the exception of cattle drovers. The decline of landlord incomes following the land war and the gradual emergence of peasant proprietorship meant a redistribution of resources from a class with high consumption of luxury products — many of them items of traditional Dublin manufacture, to one with a high propensity to save.

Table VI
Net Registered Tonnage Dublin Port

Decadal average	Overseas	Coasting and Cross channel total	
1860-69	153,874	1,260,929	1,414,803
1870-79	288,349	1,476,322	1,764,671
1880-89	277,933	1,473,146	1,751,079
1890-99	286,100	1,509,283	1,795,383
1900-09	361,171	1,630,104	1,991,276
1910-14	356,377	1,641,280	1,997,657

Table VII Major Commodities

	1860s	1870s	1880s	1890s	1900s	1910-14
Porter hhds.	225,250	329,505	382,030	412,079	494,869	592,488
		+47%	+16%	+8%	+20%	+19.7%
Wheat tons	100,075	160,182	125,320	89,895	99,621	118,637
		+60%	-21.7%	-28.3%	+10.9%	+19.1%
Flour sacks	78,108	98,713	156,080	492,919	388,176	383,096
		+26.4%	+58.6%	+215%	-23.3%	-1.8%
Cattle	168,517	197,957	234,023	276,583	316,396	286,879
		+17.5%	+18.2%	+18.16%	+14.45%	-9.32%
Sheep	179,643	240,204	250,045	412,753	394,224	261,592
		+33.8%	+4.1%	+65%	-4.5%	-33.6%
Pigs	148,134	150,906	181,998	260,548	251,091	
		+1.8%	+20.6%	+43%	-3.6%	
Coal imports	636,029	735,587	908,623	1,014,508	1,1145,084	122,780
		+15.6	+23.5%	+10.67%	+12.9%	+6.78%

Much of the relatively unspectacular market of rural Ireland was supplied by imported goods, and these goods were increasingly supplied by British rather than Irish merchants.[45] The intricate relationships which existed

12

between British and Irish railway companies, and the rail involvement in cross-channel shipping brought about the emergence of through rates for goods from British cities to provincial Irish towns, rates which were invariably less than the sum of local rates. Complaints that these rates discriminated against Irish business were frequent, and the position is admirably summarised by the *Select Committee on Railway Rates*[46]

> the witnesses from Ireland . . . . made several special complaints. They allege that the rates charged for local traffic are generally higher than on the English railways, as to agricultural produce and implements; that these local rates are high, out of all proportion as compared with those on through traffic between stations in England and stations in Ireland, to the great injury of the Dublin wholesale houses; that by action of the Irish and English Traffic Conference, including lines of steamers, a complete monopoly has been established, the rates from Liverpool to Dublin by sea being kept up to those via Holyhead. In fact, that by means of their control of the through traffic the great railway companies are enabled to prevent independent steamers from carrying at the rates which competition would naturally bring.

Allegations are voluminous, as is evidence concerning railway charges for eggs, bedsteads, fertiliser and innumerable other commodities between different Irish locations. The evidence suggests that in many instances British traders negotiated extremely favourable through rates which militated against Irish producers. However this reflected the fact that they were large customers who were capable of negotiating on an equal footing with rail and shipping companies. This was also the case for the small number of large Irish companies which existed. It was alleged that Guinness's brewery had achieved such favourable rail rates that they could undercut Cork brewers in the Kerry market,[47] while Goodbody's, the Clara jute manufacturers succeeded in having the transport cost of jute reduced from 7/- per ton, to 4/3 per ton, against a possible maximum charge of 16/4 per ton, by threatening to close their plant.[48] The structure of through rates may have injured some smaller Dublin firms.

Soap manufacturer James Crean was among those who alleged that unfavourable charges for small quantities had prevented him from developing sales in the Cork area.[49]

Despite allegations to the contrary, cross-channel shipping rates were extremely competitive with a total of forty-one sailings daily between Britain and Ireland, and 83 or 84 cross-channel sailings per week from Dublin.[50] Shipping rates were fixed by a conference with the London and North Western Company allegedly the market leader[51] but the Dublin Chamber of Commerce suggested that to deter the emergence of outside competition shipping margins were pared to the bone, and this was compensated by high rail charges.[52] Many non-Dubliners, especially Cork businessmen alleged that the system of rates 'diverted traffic via Dublin port',[53] while the absence of through rates for cattle from Cork diverted cattle shipments to both Dublin and Waterford.[54] The rates structure appears to have favoured Dublin port, though not necessarily the city's importers and distributors who alleged that they were undercut in the rural drapery trade by the cheap through rates granted to Manchester distributors.[55]

The one documented instance where transport companies attempted to channel business away from Dublin was successfully challenged in the courts by the Dublin Port and Docks Board.[56] The Great Southern and Western Railway, which had previously only operated a Dublin-Cork route with branch lines to the west, gained control in partnership with the English Great Western Railway, of the small railway lines running east of Cork towards Waterford and Rosslare.[57] The Great Western Railway opened the Fishguard Rosslare shipping route and the Great Southern line began to feed trade through Rosslare and Waterford rather than Dublin by granting rebates on freight charges, a practice prohibited by the courts.[58] The London and North Western Company advanced £100,000 to the Dublin and South-Eastern line to channel business from the Wicklow Wexford area which might have been shipped through Rosslare to Dublin. This was not subjected to legal contest.[59]

The examination of Dublin's trade suggests the extent to which it was dominated by cross-channel transport interests, notably the steamship companies and allied railways. While these interests would seem to have comparatively favoured

14

the port of Dublin the evidence suggests that their influence was not wholly beneficial to the city's economy. Dublin corporation, a body which was increasingly nationalist in its composition, made successive efforts to reduce the degree of shippers' control over the Port and Docks Board. In 1879 the steamship companies controlled 101 of the 197 votes for the Board, while 14 of the 25 Board members were directors of steamship or railway companies.[60] An alliance between Dublin corporation and the Dublin Chamber of Commerce eventually resulted in a reform of the electorate in 1898,[61] though with no obvious long-term effect on overall port policy.[62]

The lack of dynamism from the rural Irish economy and the failure of Dublin businesses to manufacture, and, in some cases, even to distribute the manufactured goods which rural Ireland needed, plus the apparent stagnation of the port in the third quarter of the nineteenth century all meant that Dublin failed to provide adequate employment, either for the indigenous Dublin population or for even a small proportion of the surplus population of rural Ireland. The percentage of the Dublin workforce employed in transport was less than in cities such as Cardiff or London.[63]

Irish cities, with the exception of Belfast, are notable in the late nineteenth and early twentieth centuries for the high proportion of male workers describing themselves as 'general labourers'. Labourers accounted for almost one-fifth of the Dublin male workforce in 1911 and for over one-fifth of the Cork workforce in 1901.[64] In both cities the proportion of general labourers, compared with British cities may indicate some difficulty which Irish workers faced when confronted with census forms, but it is more likely to suggest a workforce which drifted through a variety of occupations with no clear industrial affinity. Evidence suggests that Dublin labourers derived their existence from transport, building and some occasional agricultural work as the situation offered. At a time when the status of 'unemployed' was still relatively unknown, and when state support for the unemployed was available through the workhouse, it seems probable that the ranks of the general labourers concealed many who were either under-employed or unemployed. In turn this depressed labourers wages and left many on subsistence living standards. The labouring population constituted the hard-core of the Dublin tenement problem, were dispro-portionately represented among tuberculosis victims while their children were those most likely to die in early child-hood.

Given these unpromising conditions it is not surprising that Dublin failed to attract many of the millions who left rural Ireland in the post-famine decades. The percentage of migrants in the city's population peaked in 1851 and was not markedly higher in 1911 than in 1841. A total migrant population of 97,145 in the city in 1901, the highest ab-solute figure reached, is insignificant in the context of a national emigration outflow of 430,993 in the previous decade. Crude calculations of the flow of city-ward migration suggest that it was generally less than 10% of Irish emigration. The pattern of migration also suggests that the peaks of movement to the city reflect an emergency rather than a calculated choice. In 1851 the percentage of migrants reached a record level, almost 40% of the total population, many of them starving famine victims in search of short-term relief. The substantially lower proportion in 1861 suggests that many had left by that date, presumably emigrating when resources permitted. A second, lesser peak, occurs in 1881, again a year of acute distress in rural Ireland and a time of recession in Britain which followed a cut-back in emigration to the U.K. The city's workhouses were thronged with tramps from rural Ireland, mostly Leinster, while the year was marked by considerable distress for the city's indigenous population.

In contrast to those who arrived in emergency years, the long-term migrants tended to be employed in relatively secure, sometimes even privileged occupations as servants, shop assistants, policemen or civil servants. The proportion of migrants in the middle-class suburbs exceeded that in the more working-class city centre; 23% of migrants, mostly in the elite public service and business positions, were born outside Ireland, indicating Dublin's position as a colonial city where many of the most privileged occupations were filled by outsiders.

Dublin's economic malaise gave rise to political discontent. As early as the 1820s the city's artisan class attributed economic distress to the Act of Union, an argument force-fully put by Daniel O Connell in his Repeal campaign.[65] O Connell used his capture of the position of Lord Mayor in the newly-reformed Dublin corporation as the basis for launching his repeal movement. The evils of British rule become a regular theme in the increasingly-nationalist cor-poration, a convenient scapegoat for a body which proved singularly unsuccessful in tackling the city's numerous health and sanitation problems. Discontent with British rule was not common to all Dublin's citizenry. The prosperous Protestant middle-class, rather than fight this issue in the cockpit of municipal politics withdrew to their comfortable middle-class suburbs where they pursued separate interests and separate development. The alienation of the Protestant community from the political process, and the slow erosion of their positions of economic and social privilege mirror changes which took place at this time within Ireland as a whole, while the rise of religious tensions, and the intrusion of religious interests into politics, particularly during the reign of Cardinal Cullen, are themes common to both local and national history. While sectarian tensions in Dublin were expressed in places such as the City Hall rather than in street rioting as in Belfast, they were nonetheless acrimonious.

The story of Dublin therefore provides insights into various key aspects of late nineteenth century Irish history. It affords an opportunity to examine the impact of British rule in an urban context. Finally it affords an opportunity to examine the complex interaction of social, economic and political forces at a critical period in the history of Ireland's major city.

Table VIII Occupational Structure City of Dublin 1841-1911

	1841	1851	1861	1871	1881	1891	1901	1911
Agriculture M	2.55	2.41	2.57	2.29	2.31	1.75	2.14	2.41
F	—	—	—	—	—	—	—	—
M and F	1.57	1.47	1.61	1.45	1.49	1.2	1.46	1.75
Transport M	2.97	9.19	11.74	14.6	12.39	14.3	14.98	15.46
F								0.38
M and F	1.78	5.54	7.08	10.6	7.75	9.2	9.83	10.73
Domestic Service M	8.75	7.19	6.22	4.6	4.27	4.39	3.39	3.66
F	50.37	50.49	45.3	44.7	50.48	45.75	44.2	38.7
M and F	25.49	24.6	22.0	20.04	21.96	19.4	17.6	14.66
Building M	8.16	7.51	7.28	8.36	10.65	10.15	11.76	9.78
M and F	4.9	4.49	4.34	5.14	6.59	6.48	7.67	6.72
Industrial Service I M	5.4	3.66	4.18	4.18	4.54	5.54	7.07	6.33
F	—	—	—	—	—	0.5	1.91	4.4
M and F General	3.23	2.19	2.5	2.64	2.85	3.72	5.27	5.72
Labour M	16.3	20.56	17.08	17.2	17.97	17.79	17.47	19.5
M and F	10.19	12.38	10.52	10.64	11.22	11.51	11.4	13.4
Dealing M	12.46	13.04	13.71	15.25	14.65	14.16	13.87	12.9
F	11.82	10.4	16.2	14.22	12.38	13.72	15.18	13.9
M and F	12.2	11.98	14.72	14.85	13.79	14.0	14.3	13.2
Manufacture M	33.4	28.5	27.2	25.2	23.9	22.8	20.95	20.4
F	34.4	34.4	35.7	35.8	32.24	34.5	31.23	31.73
M and F	33.8	30.9	30.6	29.3	27.1	27.1	24.5	24
Professional M	8.43	7.72	11.04	12.58	12.8	11.8	12.37	9.16
F	2.92	3.3	3.8	4.06	3.8	5.97	6.53	10.00
M and F	6.17	5.95	8.19	9.39	9.45	9.7	10.75	10.6

Table IX

London 1861 and 1891. Selected occupations as % of total occupied

	1861		1891	
	M.	F.	M.	F.
Professional Adm. etc	9.74	7.46	8.53	7.31
Personal Service	5.29	55.4	5.77	34.1
Transport	15.64	—	17.3	—
Building	9.69	—	9.17	—
Retail and Distribution	11.63	3.54	11.19	4.15
Manufacturing	33.1	32.6	29.05	32.4
Labouring	6.8	—	7.31	—

Calculated from figures in Gareth Stedman-Jones, *Outcast London* (Oxford 1971) Appendix.

Chapter II

DUBLIN MANUFACTURING INDUSTRY

The story of Dublin industry from the famine to the 1930s[1] is marked by a decline in many long-established luxury crafts, a failure of the clothing industry to adapt to modern methods, the comparative success of printing and metal and engineering, and the sharp increase in numbers employed in food and drink which was mainly attributable to the success of the brewing industry.

Dublin was not unique in experiencing a fall in industrial employment at the apparent peak of the industrial revolution. London and Edinburgh also show a decline, though at a lesser pace,[2] and London shares many of Dublin's characteristics: notably a declining clothing industry and rising print industry. Cork too experienced a fall in its industrial employment of an equally significant scale.[3]

Much of the Dublin area's industry was situated outside the city boundaries. The traditional location was to the west of the city to take advantage of the water power of the rivers Liffey and Dodder and their tributaries. A report on the city's water supply in 1854 stated[4]

> The principal seat of manufacturing about the Metropolis is between Old Bawn and Dublin. Here we have calico printing, iron manufacture, cotton spinning, cutlery, paper making, cloth making as well as saw mills, flour mills, oil mills etc.

The water power was not satisfactory and in many cases was supplemented by steam.

> The present water power is quite irregular — mills are not only silent about one-third of the day, but each mill-owner is dependent on those above him, for when

he lets down his sluice to refill his pond, he immediately cuts off the water of all below.

Another report produced in the same year noted the existence of twenty-four water powered plants on the Liffey and adjoining courses. Four were paper mills, eleven flour mills, the remainder were saw mills, textile plants or were engaged in metal working.[5] With the spread of steam power the importance of river-side locations declined, but as late as 1879 a total of forty-five plants existed along the Liffey and neighbouring rivers. The other traditional industrial area was Ringsend, to the south of the city at the mouth of the river Liffey. It owed its existence to the poor state of Dublin port in the eighteenth century and was the location of salt works, boat builders, foundries and glass works, many using imported coal.

During the nineteenth century the area directly to the west of the city which had traditional importance in textiles developed further industrial strength with the establishment by the Great Southern and Western Railway Company of Dublin's largest engineering works at Inchicore in Kilmainham township.

All these industries must be regarded as part of the Dublin industrial structure. This is particularly true of those located at Ringsend and Inchicore which directly adjoined the city. An examination of employment in Co. Dublin in 1861 reveals a total of 4,816 men and 4,484 women engaged in manufacturing industry, the majority in the county rather than in the suburbs. Industrial employment in county Dublin declined in both 1871 and 1881 to 4,568 for men and 3,875 for women but recovered by 1891 to 4,795 for men and 4,187 for women indicating that the experience of firms situated outside the city may have been somewhat more favourable than those within the city. The structure of county Dublin's industry differed somewhat from that in the city proper. Female employment was concentrated in textiles, dress and paper. For men, paper was also important as was metal and engineering. The glass works at Ringsend with its somewhat erratic fortunes is also worthy of mention.

Within the city industry tended to concentrate in the south-western area which had access to water power. A report on Smoke Nuisances compiled in 1864 can be taken as indicating the location and variety of factories using steam power.[6]

Variety of factories using steam power[6]

	Total	A	B	C	D
Metal Works	31	15	1	1	14
Brewing & malting	19	16		1	2
Distilling	7	6			1
Corn & flour	5	1	3	1	
Printing	11	4	7		
Chemicals	12	6	5	1	
Coffee mill	1	1			
Saw mill	7	2	3	2	
Animal products	12	8	2	2	
Bakery & biscuits	11	11			
Paper	2	2			
Textiles	1	1			
Bottles	1				

There is a high degree of locational specialisation. Brewing was primarily concentrated in the James St. area, baking in the Camden St., Peter St. area, printing in the area beside Dame St. and metal working north of the Liffey in the region of Blackhall Place. Gas-works, chemical, fertiliser and vitriol plants tended to be located in the vicinity of the river Liffey. Workshops and plants not using steam power were equally specialised in their locations. The traditional centre of the city's silk trade was the Liberties, while on the north bank of the river Liffey, the Liffey St. area was the traditional centre of cabinetry. The dressmaking and millinery trade was found throughout the centre city with a special concentration of workshops in the vicinity of Grafton St., Dawson St. and Henry St.[7] Some shifts took place in this pattern during the later nineteenth century. Slum clearance and re-building, combined with a decline in traditional industries led to the virtual disappearance of industrial areas such as the Liberties or Liffey St.. Blackhall Place, centre of the metal working trades also declined and was subjected to redevelopment during the closing decades of the century. The traditional James St.—Thomas St. area retained its industrial importance, though many of the industrial concerns disappeared their sites were absorbed by the rapid expansion of Guinness' brewery.

The only major area of new industrial growth was in the vicinity of the docks, especially the North Wall. This newly cleared slobland gradually attracted a number of industrial concerns, many relying on imported materials such as timber works, or fertiliser plants. Unlike cities such as London however, there was no forced displacement of industry by commercial buildings, and site values, though more expensive than on virgin suburban land did not force firms to re-locate away from the city centre.

The most publicised area of industrial success was the city's brewing industry. This story revolves mainly around the fortunes of Guinness's brewery, but it is important to take account of the trend in the industry as a whole. As early as 1810 Guinness had become the largest brewery in Dublin and after 1833 it superseded the Cork-based Beamish and Crawford as the leading Irish brewery.[8] The 1864 list of factories records eight breweries in the city: Mr. D'Arcy of Usher St; Charles Brennan, 67 Watling St., P.J. Sweetman, Francis St., Fortune and Co., Golden Lane, Guinness's of James' Gate; Manders, James Gate; Mr. Caffrey Summer St. and Mr. Watkins, Ardee St. During the 1860s two new breweries were established, the Greenmount Brewery, outside the city and the City of Dublin Brewery at Blackpitts, close to the traditional brewing area.

The optimism indicated by the founding of new firms was apparently justified by market growth. Exports of Dublin beer rose from 90,000 hogsheads in 1855 to 258,000 in 1868 and the benefits of these rising exports were not exclusive to Guinness; exports of some competitors rose even faster.[10] Sales of Guinness within the rest of Ireland also rose sharply from 17,000 hogsheads in 1855 to 230,000 by 1880. As early as 1864 over half the beer sold in Ireland outside Dublin was Guinness.[11] Some of this growth undoubtedly reflects an expanding market in a more prosperous rural Ireland, combined with a shift from spirits to beer in response to Gladstone's penal spirits taxation, but despite the claim that 'it does not appear that Guinness took trade from other breweries'[12], this seems somewhat implausible.

Within Dublin the main emphasis was on increasing Guinness's share of the city market. The Dublin brewing trade operated a system of price regulation which removed the possibilities of price competition. However by the 1860s Guinness effectively controlled this agreement and used their powers to cut prices. In 1868 the long-established Manders brewery left the price agreement[13] presumably because of the pressure which Guinness was putting on their margins. They were obviously facing economic difficulties and failed to capitalise on the growing export market of the 1860s. In 1883 they were declared bankrupt.[14] By the late 1880s, the North Anne St. brewery had absorbed several older firms, such as Jameson Pim and Co.,[15] while the long-established Sweetman's brewery was demolished by Lord Iveagh, the Guinness chairman in 1900 to make way for an old clothes market.[16] In 1895, no doubt in a further effort to escape Guinness's competitive clutches, Charles Brennan, proprietor of the Anchor brewery built an ale plant.[17] Within ten years however the brewery was declared bankrupt,[18] while the year 1904 saw Joseph Watkins and Jameson Pim merging.[19]

The impression is thus of a successful giant, Guinness's, whose success threatened the very existence of competitors. The second largest plant described by Alfred Barnard in 1886, D'Arcy's Anchor Brewery, produced a total of 250,000 barrels. In 1881 Guinness had produced one million barrels and output had steadily increased after that date. The output of the other city breweries does not seem to have exceeded 100,000 barrels.[20]

The key years in the growth of Guinness were the immediate post-famine decades. This can be traced by the brewery's physical expansion and rising profits. In 1860 Guinness occupied four acres on the south side of James St. and Thomas St. but was short of space, so adjoining property was bought. In 1873 a massive area between James St. and the river Liffey was acquired.[21] New machinery was introduced during the 1860's which mechanised processes previously carried out by hand.[22] Between 1870 and 1878 the brewery was completely reconstructed. This investment resulted in a dramatic increase in production. Output doubled between 1868 and 1876,[23] and again between 1879 and 1886.[24] Between 1868 and 1879 average investment was £68,000 per annum, mostly net investment.[25] During the course of this expansion the rate of profit was reduced, as margins were slimmed down, but the overall profit level rose substantially. In 1869 the value of the brewery was estimated at £80,000; by 1879 this had risen sharply to £500,000[26] while at its Stock Exchange launch in 1886 the company was valued at £5m. and the shares were rapidly at a premium.

The significance of Guinness's success in terms of employment merits some attention. The figures returned in the Census for brewing workers are certainly too low, many brewery workers apparently returning themselves as labourers, draymen of porters. The 1895 Factory Returns for brewing, distilling, maltsters and bottlers are substantially in excess of the Census totals for these occupations[27] but unfortunately it is impossible to disentangle the brewing component of the total. The best indications for overall employment in brewing are the figures given by Barnard for 1886.[28] He recorded employment of 300 in the Anchor Brewery, 175 in North Anne St brewery of Jameson Pim and Co, 120 in the Mountjoy Brewery and 2,650 workers in Guinness's including clerks. It is possible that the figures for other breweries also include clerks. In 1871 Guinness had employed, 130 coopers, 900 permanent men and 90 gentlemen, presumably clerks.[29] Employment had therefore more than doubled by Barnard's visit, during a period when output had probably quadrupled. Wages accounted for a relatively small proportion of Guinness's expenditure. Of total receipts between 1871 and 1876 of £7m., only £0.3m. was spent on wages and salaries and salaries accounted for a larger share than wages.[30] Guinness continued its commercial success following the Stock Exchange launching. Dividends seem rarely to have been less than 15% and in the years 1905,6 and 1907 amounted to 20%, 22% and 25% respectively.[31] However the most rapid expansion of the brewery had already taken place. The firm was capitalised at £5m. in 1886 and this sum was not increased to £7m. until 1908.[32] Employment which stood at 2,650 in 1886, including clerks, was 2,506 in 1910, excluding clerks. By that date the company employed a total of 379 skilled workers and 44 apprentices and 2,083 unskilled workers. In addition a further 150 labourers were hired during the summer season from Powers Distillery who went through a slack period at that time.[33]

In terms of output, profitability and sales outside Ireland brewing was of major importance in the Irish economy. In the 1907 Census of Industrial Production, brewing with a Gross Output of £5.9m. was second only to textiles. In terms of Net Output, its place was even better.[34] Most of this beer was produced in Dublin and Guinness was the major producer. However the proportionate contribution to total employment was slight. With a capital value of £7m. Guinness employed 2,500 manual workers; the York St. Spinning Co. of Belfast, with a capital of only £500,000 workers employed 4-500 workers in the 1890s.[35] The overwhelming majority of brewery workers were unskilled and although, as Lynch and Vaizey emphasise,

> The brewery had at this time enjoyed for many years a reputation of being a good employer and the provisions for tradesmen and labourers — as the skilled and unskilled workers were called — was extremely generous. Their wages were generally above those prevailing in Dublin and their security of employment was substantially greater[36]

the predominance of labourers had implications in terms of wage rates and living standards at a time when the gulf between the skilled and unskilled was much greater than at present.

The spin-off of employment in related industries would also seem to have been limited. The shipping of Guinness through the port and the bottling of the finished product would seem to have been the major benefit. However no capital goods industries emerged to serve the brewing industry's needs, though the engineering firm of William Spence of Cork St. provided some equipment for the expanded brewery of the late 1870s.[37]

The brewing industry's success provides an interesting contrast with the distilling industry. This too was a traditional activity, located in the same part of the city, catering for a similar market and using similar materials. By the 1860s there were five distilleries in Dublin: John Power,

John Jameson, William Jameson, George Roe and a firm of J. Busby, Blackpitts which apparently did not long survive. Two distilleries were subsequently established, the Dublin Whisky Distillery Co. built a large plant at Jones's Road in 1872,[38] and the Chapelizod Distillery, established in 1873 in disused flax mills which was subsequently taken over by the Distillers Co. of Scotland and renamed the Phoenix Park Distillery.[39]

At the same time the existing plants were expanded. George Roe invested an estimated £70,000 in the 1860s and 1870s. In 1872 four additional stills were added[40] so that by 1887 output amounted to two million gallons annually, making it the largest distillery in the city. By 1887 the plant of William Jameson of Marrowbone Lane covered fourteen acres and £100,000 had recently been invested in expanding output to 900,000 gallons. Power's John's Lane distillery had also been extended after 1871 to achieve an output of 900,000 gallons, three times the level of 1833.[41] The only firm which apparently did not engage in major expansion was John Jameson, but its output was already in the region of one million gallons.[42] This wave of investment would seem to indicate a buoyant market. This was not however the case. Whiskey, or spirits had been consumed in large quantities by the Irish peasantry in the early nineteenth century. In 1838 the peak year, consumption reached 12.296 million gallons, by the 1860s it averaged only 4.4m. gallons.[43] The decline was due to Fr. Mathew's temperance campaign, famine population decline and the savage increases in spirit duty introduced by Gladstone in his budgets of the 1850s which harmonised the lower Irish duties with those of England. In 1823 Irish excise duty was 2/4¾, compared with 7/- in England. In 1858 this reached 8/-.[44] Drinkers gradually recovered from the swingeing duty increases and consumption rose until 1876 but declined for the remainder of the century.

Irish distillers therefore had to look abroad for increased sales. The most promising market was England where spirit consumption continued to grow. However English consumers generally preferred gin.[45] A key factor in the fortunes of the distilling industry was technological change. Traditional whiskey was produced by pot stills, a slow process requiring care and time to produce high-quality, well-flavoured whiskey. Irish whiskey was generally subjected to three successive distillations and then matured before sale.

The invention of the patent still by Dubliner, Aeneas Coffey provided the possibility for large-scale continuous batch production. The resulting product had less flavour, but was more uniform in quality, cheaper to produce, and could use varied materials, particularly maize. Patent still whiskey could be blended with a small quantity of pot still whiskey to give it greater flavour or transformed into gin. As a result of this new invention the total output of the Irish distilleries, which had fallen between 1830 and 1860 began to rise. In 1860, 6.4m. gallons were produced, 35% by patent stills, by 1900 this had soared to 14.5m. gallons, 71.5% produced by patent stills.[46]

The Dublin distillers continued to produce pot still whiskey while patent still whiskey came from Belfast and Dundalk.[47] The response of the Dublin distillers was one of complete hostility to the new product. In a book entitled *Truths about Whiskey*, a joint production by John Jameson, William Jameson, John Power and George Roe, they alleged that only pot-still whiskey was 'real genuine whiskey'. Patent still whiskey they referred to derisively as 'silent spirit'.

> In these circumstances the authors have only two courses open to them. It is much more costly to produce whisky than to produce silent spirit; and, as long as both were supposed to be essentially the same liquid, and were in competition with one another, the silent spirit lowered the price of whisky until the latter could scarcely be sold at a price to pay for its manufacture. The Dublin firms might have thrown down their pot-stills, replaced them by patent ones and gone into the silent spirit or fictitious whisky trade with other advantages which would have enabled them to defy the competition of smaller and newer establishments.[48]

Instead they concentrated on attacking the authenticity of patent still whiskey, with parliamentary questions raised by Irish M.P.s[49] or demands for mandatory bonding of whiskey for a specific length of time; patent whiskey could be sold without long maturing. The matter was still being contested as late as 1909 when a Royal Commission investigated whether it was legitimate to call spirit produced by a patent still, 'whiskey', and whether such whiskey produced in Ireland from maize could be termed Irish whiskey. Its report broadly favoured new technology versus the traditionalists,[50] though Dublin producers remained unconvinced. In evidence, Sir James Talbot Power, of John Power and Co. stated

> Having discovered by long experience how to make first class whiskey the firm is not prepared to risk its reputation by using cheaper methods.[51]

Yet as statistics indicate, by 1900 the majority of whiskey produced in Ireland came from patent stills. Lloyd George, commenting on the controversy amusingly and accurately summed up the battle between pot and patent stills as 'really a fight between Belfast and Dublin.[52]

Popular taste seems to have favoured lighter whiskies, either patent, or blends of patent and pot still. However a small minority of conoisseurs preferred pot still products as did most Irish consumers.[53] The response of the Dublin producers was to emphasise the distinct quality of their product. They were hampered in this however by the structure of the whiskey trade. Dublin distillers did not bottle whiskey themselves, except belatedly for export markets.[54] Whiskey was sold in barrels to publicans and merchants who bottled it, or more frequently blended it and sold it under their own label. The hostility on the part of Dublin distillers to blending ignored current market preferences, while failure to directly market their product weakened consumer identification. Many people bought whiskey blended by a merchant without any awareness of whether they were consumers of Power's, John Jameson or some other product. Ceding blending and bottling to outsiders also opened up possibilities for fraud, particularly mis-labelling, or dilution with inferior spirits. It is not therefore surprising that the battle waged for old standards and 'quality' on the part of Dublin producers failed. This provides a marked contrast with the brewing trade, where Arthur Guinness also traded on quality but with the advantage of a strong market identity.

The output of Irish pot stills continued to rise until 1900 despite the switch to patent stills. Much of the increased output came from new distilleries outside Dublin which ran pot and patent stills side by side and blended the product. It seems unlikely that Dublin whiskey output expanded from 1880. By 1889, three of the city's largest distilleries, William Jameson, George Roe and the Dublin Whiskey Distilleries Co. were forced to merge.[55] However it proved impossible to utilise their full capacity and lean years continued. By 1902 the company was over-capitalised and paid no dividend, while the quantity of spirits in bond was excessive.[56] By 1904 stocks equalled five years consumption and production and consumption were falling.[57] An already hard-pressed industry received a further blow from the spirit duties imposed by Lloyd George in 1909. The distilling industry resembled brewing in being highly capital intensive, and, with the exception of coopers, employing mainly labourers. Even prior to the onset of depression employment was relatively low. The Phoenix Park Distillery, owned by Distillers Co. employed only sixty workers to produce 350,000 gallons; John Power and Son, with an output approximately three times that level employed 250 workers and 25 clerks. The giant George Roe plant was said to employ 200 workers and 18 coopers, while William Jameson employed a further 200, apparently including coopers and other tradesmen.[58] It seems unlikely that employment in distilling could at any stage have exceeded a thousand workers. The majority were labourers and much of the employment was seasonal, with a winter peak. Powers Distillery had an arrangement whereby they employed river fishermen from Wexford in the winter months.[59]

Both beer and whiskey were sold in either barrels or bottles. Barrels were produced by coopers directly within the breweries and distilleries but bottle making was an outside activity and bottling was left to outside firms. Producing bottles for the drink trade was the mainstay of the Dublin glass producers. There were some firms such as Pugh's which concentrated on producing high quality table glass,[60] but they catered to a limited luxury market and seem to have declined.

Dublin glass works were traditionally sited at Ringsend and this remained a key location. The 1870 Factory Returns indicated five firm involved in glass work, employing 249 workers; by 1895 there were eight, one made no return, but the remaining seven employed 327 workers. The population statistics also indicate rising employment. In 1861 employment in the city and county was 222; by 1881 this was 351 though it had declined somewhat by 1891. The Dublin industry faced various difficulties. The process was a heavy user of coal and raw materials though firms relied heavily on recycled glass. Scottish and English glass works, with access to much cheaper coal proved highly competitive, though transport costs for bottles were high.[61] By 1874 the industry faced severe competition. One owner alleged that English and Scottish firms were undercutting Dublin prices and 'sowing disaffection among the Dublin workers'.[62] Further problems were presented by the need to adapt to new production methods. The traditional 'coal tank' method was superseded by the Siemens gas system which produced a purer type of glass in addition to fuel savings of fifty per cent.[63] However the Dublin firms were slow to adopt the new technology, despite a growing demand for bottles and a shortage of local supplies.[64] The industry was thus faced with an expanding market but falling prices due to increased competition from British and continental suppliers.[65] This reduced profits and made the financing of new technology more difficult. The long-established Ringsend Company, in an effort to find sufficient capital launched itself as a public company. Of the fifteen thousand shares, only three thousand were initially taken up.[66] Labour unrest was frequent due to pressure on prices leading to downward pressure on wages. The industry did however have the inestimable benefit of a relatively secure and growing market from the drink trade and it is therefore not surprising that by 1895 one of the Ringsend plants was owned by E. and J. Burke, bottlers and exporters of Guinness.[67]

The food industry, in contrast was not traditionally prominent in Dublin. Irish provision exports of the eighteenth century came from south-coast ports such as Cork and Waterford, though Dublin had an eighteenth century sugar refining industry. This was revived in 1866 by Bewley Moss and Co.[68] and by 1870 employed 120 workers. By 1880 the firm had changed hands and following a period of contraction again employed 120 workers,[69] however it closed during the following decade.

The sharp rise in live cattle exports using the port failed to generate any related industries but the transformation of the milling industry with the introduction of roller milling and the switch from using domestic to imported wheat meant a relocation of milling in large ports. The 1887 Factory Inspectors Report on Ireland commented that corn and flour mills were 'about the most depressed of all the trades in the country. I have seen large numbers of large corn and flour mills closed, not to be reopened and numbers are closing every day'.[70] Dublin, which had not been traditionally prominent in the industry was probably a net beneficiary from the transformation. Several existing mills were refitted,[71] while the North City Milling Co. whose directors included the Land Leaguer Michael Davitt opened a new mill in 1888.[72]

Baking and confectionery, mainly supplying local needs was the strongest component of the Dublin food industry. Technological change and free trade had little significance for the bakery industry until the 1890s.

> Save for the odd dough-mixing machine introduced in the early part of the nineteenth century, the Dublin baking trade remained unaffected by machinery until towards the end of the century. Neither did the extension of markets affect the trade much, bread being made for local consumption and not for export.[73]

The traditional structure was one of small units: in 1834 there were 131 bakeries in the city.[74] In 1864 Dublin Corporation recorded the existence of seventy-six bakeries,[75] however the 1895 Factory Returns noted only 26 factories and ten workshops engaged in producing bread biscuits and confectionery in both city and county. These figures, though not directly comparable suggest a tendency towards fewer and larger units. In 1888, Boland's, one of the city's largest bakeries completed a major extension to its Capel St. plant and the firm's total employment including a flour mill at Ringsend reached eight hundred workers. The following year, three of the city's larger bakeries merged to create the firm of Johnston, Mooney and O Brien.[76] These two firms were in the forefront of technological change. Patent ovens and dough-mixing machines increased productivity and reduced employment. The number of male bakers declined during the nineties.

The bakers union strongly resisted measures which would lead to redundancy and in 1889 negotiated an agreement which restricted output per man to 320 two lb. loaves per day. Not all bakeries were unionised and there was considerable pressure for an agreement permitting a higher output per man. As a result there was a bakers lockout in 1904 and a strike in 1911 which ultimately resulted in the acceptance of new production methods.[77]

The biscuit trade grew in importance with the rapid expansion of the firm of W. and R. Jacob. This firm opened a plant in Dublin in 1851 having previously been engaged in business in Waterford. Like virtually all the English biscuit manufacturers the family belonged to the Society of Friends. Biscuits were a new and growing consumer commodity and from mid-century fancy biscuits were produced in large batches by mechanical processes. Jacob's was an early mass producer and it grew in line with the industry. In 1883, ahead of Guinness's brewery, the firm became a public company.[78] By this date they were heavily involved in the U.K. market and scored a further success with the introduction of cream crackers in 1885. By the beginning of the twentieth century Jacobs had over 2,000 employees and was ranked among the top five biscuit producers in the U.K.[79] As a result of their success Ireland exported considerable quantities of biscuits. In 1912, exports through the port of Dublin amounted to 18,012 tons, compared with imports of 1,243. By 1911 the firm employed approximately 3,000 workers, two thousand women and girls and a thousand men,[80] a proportion of women which seems to have been substantially greater than in English firms such as Huntley and Palmer's. A measure of the importance which they attached to the English market was the announcement in 1914 that they planned to open a factory at Aintree near Liverpool. This may have been a reaction to the labour unrest which they suffered in 1913; alternatively it reflected their fear of Irish Home Rule.[81]

Capital goods and metal working firms were a key component of the city's industrial structure and a major employer of skilled workers. The 1870 Factory Returns indicated the existence of twenty-five metal foundries employing a total of 1,508 workers in city and county. By 1895 this had dwindled to 19 plants with a total of 427 workers. Given that the 1870 returns were probably less comprehensive than those of 1895 there was undoubtedly a substantial decline in metal-working plants, particularly in iron foundries and bell foundries. The 1884 *Report on Industries (Ireland)* noted that iron foundries had disappeared due to greater specialisation, increased imports and a decline in other areas of manufacture.[82] By 1895 more than half the foundry employment was provided by ten brass foundries which were probably supplying the drink industries.

In contrast the engineering industry registered growth. The 1870 returns indicated a total of twelve firms employing in excess of 900 workers, figures which exclude the Inchicore railway engineering works with a total of 625 employees. By 1895 there were 37 plants employing a total of 2,654 workers. However the majority were in railway engineering firms and other plants would appear to have been small.

The Dublin industrial scene did not automatically generate a capital goods industry, however many firms produced agricultural implements, while others produced machinery for grain mills, probably the most common form of industrial plant in Ireland. Firms dependent on the agricultural sector suffered from the recession of the late 1870s. As tillage acreage declined demand for equipment fell, while competition from imports apparently grew. A letter in the *Irish Times* in 1880 claimed that in 1856 cross-channel imports of agricultural equipment were estimated at £80,000 per annum. By 1869 this had risen to £150,000 while domestic production, previously worth £30,000 had fallen to £5,000 by 1880. Employment in the five major Dublin firms which had amounted to 250 had dwindled to 50 by 1880, half of this being accounted for by repair work.[83] In most cases the firms survived but concentrated on repair and sales rather than production. The combination of sales and production may have acted as a disincentive to developing new products as profits and continuity of business could be guaranteed simply by concentrating on sales.

The production and servicing of flour milling equipment suffered from the rising imports of flour and the closure of native mills, though there was a temporary revival in the mid

1880s due to the introduction of roller mills in a few larger mills.[84] However the Blackhall Place firm of Courtney Stephens and Co., which had employed up to three hundred workers in the 1870s and was heavily engaged in producing flour milling equipment went bankrupt in 1884.[85] The machinery was sold in a total of five hundred lots and the workers were left without employment.[86]

Some of the mills being re-equipped bought machinery from English or Belfast firms. The Custom House mill which re-opened with roller mills in 1886 was fitted by a Manchester firm and its engines produced in Belfast; only the boilers were produced by the Dublin firm of Bewley Webb and Co..[87] With increasing sophistication of equipment and growing specialisation such a tendency to import is not surprising.

Many of the other engineering firms catered for growing needs in plumbing, gas-fitting and electricity. Such firms were engaged in services rather than manufacturing and they expanded because the market grew and survived because needs could only be met locally. In some instances such services were provided by Irish branches of British firms; in others, new technology such as electrical work required the importation of outside skilled workers. An electrical engineering firm of Macready Eaton and Davidson which was established in 1903, was founded by the manager of a British firm which had a Dublin branch.[88] The structural iron firm of Smith and Pearson was established in 1902 by John B. Pearson, for more than twenty years manager of the Irish branch of a Staffordshire firm.[89] In 1907, following protests by Dublin Corporation against the employment of 'only Scotsmen and niggers' in Hammond Lane foundry, the manager explained the employment of fifteen Scotsmen and one American in addition to eighty-seven Irishmen as due to the lack of specialist skills in the native work-force.[90]

The survival of the general engineering industry in Dublin reflects the need to service and repair capital equipment in the locality. It cannot really be regarded as a self-contained industrial sector capable of withstanding outside competition. Michael Davitt, in a somewhat depressing survey of the Irish engineering sector in 1886 concluded that true manufacture was now confined to railway engineering companies.[91] These

35

too, can be seen as surviving due to special circumstances.

Several railway companies built locomotives in Dublin at different times, the two most substantial being the Midland Great Western which built 126 engines between 1869 and 1927 and the Great Southern and Western Railway which built 403 engines from 1852.[92] Many engines were also rebuilt while cattle wagons, coal wagons and passenger carriages were also constructed. The most important plant was that of the Great Southern and Western Railway Company at Inchicore. This was established in 1852 but was still under construction five years later[93] and not until 1861 were the first engines commissioned.[94] The company continued to buy engines from England[95] and most early work concerned the building and repair of wagons,[96] though both passenger carriages and goods wagons were also bought from outside companies.[97] Precisely what determined the balance between domestic production and outside purchases remains unclear. Possible factors might have included the need for specialised equipment, the capacity of the Inchicore plant and the relative costs of home produced equipment. There was an apparent reduction in outside purchases after 1879 when a new wagon shed opened,[98] while at a celebration to mark the completion of the hundreth engine it was stated that Inchicore-built engines were £400 cheaper than those bought from outside.[99] By this date employment had reached over 1,200 workers, compared with 625 in 1870. This marks a peak, employment ten years later was at an identical level.[100]

The growth of Inchicore was paralleled, though on a smaller scale by the Midland Railway Company. It engaged in a major expansion in 1879 when the old canal harbour at Broadstone was filled in and a new carriage shop was constructed.[101] By 1881 this employed over six hundred workers.[102] The momentum behind the growth of home production of railway equipment is unclear, but by 1885 all carriages and wagons on the principal lines were made in Ireland.[103] In 1882 the Dublin United Tramway Company opened a workshop at Inchicore for repairs and building, a move in tune with the 'buy Irish' obsession of the decade. In 1885 there was considerable criticism of the tram company for importing five cars from England. However they claimed that facilities at Inchicore were already 'taxed to the utmost' and the company was unable to undertake work for outside concerns.[104] The Tram company do not appear to have extended their plant. In 1897 they were again criticised for further imports, though they argued that the Inchicore plant, even when working overtime could not turn out cars in time.[105] The onset of electrification seems to have marked the end of tram building in Dublin. The Great Southern Railway Company also resumed importing in 1903[106] but the reasons for this decision remain obscure. Company minutes are singularly uninformative but it does appear that they were suffering from industrial unrest centering on questions of union recognition and wage rates and that this may have deterred them from local production.

The development of a railway engineering industry may seem somewhat surprising given the lack of any strong tradition in metallurgical industries in the Dublin area, however the industry had some links with the traditional carriage-making industry. Despite occasional outbursts of gloom the carriage industry survived, mainly as a result of developing new markets. Traditionally it had been a luxury trade, providing purpose built carriages, however by 1805 new carriages were no longer usually made to order.[107] By the mid 1880s there were an estimated forty firms in the trade, many very small.[108] However a majority of the estimated 500 workers, produced vans, cabs, rail and tram cars rather than carriages.[109] In later years some firms diversified into bicycle production, thus displaying a versatility rare in Dublin industry.[110] This flexibility ensured stability of employment but at the expense of a declining status for workers. The traditional carriage workers had been highly skilled craftsmen producing specialised products. They survived as less skilled producers of utilitarian objects. This transition is reflected in declining wage rates; body builders for example, earned up to fifty shillings in 1860, making them the elite of the city's craftsmen. Twenty years later this had declined to forty shillings.

The final branch of heavy industry represented in Dublin was shipbuilding. This is virtually impossible to identify from census returns as fewer than one hundred men recorded themselves as shipyard workers which seems an underestimate. Dublin had a traditional association with boatbuilding which was located to the south of the Liffey in Ringsend. In 1830 there were four builders. However the trade declined, reputedly due to disputes concerning the number of apprentices permitted.[111] The working shipwrights also contended that restrictions on access to the graving docks were a factor. The graving dock at Ringsend was owned by the Grand Canal Company and had generally been available to a number of companies. However a change in policy, due to thefts and feuds between rival groups of workers led to exclusive use being granted to the firm of Pike, Barrington and Good,[112] though following representations by the Dublin Chamber of Commerce it was agreed to open the docks as formerly.[113] However the Ringsend docks were small and suited only to small-scale operations. Of greater interest was the building of another graving dock on the north side of the river. This was commissioned by the Ballast Office and was built by William Dargan, but though planning commenced in 1851,[114] the dock was not opened until 1859.[115] It was then leased by the firm of Walpole Webb and Bewley who embarked on a relatively ambitious programme building ships of up to 1500 tons.[116] Employment rose to 550 by 1864[117] and the firm produced its own ships boilers and commissioned a number of engines from the local firm of Courtney, Stephens and Co.[118] The expansion came to an abrupt halt in 1870 with the suspension of the company with liabilities totalling £150,000[119] The *Irish Times* rather stridently blamed the failure on 'want of patriotic support from many Irish companies', yet a creditors meeting revealed that of 58 ships built, 17-20 showed a gross loss. In addition the company had lost money in somewhat maverick ventures involving the salvage of sunken vessels under an Australian patent.[120] The firm retrenched and concentrated mainly on repairs and building small vessels. In 1872, as an example of the new caution they declined to build a large Holyhead steamer, 'owing to the uncertainty of the labour market'.[121] Employment dwindled accordingly and the death of John Bewley in 1890 led to the sale of the shipyards.[122] The industry lapsed at this stage, surviving only in two small boat-building yards.[123] In 1902 however, two Scotsmen, Scott and Smellie reopened the North Wall yard concentrating initially on repairs.[124] They subsequently built ships and employment rose from 250 in 1902 to 1,000 in 1920 shortly before the yard's closure.[126] However Dublin's shipbuilding role was diminutive compared with Belfast. The graving dock was small and facilities were poor for handling heavy boilers, which ruled out the repair of larger vessels.[127]

Heavy industry in Dublin is therefore of limited significance, though it should not be ignored. It provided more stable skilled employment than many consumer industries. Its main markets lay within the city or the country. As such it was somewhat insulated from the full blast of competition. The weakness of the capital sector reflects the lack of demand from Irish industry or agriculture. With the decline of tillage and the growing imports of American and British farm implements the city's role as supplier of equipment to the agricultural sector diminished.

The chemical and manure industry however expanded to supply agricultural needs. The growing use of artificial manure provided many commercial opportunities despite the overall decline in tillage. In 1870 there were apparently four artificial manure plants, by 1895 this had risen to seven while employment rose from 347 to 463. The most successful firm was W. and H. Goulding, founded in Cork in 1858, which opened a Dublin plant in 1869.[128] This plant prospered; in 1871 Gouldings became a public company and manure sales which had averaged a mere 8-900 tons in 1861-2 had exceeded 16,000 tons.[129] The Dublin plant doubled in size in the early 'seventies, and in addition to domestic sales, the firm had extensive agencies in Britain and overseas. By 1881, a depressed period for agriculture, output had reached 30,000 tons, half sold at home and half overseas, while employment reached two-hundred workers at the spring peak.[130] Despite the agricultural depression of the 1880s the Irish market grew at an annual rate of 4-5% per annum, reflecting presumably a shift to artificial manures. Goulding's produced half the total Irish output and 15-20% of domestic sales. In 1884-5 it was estimated that up to 40,000 tons were imported annually.[131] Other Dublin firms benefitted from the buoyant market. Morgan Mooney's exported 20% of its output,[132] while the Dublin and Wicklow Manure Co. announced record sales, a plant extension and a 5% dividend in 1885.[133] By 1888 Goulding's employment had risen to 300 workers and overseas sales had further expanded.[134] However the predominant employment in the industry was unskilled and workers were also subject to seasonal unemployment.

Other than fertilisers the chemical industry was limited. Maguire and Patterson's match factory, an offshoot of a Belfast firm, employed mainly female workers and though engaged in a process which provoked innumerable complaints concerning workers health, never occasioned an adverse comment from Factory Inspectors. The city boasted a number of soap factories, all relatively small. The largest was the long-standing firm of John Barrington and Sons, owned by a Quaker family, one of whom, Sir John Barrington became Lord Mayor of Dublin. Barrington's produced 'bar soap of good quality which sold in both town and country markets'[135] and they also sold soap to Scotland. However the soap industry became increasingly competitive with the emergence of giant firms engaged in mass advertising. One consequence was low prices and over-production leading to efforts at market sharing. In 1903 Barrington's became party to such an agreement and in 1910 it was acquired by the giant conglomerate Unilever.[136]

Another chemical giant, United Alkali acquired the Dublin chemical and manure plant of Boileau and Boyd in 1890, though the firm continued production in other areas such as paint mixing, drugs and medicine and imported chemicals.[137] The experience of Boileau and Boyd, and of Barrington's emphasise the problems facing small Dublin companies in the large-scale conglomerate markets of the late nineteenth century.

In terms of total employment, both male and female, the textile and dressmaking industry was the largest. Most textile mills were outside the city; within the city the silk industry which was a workshop cum domestic industry was dominant. The early decades of the nineteenth century had proved seriously disruptive for the textile industry. However the 1862 Factory Returns suggest a measure of stability. Between 1839 and 1862 while employment in linen and cotton had grown, the woollen industry had declined.[138] However

40

the cotton famine; resulting from the American Civil War revitalised the woollen industry and several deserted mills reopened,[139] though this proved a temporary phenomenon.[140] By 1870 the Dublin area contained two cotton mills, eight woollen spinning and weaving mills, four flax and two worsted mills with a total employment of less than a thousand. By 1895 the cotton industry had apparently vanished and the number of linen and woollen plants had declined, though total employment had increased slightly.

The silk industry had long associations with the area known as the Liberties. Silk differed from other branches of textiles in remaining largely unmechanised. Weavers — exclusively men — worked at home, on piece rates, using only foot power.[141] The weaving section operated on a putting out system, with a small number of large firms, Pim, Fry, Atkinson and Elliott, controlling winding, silk throwing and dyeing. They assigned thread to weavers and retained responsibility for finishing and marketing. The industry, after decades of depression underwent a limited revival in the 1860s. In 1864 Messrs. Pim employed 148 weavers, by 1871 this had risen to an estimated 250.[142] Fry and Fielding built a new warehouse in 1870 and were at this time apparently employing 300 weavers.[143] By 1876 however, Mr. Elliott, manager of Fry's described the industry as 'not very extensive', while the firm's employment had fallen to fifty weavers.[144] In 1861 the Census records a total of 256 silk weavers, rising to 396 in 1871 and falling to 140 by 1881. There was however a partial revival again in the early years of the twentieth century and the number of looms rose from 60 in 1890 to 193 by 1910.[145] The industry catered for a limited luxury market. A not-untypical order of the 1880s was the upholstery for seven carriages being made for the Mikado of Japan and a state coach for the Lord Mayor of London.[146]

In terms of total employment dressmaking and shoe-making were of considerably greater importance. Dressmaking consistently employed the overwhelming majority of female industrial workers and was the largest single source of male industrial employment. Both male and female dressmaking employment showed a long-term decline; in the case of men, this dated from 1861, for women from 1871. The trend in the suburbs was somewhat different; male employment fell but female employment rose.

As the clothing industry was organised in small workshops, often in individual houses it is very difficult to chart the changes. The critical technological event was the invention of the sewing machine. This was in widespread use by the 1860s and transformed the structure of the industry as one contemporary observer noted.[147]

> The sewing machine had led to a new order of factories which bring together in large work rooms artisans whose calling had previously been carried on in their own work dwellings.

The sewing machine, combined with the emergence of department stores, or 'monster houses', as they were called, generated the mass production of ready-made clothing.[148] The department stores were alleged to import large quantities of ready-made clothing and by the 1860s English made clothing was being sold in Dublin at low prices.[149] The only possible response was the introduction of machinery by Irish tailors to reduce costs. However the Dublin tailors opposed mechanisation largely on the grounds of the reduction of skills but also because this opened the possibility of employing more women and children.[150]

Statistics suggest a declining share of the clothing industry in the hands of men and a greater proportion of women employed. The new-style clothing industry had two different, though frequently overlapping methods of organisation. Some large workshops, employing from fifty to two hundred women emerged,[151] but the rest of the trade operated on the putting out system. The 1870 Factory Returns indicate a total of 893 operatives employed in various clothing factories, over two thirds of these women. Most factories were attached to the much-maligned monster houses, but these also employed outworkers and there is considerable evidence of the existence of a sweating industry in the 1860s and 1870s. Garments partly sewn by machine were sent out for finishing by hand on payment of a deposit.[152] In other instances, branches of the clothing trade survived as outworking due to custom or the wishes of workers. Waistcoats remained an outworking trade[153] because the women workers resisted 'the restraint of the work-room' and could make as much as 10/- per week at home.[154]

Some of the more lurid allegations concerning Dublin's sweating industry must be ignored. The clothing industry was in a transitional period when new technology and organisational methods were undermining traditional practices and the incursion of women workers into areas hitherto male preserves was strongly opposed. The city's Factory Inspector admitted the existence of sweating and graphically described its working conditions, but claimed that in most cases only family labour was involved.[155]

> The outworking tailor or sweater works in his own house and employs his own family, or else hires in strangers to work; his trade is a very fluctuating one and he is often reduced to the greatest distress in the dull season and thankful to accept work on any terms. The poorer class of outworkers have only one room which, as I have mentioned above, will at once serve the purpose of bedroom, sitting room and workshop; the room is often small, dirty and ill-ventilated, was never intended for and is utterly unfit to be used as a workshop.

Many such workshops were among the casualties of the recession of the late 1870s. The 1879 Factory Report noted that Dublin dressmaking 'appears to have suffered much in sympathy with other trades',[156] while the report for 1888 noted[157]

> the chief falling off, I find, has been among the workshops, dressmakers in particular. On my visits this year, I have found numbers of workrooms in Dublin closed, workrooms which a few years ago contained numbers of workers. The principal trade of the city is chiefly confined to a few of the large establishments.

There is no evidence of any subsequent revival. Census figures indicate a decline which continues at a steady pace. The publicity given to sweating in London in the closing years of the century would almost certainly have led to similar statements in Dublin if they were justified. Jewish immigrants did enter the city's tailoring business — in 1909 a case of boycotting among Jewish tailors came before the Police Courts[158] — but their scale of involvement appears to have been limited. Virtually all contemporary statements from the 1880s allege that the bulk of ready-made clothing

43

was imported.[159]

However the substantial discrepancy between the returns on clothing employment in the 1891 Census indicating 13,691 female dressmakers, compared with 4,331 female workers in dressmaking factories and workshops according to the 1895 Factory Returns suggests that many women worked in their homes, not as sweaters but as self-employed workers doing repairs and making garments for a small number of personal customers. Their earnings were presumably low and highly uncertain while unemployment must have been a common phenomenon.

The story of shoe-making parallels that of clothing in that both were affected by the sewing machine and suffered from the division of labour and the substitution of female semi-skilled workers for skilled men working on their own account. The introduction of machinery led to the establishment of the 'bench' system by which each worker, instead of making a complete shoe specialised in a particular task. Women workers were hired to perform less skilled jobs such as finishing and closing. This system was introduced to Dublin as early as 1860 and by 1870 one factory employing 120 workers existed in addition to 32 workshops. Total employment was 445, approximately two-thirds male. By 1895 factories employed 238 workers, but workshop employment had fallen to 115. Many shoemakers continued to work on their own account, concentrating on repairs.

The decline of shoemaking employment took place despite the relatively early introduction of the 'bench' system. The Dublin industry favoured the production of high-price, high quality shoes and failed to adopt the cheaper materials being used in English factories. By 1885 English shoes sold at 10-12/- and Irish shoes at 14-16/- and by 1880 only 25% of shoes sold were Irish made.[160] In 1889 a long-established city shoe factory was taken over by the Leicester firm of John Tyler and Sons, and this was among the most successful industrial survivors.[161] The adoption of new machinery by Dublin shoemakers is not in doubt, nor is the quality of their product; however in terms of price and consumer requirements they do not appear to have met modern needs. C.S. Andrews, describing a shoe-buying episode of childhood

44

makes some pertinent comments[162]

> I had the misfortune to have had my boots made to measure (in Winstanleys of Earl Street). Of course the boots never wore out but neither did my feet stop growing and the consequences were disastrous from the point of view of feet formation.

A further factor which cannot have assisted the industry was the inexorable decline in the city's tanning industry. This was in part a casualty of the growing export of live cattle, which reduced the local availability of hides. Hides were increasingly imported from South America via Liverpool, which reduced the natural advantages of the Irish industry.[163] The Irish hides which were used for finer work tended to be sent abroad and returned to Ireland for finishing. The industry was also handicapped by its failure to adopt new technology. Traditional tanning methods using bark required that hides be steeped for twelve months; modern methods reduced the time scale considerably[164] but required an initial investment of perhaps £20,000.[165]

The final industries deserving some comment are the paper and printing industries. Paper mills were located in rural county Dublin where they were powered by local rivers. The industry suffered significant contraction in the 1880s and 1890s. The Factory Inspector's report for 1888 noted[166]

> In 1875 there were ten paper mills in and around Dublin, now only six are working.

By 1895 the number had fallen to five and one was on the point of closure, while one manufacturer stated that 'the price of the class of paper made by him has declined by 55% within the last ten years.'[167] However the printing industry situated in the city seems to have thrived and employment in both printing and bookbinding expanded for both men and women. Printing was of traditional importance in the city. In 1864, eleven of the factories identified by Dublin Corporation were print works, using the relatively new technology of steam presses.

The 1870 Factory Returns indicated the existence of 73 print works, employing 1968 workers. This accounted for almost one-third of all print works, virtually half of all employment and more than half of all machinery used in this industry in Ireland. In addition 25 binding plants employed a further 867 workers, the majority of these women. The number of plants shows remarkably little change by 1895 but employment had grown to 2997 printers, 276 lithographers and 811 binding workers.

Printing work can be divided into two distinct categories. Firms such as James Duffy, M.H. Gill and others printed a variety of books and pamphlets. Their major strength lay in catering for a Catholic nationalist market. Gill's, founded in 1858 and subsequently directed by H.J. Gill, the Home Rule M.P. was described in 1888 as 'the chief publishing house of the Catholic hierarchy, many of the publications being works on Catholic devotional subjects'.[168] Among its publications were a Catholic magazine called the 'Irish Monthly' and 'Irish poetry, fiction and romance, political pamphlets and history'. The customers of Browne and Nolan were said to include the Roman Catholic clergy, convents and priories. The firm of James Duffy, among the oldest publishing houses in the city, directed by another Home Rule M.P., Thomas Sexton published 'the newest Catholic and national publications, as well as the choicest gems of literature which Irish genius and Irish piety have given to the world'. It would have been virtually impossible for English firms to have catered to such a market, given the marked differences in religious and political sentiment. Not all firms served this market. Alexander Thom derived much of its income from being government printer.

The other aspect of the market was much more mundane. It included the growing demand for miscellaneous items of printing and stationery such as account books, commercial bill-heads for shops, commercial circulars, posters, private visiting cards, calendars etc. This market again required local contact with clients and Dublin firms supplied not only the city, but the remainder of Ireland while a firm such as H. and R. Wood established 1874, also claimed to supply English customers. Firms such as Hely's who specialised in producing stationery were also large employers, in 1888 it was estimated that their workforce amounted to 200, while the firm of Cherry and Smalldridge, who specialised in producing paper bags and other forms of trade stationery, including the inevitable almanacks were one of the largest sources of female employment. Bookbinding also proved an expanding

46

industry as a result of printing needs and there was a growing employment of women in jobs previously held by men.

In general the Dublin industrial scene is characterised by some industrial successes, side by side with failures. The major success story was Guinness's brewery; in contrast the distilling industry lost out in terms of growth of output to Belfast and other towns which adopted patent stills and blended whiskey. Consumer industries such as dressmaking or shoemaking largely failed to adapt to modern standards of mass production with an emphasis on price rather than quality. In this respect there seems to have been a common strand between the major Dublin industries, whether successful or not. Guinness's brewery produced a high quality product which commanded a premium price on the British market. In this it succeeded, partly because of strong product identity, but ultimately because a market for such a product existed. The whiskey industry also concentrated on quality and old fashioned products but with less success. Jacobs were numbered among the quality biscuit producers; Dublin shoe manufacturers were similarly quality conscious but saw their market decline. The Barrington soap factory concentrated also on quality soaps and earned modest profit in the process. Other industries which we have not examined in detail such as cabinet-making concentrated on craftsmanship while condemning cheap import products[169]

> inferior London manufactures are hand-made, turned out by garret masters of the East End and the only cause of its rivalling Dublin is its cheapness due to inferior work.

It would be superficially simple to condemn the Dublin industrial sector as characterised by obscurantist attitudes and an inexorable resistance to change. Resistance to economic change was not unique to Dublin, or indeed to Ireland, but it does seem to have been more deep-seated. Some writers see the main reason for this in the intransigence of the city's workforce and this is commonly put forward as a factor in industrial decline. Yet in many instances employers and workers were at one in their general attitude. Both seem to emphasise quality as opposed to mass production, or as in Guinness, quality and mass-production. This may reflect their perception of the Irish and the Dublin economy, which was not a rapidly growing one, and which had a population with a much lower level of disposable income than pertained in Britain. There was an expanding and prosperous market in existence on the other side of the Irish Sea, but it must have seemed a daunting prospect to a small, and perhaps under-capitalised Dublin company. Mass sales, particularly of consumer products, by the end of the century required a network of travellers, agents, advertising expenditure and perhaps the ability to negotiate market-sharing arrangements with rival businesses. The result of the changing scale of consumption and production was the swallowing up of small firms by giants, as in the case of Barrington's soap factory, or their extinction as a result of ruthless price-cutting by large competitors as happened when Manders brewery faced the challenge of Guinness. In such circumstances the urge to opt out of cut-throat mass markets, to concentrate on what a firm had successfully done in the past was no doubt irresistable.

Those industries which expanded their employment all had some special features. In the case of beer and biscuits it was an ability to compete with British giants on their own terms, and the importance of the U.K. market for both Guinness and Jacob's is emphasised by the decisions which both firms made in 1913 when Home Rule threatened, to open British plants.[170] Other industries which were moderately prosperous had effective protection against outside competition. The railway and tram companies decided to produce their own equipment, servicing and repair of capital equipment, the installation of plumbing and electrical facilities all required on the spot attention. In publishing, Irish newspapers, and to some extent books and pamphlets were products which could not have been readily supplied from elsewhere. As to the industries which might have appeared but did not, we can only speculate. The only case which merits attention is the cycle industry. As a plaque on a city street informs us, the world's first cycle factory was opened by Dunlop in Dublin in 1888. This was among an amazing total of 25 cycle companies launched on the Dublin Stock Exchange in the closing years of the century. The Dublin Stock Exchange cycle boom reached fever proportions in the year 1893 and innumerable companies, a few ultimately successful were established. Most of the early Dunlop share-holders were Irish, and they must undoubtedly have bene-fitted considerably when the company was sold for £3m. in 1896. Until that year it had been 'guided by Irish brains and developed by Irish dash and pluck'.[171] Yet as early as 1891 the bulk of production was concentrated in Coventry and London,[172] some alleged because of labour problems, but perhaps because both the market and the relevant industrial skills existed there.

DUBLIN MANUFACTURING EMPLOYMENT, MALE AND FEMALE 1841-1911. Table I

	1841	1851	1861	1871	1881	1891	1901	1911
Male Manuf. workers	20,110	20,992	20,192	18,580	17,628	16,751	17,755	18,067
% M. workforce	33.4	28.5	27.2	25.2	23.9	22.8	20.95	20.47
Metal workers	2,918	3,130	3,088	3,287	3,153	2,751	3,217	4,065
% Manuf. Empl.	14.5	14.9	15.29	17.69	17.88	16.4	18.3	22.49
Tanning	1,247	1,268	972	758	491	360	194	164
% Manuf. Emp.	6.2	6.04	4.8	4.07	2.78	2.14	1.1	0.9
Furniture	2,513	2,575	3,216	2,663	2,139	1,993	2,112	2,133
% Manuf. Emp.	12.49	12.26	15.92	14.3	12.13	11.89	12.0	11.8
Carriages etc.	1,133	1,120	1,051	1,193	1,061	1,099	1,402	1,238
% Manuf. Emp.	5.63	5.33	5.20	6.42	6.01	6.56	7.97	6.85
Textiles	1,749	1,350	1,086	942	547	406	273	308
% Manuf. Emp.	8.69	6.43	5.37	5.06	3.10	2.42	1.55	1.70
Food Drink etc.	1,102	1,592	1,339	1,411	1,870	2,250	2,472	2,234
% Manuf. Emp.	5.47	7.58	6.63	7.59	10.6	13.43	14.06	12.36
Printing	1,007	1,279	1,563	1,841	1,899	2,176	2,154	1,950
%	5.0	6.09	7.74	9.9	10.77	12.99	12.25	10.79
General Manuf.	185	167	265	383	846	1,019	1,576	1,950
%	—	—	—	—	—	—	8.96	10.79

Table I Cont.

	1841	1851	1861	1871	1881	1891	1901	1911
F. Manuf. Workers	13,940	16,968	17,977	16,543	14,744	14,389	14,007	14,250
% F. workforce	34.4	34.4	35.7	35.8	32.24	34.5	31.23	31.75
Furniture	185	428	957	795	770	688	733	517
% Manuf. Emp.	1.32	2.52	5.32	4.8	5.22	4.78	5.23	4.03
Paper	21	9	79	256	429	433	457	486
	—	—	—	1.54	2.9	3.00	3.26	3.79
Textiles	1,276	1,507	1,056	910	908	606	608	705
%	9.15	8.88	5.87	5.5	6.15	4.21	4.34	5.50
Dress	10495	13,024	14,324	11,835	10,339	10,308	9,198	7,400
%	75.2		79.6	71.5	70.1	71.6	65.6	57.73
Printing	176	330	549	720	712	857	854	764
%	1.26	1.94	3.05	4.35	4.82	5.95	6.09	5.96
Food	233	343	425	336	366	514	673	866
%	1.67	2.02	2.36	2.03	2.48	3.57	4.8	6.75
Gen. Manuf.	449	38	12ᶠ	1,081	927	738	1,296	1,735
%	—	—	—	6.53	6.28	5.12	9.25	13.5

Table II COMPARATIVE MANUFACTURING EMPLOYMENT 1841-1901. London 1861, 1891
Selected occupations as % of manufacturing employment

	1861		1891	
	M.	F.	M.	F.
Furniture	17.6.	5.69	16.8	5.1
Metal Engineering	16.8	0.72	17.1	0.8
Ships	3.7	–	2.0	–
Print and paper	8.56	4.0	13.1	10.0
Precision Inds.	6.67	0.47	7.48	0.85
Tanning	4.3	1.3	4.1	1.98
Food, drink	5.2	1.3	4.97	5.1
Textiles	5.1	8.3	2.2	4.8
Clothing	23.1	74.8	18.8	61.9
Chemicals	3.8	0.5	3.9	1.2
Misc.	5.1	2.8	9.5	8.2

Edinburgh, 1841-1901. Selected occupations as % of total manufacturing workforce.

	1841	1861	1881	1891	1901
Printing	10.19	14.05	16.42	15.69	17.44
Metal engineering	12.9	13.75	14.12	14.17	17.71
Clothing	47.23	41.33	33.3	32.3	27.66
Furniture	10.99	9.55	9.12	7.19	7.97
Leather	2.38	2.29	2.08	2.00	1.65
Food, drink	8.11	8.53	10.02	12.23	10.89
Paper	0.13	0.65	1.65	2.11	2.99

Sources: Gareth Stedman-Jones, *Outcast London* (Oxford 1971) R.Q. Gray, *The labour aristocracy in Victorian Edinburgh* (Oxford 1976)

Chapter III

ECONOMIC FLUCTUATIONS, LIVING AND WORKING CONDITIONS

This chapter examines the booms and depressions in the Dublin economy and the changes in wages and in working class living standards. The factors influencing the Dublin economy were complex. The state of Irish agriculture was crucial, given her position as a leading port for both imports and exports and her role as distributor and supplier to rural Ireland. Changes in the British economy were also important as were broad factors which impinged on the economies of Europe and the United States. By virtue of her membership of the United Kingdom, Ireland was part of a large free trade area open to a variety of influences from external sources. Hence the indirect impact of the American Civil War which led to the reopening of disused woollen mills in Co. Dublin. The Irish and British banking systems were highly integrated so that changes in interest rates, or speculative booms or slumps were readily transmitted across the Irish Sea.

Prices and wages tended, with slight variation to move in line with those prevailing in Britain. The *Royal Commission on the Poor Law* remarked on the link prevailing between the British and Dublin economies[1]

> Indications are afforded by charts of a trade cycle corresponding to England, with only very slight differences in the general movement. Prosperity of the year 1897 was relatively greater than in England — very noticeably in the building trade. 1893, the most prosperous year so far as unemployment percentages was very prosperous in Ireland but there was a slight decline in the building and printing trades. In smaller towns, Limerick, Galway and Drogheda, there is nothing

in the movement of trade corresponding to the clearly defined trade cycle in England. They are affected by conditions of the farming industry.

The above quotation would seem to suggest that Dublin was less influenced by the fluctuations in the agrarian economy than was the case in smaller Irish towns, yet all evidence suggests that agricultural depression could act as a key factor of the city's economy. Changes in the volume of agricultural exports travelling through Dublin port was the most direct link. Bad harvests, leading to higher food prices impinged on the living standards of the city's workers and might generate distress. Agricultural depression also brought an influx of rural migrants to the city in search of work or relief, a phenomenon of particular importance during the famine of the 1840s and also during the agricultural recession of 1879-82.[2] Other links emerged from the city's role as producer or supplier to rural Ireland. Unlike Cork or Limerick, Dublin had a very insignificant role as processor of food products, with the notable exception of beer and whiskey. However the city's fertiliser and farm equipment firms supplied the agricultural community and the sharp decline in tillage during the 1880s caused a loss of employment in agricultural engineering firms.

The largest connection between the city and Irish agriculture is the most difficult to document. The Dublin manufacturing sector and Dublin distributive firms traditionally supplied most of the consumer needs of rural Ireland via wholesaling agencies. Other firms acted as suppliers to Irish landlords. Serious agricultural recession, as in the late 1870s, plus increased competition from English wholesalers produced sharp drops in the profits of Dublin drapers and protests from those who sold mainly to the landlord class.

The impact of shifts in the British economy was also critical. Britain was the supplier of most imports and the destination of the principal exports. The relationship between British and Irish financial institutions was extremely close in terms of interest rates and financial confidence. The financial panic of 1866, which originated in London brought in its wake the collapse of several Dublin speculative ventures. The Dublin Central Railway station and proposed building ventures by Mark Bentley at Foxrock were among

54

its indirect victims. The *Dublin Daily Express* noted[3]

> The high bank rate has depressed business, also dis-
> turbances in the country and fear of cattle plague.
> Negotiations which have been on foot for certain loans
> for construction of works of an important public nature
> have not up to the present been brought to a successful
> conclusion and several of our leading wholesale firms are
> beginning to contract their business operations.

In contrast the 1893 Stock Exchange boom originated in
Dublin with massive speculation in bicycle shares and spread
from there to British Exchanges, notably Birmingham.[4]

One matter worthy of investigation is the Dublin building
cycle and its relationship with British building cycles. Figures
for the number of building plans submitted to Dublin
Corporation exist from 1884 but they do not take account of
suburban building activity. Prior to this period an
examination of the city directories for evidence of new
houses suggests a very low level of activity during most of the
1860s but a rise from 1869, peaking in 1872. Building fell
back somewhat but remained at a high level until 1880, a
trend which matches the English experience.[5] The high level
of planning applications in 1886 contrasts with England but
they reflect building, not by private enterprise, but by the
philanthropic Artisans Dwelling Co. The graph is further
complicated by the boundary extension of 1900. However
the sharp decline in building activity after 1908 is very
obvious, a trend also experienced in Britain. The Artisans
Dwelling Co. ceased building in 1907 due to high interest
rates. The decline in building activity at this period led to a
sharp rise in unemployment.

Slumps and Prosperity 1860-1914

This section attempts to sketch the chronological cycles, as
they were perceived by contemporaries. In addition to the
factors discussed above, more mundane matters such as bad
weather often proved critical in bringing economic activity to
a halt.

The early years of the 1860s afford an interesting indication of the relations between urban prosperity and the
agrarian economy. They were marked by considerable
agrarian depression due primarily to unfortunate weather

conditions and one writer at least[6] has argued that the decline in agricultural output was greater than during the depression of the late 1870s. Conditions were further complicated by business uncertainty resulting from the American Civil War and tight monetary conditions. Contemporary accounts suggest a recession which intensified as poor agrarian conditions persisted, though business confidence was still moderately high if the attitude of the *Dublin Builder* is typical[7]

> though money is scarce, discount high, material provisions dear, workmen scarce and wages high — yet we prosper.

However the report for 1861 by the Collector General of Rates emphasised the existence of a trade depression due to a second deficient harvest.[8] By 1862 the long-established charity, the Sick and Indigent Roomkeepers Society was once again chronicling a tale of gloom, noting the adverse impact of the American Civil War and[9]

> the International Exhibition (which) has left Dublin during the past summer comparatively empty and the successive previous bad harvests.

Economic depression and an apparent decline in private building, the result of a large number of vacant houses, were partly compensated by higher public investment. By 1863 the city waterworks was employing 578 men. This was regarded as 'most opportune at a time when distress was beginning to be most severely felt'. The city cattle market was another substantial source of employment.[10]

By 1864 agricultural conditions had improved and economic activity increased; 1865 was a cyclical peak in the British economy.[11] However the financial panics of 1866 caused some temporary problems for a number of business and speculative ventures. By 1868 the recession had ended and the *Irish Builder* could remark[12]

> In Dublin the artisan classes have been with few exceptions fully and remuneratively employed.

This recovery continued into the economic boom which coincided with the Franco-Prussian war. By the end of 1870 house rentals had risen sharply and the year overall had been favourable.[13] The street directories record steeply rising levels of house-building. Investment in infrastructure was also

56

at a high level. Dublin Corporation was completing its water scheme and planned an ambitious main drainage system. The Dublin Port and Docks Board was in the throes of a decade of major improvement while the Spencer Docks of the Midland Railway Co. employed 6-700 workers during its construction in 1872-3.[14] However the inflationary boom itself created problems. The price of industrial raw material such as iron and steel rose to such an extent that the main drainage scheme proved too expensive for Corporation finances and had to be deferred. Pressure for wage increases and strikes were almost endemic. However the *Irish Times* was almost lyrical in its review of the year 1872[15]

> Notwithstanding the dearness of money, as well as all other articles in daily use, trade and commerce of the city are in a most healthy condition. On the quays business is in a progressive state. Factories send up their lofty chimneys in many directions and suburbs on two sides are likely to become identical with the city.

The period of falling prices which followed from 1873 has become known to history as the 'Great Depression'. However its immediate impact on Dublin proved slight. Building activity fell back somewhat from the record levels of earlier years but remained substantially above the levels of the early 1860s. The absence of references to distress and recession suggests that the overall economic climate was favourable. By the end of 1877 however the *Irish Times* was talking in terms of trade depression.[16] However most commentators initially saw this as a short-term phenomenon. The President of the Dublin Chamber of Commerce affirmed that 'many who have been idle or partially employed will work full time' and he felt that 'the worst of the present crisis has passed away'.[17] Some months later the *Irish Times* wrote that 'Comparatively speaking Ireland has suffered much less than the sister country'.[18]

Unfortunately this optimism proved ill-placed. The year 1879 proved climatically disastrous and reinforced the agrarian depression which had already emerged. The first indication of agrarian depression impinging on the city emerges in the annual report of Arnott and Co. the Dublin drapery firm. In March 1878 it reported depressed trading conditions resulting from the poor state of the wholesale business which supplied rural Ireland.[19] Throughout 1879 and 1880 reports of recession and lack of work became continual.

The reports of the Factory Inspectors which had not hitherto remarked on the existence or otherwise of recession noted its severity particularly in the dressmaking and tailoring trades.[20]

> Dressmaking appears to have suffered much in sympathy with other trades, the cause not being only the depression in trade, but also the inclemency of the weather, the summer having been so cold.

The Inspector concluded

> I may say all through this district there appears to be the greatest want for work to do in every trade.

Evidence of the exceptional nature of the recession of the winter of 1879-80 is provided by the emergence of a working class protest movement which had not hitherto been a feature of Dublin life during the post-famine years. In January 1880 a meeting of 2-3,000 men, mostly labourers and building craftsmen assembled at Harold's Cross.[21] A police file commented on the initial meeting[22]

> They presented the appearance of men out of employment — all extremely quiet and well behaved. None of the men who are accustomed to take part in political demonstrations were recognized in the crowd.

Their demands reflected the scarcity of employment particularly in the building industry. A meeting early in February which was addressed by Mr. Mooney of York St. workmen's club and by McCormick a jobbing painter demanded that immediate work be provided and that a portion of the £10,000 which had been saved in Corporation budgetary pruning be used to commission small-scale public works.[23] A further grievance, particularly among building craftsmen was the awarding of a Corporation sewer contract to a Scottish company.[24] Hostility to outside workers and demands that contracts be given to local rather than outside employers became common at this time. Dublin Corporation was subjected to a deputation of bricklayers demanding that the proposed building contract at the Mansion House be given to a local contractor who would employ local labour.[25] The awarding of the contract for the

South City Markets to an English firm led to a claim by workers that it was 'likely to relieve unemployment in Birmingham'[26] rather than Dublin.

This hostility to outsiders is part of the Dublin working class reaction to the recession of 1879-80. Its second dimension is the impact of the land war and the reaction to this. The most obvious impact seems to have been on the city's wholesale businesses. As early as 1877 Arnott and Co. experienced reduced turnover from rural Ireland. However this firm provided sufficiently strong to weather the crisis. Its most serious victim was the Sackville St. store of Mc Swiney and Co., owned by a former Lord Mayor. By August 1881 it proved unable to declare a dividend and recorded a small loss due to the depressed country trade.[27] The following year Peter Paul McSwiney retired, ostensibly due to ill-health, and the company which had again failed to declare a dividend attempted to restore its fortunes by changing its name to the Dublin Drapery Warehouse.[28] This also proved unsuccessful and the following year this company was wound up before the Master of the Rolls and sold to a Mr. Cleary of Limerick for a mere £32,000.[29]

The Dublin workforce was fully aware of the relationship between unemployment and land agitation and the result was a singular lack of sympathy for the problems of the rural peasantry which was reinforced by the numbers of rural migrants who streamed into the city. The meeting of unemployed workers at Harold's Cross in January 1880 protested against the 'unfairness of raising money in the City and sending it to Connemara'[30] and the Lord Mayor was forced to distribute some relief in the city from his Mansion House Fund. A deputation from the City Labourer's Association to the Lord Mayor emphasised that their lack of employment was due to agitation in rural Ireland and the consequent reduction in merchant incomes,[31] while a builder's foreman, J. Doonen claimed in a letter to the *Irish Times*, that the artisans of Dublin resented the economic theories of the land reformer Michael Davitt.[32] Some years later in 1889 a meeting of the Dublin Trades Council listened to a denunciation of the Plan of Campaign which had both reduced landlords' incomes and led to a cessation of hunting. In consequence the market for hunting boots was very poor.[33] Similar attitudes of hostility towards tenant agitation were also expressed by Cork artisans.[34]

A further response to the crisis was the renewed interest in promoting Irish industry. This was a perennial topic, guaranteed to receive greater interest in times of recession as had happened in the 1820s. It reached a peak in the early 'eighties, with the interest of the Home Rule movement in tariff protection and the movement to exhibit goods of Irish manufacture. Industrial exhibitions were a typical Victorian institution given a major boost by the 1851 London Exhibition. Previous exhibitions had among their purposes the furthering of Irish industry[35] but they tended to retain an international flavour showing goods which were both Irish and foreign.

The proposals in 1881 were for an exhibition restricted to goods of Irish manufacture and this aim received widespread support from the city's artisans. The tone behind their support was nostalgic, Mr. McCormack a local artisan encouraged such an exhibition, recalling that at the time of the Union there were 2,400 looms working in the city, but that numbers had now fallen to ninety.[36] The exhibition organisers were extremely careful to ensure the purely Irish nature of all exhibits[37]

> in cases which are numerous where the materials are produced elsewhere in a partly manufactured state and put together in Ireland, each exhibitor must state in writing what part of the manufacture was executed in Ireland; a copy of this statement to be attached to each exhibit and such statement to be on a printed form setting forth that any misrepresentation will involve the removal of all the exhibits of the offender.

There were some delays in actually launching the exhibition, partly due to nationalist prejudices against the use of the term 'Royal' and Belfast wishes that a member of the Royal Family should open the exhibition,[38] but it ultimately opened in 1882. Efforts were made to use the exhibition as a long-term agency for the promotion of Irish industry. It was proposed that a banking and trading company be established on the nucleus of the national exhibition company. They were to act as bankers, factors and brokers and principal agents for the purchase and sale of Irish

60

manufactured goods of all descriptions.[39] It was also proposed to provide loans for industrial investment. The ambitious plans remained unfulfilled. In January 1883 the Exhibition closed[40] and some months later the company was wound up.[41] However campaigns to promote the purchase of Irish goods and denunciations of imports remained a characteristic of Dublin industrial policy, particularly on the part of the city's labour leaders.

> Much energy was spent in endeavouring to protect moribund trades by denouncing the import of goods of non-Irish origin.[42]

They also adopted the Land League weapon of boycott, with some limited effect. The South City Market Co., which had rebuilt a large area of South Great George's St. and vicinity faced a boycott of its shops due to the fact that an English architect and English workers had been employed on the site.[43]

By 1883 there was evidence that the immediate recession was lifting somewhat. The *Irish Times* noted[44]

> There is talk of impending or existing distress in the city amongst the labouring classes who are able and willing to work but cannot find the opportunity to use their hands. But poverty and privation do not exist now as they did a short time ago.

The revival, if it materialised, proved short-lived. Building was apparently in a depressed state.[45] Although a number of large-scale works were in progress such as a new railway terminus at Amiens St. there was an absence of speculative building. By 1886 conditions had apparently worsened. Newspapers contained many letters documenting the severe unemployment among artisans and labourers.[46] The *Evening Telegraph* alleged that unemployment was greater than at any time in the previous quarter of a century.[47] The distress was occasioned by further agricultural depression and severe weather conditions.[48] A contributory factor may have been the uncertainty resulting from the possible passage of the Home Rule Bill. The hostility of the business community to this measure is not in doubt. The *Report of the Dublin Chamber of Commerce* for the year 1885 stated that[49]

> any measures calculated to weaken the Union at present

existing between Great Britain and Ireland would be productive of consequences most disastrous to the trading and commercial interests of both countries.....
Their address to the Lord Lieutenant, Lord Carnarvon emphasised this point[50]

> The mercantile community which we represent feel that it is only under the security of the Constitution and surrounded by the assuring influence of peer and order that industry and commerce can flourish.

Certainly the defeat of the Home Rule Bill resulted in a Stock Exchange boom[51] and subsequent reports of improved economic conditions. Whether it was responsible for the upsurge of housing planning applications which ensued is unclear. By December 1886 it was stated that the city's trade was[52]

> very lively despite the disturbed conditions of agrarian interests. The poorer class of labourers in Dublin are pretty fairly employed.

Within two months however the unemployed were once more demonstrating on the streets to demand work.[53] The principal problem at this stage appears to have been the steadily falling price level which put pressure on profits and the failure of new sources of employment to emerge in place of industries which had failed. The drapery firm of McBirney and Co. reported in 1888 that[54]

> the season had been a peculiar and unusual one. Trade for the half year was in excess of any half year since 1885, but profits were smaller in proportion to the amount of trade done, owing to the exceedingly keen and severe competition.

The report of the Factory Inspector for 1887 confirmed the picture of depressed business conditions.[55]

> During the last year there has been no improvement in trade in this district. In some of the factories at times they have been kept busy but the one complaint is the continuing fall in prices, and the consequent unremunerative profits.

The subsequent years however seem to have brought a revival in industrial activity. The number of factories in Dublin city and county rose from 290 in January 1889 to 302 by the following October,[56] compared with 306 in

1872.[57] By January 1890 the inspector recorded 316 factories; by October 1891 this had risen sharply to 345,[58] and despite some evidence of recession in 1892 the number of factories continued to grow[59] while large-scale building works were once more in evidence.[60] The extensive reconstruction of Switzers department store seemed to indicate prosperity in the distribution trade.[61]

The renewed threat of Home Rule however provoked another business scare. Bank of Ireland securities and other stocks dropped seriously on the market,[62] while an architect alleged that building works were being abandoned on a wide scale. Harsh weather proved a more serious problem. The winter of 1893-4 was difficult and depression in the building industry persisted until April.[63] A further bad winter in 1894-5 once again caused problems for building activity.[64] Bad weather seems to have been the most common cause of economic distress during the 1890s. Falling interest rates and the successful conversion of Dublin Corporation debts into stock permitted the much-delayed beginning of the city's main drainage scheme. A further source of employment was the Portrane Asylum, though its somewhat remote location, coupled with a scarcity of agricultural labouring jobs apparently meant that farm labourers, rather than city workers took many of the jobs available.[65] The emerging impression of the 1890s is one of qualified prosperity. This is confirmed by the city's demographic pattern. The population increase registered during the 1890s reversed the decline experienced during the 1880s. The closing years of the century and opening 1900s seem to have been marked by a high level of building activity, though the industry would seem to have fallen off sharply after 1906, and even earlier, if Corporation and Artisans Dwelling schemes are excluded. The winding up of two of the city's largest building firms, Meade and Pile led to a dramatic increase in unemployment among building workers.[66]

Contemporary accounts of economic conditions in the early years of the twentieth century are a monotonous reiteration of woe. By 1907 the suburban housing expansion had apparently ground to a halt and there was a 'prolonged depression'.[67] By 1910 the *Irish Builder* was talking in terms of depression which had lasted for eight years[68] and there is no record of any revival until the year 1912.[69] Evidence from other sources fails to dispel the impression of unemployment and depression. The question of unemployment relief works was a major preoccupation at this time.

The impression which emerges therefore is of a growing sense of economic crisis from the middle of the first decade of the century, one which does not appear to been caused by agricultural recession as in the 1880s, but seems somehow endemic to the city. In 1906 one leading article stated[70]

> Distress in Dublin due to unemployment is not as it is in some more favourable cities, sporadic and occasional, but endemic and permanent.

The sense that this was a long-term problem is something which had been absent during the depression of the 1880s but had apparently grown by the early twentieth century. This depression was not unique to Dublin but was common to the majority of U.K. cities, one which was ultimately resolved by the onset of World War One which generated a host of business opportunities. In the early twentieth century however there was little evidence of economic growth: successful industries such as Guinness's had reached an apparent plateau, new firms were slow to emerge, while other major employers such as the port and the building industries were providing insufficient jobs.

Social structure and wage levels

The impact of economic cycles varied enormously between different sections of the population. In times of recession the unskilled working class would seem the most likely victims, but even the city's skilled workers, particularly those in the building industry were subject to considerable disruption. The occupational statistics give some indications of the proportion of workers in vulnerable sectors such as building or general labouring. The industrial classification gives an imperfect picture of social groups. Fortunately the 1881 census commissioners were asked by the *Dublin sanitary association* to provide an occupational breakdown which would form the basis for dividing the population into various social categories. These figures were subsequently used as a basis for calculating the mortality levels of the different social classes. They were compiled for the city of Dublin, and for the suburbs which are included in the Dublin Registration District.

The resulting tables distinguish between employers and employed and specially segregate the workhouse population.[71] Dependents are also assigned an occupational category. It is therefore possible to allocate the total population according to social class. We have re-tabulated the data, dividing the population into five social classes corresponding with those used by Armstrong which are based on the Classification of Occupations used by the 1951 English Census Commissioners.[72]

I Professional

II Employers, managers and senior clerical such as civil service.

III Skilled workers shop assistants and clerks.

IV Semi-skilled workers, domestic servants, carters and many engaged in transport.

V unskilled workers, hawkers etc.

The early Irish Census, from 1841 to 1861 also attempted a crude social classification into three categories.

I. Vested means and professional, described as

Heads of families possessing capital in wealth, or professional knowledge or whose means of subsistence enabled them to live without labour.

This would broadly correspond to Armstrong's Class I, with perhaps some of the larger employers, Class II, also being included.

II. Direction of labour

Heads of families directing income or employment also artisans who possess acquired capital in the knowledge of some trade; neither wholly exempt from labour.

corresponding to Armstrong's group III and much of group II.

III. Own labour

Heads of families without capital, either money, land or acquired knowledge. Labourers or those employed, little or no instruction.[73]

Armstrong's groups IV and V.

Social structure city of Dublin 1841-61

	Vested Means	Direction of Labour	Own Labour	Others
1841	9.5%	56.5%	26.2%	7.8%
1851	5.7%	24.7%	59.1%	10.5%
1861	7.2%	44.2%	35.0%	13.6%

Social structure city of Dublin 1881 and 1911

	1881	1911
I	4.55%	5.5%
II	7.4%	8.9%
III	38.6%	34.2%
IV	15.6%	13.5%
V	21.8%	25.4%
X (Students not living with family, pensioners etc)		
	1.65%	2.2%
Workhouse inmates and those of unspecified but limited means		
	10.2%	10.3%
Domestic servants, Class IV as percentage of total		
	8.2%	5.5%

Unfortunately it is impossible to discover the basis by which the Commissioners grouped the various categories. This makes it difficult to interpret the changes in relative shares, particularly between 1841 and 1851. However the general trend would appear to be a decline in the professional and gentleman population and in the skilled worker category and a rise among the unskilled and semi-skilled group without any means.

The proportions in classes I and II rose between 1881 and 1911, perhaps due to the incorporation of some suburban areas such as Drumcondra and Clontarf in the city in 1900. However the proportion in category III fell while the share of Category V rose. The declining skilled and rising unskilled share of the population corresponds with the trends in industrial occupations. If we add Category V those who were in the workhouse and those with limited means plus Category IV workers, excluding domestic servants we are left with a group amounting to more than 40% of the city's population, including servants — amounting to 50% in 1911, a group which can be regarded as impoverished and vulnerable to economic and personal crises.

The somewhat inconclusive figures available from 1841 seem to suggest that the proportion of the population in the unskilled and semi-skilled classes rose while the proportion in the skilled class fell. If correct, this would indicate a worsening environment for much of the population. However to decide this we must take wage and price levels into account.

Wages 1855-1914

Information on wage rates is not wholly satisfactory. We are dependent on the vagaries of the past, whether official reports or contemporary writers chose to record wages in certain trades. The problems are also compounded by piece rates and by changing hours of labour. Information concerning female wage rates is virtually non-existent.

A number of general comments are in order. A wide variety of rates are frequently quoted for a particular occupation. Workers were graded and paid according to grade. Hence in a traditional industry such as carriage building, wages of painters in 1855 varied from 3/4 per day for a second class painter to 5/8 for a first class worker.[74] Members of the United Society of Cordwainers, who manufactured the humble leather buskins of the poor earned 10-15/- approximately one half the income of members of the Gentlemen's Boot and Shoe-Making Society, who earned from 30-45/- per week.[75] Piece rates also pose a problem and many of the wages quoted in fact assume a standard output for a worker on piece rates. Over time there appears to have been a reduction in the variety of grades and a tendency to switch from piece rates to standard rates. The other point of note is the wide gap which existed between skilled and unskilled wages, though this narrowed over time. Bowley, a leading historian of wages remarked[76]

> It appears that the wages of Irish town labourers have been like those of agricultural labourers considerably lower than the wages of men doing similar work in England and Scotland, but that artisans on the other hand have been as well paid in Ireland as in any English or Scottish town other than Ireland.

The wages of skilled workers in the building industry were almost identical with those in England or Scotland in the 1890s.[77] Engine drivers and other skilled railway workers received wage rates comparable with those in Britain, while unskilled rates were considerably lower. In 1886 4.2% of English rail employees received 40/- per week and over, compared with 0.3% in Scotland but 3.7% in Ireland. Of those paid less than 20/-, the proportion in England was 41.8%, Scotland 52.8% and Ireland 78.4%. The majority of low-paid Irish workers received 10-15/-, whereas their English and Scottish counterparts received 15-20/-.[78]

The second half of the nineteenth century saw a significant shift in relative wage levels and in disparities between various skills. At the end of the 1850s the elite of skilled workers was in the carriage industry while poplin weavers were also high earners, though their employment was uncertain. Brewery workers earned substantially more than the generality of unskilled workers but considerably less than skilled workers.

The late 1850s were marked by a general upward drift of wages which halted during the depression of 1859-60. Wages resumed their upward trend in 1867-8 with labourers employed by Dublin corporation receiving an increase in wages from 9/- to 10/6[80] and 12/- in the following year.[81] The next major round of increases coincided with the price inflation of the early 'seventies. The years 1870-72 were marked by a rash of strikes demanding increased wages and reduced working hours. Those in dispute included

Wage Rates Dublin 1855-1905 [79]

	1855	1860	1877	1880	1883	1893	1905
Carriage ind.							
Vicemen trimmers							
Painters	12/-28/-	16/-34/-	23/6-32/5	24/-32/-	24/-29/-	—	—
Smiths	34/-60/-	40/-82/-	35/4-37/10	40/-48/3	40/-46/-	—	—
Printers	24/-36/-	35/-40/-	35/-40/-	—	33/-39/-	32/-35/-	32/-35/-
Cabinet makers	—	28/-30/-	—	—	—	35/-	35/-
Building crafts	—	28/-30/-	36/-	36/-	36/-	34-36/-	36/-38/3
Iron workers skilled	—	22/-36/-	—	—	—	34/-	—
Brewery workers	—	12/-21/-	—	—	—	—	—
Porters, carters	9/-15/-	10/-13/-	23/-	21/-	18/-	—	18/-20/-
Labourers	—	10/-12/-	15/-18/-	16-18/-	15-18/-	—	16/-18/-

building workers, both labourers and carpenters, telegraph clerks, scavengers, tram labourers, quay porters, tailors, bakers, chandlers and cordwainers. At the Lord Mayor's banquet in 1873 the Lord Lieutenant commented on the 'very remarkable increase in wages', increases of the order of 5/- for skilled and 3/- for unskilled workers.[82] Further demands for increases of the order of 2/- emerged from bricklayers carpenters and coachbuilders in 1876.[83] For most of the 1880s wages tended to fall. Insofar as there were strikes they were occasioned by resistance to wage reductions, as was the case with coal workers employed by Messrs. Tedcastle in 1884.[84] An attempt to organise quay labourers into a trade union, the Emmet Amalgamated Quay Porters Society, and to enforce a closed shop for its members and higher wages foundered because of the high level of unemployment and availability of non-union men.[85]

The reduction in wages seems to have been most prominent among building workers and unskilled labourers. Stonecutters employed on the building of the National Museum were hired for 30/- per week, compared with the going rate of 35/-.[86] In 1883 the general level of carpenters' wages was reduced from 36/- to 34/-.[87] Dublin corporation labourers suffered a substantial wage reduction of 4 to 6/- per week with wages falling to an average of 14/-.[88]

The years 1889-91 were marked by unprecedented labour unrest. The initial strikes were concerned with wage increases and the reduction of the working week. Seamen demanded a rise to 30/- from previous rates of either 25 or 28/- which some firms conceded. Others hired alternative labour[89] while bricklayers campaigned for an increase from 34 to 36/- for summer working and gained 35/-.[90] In the spring of 1890 building labourers achieved an increase in wages from an average of 15/- to 16/6 with summer rates of 18/-.[91] However labour unrest spread and the issues at stake became more contentious matters such as trade union recognition.

The strikes of these years are closely related to the London dock strike of 1889 which provided an example to unskilled workers of the possibilities of trade union organisation. However the results in Dublin, due primarily to the availability of alternative workers were unsuccessful. A coal porters' strike on the question of union recognition in 1890 ended on the basis of 'free labour, free trade, weekly notice and arbitration.'[92] Hope of men such as Michael Canty, organiser of the gas and coal labourers, for union recognition and standard wages in all firms was dashed. A similar strike the following year among corn porters also ended 'on the principal of free labour'[93] and an undertaking that 'all men for whom jobs can be found will be taken back'.[94]

Wage levels in 1893-4 in many instances were below those of the late 'seventies though rates for skilled workers compared favourably with Belfast or English cities such as Manchester. A comparison of skilled wages revealed that rates in six trades were identical in Dublin and Belfast, lower in Dublin than in Belfast in three, and higher in five trades.[95]

The 1890s brought wages increases and reduced working hours for a substantial proportion of the Dublin workforce. The Board of Trade noted that wages in Ireland had increased in the years 1894-7, though they had fallen in 1893.[96] This tendency continued in 1898, but though 1899 and 1900 were years of 'unprecedently high' wage increases in the U.K. this did not apply to Dublin.[97] A sixty hour week had been conceded in the 1860s and for some groups of workers this fell to 56 or 58 hours by the early 1870s. In many cases no further reduction was achieved until the 1890s. By the end of that decade a 54 hour week was the norm, and some groups worked shorter hours, 52½ hours in printing and 51 hours in tobacco manufacture.[98]

Not all concessions were gained without dispute. A strike of building workers in 1896 demanded restoration of the cut in wages from 36/- to 34/- which was made in 1883. This dispute involved a total of 4,500 workers and resulted in a loss of 114,000 man-days.[99] Skilled workers left for jobs in Manchester[100] but labourers were forced to beg for charity.[101] The settlement conceded 36/- for a summer week of 54 hours while labourers received increases of from 3 to 4/- per week.[102] The building trade rates became the norm for Dublin skilled workers.

The wages of unskilled workers remained low and in some cases they worked longer hours. Local authority labourers were paid between 15/- in Clontarf and Pembroke and 18/- in Rathmines. Pembroke workers were not paid for days when rain broke their work, while Clontarf workers were denied overtime. Efforts to gain a wage increase in 1897 proved unsuccessful.[103]

An earlier effort by Rathmines labourers to gain a wage increase was rejected and the commissioners replied that they had several applicants for labouring positions.[104] Dublin corporation workers received higher wages for longer hours. Street sweepers were paid 17/6 for 59 hours, carters £1 for a 54 hours night work.[105] These rates increased by 1/- in 1898 and were further increased in 1900. By this stage all corporation workers were given a minimum of £1.[106]

The rate of wage increases tapered off sharply during the early twentieth century. The Board of Trade noted the years 1901-3 as a time of wage decline[107] while Bowley remarked that 'if we had not allowed for some shifting of occupations towards higher wages we should have found a definite fall in real wages after 1902'. Wages in 1905 were virtually identical with 1900 and remained unchanged until 1912-13.[108]

The years from 1905 were marked by a further wave of labour unrest, much of it concerning trade union recognition and working practices. Most disputes ended in victory for the employers. Thus the 1905 building dispute on the question of piece work and the employment of outside craftsmen was a victory for the master builders.[109] The 1908 dock strike on trade union recognition was also a victory for the employers. The conference which settled the dispute agreed[110]

1. Questions affecting individuals only shall be settled by the individual and the firm.

2. Freedom of the employer as to the persons whom they employ is admitted.

3. No distinction as to work (including the delivery and reception of cargo) between union or non-union men to be made by either employer or employed.

4. Questions affecting general conditions of employment hours, rates of wages etc. shall in the first place be communicated in writing by the men to the firm. If no arrangements, the men through the General Secretary of the National Union of Dock Labour may make representations.

5. Then to the Conciliation Board of the Board of

Trade.

6. No distinguishing badges to be worn at work.

While some disputes produced gains in wages and working conditions the impression is one of wage stability and employers' victories. A railway strike on the issue of 'blacking' ended in complete victory for the Great Southern and Western Railway Company.[111] Wage stability ended in 1912-13. The wages of building and printing workers, unchanged from 1905 rose in 1913.[112] Rathmines workmen received a maximum of 19/- in 1912 and a further increase of 1, 2/- in the following year.[113] By 1914 building and printing craftsmen wages ranged from 36/- to £2. This was the peak of skilled earnings, with brass founders gas fitters and engineering workers earning 33-36/-.[114] Earnings of unskilled workers varied more considerably. £1 was a typical sum by 1914 though David Chart estimated the average labourer's wage at 18/- with 15-16/- 'not unknown' and building labourers earning 20/10, though subject to short-time working.[115] Labourers employed in government institutions who were members of the Irish Government Workers Union earned from 21/6 to 30/-.[116] The timing of wage increases reflected the rising cost of living and increases were accompanied by a substantial rise in trade union militancy especially among unskilled workers who rallied to the charismatic Jim Larkin's Irish transport workers union. The bunching of wage increases in a relatively short timespan was not unusual, however its occurrence at this time enhanced Larkin's reputation and intensified employers' intransigence. We do not propose to examine the 1913 lock out, simply to note that its failure was not surprising given the apparently chronic surplus of unskilled workers and the unsuccessful experience of similar disputes in the past.

The discussion of wages leaves two interpretative problems. The first relates to price changes, the second to questions of unemployment and short-time working. No comprehensive price index exists for 19th century Ireland and the only index available deals exclusively with agricultural prices.[117] The alternative approach was to collect price-lists from Dublin markets. In the interest of simplicity these were limited to four commodities, three of which accounted for 66.5% of total food expenditure in the average labouring household in 1904.[118] The other major budgetary item, rent, accounted for 16% of total expenditure.

It would be impossible to compile a rent index for tenement housing, though we may assume that rents increased over the period partly due to an improving standard of accommodation.

Commodity Price Index 1864-1914 1865 = 100

	Bread	Potatoes	Beef	Weighted Average
1854	95	92	106	99.8
1865	100	100	100	100
1866	113	115	112	112.9
1867	137	149	109	126.5
1868	137	149	107	125.6
1869	113	133	114	116.4
1870	113	126	112	114.5
1871	125	118	123	123.1
1872	133	172	123	134.5
1873	133	192	135	142.7
1874	133	146	123	130.6
1875	117	115	125	120.2
1876	117	144	123	123.7
1877	133	162	124	133.4
1878	129	190	125	136.4
1879	117	162	114	122.4
1880	125	177	126	133.2
1881	125	110	116	118.8
1882	121	100	130	121.8
1883	117	131	132	125.7
1884	104	95	123	111.0
1885	100	85	109	101.7
1886	92	92	100	95.5
1887	92	110	90	93.8
1888	100	77	102	97.4
1889	104	87	100	99.7
1890	100	90	104	100.3
1891	113	118	104	109.8
1892	104	77	96	96.4
1893	96	85	93	93.0
1894	71	108	91	85.4
1895	71	105	96	87.1

1896	84	74	90	85.1
1897	96	95	90	93.2
1898	104	113	90	99.2
1899	87	90	98	92.3
1900	87	113	103	97.9
1901	87	102	100	95.0
1902	92	92	106	98.2
1903	92	120	106	102.4
1904	96	115	98	99.7
1905	100	87	95	95.9
1906	92	97	97	94.9
1907	96	146	100	105.3
1908	100	110	100	101.5
1909	104	92	105	102.6
1910	100	108	106	103.8
1911	100	110	105	103.7
1912	108	118	112	111.3
1913	100	146	109	110.9
1914	100	103	105	106.0

Index is based on a weighted average of food expenditure derived from Stafford.

Prices 1864-70 come from *Thom's directory 1875*, the remainder from *Supplement to the seventeenth Report of the Registered General of Births, Marriages and Deaths in Ireland Decennial Summary* 1871-80, (c. 4153) 1889, xx, p.44. ibid., 1881-90, (c. 2536) 1894, xxv, p. 45, ibid, 1891-1900, (cd. 2089), 1904, xiv, p. 46, 1901-10 (cd. 7121) 1914, xv, p. 50.

There are a number of drawbacks to this crude price index as a measure of working class welfare. Pork and bacon comprised a high proportion of meat consumption, unfortunately figures for this are less readily available while the index does not allow for any measure of substitution between bread and potatoes in years when one is extremely expensive. Nevertheless it reveals the general trend of food prices. A steady rise throughout the 1860s to a peak in 1873, thereafter fluctuations in a downward direction with price declines not becoming significant until after 1883 and a picture of considerable price instability. In a total of twenty-two of fifty-one years, the index moved by more than five points over the previous year. In eleven cases this move was in an upward direction; several of these years, notably 1870-73, 1891, 1898, 1907 and 1912 coincide with periods of labour unrest.

The table of wage increases reflects price changes. Wages rose through the years 1867 and the early 'seventies, tended to decline in the early 'eighties, rose in the 1890s but then remained relatively static until 1912-13.

It is difficult to comment with precision on overall trends in real wages. The Dublin corporation labourers who earned 12/- in 1867 had distinctly lower real wages than those earning £1 in 1900 or 28/- by 1913, while a printer earning 35-40/- in 1877 and 35/- in 1905 also had a higher real wage due to falling prices. In general periods of falling prices were marked by gains in real wages whereas times of price increases, though followed by rising wages were years of strain. This pressure on living standards was reflected in labour unrest. Over time the gap between labourers and skilled workers closed. Many skilled workers in 1914 had monetary wages identical to the late 1870s, virtually all unskilled workers had higher money wages by the eve of World War One.

This optimistic picture of real wages ignores the 4.2% by which the city's skilled workforce declined, which was almost exactly matched by a rise in the proportion of unskilled and semi-skilled workers. A family descending from the ranks of the skilled to the unskilled would have suffered a distinct decline in living standards.

If £1 per week had become the common unskilled wage by 1914 there is evidence that many household heads earned less. A total of 11,305 heads of tenement households earned 19/- or less, 2,784 of these 10/- or less, of a total of 28,079 tenement households[119] while detailed budgets indicate that many earning £1 still lived in conditions of poverty. A survey of budgets in 1905, when food prices were lower suggested that there was no margin on £1 a week for a family of five for spending on unnecessary items.[120] While statistical data of this nature is not available for earlier years there is little reason to assume a smaller proportion living in poverty in earlier years.

Chapter IV

POVERTY UNEMPLOYMENT CHARITY AND RELIEF

The problems of poverty in Dublin were a localised reflection of those which plagued other cities at the time. Illness, disability drunkenness or simple misfortune plunged many families into distress. Large families of young children, widowhood or old age frequently meant distress. These causes were due to personal circumstances rather than economic causes; in addition economic forces gave rise to problems of unemployment, or underemployment whether long or short-term.

The most important economic factor was the city's abnormal proportion of casual workers and the consequent high level of chronic under-employment. Casual labouring was partly a consequence of the city's occupational structure. The emphasis on transport and distribution, the importance of port and railways all served to reinforce the predominance of casual working. This situation was exacerbated by the city's dominant industries, brewing and distilling, both of whom employed casual workers during busy seasons who were discharged in slack times. Precise evidence remains impossible but a substantial proportion of the city's working class apparently lacked steady employment. An account of the Church Street area in 1884 noted[1]

> The population is mainly composed of those who live by chance employment. Of twenty houses in tenements only one is an artisan — a carpenter in regular employment. Men sometimes work. Children sometimes sell wares, fish and fruit. Many men work in the markets in the morning. Not one of the males is in constant employment (of the eight families in this house).

A more colourful account of a tenement area on the south side of the River Liffey noted[2]

> Golden Lane and Bride Alley are inhabited by vagabonds and birds of prey. Street musicians, old clothes dealers, and hawkers.

while the report of the Sick and Indigent Roomkeepers Society for 1857 noted of the city's labouring class

> how small a proportion of that number can find profitable labour and by how much smaller a proportion is employment attainable with any degree of permanence. They live, as was expressed in a former Report 'by employing every mode which industry can prompt or human ingenuity devise in order to procure even the meanest supply of the common necessaries of life.'[3]

The number of casual traders was constantly being increased by destitute widows, or by men unable to continue with their existing jobs. One widow wrote to the city's Mansion House Committee in 1880 asking for money 'to get a food thing, a basket to sell milk and eggs',[4] and while there is no evidence that help was forthcoming in this instance, the desire of charitable societies to help people to help themselves, as opposed to providing hand-outs led to many dealers being funded. The Sick and Indigent Roomkeepers noted that one of their major forms of assistance was[5]

> catering to the wants of poor industrious persons, particularly females who have been awarded small sums to trade in delft, glass, vegetables, fish and fruit, whereby they have carved a decent livelihood.

In 1895 the Society of St. Vincent de Paul, the leading Catholic charitable organization noted that the centre-city, Pro-Cathedral branch replaced the capital of dealers and pedlars, while the Rathmines conference provided a labourer who was disabled with rheumatism with a donkey and established him as a vegetable dealer.[6]

Dealing was predominantly the refuge of women and the proportion of females engaged in distribution in Dublin was far in excess of most other cities. Many were widows, a situation all too common in a city where the adult male death-rate, due mainly to tuberculosis was far in excess of the U.K. average. Others became charwomen or washerwomen. One widow who approached the Mansion House

Committee requested a mangle to permit her to become self-supporting.[7] However the casual earnings of such women were rarely adequate for family support and in many cases children were forced to engage in street selling. The *Report on Street Trading Children* discovered that in one-sixth of cases, one or both parents were dead. Typical of such households was a twelve year old girl who sold matches earning 3/- a week to supplement her widowed mother's earnings of 5/- as a dealer,[8] or the fourteen-year old paper seller, whose widowed mother and four other children were supported by his earnings of 5/- in addition to outdoor relief.[9] In cases where both parents were alive child dealing was either attributable to chronic illness, such as the case of a 13 year old news vendor whose mother worked in a laundry to help support an invalid father,[10] or to drunkeness or unemployment.[11]

The ultimate outlet for the desperate was begging. A tourist account of the city in 1853 noted the number of beggars as 'frightful'.[12] By the end of the century the situation had not obviously improved and the *Irish Independent* claimed that certain streets were 'literally infested with them, especially Gardiner's Place and Gardiner's Row, also Merrion Row and the Club side of Stephen's Green'.[13] Some of the women and children ostensibly selling flowers and other articles were really begging.[14]

It is difficult to decide whether the number of casual workers showed a long-term tendency to increase. The rising share of general labourers and the high proportion of workers in dealing suggests that it did. Numbers were swollen by craftsmen whose skills became redundant and the problem became particularly acute during times of recession. An eighty-year old man who applied for assistance to the Mansion House Committee noted that his son 'a rope maker by trade' was unemployed for several months and had been seeking casual labouring work.[15] The existence of a chronic surplus of workers is indicated by the ease with which striking workers were replaced. This was a regular occurrence in the case of labourers, as the many unsuccessful dock strikes indicate. One such strike in 1886 was dismissed by a newspaper with the comment that 'no inconvenience was caused to the company. Alternative workers were easily hired'.[16] Though common to unskilled workers the replacement of striking skilled workers also occurred. In 1864 striking stonecutters bricklayers and paving workers employed in the restoration of St. Patrick's Cathedral were replaced by others.[17] This chronic surplus of workers militated against efforts to increase wages or enforce trade union recognition.

Seasonality

Seasonal periods of slack working were common to a variety of occupations such as tailoring and dressmaking and the building trades. This particular aspect of working class employment has been analysed in detail for London[18] and it is not proposed to repeat the exercise. However the dependence of the port of Dublin on agricultural produce for a large proportion of its exports meant heavy seasonal fluctuations while the fertilisers factories were subject to peak demand concentrated in a short spring season.

Bad weather, particularly harsh winter conditions could pose serious problems for the city's poor, both because of diminished work opportunities and the increase in food and fuel prices. Coal famines were frequent until sail colliers gave way to steam in the 1880s. However as late as 1894 the high price of coal, coupled with the harsh weather conditions gave rise to the launching of a Lord Mayor's fund.[19]

Bad weather interrupted normal working patterns. The harsh frosts in the early months of 1895 led to widespread unemployment among building workers.[20] Harsh weather often meant greater sickness and consequent loss of work, factors which pushed otherwise self-sufficient families to the brink of destruction. The Report of the city-centre Pro-Cathedral conference of St. Vincent de Paul society for the year 1895 noted

> Many families were tided over the winter and through sickness until the workers were enabled to obtain decent employment with wages of from 20/- to 25/- a week. Were it not for the aid thus given, many of these families would have been obliged to go to the workhouse.

The reports of the other major charitable agency, the Sick

80

and Indigent Roomkeepers Society almost invariably contain a comment on the year's weather and there appears to have been a strong association between harsh weather and personal distress. A negative instance of this emerges from a report for the year 1874

> no cause for special appeals for assistance became necessary. The weather as a general rule was mild and genial.

More typical however is the report for the year 1860

> It has been truly stated that since 1812 the rigors of this season have not been equalled and this resulted in the most disastrous consequences to the humble but honourable industry of the poorer classes. The heavy snows and frost prevented the poor from carrying on the sale of their little wares in the street, suspended to a great extent out-door labour of all kinds and owing to the very high price of fuel, rendered the conditions of the poor deplorable in the extreme.

Drunkenness

The importance of drink as a contributory factor in poverty is impossible to estimate. The various detailed working class budgets are curiously silent on this question. Of the twenty-one families studied in detail on this question. Of the twenty-one families studied in detail by Stafford[21] only three specifically noted purchases of porter, and the largest of these only amounted to 2d per day. Three of the budgets note sums of money kept by the husband, in one case as much as 8/- per week, another an average of 5/-, and in three other budgets there exists a surplus item, not specifically accounted for. However this tells us little of value.

Convictions for drunkenness, though apparently much higher than Belfast or Cork[22] were relatively low. In 1910 there were 2,462 charges of drunkenness in the Dublin Metropolitan Police district, while a total of 3,758 people were drunk when arrested.[23] Attitudes towards drink varied among commentators and charitable organisations depending on their ideological preferences. The reports of the Sick and Indigent Roomkeepers Society are totally silent, perhaps because it was alleged that many of the Society's organisers were publicans who paid out money to clients who frequently spent it in their establishments.[24] This specific allegation was subsequently withdrawn, but similar statements were made by other sources.[25] The official statement of the Society's policy claimed to assist only those who were 'sober honest and industrious'.[26] One city conference of the Society of St. Vincent de Paul claimed that of 114 families assisted during 1894, twenty 'would not have required relief but for the intemperance of the head of the family'. They also added; 'It is possible that intemperance may be the root of evil in double that number'.[27] This society made consistent efforts to enforce temperance in the families assisted and the Rathmines Conference noted the successful rehabilitation of a man who had been dismissed from a 'respectable position' due to intemperance. He became a teetotaller and was found employment as a railway porter. Six years after his downfall he was appointed station master in a country town.[28]

The National Society for the Prevention of Cruelty to Children was emphatic that drunkenness was the main factor in the majority of cases which it handled.[29] The majority of families reported earned incomes above the working class average. In the year 1900, 1299 of the 1507 cases reported had an average income of 23/10.[30] The society claimed relatively few dealings with the city's destitute families[31]

> The men with whom we have altogether to deal are, or could be, earners of good wages. The utmost fringe of the 'submerged tenth' we rarely touch. They, sharing their misery and destitution with their children, can hardly be said to be cruel.

The evidence of this society, though undoubtedly correct as to the role of alcohol, may underestimate its importance in child maltreatment among the poorer families. The overwhelming majority of cases which it handled were reported by the public. Children neglected in more 'respectable' areas were more likely to be reported than those in the depths of the slums. In many of the records of street trading children, one or both parents were drunkards. Drunkenness was frequently combined with long periods of unemployment and both factors were related. Which was the initial cause we cannot say.

Most commentators remarked critically on the large number of public houses in the city and the heavy incidence of drink. Sir Charles Cameron, the medical officer of health was relatively tolerant, noting the overcrowded housing and the consequent urge to escape, adding that the pub was simply the poor man's club.[32]

Agencies for relief of distress

Distress, regardless of its causes was an ever-present fact of working classe life. The consequences of unemployment sickness or death were partly relieved by a variety of sources. Many of these escape adequate documentation. Assistance in money and kind from family and neighbours, and short-term credit from small local stores must have been the first call of many in distress. The Philanthropic Reform Association noted[33]

> A very large proportion of the applicants have received help from one or other of the great Dublin charitable societies and another very noticeable point is the extent to which these poor people help one another.

The pawnshop was a flexible, if expensive source of short-term assistance and there were approximately 2.8m. tickets issued annually in the city.[34] The pawnshop however was only appropriate to a brief period of slack work. A more lengthy recession frequently left families unable to redeem possessions with further disastrous consequences. A regular form of assistance by the Sick and Indigent Roomkeepers Society was the provision of cash to permit tradesmen to redeem pawned tools. In other instances clothing and boots were pawned which prevented men from seeking work and wives and children from leaving home. One un-employed tradesman noted that as a result of pawning all possible possessions[35]

> My own clothes are so worn that it is questionable whether I would be taken into any firm.

while of his wife and six children he noted that

> none of them are able to go outside the door for want of clothes. None of the children could attend school or their place of worship for the last four months.

The official agency for the relief of distress was the Poor Law and the workhouse provided an umbrella institution which relieved the sick, the aged, invalids, acted as a refuge for unmarried mothers, battered and deserted wives and abandoned children in addition to able-bodied unemployed. It was a somewhat inappropriate method of assisting many types of distress due to the requirement to enter a workhouse. A subordinate problem was the social stigma attached. There is some evidence that the so called 'respectable' poor tried to avoid it. An elderly house painter who had apparently seen more prosperous days when he was an active member of the O Connell memorial committee and a friend of the leading politician Sir John Gray begged help to keep him out of the South Dublin Union, a fate which would break the heart of his daughter, 'a professed nun for more than twenty-eight years in Castleisland convent.'[36]

Table I. Numbers in receipt of indoor and outdoor assistance, North and South Dublin Unions

	Indoor	Outdoor	Total
1870	15.124	1,644	16,768
1871	15,301	1,618	16,919
1872	16,935	1,764	18,803
1873	16,132	1,596	17,804
1874	15,860	1,450	17,398
1875	15,950	1,410	17,432
1876	16,199	1,298	17,570
1877	16,507	1,404	17,990
1878	18,807	1,368	20,253
1879	22,639	1,816	24,537
1880	32,072	6,555	38,710
1881	28,294	9,270	37,650
1882	34,677	6,853	41,613
1883	24,741	7,227	32,067
1884	22,183	5,191	27,480
1885	20,455	4,875	25,456
1886	20,352	5,673	26,152
1887	23,141	5,661	28,947
1888	27,265	6,985	34,392
1889	26,320	7,957	34,411
1890	23,421	5,437	29,002
1891	18,364	5,445	23,958
1892	20,125	6,189	26,458

1893	19,902	5,970	26,021
1894	22,163	5,919	28,237
1895	23,402	7,217	30,774
1896	24,931	6,292	31,364
1897	31,987	6,518	38,648
1898*	32,864	7,219	40,231
1901*	31,956	10,312	41,440
1902	33,575	6,343	42,563
1903	37,217	9,203	46,598
1903**	35,805	8,779	44,955
1904	32,039	9,282	42,073
1905	33,407	10,524	44,605
1906	31,097	10,615	42,245
1907	30,175	11,060	42,007
1908	32,429	11,669	44,969
1909	32,680	11,660	45,098
1910	31,538	13,376	45,552
1911	32,701	14,748	48,365
1912	36,232	13,947	51,364
1913	35,800	12,729	49,248
1914	32,653	10,218	43,768

*This series breaks at this point and only figures for the half-year ending March 1899 are available. Those from 1870 to 1898 relate to year ending Sept. In 1901 to 1903 they relate to year ending March. ** and subsequent figures, year ending Sept.

Table II. Sex distribution of workhouse inmates South Dublin Union. %

	Males	Female	Child*	Accompanied**
1875	40.47	41.74	17.77	24.92
1880	53.99	30.35	15.64	18.23
1904	54.6	31.5	13.84	17.4

* Less than fourteen years.
** One or more members of immediate family also in workhouse.

Table III Civil status %

	Male			Female		
	Single	Widowed	Married	Single	Widowed	Married
1875	50.8	23.8	25.4	36.1	35.8	28.1
1880	74.2	11.55	13.74	37.5	31.7	29.7
1904	62.1	17.5	19.88	29.0	35.5	35.5

Table IV Age distribution of adult inmates

	Male			Female		
	1875	1880	1904	1875	1880	1904
14-19	4.72	12.8	4.94	4.59	5.29	5.2
20-29	14.17	27.9	16.15	21.07	23.6	25.06
30-39	20.86	21.37	19.9	16.09	22.39	25.06
40-49	16.14	13.6	17.46	15.32	16.4	14.64
50-59	13.77	8.94	14.7	11.11	13.05	12.15
60-69	16,92	11.92	20.96	21.45	13.05	15.63
70+	13.38	3.37	5.82	10.34	6.17	7.69

Table V Percentage dying in workhouse

	Male	Female	Children
1875	12.15	13.3	5.35
1880	3.58	6.37	7.39
1904	4.29	6.69	3.38

Table VI Occupational status of inmates

	Prof. white collar etc.	Skilled worker	Males Semi-skilled	Unskilled	No occupation
1875	4.33	35.03	16.14	37.4	7.08
1880	2.09	32.86	6.87	55.8	2.29
1904	3.47	19.9	8	63.8	4.68

	Dress-maker	Other skilled	Females Semi-skilled*	Un-skilled	Prostitutes	No occupation
1875	5.22	14.0	41.76	1.2	4.41	37.3
1880	7.32	8.92	38.57	2.32	6.25	36.07
1904	3.75	7.76	42.8	3	0.5	42.1

*mostly domestic servants

Table VII Duration of stay in workhouse

	Male		Female		Children	
	1-12	1yr.+	1-12mos.	1yr.+	1-12mos.	1yr.+
1875	33.23	7.45	31.17	10.26	33.92	6.25
1880	15.53	2.09	23.53	5.48	17.95	3.52
1904	21.48	3.72	18.36	9.42	16.38	2.82

Table VIII Tramps and no abode as % total inmates

	Tramps	No abode or refuge
1875	4.12%	11.42%
1880	35.8%	11.07%
1904	5.32%	15.72%

The workhouse is surrounded with such a degree of folk mythology that it is difficult to disentangle its precise role in relieving need. Published figures presented in Table I show some dramatic fluctuations in admissions — a particularly spectacular increase took place in the year 1880, coupled with a long-term trend of rising admissions. This long-term rise was not a uniquely Dublin phenomenon, but one which also happened in the U.K. where it gave rise to political concern.[37] The numbers in receipt of outdoor relief also showed a long-term tendency to rise as criteria for its receipt were relaxed. Those given outdoor relief were not able-bodied workers; it was restricted to the disabled, aged men and women and their dependents, and able-bodied widows with two or more children. Only in the depression years 1880 and 1881 was outdoor relief conceded to the able-bodied as an exceptional measure.

A more precise understanding of the role of the workhouse necessitates examining admission registers, though even this source leaves many unanswered questions. A one in ten sample of all admissions was taken for three years; 1875, a year of very low admissions; the emergency year of 1880, and 1904, which appears reasonably typical of the years of heavier intake in the early twentieth century.[38] Tables II to VIII give some indication of the various categories of admissions and their changing pattern over time.

In 1875 the numbers of men and women were evenly balanced and over 30% of adult inmates were over sixty years of age. Many of these were ill and accounted for the 12-13% of adult inmates who actually died in the workhouse. The pace of life was very relaxed; over 30% spent in excess of one month there, with 7% of men and over 10% of women, mostly, but not exclusively elderly, staying for more than one year. Only 4% of inmates were from beyond the area of the South Dublin Union.

There is a clear contrast between 1875 and 1880. The proportion of tramps rises to 47.44% of male inmates as the recession sent men from other parts of Ireland in search of work. The influx of tramps sharply reduced the mean age of inmates, with the largest proportion aged between 20 and 29, while the proportion of those over sixty fell sharply. The overwhelming majority were only accommodated for a single day, many were only fed not housed, though some returned for repeated visits. They came overwhelmingly from the neighbourhood of Dublin. County Kildare accounted for 29.75% of male tramps, Wicklow for 24.5%, Co. Dublin, outside the Union for 11.5% and the remainder of Leinster for 13.96%. In the case of women, where tramps formed a much small proportion, 35.2% came from Dublin, 25.4% from Kildare, 12.29% from Wicklow and 25.4% from the remainder of Leinster.

While many tramps were labourers a substantial number claimed skills such as carpenter, mason, shoemaker and whipmaker. The proportion of skilled workers, 32.86% of male inmates is only fractionally below the 1875 level. Male domestic servants and gardeners who were important in the 1875 intake were poorly represented, while the number of labourers rose. The female tramp contingent, at 21% of the total was less significant. The majority were women on their own, or perhaps accompanied by a child, though some travelled with husbands.

The phenomenon of tramping was a traditional Irish reaction to famine and depression and it accounts for a major portion of the increased workhouse numbers in 1880. Ad-

89

missions almost trebled between 1875 and 1880, in the case of men the increase was almost four-fold. Tramps accounted for half of the increase in total admissions, almost two-thirds of the increase in male admissions. This gives a new perspective on Dublin's role at a time of economic distress. Much of the distress to be relieved was imported from outside the city, and, many of the unemployed demonstrating for work may also have been strangers. This gives some justification to the city's complaints about the unfair burden of poor relief which it carried. Much of it should have been a national rather than a local charge.

The depression of 1880 also appears to have posed increased pressure for the family unit. The number of deserted women and children rose to nineteen, the number of children deserted by both parents to six. Many women who entered the workhouse with children noted that their husbands were seeking work elsewhere, while for some inexplicable reason the proportion of prostitutes also showed a rise.

The register for 1904 is considerably more informative than the earlier registers and in many cases records the precise reason for admission. A total of 41.69% of male admissions arrived with a medical recommendation, either from a doctor, or in a minority of cases from a hospital. This was also true of 39% of women and 13.55% of children. A further 6.77% of children were admitted because a parent had been admitted on medical advice while 3.38% were born in the workhouse. These figures suggest the workhouse fulfilled a key role in the city's medical services. A contributor to the social services handbook of the Church of Ireland remarked of the workhouse hospital[39]

> originally intended to accommodate only the sick inmates of the workhouse, it has by degrees developed in many cases, into the public infirmary of the district.

The medical complaints suffered were of a varied nature. Many were minor injuries incurred in the course of work, i.e. 'sore arm'. Fourteen per cent of men and 17% of women suffered chest ailments, either tuberculosis, bronchitis or pneumonia; others suffered rheumatism, or the indefinable 'debility'. As a result of the high proportions of sick, elderly and children, a very high proportion of workhouse inmates were economically inactive. Evidence given to the Vice-Regal Commission revealed that on 11 March 1905 only 364 inmates of the 3,139 at the North Dublin Union were classified as able-bodied, and two-thirds of these were women. In the South Dublin Union, 1,032 of a total of 4,105 inmates more than half of them men, were able-bodied.[40]

A factor of some importance, in many short-stay admissions was lack of accommodation, perhaps evictions. Over ten percent of all inmates in each year were classified as having no abode or as coming from a refuge. In 1904 the figure had risen to 15% and many specifically mention having been evicted. Thus the housing problems of the city contributed to workhouse numbers and did so to an increasing extent by the beginning of the twentieth century. However it is interesting to note a distinct change in the category of workhouse inmate. In 1875 the proportion of men belonging to skilled trades was virtually identical to admissions from the unskilled labouring class. By 1904 the proportion of skilled workers had fallen sharply while the share accounted for by the unskilled had almost reached two-thirds. This partly reflects the decline in the city's skilled workforce, but also seems to indicate that the workhouse taboo was extending among the skilled working class.

On the other hand, by 1904 the workhouse had undoubtedly acquired a hard core of inmates who could be classified as the 'residue' of the working classes, unemployed men and women with little capacity for work and no alternative accommodation. Many of the men in their twenties and thirties fell into that category, as did a more limited number of women. The *Royal Commission on the Poor Law* noted[41]

> evidence of relieving officers of the North and South Dublin Union that the labourers however casual and the frequenters of the workhouse belong to two distinct classes

This can be documented from the register which records the admission in November 1904 of a 45 year old servant who had left the workhouse the previous day. On this occasion she stayed until March 1906, or the case of a 36 year old single labourer with no abode, whom the clerk records as 'in and out of the Union for ten years'. He stayed one week on this occasion. Many of the long-stay cases were

91

handicapped, either physically or mentally, but some of the records can only perplex the reader. Among the admissions in the 1904 sample is that of a 63 year old carman who was accompanied by his 58 year old wife and 18 year old daughter. They are listed as having no abode. The carman remained until his death in March 1909; his wife until her death in 1911 and the daughter until her death in 1947.

While these are the more striking cases, a substantial proportion used the workhouse for short-term relief when faced with illness, eviction or lack of accommodation. Women and children seem to have used the workhouse to tide them through a husband's absence seeking work, or a bout of domestic friction. Every register records the admission of several 'marriage cases'. The care which the workhouse provided may not have been popular, it was in most cases a last resort, but it must be seen as an integral part of the relief mechanisms available to the city's poor.

Charities

Charities provided an alternative, and for those on outdoor relief, a supplement to the Poor Law. Dublin had a reputation of being a city with innumerable charities[42] and this belief was reiterated by the Royal Commission on the Poor Law.[43] While innumerable charitable agencies existed, many were proselytising bodies, such as St. Michan's Bible Women's Mission, a body which distributed charity and bibles in equal proportions.[44] The majority were concerned with specific needy groups, such as the A.F.D. Society which assisted the poor clergy of the Church of Ireland and their families, the Dublin Garrison Needlework Association which employed the wives and widows of soldiers in sewing, or the Association for the Relief of Ladies in Distress through non-payment of Rent in Ireland, which by 1902 had merged with the Irish Distressed Ladies Fund.[45]

The largest single group of charities were orphanages which catered for every possible religion and social class. Dublin boasted forty-four, among them the Dominican Orphanage Eccles St. which catered for Catholic orphans of 'professional and mercantile families', the neighbouring St. Brigid's R.C. orphanage, also in Eccles St. caring for 'destitute children in danger of loss of faith' and Miss Carrie's home for destitute children, again in Eccles St. which provided evangelical christianity. Female rescue agencies and homes for distressed gentlewomen were also extremely plentiful. An awareness of the confusion of existing agencies led to the formation of the Association of Dublin Charities under the auspices of the Church of Ireland and the compilation of a register of charities and eligible groups. In his introduction however, G. Williams, the compiler of the handbook wrote of 'vast overlapping of intention (which) existed, resulting in wasted energy' and he called for more cooperation, closer scrutiny and in some cases amalgamation. Only four agencies were listed which provided assistance to all categories of people in their own home: the Society of St. Vincent de Paul, the Sick and Indigent Roomkeepers Society; the Strangers's Friend Society and the Association for the Relief of Distressed Protestants. In addition many families would have sought help from local convents, monasteries and parish churches. Dr. Walsh, Catholic Archbishop of Dublin claimed that[46]

> The clergy and nuns of Dublin have been providing for years past food and clothing for the children of the poor and have been doing so at an extent totally unknown by the ordinary citizen.

The largest agency providing assistance was the Society of St. Vincent de Paul, founded in Paris in 1833, which opened its first Irish branches in 1845. The society combined strong impulses for religious regeneration — both of those to be assisted and those providing help — with the provision of material relief, and on occasions when the two impulses came into conflict, the religious goals took precedence. 'Visitation of the poor in their abodes' was the fundamental and essential work of the society',[47] and the granting of assistance without visitation was condemned as in breach of the society's traditions. Visitation provided opportunities for religious work, the only work reported by the city-centre conference of St. Michael in 1906 was the distribution of religious publications such as the *Messenger*; it also afforded the society greater control over those relieved, the ability to make observations on the sobriety of families and the condition in which rooms and children were kept. Those receiving relief were urged to abstain from drink, to improve their religious attendance and to join religious sodalities. The most revealing statement concerning the primacy of spiritual matters appears in the 1912 report from a conference whose area included the depressed city quays.[48]

> So numerous were the applications for relief that the members were inclined to look to the temporal needs of their friends to the entire exclusion of their spiritual necessities. Bearing in mind that the object of the Society was not to remove poverty but to raise the moral tone, both of the visitors and the visited, the Conference therefore, adopted no new cases but devoted itself to the spiritual interests of the families whom they had already on their books.

Running through the reports is an unstated implication that material benefits in the form of employment or greater prosperity will follow from closer attention to religious duties, as in the case of the unemployed drunkard who took the pledge, joined the sodality and found employment as a country stationmaster.[49]

Active members of the society were men of professional or mercantile background. Funds were gathered by bequests, private donations from honorary members, concerts, church gate collections, an annual bazaar and sales of their 'Bulletin'. A major source was the secret bag, passed to all active members at meetings when each was encouraged to contribute. With the exception of special activities such as the orphanage at Glasnevin, funds were raised and spent within each individual parish. This posed difficulties as there was little surplus money in the poorest areas, while branches in the middle class suburbs of Blackrock and Rathmines appear to have been extremely active. The conference attached to St. Mary's Pro-Cathedral, a parish containing some of the worst slums noted[50]

> Owing to the increase in the population of the poorer classes in our district and to the continued exodus of the moneyed classes to the fashionable south side of the city the demands upon our resources have increased while the sources of our income in the way of subscriptions and donations have become seriously re-

duced. We are now constantly in the habit of giving relief to destitute Roomkeepers who occupy the houses from which we formerly received generous contributions towards our work.

A similar problem was reported from the south-city parish of St. Kevins,[51] while the conference of St. Michan's was forced to suspend relief in 1905 for want of funds. Efforts were made to tackle the problem by persuading those who moved to the suburbs to retain membership of a city branch, while a branch founded among employees of Guinness's brewery was assigned responsibility for the Francis St. area.[52] Nevertheless it seems probable that prospects for relief were greater in Rathmines and Terenure than in Marlborough St. Assistance was generally granted in kind, though money was occasionally given, as when an unemployed clerk was assisted to emigrate to England and another unemployed man's removal to the country was financed.[53] Others were found employment frequently through the personal influence of society members.

The society maintained strict rules of confidentiality and reports indicate neither the total numbers assisted nor any details as to their occupational background. It would appear from reports however that much help went to those of 'respectable' background. Thus in 1894, in addition to the clerk already mentioned, there is a record of assistance to the 'widow of an official who held a good appointment' and to 'a respectable man who earned his income from private tuition'. A police report claimed that the society[54]

gave relief to a class of people who would not enter a workhouse, and if possible would not let their poverty be known.

It seems possible by virtue of the social background of members and of the emphasis which was placed on the practice of religious duties that middle class families in distress, or those working class families who subscribed to Catholic middle-class mores concerning temperance and religious attendance were more readily assisted than the hard core of destitute working class.

In addition to assistance in the home the society operated two orphanages to which it regularly dispatched children encountered in the course of visitation. Others were sent to industrial schools. Many were the children of widows or of fathers suffering long-term disability. The society seems to have favoured separating the family into institutional care rather than providing maintenance in the home. Thus in the case of a man suffering mental illness and incapable of work the children were dispatched to institutions and a permanent position was found for their mother, who had been 'freed from her domestic responsibilities'. The report concluded that the family was no longer in need of assistance.[55] In splitting up families in need, the society differed from the policy expressed by the National Society for the Prevention of Cruelty to Children.[56]

> This Society differs in its aim from all other Societies seeking the welfare of unhappy children in that, whilst others seek to house and provide for the wanderer, homeless destitute, it seeks to furnish aid to those worthless parents who make children wanderers homeless and destitute and to render other provisions than their own home less necessary.

However in providing institutional care for children the St. Vincent de Paul Society was reflecting the more common urge at that time; to remove such children from the home and the provision of places was particularly important in a city where the fear of proselytising remained strong and allegations of such practices were rife until 1914. The Reports of St. Brigid's orphanage contain many instances of children allegedly rescued from proselytisers and they emphasised the increased danger on this front as a result of the unemployment following from labour unrest.[57] The society of St. Vincent de Paul are not therefore alone in this concern. In one instance where the society resisted pressure from a widow to have her seven children taken into institutions, and provided her with a weekly sum of 3/6 to supplement her outdoor relief, the woman arranged to hand the children to a proselytising agency, though a last minute intervention placed them in Catholic orphanages.[58]

The boys at St. Vincent's orphanage were educated in trades and some sat their intermediate certificate examinations, which was unheard of among the Dublin poor.[59] Non-residential education for poor children proved less effective. Two night schools were founded in 1898 to remedy

96

the educational deficiencies of boys forced to leave school at an early age. However they were caught between the relative needs of religious and secular knowledge and because the time for religious instruction was felt to be too limited they broke with the national educational commissioners and in the process lost necessary financial assistance.[60] The schools closed within a relatively short period.

The Sick and Indigent Roomkeepers Society was an eighteenth century institution of exclusively Dublin origin. Unlike the Society of St. Vincent de Paul it was non-sectarian and had no moral or religious purposes. It would appear that its non-sectarian status was difficult to sustain in the climate of nineteenth century Dublin. The decline in the Protestant working class, the movement of many Protestants to the suburbs weakened their participation both as donors and recipients. A major source of income was charity sermons, including an annual one in St. Patrick's Cathedral; however by 1874 this only yielded £16, and there is considerable evidence of reluctance on the part of the Church of Ireland towards continuing this tradition.[61] There are also unproven allegations that the society discriminated against Protestants.[62]

They also seem to have offended the sense of propriety of respectable citizens, both Catholic and Protestant. In 1864 the Lord Lieutenant declined to attend the annual charity ball which was their main source of funds. This refusal was, according to the Lord Mayor, P.P. MacSwiney due to 'the admission of improper characters which of late years was increasing'.[63] Matters reached a crisis in 1877 when the Church of Ireland Archbishop of Dublin resigned as treasurer and the Lord Provost of Trinity College and the editor of the *Freeman's Journal* and prominent city politician E. Dwyer Gray withdrew from the committee. Lord Randolph Churchill private secretary to the Lord Lieutenant wrote demanding an explanation of the scandal.[64] The problem focussed on the occurrence at the annual ball of[65]

a lot of curious or objectionable freaks gone through, some of them by men appearing in female attire to characterise whose articles, adjectives were not strong enough.

A reform of the society which included replacing the ball

97

Table IX Numbers relieved by the Sick and Indigent Roomkeepers
Society[69]

	Families	Persons
1856	6,280	21,205
1857	6,107	20,369
1858	6,430	20,888
1859	6,243	19,769
1860	6,116	19,949
1861	7,690	25,187
1862	7,976	27,015
1863	9,242	30,622
1864	7,852	25,910
1865	8,112	26,587
1866	7,023	23,896
1867	6,742	22,861
1868	7,731	26,078
1869	8,087	26,793
1870	7,053	23,717
1871	8,123	26,582
1872	9,947	33,462
1873	10,504	35,465
1874	9,651	33,684
1875	8,264	26,422
1876	7,911	25,275
1877	7,338	24,147
1878	8,177	28,003
1879	9,816	35,531
1880	10,907	41,583
1881	7,888	30,887
1882	8,073	31,403
1883	8,873	35,528
1884	8,880	35,748
1885	8,553	34,457
1886	11,961	51,751
1887	11,859	53,269
1888	9,713	44,048
1907	6,826	24,438

with a rather decorous temperance picnic ensured that their
efforts reached new peaks in the depression of the 1880s.
The scandal would seem to have had repercussions; while
they were granted funds of £630 to disburse by the Lord
Mayor during the depression of 1863[66] in the 1880s they
were restricted to the funds which they could collect themselves. Unfortunately no reports for the society survive for

the 1890s, or for the first decade of the century with the exception of 1907. This shows a much reduced level of activity, at a time of considerable distress, suggesting that the society was in long-term decline.

There is some correspondence between fluctuations in numbers in the workhouses and those assisted by the Sick and Indigent Society.

It is by no means exact as the society was frequently constrained in its activities by lack of funds. A difficult year increased demands on resources, while reducing the surplus available for contributions. In 1880 for example it proved difficult to collect subscriptions and the society was forced to curtail its activities.[67] The assistance provided was limited to one donation per family in a six month period.[68]

Some families drew assistance both from the Sick and Indigent Society and the Society of St. Vincent de Paul. Both had heavy involvement with local clergy in centre city parishes. As they catered for the constant needs which arose from personal circumstances, exceptional distress posed heavy burdens which they had difficulty in meeting. Years of special need generally gave rise to special funds, either initiated by newspapers or by Dublin Corporation.

In January 1867 the *Irish Times*[70] launched a fund for the relief of distress caused by bad weather, but there are no records of any other exceptional schemes prior to 1879 if we exclude the £630 contributed to the Sick and Indigent Society by Dublin Corporation in 1863.

In contrast the autumn of 1879 was marked by serious official concern. On 13 November the South Dublin Union passed a resolution noting the need for public works and this was forwarded to the Chief Secretary's office.[71] Distress was not unique to the city, but was common throughout rural Ireland. In response to the pressure on Poor Law Boards, the *Relief of Distress Ireland Act* was passed in March 1880 empowering the granting of outdoor relief in the form of food and fuel for a limited period to able-bodied men and their families. These provisions were restricted to areas of exceptional distress, mostly unions in the west of Ireland, but were subsequently extended to include the South Dublin Union.[73] Men applying for relief were put to work in the Union stoneyard as a requirement for receiving aid.[74] Further evidence of the extent of unemployment is afforded by the demonstrations of unemployed workers and the deputations who visited Dublin Corporation demanding work. A DMP member who observed one demonstration commented[75]

> They presented the appearance of men out of employment — all extremely quiet and well behaved. None of the men who are accustomed to take part in political demonstrations were recognized in the crowd.

The winter of 1880-81 again saw allegations of serious destitution and proposals by a Poor Law doctor, Dr. McCabe that extraordinary public works be established.[76] However while the *Relief of Distress Ireland Act 1880* was renewed in many western unions, this did not happen in Dublin. At a meeting of the South Dublin Union it was stated that unemployment was 'nothing like last spring', though the Lord Mayor was still receiving deputations of labourers looking for work. The Union was unable to extend outdoor relief unless the workhouse was full and numbers, though high, had fallen from the record levels of 1880.[77] However the serious level of unemployment is indicated by the fact that in July 1881, normally a time of peak labouring employment Dublin Corporation received a letter from a committee of unemployed labourers requesting the establishment of public works.[78] The same day a demonstration of unemployed labourers met at Harold's Cross.[79]

References to unemployment persisted, though at a declining rate in the years 1882 and 1883, but there is indirect evidence of some easing of the situation. Workhouse numbers dropped from 1883 onwards and concern does not re-emerge until 1886 when a chorus of statements recording distress and unemployment emerge. The *Evening Telegraph* alleged that there was more unemployment 'than for the last quarter of a century and no sign of improvement'. Among recent union inmates, were, it was alleged tradesmen such as painters, tailors and shoemakers in addition to building labourers.[80] On 11 March a Mansion House meeting opened a distress fund[81] and Dublin Corporation established a limited system of unemployment relief works while processions of unemployed reappeared.[82] Perhaps of greater

100

interest is the existence in the Chief Secretary's files of a report on *Poverty in Dublin* compiled by 'two very experienced officers of the Detective Division' of the DMP and dated 10 March 1886. These officers[83]

had made inquiries through the different charitable institutions in the city and find that poverty amongst the artisan and labouring class is by far greater at the present time than it has been for many years past. The St. Vincent de Paul society which gives relief to a class of people who would not enter a workhouse and if possible would not let their poverty be known. A man in the office of the society informed us that there is more people looking for charity this year than he ever had known before. The strain is so great at present on the funds of the society that it is heavily in debt and some of their branch offices are closed from want of funds. He would not inform us what class of people were in most poverty as society rules are strictly private.

North Dublin Union has 900 more inmates than at the same period last year and there are £12 per week more expended on outdoor relief. The Master has informed us that a workhouse is not test of existing poverty as it is nearly always the one class of people who frequent it. At the same time there are more labourers in the house than there were for years passed (sic) and has noticed more poverty amongst that class of people.

The Roomkeepers Society in Palace St. is frequented daily by numbers of poor people looking for relief and we are told that the funds of the society are not able to meet the number of calls on them and are increasing every day. The majority of people who are seeking relief from this society are of the artisan and labouring class. From other information and our own knowledge of the city we have never seen so many artisans about the streets or business so much depressed as at present. Every persons who we talk to are complaining of doing nothing in their trade or calling. (Signed Thomas Simmons Sergt. and James Sheridan).

A further demonstration in February 1887 protested against the Corporation discharging men from relief works,[84] but otherwise interest in unemployment waned. There are no further official steps to relieve distress until the early months of 1894 when harsh weather conditions were apparently the key factor.[85] The following winter proved 'the most miserable on record since the 1840s'[86] but with the exception of these two years, when distress was due to natural causes, the 1890s appear to have been relatively prosperous. One city branch of St. Vincent de Paul Society remarked in 1898 that [87]

> distress in the district is not very great, a large number of labourers are employed on Main Drainage and the electrification of trams..

In contrast the first decade of the twentieth century brings a volume of activity on unemployment which far surpasses that of the 1880s. Building activity began to slacken in the years 1902 and 1903,[88] and many workers were left unemployed with the winding up of the large building firms of Meade and Pile.[89] From 1904 references to unemployment became almost continuous. In July 1904 Dublin Corporation discussed the problem of allocating the contract for the city waterworks to a provincial firm, which it was feared, would import labourers at a time of serious local unemployment.[90] Some weeks later a procession of unemployed duly lobbied the Corporation,[91] the first such incident since 1887. By the autumn the position had so deteriorated that the Board of Guardians of the North Dublin Union met Local Government Board officials to consider acquiring the Linenhall Barracks as an overflow workhouse.[92]

Attention also focussed on the possibility of providing public works or an extension of outdoor relief. Under Section 13 of the 1898 *Local Government Act*, permanent statutory provision was made for exceptional distress. Boards of Guardians in conjunction with local authorities were empowered to give financial relief to unemployed tradesmen and labourers, provided that the need was accepted by the Local Government Board.[93] The workers were to be employed in public works schemes such as street cleaning. The North Dublin Union proposed implementing these provisions and in response Dublin Corporation promised to cooperate and also to advance their normal capital expenditure programme. When the topic was discussed by the South

102

Dublin Union, the Chairman, William C. Crimmins remarked that[94]

> not within the memory of any member was there so much distress in the city due to lack of employment for the working class.

In response to their commitment to accelerate public works Dublin Corporation advanced its proposals to build a technical school on the north side of the city[95] and undertook to spend £2,775 on street repairs,[96] a sum, which, incidentally amounted to little more than 1d on the poundage of the North Dublin Union. The response to this was a deputation from the North Dublin Union charging the Corporation with 'trifling with distress'. The Union also approached the Local Government Board for power to extend outdoor relief to the able-bodied.[97] Other groups in the city set up a special distress fund.[98]

Concern with unemployment then lapsed until the following winter when a special meeting of Dublin Corporation decided to spend £2-£3,000 on road works in excess of current estimates.[99] However following a demonstration of unemployed at the City Hall, proposed expenditure was raised to £7,650.[100] These were the first special funds raised by Dublin Corporation for unemployment relief since the 1880s and they employed 480 men for a total of 7,000 days during the month of December.[101]

Dublin Corporation refused to adopt the 1905 Unemployed Workmen's Act.[102] This measure extended throughout the U.K. a scheme which had operated for several winters among the London unemployed. It provided for the establishment of Distress Committees who would in turn compile a register of unemployed. These were investigated to ensure thieir bona fide state and were then set to various forms of relief work. Funds for relief works would be provided by charitable subscriptions, with the administrative costs of the Distress Committee and the unemployment register being paid by local rates. In addition to distress works the legislation envisaged the establishment of labour colonies and schemes for the migration and emigration of the unemployed. Dublin Corporation's objection to the act was political: they resented having to supplement local charitable sums from the rates and believed apparently that costs should be borne by central funds.[103] Other Irish towns apparently shared their suspicions because none applied during the first year of the act's operation.

In the spring of 1906 a body called the Philanthropic Reform Association, which had been concerned with social reform matters such as conditions in the city's police stations, control and care of children on the city streets,[104] focussed its attention on unemployment. They raised some funds locally and in July applied for a grant from Queen Alexandra's Fund, a fund established in 1905 to contribute to unemployment relief works.[105] They opened an unemployment register and within three days had received 1,316 applications. The work of the Philanthropic Reform Association proved the need for such a service and also demonstrated that those applying were not merely the 'residue' of the population. A total of 320 applicants were found unsuitable for work; 98 found alternative employment and 296 did not attend for work. Of the remainder however, 407 were classified as first class: of good character and willing to work; 127 were classified as decent but not particularly capable, 22 were regarded as incapable and 38 as doubtful. While the overwhelming majority were labourers or porters, approximately 10% were skilled workers.[106]

This limited activity may have helped Dublin Corporation to drop its inhibitions, but of greater importance was the fact that the Liberal Government which came into office in 1906 decided to make a parliamentary grant of £200,000 towards the administration of the Unemployed Workmen's Act.[107] With the prospect of state money becoming available, Dublin Corporation duly adopted the act and established a Distress Committee.[108] They succeeded in putting the first batch of men to work by 17 December. A total of 3,500 applied and of these, 1,663 were offered work. Reflecting hostility to outside workers, applications were limited to those who had resided in the city for more than two years.[109] Most were employed in street cleaning and a total of £2,149 was spent of which £192 came from the rates, £207 from voluntary receipts and the balance from government funds. The maximum number employed in any one week was 797, most however only got work for 4-5 days.[110]

The act was used once again during the winter of 1907-

8 when according to the city's Recorder conditions were worse than in the previous year. Expenditure amounted to £2,612 with a substantially greater voluntary contribution.[111] In 1908-9 the funds available were increased to £300,000, and Ireland's share to £13,750.[112] As a result the scale of operations in Dublin was substantially increased and a total of 3,272 applicants were given work with total spending amounting to £6,550.[113] In addition the City Treasurer was authorised to raise a loan of £10,000 to provide further work on street repair.[114] It was alleged that statistics of distress in December 1908 were 'at least 20% up on normal',[115] and conditions were exacerbated by a long-running carters strike.

Unemployment remained a major concern as late as the following March when a Trades Council deputation lobbied the Lord Lieutenant and the Dublin Distress Committee, arguing that though the register contained a total of 4,000 names, true unemployment in the city was 12,000. The register had been closed because funds could not employ existing applicants for more than two weeks.[116] In response to this deputation the Lord Lieutenant provided a further £1,000 for relief works.

The unemployment problem of the spring of 1909 was undoubtedly worsened by strikes of carters and dock labourers, nevertheless the underlying position gave rise to considerable concern. The *Irish Times* in a leading article in June noted,[117] 'Formerly the cry of unemployment was heard only in winter months', by this stage it was becoming virtually continuous.

In 1909-10 though total government spending on unemployment had been reduced to £200,000, Dublin's sum, at £6,346, remained virtually identical with the previous year's. By this stage unemployment relief was becoming an annual winter preoccupation and Dublin Corporation voted yet another overdraft of £10,000 for relief works.[118] Direct unemployment measures were costing the Corporation 1/- in the £ and the *Irish Times* criticized the

> present system of ignoring unemployment all summer and then legislating in a hurry to meet conditions which might have been foreseen.

By the winter of 1910-11 there was apparently an improvement in overall U.K. unemployment and the funds available under the 1905 Act were reduced from £300,000 in 1908-9, to £200,000 in 1909-10 and £100,000 in 1910-11. Ireland's share was a mere £5,000, as against £10,000 in 1909-10 and £13,750 in 1908-9.

Every effort was made to give the largest possible share to Dublin at the expense of Belfast. Nevertheless the government grant was little more than 60% of that available in the previous year and total funds fell to £4,379 with a consequent decline in numbers employed. A public meeting of the Dublin Distress Committee was held in the Mansion House, attended, among others, by the Lord Lieutenant and his wife, the Countess of Aberdeen. In response to their demands the Chief Secretary of Ireland announced the granting of a further £500 for relief employment. However he stated[120]

> It is not intended that the chronic distress and unemployment of a city should be met by this fund. Section 13 of the Local Government Act 1898 enables the guardians and Corporation to raise funds for relief and works for this class if they are satisfied that there is exceptional distress.

a conclusion already reached by the Irish report of the *Royal Commission on the Poor Law*.[121] Subsequent demands voiced by a mass meeting of Dublin workers[122] and a motion from Dublin Corporation[123] remained unanswered and the winter of 1911-12 saw the Unemployment Relief Act still operating with a mere £5,000 for Irish expenditure, though Dublin's share of this sum managed to increase even further to 70%, as against 63% in the previous year.[124]

The problem of distress in the years 1912-14 was seriously compounded by a wave of labour unrest which resulted in lengthy strikes. The coal strike of the spring of 1912 forced the South Dublin Union to request a special rate of 1½d in the £.,[125] while a Mansion House meeting launched a relief fund.[126] Not surprisingly requests from a citizens meeting to Parliament for further funds met with no response.[127]

There is some indirect evidence that trade in the city was reviving by late 1912, if labour unrest had not increased the level of distress. The *Irish Builder*[128] spoke of

> a most rapid and substantial revival in the building

trade in Dublin: a general air of briskness and prosperity not seen for a decade past. Most trades are very busy, unemployment has almost disappeared.

Some months later, William Martin Murphy in his address to the Chamber of Commerce claimed that the city's trade was prospering.[129] This situation would seem to be partly confirmed by the reduction in employment provided by the distress committee and the smaller proportion of state funds allocated to Dublin; only 52% of the Irish share, a decision which appears to have met with no protest.[130]

The events of 1913-14 are seriously complicated by the Dublin Lock-out and the resulting distress. Dublin Corporation raised a special rate of 3d in the £ as their relief gesture.[131] In response to representations made to the Local Government Board £10,000 was allocated to Ireland as its share of the Unemployment fund. However[132]

> Owing to the reluctance of strikers to register as applicants for work, the Dublin Distress Committee was unable to earn more under the Act.

In all, almost 3,000 were employed at a cost in excess of £7,500.[133] With the gradual ending of the lock-out employment opportunities in the city proved surprisingly good. Workhouse numbers were lower than in 1912-13[134] and although war brought some short-term disruption, the war years as a whole were a time of negligible unemployment, though inflation posed severe pressure on real wages and hence on living standards.[135]

Unemployment in Dublin: an assessment

Two periods stand out as marked by serious unemployment: the early 1880s and the years from 1904-12. Otherwise references to unemployment and distress committees are notably absent. The validity of the 1880s as a time of serious unemployment seems in little doubt, particularly as statements concerning the prevalence of unemployment and other external signs such as demonstrations disappear from 1887 for a period of almost twenty years.

The years from 1904 however pose greater problems. There was a growing awareness of the problems of unemployment, not merely in Ireland but also in Britain[136] and increased interest in measuring its extent and relieving workers who were regarded as genuinely unemployed as opposed to malingering. It is therefore possible that the upsurge of interest in Dublin reflects currently fashionable social concern. The existence of government funds to relieve unemployment from 1905 would also act as a further incentive to maximise its seriousness. Against this however must be set certain points. The problem of working class poverty failed to arouse the degree of interest and commitment in Ireland that was found in certains sections of British society at the time and there is no evidence of an orchestrated campaign by any group of Dublin citizens to focus attention if we except the Philanthropic Reform Association. A leading article in the *Irish Times* in fact suggests that the contrary was the case.

> There are large sums which Dublin contributes to the foreign missions. Why are no such efforts made to keep our children off the streets. The people of Dublin are keenly agitated over the question of whether Christian young men can play billiards without endangering their eternal welfare, but they are not interested in keeping the bodies of street children from want or their souls from vice.[137]

In addition there is the objective evidence available from rising workhouse admissions and increased numbers in receipt of outdoor relief, while the first efforts to establish relief works were initiated by the Poor Law Guardians prior to the passing of the 1905 Unemployed Workmen's Act. We must conclude, that if popular interest and government funds increased attention on the problem of Dublin poverty and unemployment they did highlight a very real problem, while the obvious sympathy shown by the Local Government Board — a body not noticeably friendly to the city or its administration — in channelling increased funds to Dublin would seem to confirm this argument.

Information on the background of unemployed workers in the 1880s is slight but indicates that they were primarily building workers, both craftsmen and labourers. Given the declining unemployment in many branches of manufacturing industry, former craftsmen must also have been among the unemployed. The Sick and Indigent Roomkeepers Society frequently emphasised the phenomenon of deteriorating circumstances for many citizens and some who applied to them were seeking relief[138]

> From a Charity to which in their days of better fortune they were not unwilling subscribers.

Information is considerably more plentiful in the early twentieth century, thanks to the files of the various distress committees. These reveal a greater preponderance of unemployed aged under forty than was the case in London. Forty per cent of applicants were aged less than thirty years, and a further 30% between thirty and forty years. The *Royal Commission on the Poor Law* noted the problem of boys being displaced from work[139]

> In Dublin there is a problem experienced by boys when they grow too old for boys wages — especially telegraph boys. Guinness' brewery has difficulty in absorbing them. Discharged soldiers are also a problem.

Somewhat paradoxically however they added. 'There is a smaller proportion of genuine workers unemployed in Ireland than in England.'

Evidence concerning the background of unemployed workmen confirms the prevalence of labourers and building workers, but also indicates a sizeable level of unemployed skilled workers. Virtually all initial applications came from unskilled labourers, men, as the Distress Committee recorded[140]

> whose want of employment cannot be set down to trade depression, or slackness, or dislocation of any particular industry.

Trade unions felt that their members did not apply to the Distress Committee, but that unemployment among skilled workers was considerable. In the winter of 1906-7 it was claimed that nearly half of the members of the carpenters union had been unemployed and that unemployment among trade union members amounted to 1,900 workers of whom 1,400 were skilled and 500 unskilled.[141] Figures available from later Distress Committees suggest that although general labourers and building workers remained the dominant groups, both skilled workers and even shop assistants applied for assistance. Skilled workers may have been attracted by the fact that wage differentials between skilled and unskilled workers were rigidly maintained. While labourers were paid 15-16/- for a 45-48 hour week, below standard wages, skilled workers with the exception of painters who received 20/- for 30 hours work, were paid full standard wages, generally 36/- for a 54 hour week.[143] Unemployment of skilled workers was not unique to Dublin but it does seem to have been greater. A graph of unemployment among printing workers in Dublin and Belfast revealed more violent fluctuations and generally higher overall levels in Dublin.[144] Explanations for the city's high unemployment level were not altogether satisfactory. J.P. Nanetti a Nationalist trade union M.P. blamed distress on the recession in the building industry and the decline in the engineering and metal trades, but tended, in common with many labour leaders to seek a scapegoat in the influx of men from the country.[145] He, and virtually all commentators emphasised that the unemployment was 'not of sudden growth', but virtually chronic in the city.[146]

In terms of overall working class living standards the existence of a seemingly serious period of unemployment in the early 1880s effectively negates most of the gains from falling prices during that decade. On virtually all heads the years from 1907 must be seen as a time of deteriorating standards for the city's working classes following apparent gains during the 1890s.

Table X Employees on Distress Works 1910-15 [142]

	1910-11	1911-12	1912-13	1913-14	1914-15
Building workers	1,535	1,350	1,678	1,721	752
Furniture	6	——	50	54	29
Engineering, ships	48	2	70	60	192
Food	12	——	9	14	37
Printing	4	18	47	83	47
Shoes, tailoring	——	——	——	10	12
Women	91	68	153	222	832
Labourers	1,420	1,270	602	777	1,272
Painters, stonecutters	——	119	47	42	——

Prices rose, with only limited wage increases until 1912-13, while it was also a time of chronic unemployment, particularly among building workers and general labourers.

110

There is strong evidence therefore of pressure on living standards in the years immediately prior to 1914. These years show a greater preoccupation with quantitative assessments of poverty and precise attribution as to its causes. In 1904, Stafford, a medical officer with the local government board carried out an investigation of the Dublin working classes consciously modelled on Rowntree's study of York.[147] A total of 63 streets containing 436 houses and 1,254 familes were investigated. The average income of heads of families was 16/- and in 650 cases, or more than half, the total family income was less than £1. Applying Rowntree's stringent budgetary standards Stafford concluded that £1 a week was the minimum necessary income for a family of two adults and two children. For a family containing four children this rose to 26/-. A total of twenty-one families, which Stafford regarded as typical of the working classes kept detailed budgets for a number of weeks. Eight of these families lived above the poverty line: thirteen below. Those below the minimum included all unskilled labourers with one exception, and, with the exception of an enterprising widowed seamstress, who was also a car owner, all families of more than two children. The families above the poverty line contained a total of ten children — five belonging to the seamstress, while the thirteen families below the poverty line contained thirty-five children.

A comparison of Stafford's budgets with those of comparable English families reveals a greater proportion of total income devoted to food, 63.38% in Dublin, 51% in York. The share of income devoted to rent; 14.5% in Dublin, 18.0% in York; fuel, 4.87% Dublin, 9.0% York and clothing Dublin 4.12% York 6.3% was also substantially lower in Dublin.[148] The need to devote a greater proportion of budget to food in Dublin suggests a lower overall standard of living. The low proportion spent on rent — London figures for workers earning approximately £1 per week also indicate a substantially higher rent expenditure[149] — may reflect the high proportion of casual workers and a need to tailor rent levels to a low permanent earning level. It also gives rise to an interesting insight on Dublin's housing problem: that some factors, either consumer preference, or insecurity of income, predisposed Dublin workers to a poorer standard of housing

111

relative to income than counterparts in English cities.

Yet even the higher proportion of budget devoted to food proved inadequate to meet basic nutritional requirements. Scientific analysis of Dublin working class diets revealed major deficiencies in terms of essential nutrients and in the overall level of calories. The city's diets emerged as considerably inferior to those of farm labourers. Urban calories were largely derived from white bread and sugar in contrast to rural potatoes, butter and brown bread. The quantity and quality of milk in the city compared adversely with that in the country. Evidence suggests that when food was inadequate a major effort was made to provide the breadwinner with sufficient nourishment at the expense of the wife and children.[150]

More detailed information concerning income levels is available in the year 1914 when the departmental housing inquiry collected detailed statistics on the earnings of tenement families. By 1914 the price of most necessities had risen from their 1904 level and the crude price index suggests that 23/- would be a comparable poverty line, a figure which one contemporary investigator arrives at independently.[151] For a family of six he suggests a figure of 30/-. In a total of 16,298 families, 71.6% of cases where earnings were ascertained, the head of the family earned less than 23/-, as did a total of 908 pensioners.[152] These figures however related only to the household head. The Stafford survey of twenty-one families showed that income was earned by more than one source in seven instances and this accounted for 15% of total income, or 39% of that earned by the seven families in question. We might perhaps assume that overall incomes in working class families were increased by 15% by supplementary earnings. However the figure of 23/- assumes a family of four. In 1911, 25% of families living in one room tenements were of more than four persons; in the appalling tenement streets of Mabbot and Tyrone Streets the proportion was 30%. While it is impossible to accurately calculate the proportion of families living in poverty, a figure of 16,000 is probably an underestimate. The basic labouring wage of approximately £1 per week in 1914 was inadequate to support any family with children in the absence of supplementary earnings and this makes no allowance for casual

112

working or low earnings.

There was no immediate solution to this problem. The 1905 *Unemployed Workmen's Act* had been regarded as a stop-gap measure pending the Report of the *Royal Commission on the Poor Law*.[153] It was also designed to relieve cyclical rather than chronic distress. The Dublin problem was widely regarded as chronic. The section of the *Royal Commission on the Poor Law* dealing with Ireland concluded that provision for relief of exceptional distress which was available under Section 13 of the *Local Government Act* — providing for outdoor relief and public works financed exclusively by local taxation was 'better adapted to the circumstances of Ireland than the Unemployed Workmen's Act' and urged that the latter be discontinued. If further state grants proved necessary to relieve exceptional distress they recommended that they should be paid in proportion to the expenditure on relief paid from local rates. They also recommended that the introduction of Labour Exchanges and unemployment insurance be deferred in Ireland until their effectiveness had been proved in Britain.[154] This report was largely drafted by Dr. Kelly, Catholic Bishop of Ross and it reflects the tendency to regard Ireland as an overwhelmingly rural country. It also indicates the conservative attitude of the Catholic clergy towards state relief of poverty. The parsimonious approach may also reflect attitudes current at the time which were determined not to burden a future Home Rule Ireland with a heavy weight of social expenditure — attitudes fully expressed on the question of Old Age Pensions.[155] The consequences of such a report were to preclude any immediate state assistance for Dublin's unemployed.

The failure to tackle the problem of casual labour and chronic unemployment was not limited to Ireland. The Liberal government as a whole ignored this element of the unemployment scene.[156] There is an even greater failure on the part of the city's government to consider possible approaches. A comprehensive building programme designed to remove the tenements would have brought multiple benefits in terms of employment and a boost to wages. However Dublin Corporation failed to even consider such an approach. Their policy — if the word is admissable —

113

was purely reactive, applying for government funds if they existed on a purely ad hoc basis.

Public interest in such matters undoubtedly increased during the closing years of the nineteenth century, but remains singularly low key. The Philanthropic Reform Association was founded in 1896 to orchestrate public opinion. It lobbied for workhouse reform, a revamping of the system of poor relief, the introduction of stringent housing bye-laws, and in 1905-6 for the adoption of the Unemployed Workmen's Act. Its attitudes strongly reflected those found in Britain at the time. A desire for rational reform coupled with the urge to coerce the working classes in some respects — such as cleansing the tenements and the segregation of the undesirable poor.[157] In 1901 the Church of Ireland published its *Social Services Handbook* to create greater knowledge and awareness of social problems among its members.[158] The initiative for this move also came from Britain. Inspired by the Lambeth Conference of 1898, the Church of Ireland Social Services Union was established. They set up a fund to help elderly ladies, took over and remodelled a tenement building, while past pupils of Alexandra College undertook similar efforts. Nevertheless they reported that there was 'a discouraging lack of interest in the study of the social question in Ireland'.[159] However the majority of the city's poor was Catholic and the responsibility for active involvement on the part of Catholics is thus correspondingly greater. The lack of interest on the part of members of the Church of Ireland may be explained by their general alienation from the city and the Catholic, nationalist impulse of a future Home Rule capital, also by the fact that Protestant social welfare efforts were frequently condemned as proselytisation.

Catholic clergy and laymen were actively involved on an individual basis and through the Society of St. Vincent de Paul. There is however a singular absence of effort to analyse the background of poverty, or to propose long-term remedies. The major social problems discussed in the leading Church journal, the *Irish ecclesiastical record*, in the closing years of the nineteenth century were alcoholism and the threats posed by socialism. The writings of Pope Leo XIII, which provided useful pointers on matters concerning the

114

working class, such as living wages[160] received little immediate attention. The Catholic Church retained an overwhelmingly peasant and rural orientation. A paper at the Maynooth Union in 1908 which examined the problem of poverty argued in terms of creating employment by 'breaking up our vast idle ranches'. To remedy the casual labour problem it was proposed to establish labour colonies, a popular solution among British reformers at the time.[161] Relief of the poor was to be organised on a local basis with locally financed Public Assistance Committees being supplemented by the St. Vincent de Paul Society.[162] The lack of sympathy with the Dublin working class and their problems is in marked contrast with the active clerical involvement in the Irish land question, a point emphasised by Walter McDonald, the controversial Maynooth professor.[163]

The second decade of the twentieth century brought growing concern and a gradual changing of attitude, or perhaps, greater publicity given to the sympathetic voices which existed. A key factor must be the emergence of mass unskilled trade unionism and the 1913 Lock out, which brought the terrors of rampaging socialism and the fear of strikers' children being sent to atheist homes. The *Irish Catholic* newspaper condemned the strikers as[164]

> members of the very lowest and most degraded section of the unemployable class who came out from the slums attracted by plunder.

However others such as the Jesuit academic, Fr. Finlay, a man actively involved in rural regeneration through the co-operative movement and also the NSPCC told a general meeting of the St. Vincent de Paul Society in the winter of 1913 that[165]

> the prospect before our statesmen is not alluring but they must find some remedy for the plight of the multitudes of poverty-stricken men struggling in our cities for standing room in which to breathe.

On October 25, 1913, the *Irish Catholic* (hitherto highly unsympathetic to the urban working class) published an article on 'the slums of Dublin'[166] which emphasised that the clergy must become involved in slum improvement. By 1914 the *Irish Messenger* launched its series of social action pamphlets and no. 13, by a Rev. Hughes updated

115

Stafford's research on minimum income levels and concluded that[167]

> An average of earnings below the standard requisite for decent living, under employment and unemployment are the primary causes of poverty prevalent in Dublin.

His concern was not exclusively material.

> Destitution is reducing thousands of our fellow Catholics to a condition of which the loss of Faith is a natural sequence.

This pamphlet marks an appreciation of the harsh practical realities of poverty at a time when the Catholic church begins a series of practical measures to assist the poor, such as the provision of welfare clinics for children and mothers.[168] By 1914 there is a belated awareness emerging of the problems to be faced. This growing awareness reflects contemporary opinion in Britain, realities such as the rising Poor Law burden in Ireland and the aftermath of the 1913 unrest in the city. There is little evidence that municipal government, or the British administration, or even the pending Home Rule leaders were prepared to tackle the problems.

Chapter V

PHYSICAL AND SOCIAL MOBILITY

A city is not a static entity and the late nineteenth century was marked by major changes in the social structure of Dublin and in the residential pattern of its citizens. There was a movement of population from the centre city to the outskirts and a shift in the religious balance of population in both occupational terms and residential location. The trend of population decline in some of the central city areas with growth on the outskirts was already evident by 1861. A comparison of population by parish in 1861 with the figures of 1831 reveals that the population declined in a total of thirteen parishes and increased in eight. The decline was most noticeable in the south-west quadrant of the city. St. Luke's in the Coombe, and St. Michael's in the Cornmarket both registered declines of over one-third, virtually half in the case of St. Michael's, while St. John's parish in the Werburgh St. area registered a fall of over 30%. Other parishes in this general area also registered losses. However parishes such as St. George's, which included the area of Mountjoy Square and part of the North Circular Road, and St. Thomas which served the area east of Marlborough St. including the docks and railway terminus both registered sharp increases, while St. Peter's parish, which included much of the South Circular Road and a considerable amount of suburban Dublin more than doubled in population. These trends are confirmed by the changes registered in the various city wards after 1861; though the decline in central areas becomes more noticeable while the population continued to grow in the areas adjoining the docks. The areas with the most severe decline in population are those which experienced a reduction in their housing stock, however in all instances the percentage decline in houses is less than the decline in population, while the increase in the housing stock is generally in excess of the increase in the population. This reflects the gradual demolition of large tenements and their replacement by smaller houses. Two areas which are exceptions to this trend are Rotunda and Mountjoy Wards, where population increased at a rate in excess of the increase in the housing stock, reflecting the gradual transformation of parts of these wards from large middle class houses, to multi-family tenements. This tendency is further confirmed by the fact that Rotunda Ward is the only city ward whose rateable valuation in 1901 was lower than in 1860. For city wards as a whole the increase was of the order of 34.71%; Rotunda Ward's valuation fell by 6.95%. The figures for rateable valuation also suggest that the population decline in the central city wards was by no means fully compensated by the erection of extensive commercial premises. Although valuations rose in all wards other than Rotunda, the rise was below average in Mansion House (6.54%), Royal Exchange (29.03%), South City (21.97%), and Trinity (17.07%). The wards experiencing the largest increases were the dock wards — North Dock (80.91%), South Dock (38.71%), Arran Quay Ward (90.73%) and the area containing Guinness's brewery and the distilleries, Ushers Quay (68.81%) and Wood Quay (46.81%). The area of most significant expansion in population, housing and valuation however was beyond the city boundaries. Suburban growth was significant both in terms of rising rateable valuation and population.

The move to the suburbs was initiated by the professional and upper middle classes seeking new residences which were physically removed from the dirt, smells and congestion of the city centre. It also reflects the expansion of the middle class population. There were real limitations to the provision of first class housing within the city boundaries. The city was confined within the two canals and although some vacant land remained, much of it was inappropriately located. In particular the fashionable quarter adjoining Merrion and Fitzwilliam Squares was virtually all developed by the 1840s. Much of the city's vacant land was low lying in the neigh-

118

Table I Population change in city wards 1861-1911

	1861	1911	% change	% change houses
Arran Quay	27,726	35,019	+26.3%	+56.54%
Inns Quay	21,188	23,505	+9.99%	+42.64%
Mountjoy	15,421	25,998	+69.59%	+55.46%
North City	14.150	7,886	-44.27%	-25.21%
North Dock	18,573	24,506	+31,94%	+62.26%
Rotunda	12,059	15,627	+29.5%	+11.68%
Fitzwilliam	10,187	12,404	+21.76%	+40.13%
Mansion House	13,526	11,189	-17.28%	-11.73%
Merchants Quay	22,417	25,705	+14.67%	+78.45%
Royal Exchange	13,990	6,532	-53.31%	-40.35%
South City	9,370	3,857	-58.84%	-38.78%
South Dock	13,515	15,074	+11.54%	+13.74%
Trinity	17,267	11,081	-35.83%	-24.72%
Ushers Quay	22,864	25,793	+12,81%	+51.77%
Wood Quay	22,260	21,986	-1.23%	+31.42%

Table II City and Suburban Valuations

	City	Neighbouring Suburbs
1871	£596,145	£177,633
1881	£657,578	£235,460
1891	£690,619	£273,874

Neighbouring means, Rathmines, Pembroke, Kilmainham, Clontarf and Drumcondra — those suburbs adjoining the city. The figure for 1871 does not include Drumcondra which did not become a township until 1878).

bourhood of the port and in need of reclamation. In time this provided new housing but the locations, surrounded by industrial and transport facilities, near railways and gasworks meant that only working class housing was developed. Other vacant city land, such as the north west quadrant, suffered from the vagaries of fashion. Henrietta St. for example degenerated to a street of tenements by the 1870s having previously housed the legal eminences of the city.[1] Such a change would have deterred property developers and the area was further blighted by the large number of military installations, bringing in their wake prostitution, hospitals and similar facilities and by the decision of Dublin Corporation

119

to site their cattle market in this area.

Much of the remainder of the north city area remained in a state of suspension as a result of a protracted law suit concerning the Gardiner and Blessington estates, the major ground landlords in the area.[2] When development began in the late '60s and early '70s the builders recognised market trends and provided modest housing suitable for skilled workers, clerks, policemen and shop assistants. The developers were Edward McMahon a nationalist M.P. and his partner Mr. Lombard, a director of Arnott and Co. drapery store, occasionally assisted by Sir John Arnott, managing director of this and other companies and the owner of the *Irish Times*. By 1880 at least 600 houses had been built; by 1884[3] this had doubled to 1,200, at least 200 of these valued at less than £8 and catering for artisans, renting at approximately 6/- per week.[4] They built various sizes of houses, all carefully graduated to meet different income levels and various social aspirations. Inishfallen Parade for example, whose inhabitants once included the future playwright Sean O Casey, consisted of four rooms and catered for artisans. Other streets however contained five or six rooms and catered for a somewhat more prosperous market. Houses roughly similar in character were also built during the 1860s in the vicinity of the South Circular Road, mostly by Frederick Stokes, the major Rathmines developer but also by Sir John Arnott. Although to the south of the city, the area was somewhat to the west and so was unfashionable, its status adversely affected by proximity to military barracks. Housing development within the city therefore consisted of smaller houses. Whereas the number of first class houses declined from 10,688 in 1861 to 9,067 in 1881, the number of second class houses, those from five to nine rooms rose from 10,486 to 13,061 and third class houses, those with two to four rooms from 1,740 to 2,064. There is in fact no identifiable street of first class housing in the city built in the second half of the nineteenth century.

Reflecting both fashion and the availability of first class housing the suburbs developed a social pattern which differed considerably from that prevailing in the eighteenth century city, where rich and poor tended to live in close

120

proximity. In the nineteenth century, the gulf between the classes undoubtedly widened.

The various Censuses from 1881 permit a comparison of city and suburban social structures. Table III compares both city and suburbs in the years 1881 and 1911.

The suburban predominance among the members of the professional and employers and managerial classes is immediately evident. In 1881 these accounted for 30.4% of the suburban population, compared with 11.95% in the city. The gulf had narrowed marginally by 1911, due partly to the fact that the suburbs of Clontarf and Drumcondra had been included in the city. The reverse pattern emerges in the other social categories, though the relative proportion of domestic servants, further reinforces the evidence of suburban prosperity.

Table III Social structure Dublin registration district 1881, 1911[5]

	City		Suburbs	
	1881	1911	1881	1911
I	4.55%	5.5%	18.1%	18.6%
II	7.4%	8.9%	12.3%	14.1%
III	38.6%	34.2%	24.5%	27.2%
IV	15.6%	13.5%	23.9%	20.9%
V	21.8%	25.4%	12.2%	11.0%
X	1.65%	2.2%	2.1%	2.3%

Workhouse inmates and those of unspecified but limited means.

	10.2%	10.3%	6.8%	5.9%
Servants	8.2%	5.5%	13.9%	11.5%

I	Professional and higher public service.
II	Employer and managerial.
III	Skilled manual and clerical.
IV	Semi-skilled, including domestic service.
V	Unskilled.
X	Students not living with family, pensioners.

If Class III is sub-divided into manual and non-manual, suburban residents of this class emerge as more likely to be non-manual workers than their city counterparts. By 1911 despite the expansion of the city boundaries there was a higher proportion of clerical workers among the suburban residents than in the city. The city therefore tended during the nineteenth century to lose its most prosperous residents. In 1891 the suburbs contained nine-tenths as many barristers as the city did, despite having an overall population only 40% that of the city. Dublin also experienced a transformation in the religious composition of its population, a factor not totally unrelated to the middle class migration.

Table IV   Non Manual Workers

	City		Suburbs	
	1881	1911	1881	1911
As % Class III	19.78%	27.44%	30.25%	39.17%
As % total pop.	7.6%	9.38%	7.3%	10.65%

In the 1830s an estimated 27% of the city's population was Protestant.[6] From 1861, the first Census to give the religious composition of the population every decade records a decline in the Protestant proportion of the population, except in 1901 when the city boundaries were altered. In the decade 1861-71 the Church of Ireland population of the city fell by almost ten thousand or 19%.

Table V   Religious composition of the city's population, 1861-1911

	R.C.	C of I	Pres.	Meth.	Others
1861	77.23%	19.35%	1.92%	0.74%	0.76%
1871	79.24%	16.20%	1.83%	0.74%	1.99%
1881	80.44%	15.84%	1.79%	0.77%	1.16%
1891	82.21%	14.34%	1.43%	0.70%	1.33%
1901	81.77%	14.34%	1.40%	0.80%	1.69%
1911	83.13%	12.91%	1.38%	0.76%	1.82%

The decline in Protestant population was universal throughout the city, but the pace of change was not. Some areas already had a very small Protestant population by 1834, in others Protestants represented a sizeable share of

122

the community. Catholics represented in excess of 85% of the population in four central parishes, St. Michael's, St. Michan's, St. Luke's and St. Nicholas Without. These figures suggest, particularly in the case of St. Luke's, the parish containing the ancient weaving area of the Coombe, that some of the traditional sectors of Protestant craft workers, such as the silk weavers had already been seriously undermined. Virtually all the parishes adjoining those named had a Catholic population in excess of 70%. However sizeable Protestant communities still remained in parishes which contained a substantial proportion of middle class residents. Parishes with a Church of Ireland population in excess of 30% of the population were St. Andrew's, St. Anne's and St. Peter's — which included the south city squares and major streets; St. Werburgh's parish which included Dublin Castle. North of the river Liffey, St. George's and St. Thomas' parishes, which contained the north city's Georgian residential area also contained sizeable Protestant communities. In St. George's parish, 40% of the population belong to the Church of Ireland. By 1861 only two parishes had a Protestant population in excess of 30%, St. Anne's and St. Peter's, both situated in the fashionable south-east area. Those areas already strongly Catholic by 1834 showed an intensification of this trend which had spread out to absorb adjoining parishes with moderate Protestant communities in 1834. The most rapid decline in the Protestant population occurred in St. Catherine's parish, a working class and commercial community adjoining Guinness's brewery, and in St. George's parish, indicating the beginning of the middle class desertion of the north city area, though that parish's Protestant population was still above the city's average.

In subsequent decades the flight of the Protestant population continued. It was sharpest in the north city areas which had once contained a middle class population. Rotunda Ward, the only city ward to record a decline in rateable valuation between 1861 and 1901 had the highest percentage decline in the Protestant population in the decades 1861-71 and 1871-81. In 1881-91 it was overtaken by neighbouring Mountjoy Ward, though it still registered a sharp decline. The change in the middle class areas south of the Liffey was somewhat delayed. Not until the decades 1891-1901

123

do Fitzwilliam, Mansion House and Royal Exchange Wards record declines which are above the city's average.

The declining population reflected the changing social balance of the population. Areas with a substantial Protestant population were inhabited by the middle classes. The drift of Protestants from the north city wards and parishes coincided with their social decline. Some comments on the religious patterns in the various occupations are therefore in order.

This unfortunately is an extremely difficult topic and much research remains to be done. The existence of a Protestant working class in eighteenth century Dublin, concentrated mostly among the skilled workers and exercising authority through the guilds is indisputable. Research into the activities of the Dublin Protestant Operatives Association[7] confirms their continued existence, though not their numerical strength in the 1840s. However the history of Dublin in the pre-famine decades suggests the existence of economic distress particularly in industries such as silk, which were particularly associated with Protestant workers.

The 1871 Census provides the first breakdowns of the religious affiliation of different occupations for individual cities and counties. (The 1861 Census provides such a breakdown for the country as a whole). These, though of considerable interest, are arguably too late. By 1871 Protestants number approximately 20% of the city's population, a sizeable decline from the levels of the 1830s and 1840s. The figures in Table VI reveal the survival of some Protestant manufacturing workers, though their share is below that in the male working population as a whole. However the proportion was declining so that by 1911 only 10.43% of manufacturing workers belonged to the Church of Ireland.

Protestant and Presbyterian labourers were virtually unknown while transport workers were disproportionately recruited from among the Catholic population. Male domestic servants belonging to the Church of Ireland totalled 21.72% of the whole in 1871 suggesting that Church of Ireland families of the servant keeping class made efforts to recruit servants belonging to their own faith. Protestants are disproportionately numbered among the middle class occupations of professional and public service and the white-

124

Occupational breakdown of the population of the city of Dublin by religion, 1871, 1881, 1911

	1871			1881			1911		
	RC	CoI	Pres	RC	CoI	Pres	RC	Col	Pres
PP.	47.92	43.82	3.64	53.6	37.25	6.67	57.12	34.99	2.99
MF	80.55	14.04	2.77	81.71	14.09	2.6	85.14	10.43	1.69
B.	83.07	14.15	1.59	85.27	12.23	1.68	86.64	10.48	1.54
ISI	58.16	32.01	5.15	63.73	28.59	4.35	69.18	23.41	3.53
T.	78.93	12.61	1.67	85.63	10.4	1.71	88.03	8.79	1.17
D.	84.84	10.29	2.74	87.24	9.01	1.85	79.11	14.52	1.9
DSM	74.16	21.72	0.5	75.92	18.92	1.21	81.91	15.84	0.76
DSF	85.89	11.48	0.57	87.76	11.02	0.68	91.38	7.63	0.47
Lab.	96.55	2.99	0.08	95.77	3.98	0.21	97.1	2.7	0.09
Prod M	78.45	17.01	1.98	80.80	15.21	2.47	82.23	13.60	1.60

PP. Professional and public service
MF Manufacturing
B. Building
ISI Industrial Service I, clerical, banking insurance etc.
T. Transport
D. Dealing.
DSM. Male domestic service
DSF. Female domestic service.
Lab. Labouring.
Prod. M. Religious breakdown of all occupied males.
For classification see Armstrong op cit.

collar clerical and banking jobs which constituted the Industrial Service category.

These trends are confirmed when the analysis is refined to examine individual occupations. Protestants were over-represented to a substantial degree in law, medicine and civil service white-collar employment, army officers and men. In manufacturing employment Table VII isolates two sectors, printing and machinery where Protestants represented an above-average share of the workforce. The increase in the Protestant share of machinery workers in 1911 probably represents recent migrants from England employed in the new and expanding electrical sector. The residual Protestant (Church of Ireland) strength in silk is also indicated, as is its disappearance over time. Coopering on the other hand is dominated by Catholic workers, with Protestants tending to belong to the Presbyterian faith rather than the Church of Ireland.

Table VII Denominational breakdown of occupations, 1871, 1881, 1911

(100 means a representation proportionate to the share in the working population as a whole.)

	RC			Others*		
	1871	1881	1911	1871	1881	1911
Law	44.3	53.6	65.3	302.7	295.4	260.6
Medicine	38.8	47.3	58.9	322.6	321.8	289.6
Banking	44.7	43.2	57.1	301.5	338.9	298.7
Clerks	76.0	83.1	86.7	187.3	171.1	161.6
Civil Ser.	68.1	76.8	85.8	216.2	197.5	165.6
Mun. Officer	91.5	93.4	112.0	131.1	127.8	44.3
Army Officer	27.7	37.8	22.2	363.4	361.9	460.0
Army men	31.1	25.1	22.1	350.9	415.2	460.5
Police	108.7	104.8	100.7	68.5	79.9	96.9
Teacher	63.2	74.4	71.4	234.0	208.7	232.2
Draper	71.8	86.3	92.3	202.7	145.9	135.9
Printer	85.8	91.9	97.6	151.5	134.9	118.7
Machinery	72.8	90.0	71.1	198.9	141.9	233.6
Silk	92.8	97.2	107.1	126.2	111.6	67.8
Cabinet Mkr	91.8	90.3	101.5	130.0	140.7	92.9
Cooper	117.5	115.7	110.3	36.2	33.8	52.5

*Attempts to calculate these statistics on the basis of Protestant faiths other than the Church of Ireland, i.e. Presbyterians, produced very erratic figures due to the small numbers involved, hence they have been presented as Catholics and others.

Insofar as small areas with concentrations of Protestant workers can be identified, they tend to belong to the skilled sectors. In the various skilled occupations not represented on this table Catholic workers predominated. Carriage workers for example, were over 90% Catholic by 1871. Cabinet making on the other hand, is an instance of a skill in which Protestant workers were over-represented in the 1871 and 1881 returns, but one where their share had fallen by 1911.

It is impossible to state with any accuracy what happened to the Protestant skilled workers. Some, particularly in depressed trades such as silk probably emigrated in the early years of the century. In other instances it seems possible that sons failed, as in the past, to follow their father's trades due to depressed employment opportunities. It is perhaps no coincidence that the two sectors of strong Protestant representation, printing and machinery were areas which satisfactorily maintained and even increased their employment during the late nineteenth century.

The Protestant population still retained strong representation in the professions and white-collar occupations. While the proportions of Catholics rose in medicine, law, teaching and banking, the overall rise was not dramatic and Catholics remained seriously underrepresented. Their rise to over-representation in municipal employment, in marked contrast to the trend in civil service employment probably reflects the impact of political favour within municipal employment.

Evidence concerning inter-generational social mobility and the social composition of religious denominations can be derived from civil marriage registrations. This data has been examined for both the North and South Dublin Unions — an area containing the city and some adjoining suburbs plus a small rural area, for the years 1871 and 1911.[8] Occupations have been coded into seven groups in general following the practice of Armstrong,[9] though Category III has been divided into manual and non-manual while farmers have been separately distinguished to avoid difficulties of classification. In many instances the job descriptions do not distinguish between an employer or employee. A conservative classification has been adopted — assuming an employee unless there is some evidence to the contrary.

The available data confirm the predominance of Protestants in the professional and mercantile classes, a dominance only partly reduced by 1911. In cases where father and son both belonged to the professional class, 83.58% in 1871 were married in Protestant churches or in the Registry office.[10] This figure is exaggerated due to the failure of returns from Westland Row Church, but only to a minor extent. Of all sons belonging to the professional class, regardless of parental occupation, 83.33% married in Protestant churches though such returns only constitute 36.69% of the total. This social imbalance is also found among the employer and clerical classes and, though reduced by 1911 remained very significant.

On the question of inter-generational social mobility the strongest impression is one of relative stability. In both 1871 and 1911, an absolute majority of sons belonged to the same socio-economic group as their father. In 1871

Table VIII Marriages in Protestant Churches or Registry Office as percentage of total socio-economic groupings, 1871 and 1911

	1871	1911
Both Class I (i.e. father and son)	83.58%	67.34%
Both Class II	50%	38%
Both Class III	36.74%	28.9%
Both Class IV	28.57%	18.42%
Both Class V	2.18%	3.33%
All Sons belonging to Class I	83.33%	65.67%
All Sons belonging to Class II	55.55%	40.36%
All Sons belonging to Class IIIa	52.38%	43.24%
All Sons belonging to Class III	33.18%	22.36%
All Sons belonging to Class IV	33.78%	16.45%
All Sons belonging to Class V	9.78%	5.61%
Marriages in Protestant churches and registry offices as % of total marriages with useable occupation data.	36.69%	23.45%
Total no. marriages useable	774	904
Total Protestant and registry marriages	284	212

For the year 1871 the sample consists of one in two of all marriages located. The marriage series for the months April-June could not be located, while the priests of St. Andrews Church, Westland Row, R.C. failed to make any occupational returns in 1871. For 1911 a sample of one return in three was taken, though once again there were a certain number of individual cases where the occupational data, particularly father's occupation had not been entered, or more commonly, was returned as 'deceased'. Female occupational data was consistently not recorded in a majority of cases.

the figure was 56.84%, in 1911, 54.75%. Stability was most evident at both extremes of the social spectrum. In 1871, 85.8% of those in Class I were sons of men who belongd to this group, while 67.93% of unskilled workers were sons of unskilled workers. For skilled workers the figure was 58.86%. The only groups which show any degree of inter-generational mobility are clerical white-collar workers, reflecting that this was an expanding and relatively new occupation, and semi-skilled workers. The semi-skilled class seems to have had imperfect definition and sons of both skilled and unskilled workers appear to have drifted in with ease, reflecting a lack of barriers to entry, while sons of semi-skilled workers also tended to shift to unskilled or skilled employment. The

128

Table IX
Percentage of a socio-economic group who were sons of a specific soci-economic group.

1871

Sons	I Fathers	II	IIIa	III	IV	V	Farm	%	N
I	85.81	6.4	2.6	–	2.6	–	2.6	100	78
II	12.65	37.97	2.53	12.65	2.53	1.26	30.37	100	79
IIIa	16.98	24.52	13.2	13.2	7.54	1.88	22.64	100	53
III	1.66	6.38	2.48	58.85	8.86	15.24	7.09	100	282
IV	–	5.26	–	14.47	36.84	22.36	21.0	100	76
V	–	1.11	1.67	18.43	7.26	67.03	4.46	100	179
Farm	3.7	–	–	7.4	–	7.4	81.48	100	27
Total N	90	72	21	229	74	184	104	–	774

1911

Sons	1 Fathers	II	IIIa	III	IV	V	Farm	%	N
I	64.47	22.36	2.63	1.31	–	–	9.21	100	76
II	7.33	45.87	–	13.76	3.66	1.83	27.52	100	109
IIIa	10.66	20	26.66	20	4	6.66	12	100	75
III	0.78	7.05	3.13	50.19	7.45	20.78	10.58	100	255
IV	–	6.4	2.15	18.27	40.86	25.8	6.45	100	93
V	–	0.74	1.49	19.47	5.61	68.53	4.11	100	267
Farm	–	3.44	3.44	–	–	–	93.1	100	29
N	67	109	37	228	79	267	117	–	904

group with the greatest mobility were sons of farmers, but this is inevitable as the overwhelming majority had consciously opted out of a farming career by virtue of moving to the city. Class II, employer and managerial, also seems to have been a relatively open group with over 60% of its members descended from members of other groups.

By 1911 the overall picture is of somewhat greater mobility. Only 64.47% of Category I are the sons of professional men, while the immobility of Category V has also been reduced. On the other hand, classes II and IIIa record increased proportions of sons following in their fathers' footsteps. Even in the seemingly more fluid circumstances of 1911, the majority were employed in the class in which they were born and mobility when it took place was over a limited social distance. If we exclude the farmers, because it

Table X

Occupations adopted by sons of fathers belonging to a particular socio-economic group

1871

Fathers	I Sons	II	IIIa	III	IV	V	Farm	%	N
I	74.44	11.11	10	3.33	–	–	1.11	100	90
II	6.94	41.66	18.06	25	5.55	2.77	–	100	72
IIIa	9.5	9.5	33.3	33.3	–	14.3	–	100	21
III	–	4.36	3.05	72.48	4.8	14.41	0.87	100	229
IV	2.7	2.7	5.4	33.78	37.83	17.56	–	100	74
V	–	0.54	0.54	23.36	9.23	65.2	1.08	100	184
Farm	1.92	23.07	11.53	19.23	15.38	7.69	21.15	100	104
N	78	79	53	282	76	179	27	–	774

1911

Fathers	I Sons	II	IIIa	III	IV	V	Farm	%	N
I	73.1	11.94	11.94	2.98	–	–	–	100	67
II	15.59	45.87	13.76	16.51	5.5	1.83	0.09	100	109
IIIa	5.4	–	54.05	21.62	5.4	10.81	2.7	100	37
III	0.43	6.57	6.57	56.14	7.45	22.8	–	100	228
IV	–	5.06	3.79	24.05	48.1	18.98	–	100	79
V	–	0.74	1.87	19.85	8.98	68.53	–	100	267
Farm	5.98	25.64	7.69	23.07	5.12	9.4	23.07	100	117
N	76	109	75	255	93	267	29	–	904

remains difficult to rank them on a social scale, and assume that the clerical class was superior to the skilled working class, we can calculate the total numbers who ascended and descended the social scale between two generations. In both years those ascending and declining roughly balanced. In 1871, excluding farmers, a total of 121 advanced, while 126 descended, 32.6% of the total moved. In 1911, a total of 160 moved up, while 157 descended, 32.48% of all cases.

Social mobility was relatively limited, with those ascending roughly balanced by those descending. This conclusion is not surprising given the relatively poor economic prospects prevailing in the city. It is also possible that those descending the social scale were less likely to marry and this may bias our figures somewhat.

Inter-generational mobility, when it occurred was over a

relatively limited social distance. The increased openness of Class I in 1911 compared with 1871 merely reflected a greater influx of businessmen's sons into the professions, though farmers sons had by this stage also gained limited entry. Access to the professions was primarily restricted by economic factors. Medical education proved extremely expensive and the establishment of a successful career depended on access to a hospital position. One leading physician explained[11]

> his success does not depend upon private patronage.
> His selection to a hospital depends on the governor
> and the ways in the hospital . . . the hospital physician
> has pupils who become scattered all over the country
> and they send up the patients.

A son of a successful doctor, or of an otherwise well-established family would be more likely to secure the favour of hospital governors and establish a successful career.

Access to medical careers for Catholics, which could prove difficult within the established hospital system was eased by the founding of two Catholic teaching hospitals, the Mater Misericordiae and St. Vincent's hospitals which were linked to the Catholic University medical school. This may have opened up medical careers for sons of prosperous businessmen or farmers, but the financial burdens remained overwhelming. In Cosgrave and Pike, *Dublin and county Dublin in the twentieth century* (published 1908),[12] a book containing biographies of prominent city personalities, twenty-two of the sixty-six doctors listed, one third, are sons of doctors. Most of the remainder were sons of clergymen or army officers.

The other prime income earning professions were those connected with the law. The education of a solicitor which proceeded by means of an apprenticeship was less expensive than that of a doctor or barrister. As an apprentice scrivenor a young man could earn perhaps £60 per annum, which would reduce the cost of his training.[13] Entering an apprenticeship required payment of a capital fee. For those without capital the more lowly post of solicitor's clerk could perhaps ultimately lead to qualifying as a solicitor. However the solicitors as a body placed considerable obstacles against the upward mobility of clerks. Despite repeated pleas, clerks were forced to sit an apprenticeship, though this was reduced in length for a clerk of ten years standing, and they were also forced to sit the regular solicitors' examinations. Only 37 law clerks qualified as solicitors between the years 1866 and 1888, less than 3% of the total entrants.[14] Evidence on the parental occupations of solicitors apprentices for Ireland as a whole, suggests that 'country' families — families listing a country house address but no occupation, generally gentlemen — and solicitors were the most common source of apprentice solicitors. Of those apprentice solicitors coming from a trade background, 13.5% of total entrants between 1851 and 1860, many apparently came from relatively modest backgrounds having fathers listed as tanner, hatter or victualler etc.

The costs of becoming a barrister were much greater than those of a solicitor. The overwhelming majority of barristers were graduates until the early twentieth century, in contrast to less than 10% of solicitors. Until 1885 Irish barristers were required to attend for several terms at one of the London Inns of Court and this dramatically increased the expense. The ending of this requirement should have widened access, but there is no evidence of this happening. The social background remained remarkably stable over time, the only change which may indicate a lowering of social status is the falling proportion of graduates entering the profession after 1901. The social background of barristers was notably higher than that of solicitors, and was, on the whole, a background of privilege. In the years 1901-10, 26.9% were from 'country' families, 16.3% were sons of professional men — excluding barristers and 12.6% were sons of barristers. Those whose fathers were engaged in trade, a falling proportion throughout the late nineteenth century tended to be sons of brewers, merchants or businessmen of high status.

Barristers' incomes could be extremely high. At the beginning of the nineteenth century top barristers earned an average of £8,000 per annum. By 1873 George May, Q.C. estimated that only two barristers were currently earning in excess of £4,000 per annum; five or six were earning £3,000, twenty earned £2,000 and many were earning £1,500.[15] Reaching such income levels required, in addition to expensive study, a long period of poverty and it was believed that most young barristers could not survive without an alternative source of income, either earned or unearned. In addition to economic barriers other factors apparently limited access to successful legal careers. Allegations of discrimination against Catholics in the Law Library were made in the early years of the century,[16] though more precise details remain unclear. Promotion to Queen's Counsel was generally governed by the politics of the applicant and that of the Lord Chancellor. Barristers relied heavily on solicitors for work and a young barrister, with no social connections among solicitors could face considerable difficulties. These considerations only arose for the small minority who could overcome the costs of qualifying as a barrister, having first acquired the necessary education to embark on this career.

Class II, the employer and managerial class emerges as considerably more open, recruiting members from the professional class, to a considerable extent from the farming community and also to some extent from the skilled working class. This partly reflects its heterogeneity, ranging from politicians and grocers − i.e. small businessmen, to large manufacturers and financiers. The recruitment of some members from classes III and IIIa is not therefore surprising. For a shop assistant's son to become an employer shopkeeper is not a dramatic advance.

The barriers to entry were partly educational, but the primary barrier was one of capital. The higher proportion of farmers's sons, than in the professions, reflects this fact and suggests that a certain transfer of capital took place from agriculture to city businesses, especially grocery and publican businesses. This impression is confirmed by an examination of the birth-place of residents of a small sample of streets in the Census enumerators returns for the year 1911. Of 61 shopkeepers identified, 31 fractionally more than half were natives of neither Dublin city nor county, though Dubliners accounted for over 70% of the overall population.[17] In the year 1901 all the pubs identified in a sample survey of Wood Quay Ward were owned by rural migrants. This picture of strong rural representation in shopkeeping is confirmed by the recollections of C.S. Andrews concerning his school-fellows in the Holy Faith Convent, Dominick St. in the early years of the century.

They were the sons and daughters of prosperous butchers, grocers, publicans and junior civil servants. To them, and to the nuns, my accent sounded utterly of the pavement, the more so because the parents of the children and the nuns were mostly from rural areas.

The Andrews family history shows some methods of entry into the shopkeeping class. His maternal grandfather had been an inspector in the Dublin Metropolitan Police. When he died, his widow turned the front room and yard into a dairy business. His father, son of a small builder was apprenticed to a pawnbroker. Eventually a legacy from his employer, plus a similar small sum which his mother acquired permitted the family to rent a shop in Terenure which his mother ran as a creamery while his father established his own pawnbroking and auctioneering business.[18]

Clerical workers, including civil servants, were predominantly recruited from the professions, employers and managers and the clerical class with a substantial farming input. The number of clerks emerging from the skilled manual working class, 13% in 1871, rising to 20% by 1911, suggests that sons of skilled workers or policemen could aspire to clerical careers to a limited extent.

Although educational costs were lower, other factors militated against recruitment of working class applicants. Entry to a Bank of Ireland clerkship for example, was by means of an initial interview of candidates who had been nominated by governors and managers. Those deemed to have passed this interview were then subjected to an examination which was apparently of senior national school standard.[19] The initial selection by nomination and interview biassed recruitment in favour of the middle classes. In 1873 William Digges La Touche, explained the bank clerks were 'generally merchants sons, sons of gentlemen and clergymen and some few shopkeepers sons'.[20] Discrimination on religious grounds may also have acted to restrict social mobility. In 1902 a body known as the Catholic Association was founded with the intention among other aims of ascertaining[21]

as far as possible . . . the position of Catholics as regards banks, railways, government, insurance and municipal offices, local government appointments, professional openings, the press, university and Parliament.

One result of their lobbying was a change in recruitment practices in the Great Southern and Western Railways clerkships. Previously these had been filled by directorial nominations, which was undoubtedly socially restrictive and presumably religiously so, as well. In 1903 competitive examinations were instituted. Despite this, there was apparently no immediate revolution in the background of successful candidates. Working class children and small farmer or farm labourers' children both lacked the necessary educational level, or were frequently disqualified on medical grounds, such as defective eyesight or other slight disabilities.[22]

Although the educational standard for many clerical jobs was only that of national — i.e. elementary school, few children of unskilled or semi-skilled workers reached this level. National schools were poorly equipped and school attendance was extremely erratic on the part of the poorest children. The need to supplement family income by begging, selling newspapers or other sources of casual employment[23] militated against school attendance and this was particularly so after children reached ten years of age. Most working class children left school having only completed third, or perhaps fourth standard. In 1912 there were a total of 44,048 boys in Third Standard at National Schools, but only 36,596 in Fourth Standard and the higher standards were marked by a further falling off in attendance.[24] In at least one working class city centre school there was no class available beyond fifth class as the majority had left school by this stage and those of 'better class' had moved to attend the schools of the Christian Brothers.[25] Education as a path to upward mobility was not readily available to the poor, though it provided a limited avenue for skilled working class families and those of clerical background. Many of these families favoured the schools of the Christian Brothers because they had a reputation for achieving examination successes, but despite the fact that the Christian Brothers provided secondary schooling free of charge — the only body doing so — few working class children continued their education. As C.S. Andrews recalls[26]

In Synge St. (a leading Christian Brothers school) the

135

bulk of the pupils were from the lower middle class and working classes but, when the secondary school stage was reached, a great number of the working class boys dropped out. Their family circumstances required that they should contribute to the family budget.

Secondary schooling was privately organised on a denominational basis and with the exception of the Christian Brothers schools entailed the payment of fees. Scholarships were extremely rare, but even free schooling or more extensive scholarships would not have helped those who failed to complete primary schooling. Night schools were poorly developed and seem to have been unsuccessful. Those organised by the Catholic charity of the Society of St. Vincent de Paul placed considerable emphasis on religious rather than secular learning and in the process lost the financial assistance of the Commissioners for National Education. The schools do not appear to have prospered and closed after a short period.[27]

Education therefore, both primary and secondary, was generally availed of to the greatest extent by those with some surplus income. The proportion of Catholics receiving either primary or secondary schooling in the city was consistently below the proportion of Protestants.

Table XI
Percentage of the population of different religions receiving education, 1881-1911[28]

	1881 Prim.	1881 Sup.	1891 Prim.	1891 Sup.	1901 Prim.	1901 Sup.	1911 Prim.	1911 Sup.
R.C.	10.5	0.64	10.5	1.24	13.2	2.0	13.0	1.9
C of I	11.8	6.3	12.6	6.5	13.4	6.1	12.0	4.2
Pres.	12.7	6.0	14.1	8.2	10.9	11.4	12.0	9.4
Meth.	8.23	9.7	10.0	10.2	9.4	10.3	10.9	7.3

[Prim. — primary; Sup. — Superior]

Opportunities for advancement by means of education would therefore appear to have been restricted, and the discrepancy in attendance at superior schooling between the different religions does much to account for discrepancies in representation in professional and clerical occupations. On the whole when the working classes moved out of the class into which they were born, they simply moved into another segment of the working class. In 1871 almost 83% of Class III, 74% of Class IV and 93% of Class V were recruited from classes III, IV and V. Most of the outsiders came from farming, though III is of interest in having 6-7% of its recruits from the employer class.

The skilled manual class contains a number of readily identifiable groups. The majority were skilled craftsmen and in many cases sons followed directly in their fathers' footsteps reflecting the restrictive attitude on apprenticeship adopted by many skilled trades. Access was frequently limited to sons of existing tradesmen. The bricklayers union confined apprenticeships to sons of bricklayers, though some outsiders were admitted on payment of a £30 fee. In the depressed silk weaving trade only sons or grandsons of weavers could be recruited, while the stonecutters union ruled that their apprenticeships should also be confined to sons of stonecutters. Records of the plasterers union reveal 'a signficant repetition of family names'.[29] The only obvious exception to these restrictions occurs in the case of the printers union. The number in each individual craft occurring among the marriage registrations is too small to permit any examination of patterns of continuity among individual trades. However a clear picture of sons following the parental trade emerges. Of 166 cases where both father and son belonged to Class III in 1871, a group which includes a sizeable number of both soldiers and policemen who are excluded from this analysis, 63, or 38% followed identical trades. The tendency for sons to follow father was most pronounced in building trades such as plasterer, or carpenter, though it was also evident among tailors. In numerous other instances sons of craftsmen took up another trade closely related to that of their father, such as shifting from one building trade to another. Statistics indicate an influx of workers from the unskilled and semi-skilled categories. Much of this influx can be accounted for by soldiers who were frequently the sons of labourers. In a limited number of instances labourers' sons take up skilled trades. It is possible that such men were grandsons of carpenters or had connec-

137

tions with the trade through other close relations. The existence of some non-union houses would have permitted the bypassing of restrictions on the background of apprentices, but it would seem probable that these apprenticeships would be sold on the open market for a fee.

The career of policemen almost invariably attracted farmers' sons. Of the twelve policemen recorded in 1871, six were farmer's sons, two were sons of labourers, one of a skilled artisan and one each were sons of an auctioneer, an army man and a policeman. In 1911 twelve of the fifteen policemen recorded were sons of farmers, the remainder being the sons of a steward, a gamekeeper and a policeman. The preference for recruiting policemen from men of farming background was well established. An inquiry into police pay in 1873 lamented the 'diminution in Ireland of the ranks of the population from which the police is recruited',[30] but despite an apparent scarcity of farmers sons one witness expressed himself 'loath to take men from the city of Dublin, though some were occasionally accepted'; he personally favoured the farming class.[31] The evidence of policemen being recruited from rural Ireland is confirmed by independent evidence. All 38 inmates of Summerhill Police barracks in 1901 were non Dubliners, while in a small sample of streets from the 1911 Census, all the twenty-one active or retired policemen were migrants. In London Charles Booth discovered that only 30% of policemen were native Londoners.[32]

Those in Class IV consisted mainly of service workers, domestic servants and transport workers. In 1871, 21% of its members were sons of farmers, much the largest representation of farmers sons in the working classes. By 1911 this had dropped to 6%. The influx of farmers sons is not surprising given the number of jobs which entailed working with horses. Domestic servants also tended to be of rural background and the falling proportion of farmers' sons partly reflects the dwindling ranks of male servants. This also accounts for the much lower Protestant share in this class by 1911. Some of the largest recruiters of transport employees also apparently favoured rural recruits. The Dublin United Tram Co. according to one source, had a policy of not hiring Dublin men as drivers or conductors and those attached to their Terenure depot were generally from Co. Westmeath.[33] The large proportion of sons of labourers or craftsmen who shifted to semi-skilled jobs did so because of lack of barriers to entry. Apprenticeships were not an issue, nor was trade union strength a handicap to outsiders. Similarly sons of semi-skilled workers drifted to the status of general labourer or occasionally rose to the ranks of skilled workers.

The general labouring class remains, with the exception of the professions, the least mobile, with over 67% of its members in 1871 sons of labourers and a virtually identical 68.5% in 1911. The largest number of outside recruits were skilled workers confirming the numerous statements that some skilled workers dropped to the labouring class because of poor economic prospects. The numbers so declining appear to have risen over time. In 1871, 14.41% of those whose father belonged to Class III had become unskilled labourers; for 1911 the comparable figure is 22.8%.

Investigating the background of unskilled labourers permits us to view with some scepticism allegations that Dublin labouring jobs were frequently taken by migrants from the country. It is possible that some labourers, themselves sons of labourers, were in fact sons of agricultural labourers, but there is no evidence to confirm this while the proportion of farmers' sons among the labouring community is extremely low. The predominance of city-born among the labouring community is confirmed by Census enumeration returns. Thus Dubliners are overrepresented among the labourers and hawkers in Wood Quay Ward in 1901 while being underrepresented among shopkeepers and shop assistants. In the city-centre tenement streets of Tyrone St. and Mabbot St. in 1911, 86.6% of unskilled labourers were native Dubliners compared with 70% of the total population.

Allegations of rural labourers displacing native Dubliners were rife. At a meeting of Dublin Corporation in 1904 one councillor expressed fears that a certain building contract would result in the importing of a large number of outside labourers.[34] Similarly a delegate to the Trades Council in 1896 complained of an influx of labourers into the city who were taking all the jobs connected with the building of Portrane Asylum and the main drainage contract.[35]

139

Table XII Migrants and Natives in Dublin City and County*

Birthplace	City Dublin	City Elsewhere	County Dublin	County Elsewhere
1841	170,142	62,584	103,371	36,676
	(73.11)	(26.89)	(73.81)	(26.19)
1851	156,811	101,558	101,582	45,196
	(60.69)	(39.31)	(69.21)	(30.79)
1861	168,691	86,117	107,085	48,359
	(66.20)	(33.80)	(68.87)	(31.13)
1871	155,861	90,465	102,912	56,024
	(63.28)	(36.72)	(64.75)	(35.75)
1881	153,332	96.228	105,924	63,351
	(61.44)	(38.56)	(62.58)	(37.42)
1891	164,813	80,162	109,145	65,042
	(67.28)	(32.72)	(62.61)	(37.39)
1901	193,451	97,145	99,576	57,980
	(66.57)	(33.43)	(63.20)	(36.80)
1911	214,364	90,415	111,808	60,585
	(70.33)	(29.67)	(64.86)	(35.14)

* Dublin in both cases means born city *or* county. It is impossible to distinguish migrants from city to county and vice versa.

There is evidence that some labouring jobs, including some of the more secure, may have passed to rural workers. Guinness's brewery preferred rural labourers, ostensibly because 'few town-bred men could satisfy requirements of the company regarding physique'.[36] They required a height of 5' 7" - 6' 1" and a chest measurement of 37½-40½ inches. The canal companies were also said to have favoured migrant workers. This may have been due to the desire for larger and stronger workers, but one suspects that work discipline and employers' control may also have been a factor. Some contractors may also have favoured migrant workers as less likely to be unionised or to have adopted restrictive work practices.

Our evidence suggests that rural born labourers do not appear to have settled long in the city, or to have married to any great extent. The register for the South Dublin Union workhouse suggests that rural labourers tended to come to the city in times of depression, a fact confirmed by the 1851 Census, the immediate post-famine Census which records the peak proportion of migrants in the city's population. Being more mobile than native Dubliners it seems probable that they would have emigrated rather than face long-term unemployment. Unfortunately it is not possible to estimate inward and outward migration, but in a study of the German city of Bochum, David Crew noted that[37]

> from nine to twenty-five per cent of the population also left the city each year and there is good reason to suspect that most of these out-migrants had also been among that year's recent arrivals.

> The out-migrant flow was disproportionately composed of unskilled and semi-skilled workers while skilled workers were over-represented among those who remained in the city.

The evidence for Dublin is not wholly conclusive but it seems probable that the hard-core of city labourers consisted of native-born residents, the sons of labourers. H.J. Dyos examining the birth-places of the population of one deteriorating London slum street discovered a steadily-increasing proportion of London-born at a time when the overall proportion of Londoners in the population was declining.[38]

The final group deserving of comment are farmers' sons. Our picture is necessarily more fragmentary than in the case of other groups as only a minority appear in city marriage registers. They achieve a variety of occupations not seen in any other group, with strong representation in the upper groups, a substantial presence in the skilled working class and few general labourers. The variety of occupations reflects the fact that 'farmer' covers a wide economic spectrum. It also suggests that migration may have opened up prospects of social advance which were denied to the indigenous population.

While figures on migrant numbers in the suburbs are not available before 1911, these suggest an above average migration to the suburbs, particularly to the most middle class suburbs. In that year only 56% of the population of Rathmines was Dublin-born, compared with almost 64% in Pembroke and 67% in Kingstown. The high proportion of migrants in the suburbs may confirm earlier evidence of significant numbers of migrants in middle-class occupations, or it may simply reflect the large numbers of country serving girls living in these areas. An examination of the Census enumerators' returns for Palmerstown Road and Park, two of the most prestigious roads in Rathmines in 1911 confirms the predominance of migrant servants, only 27% were Dublin-born. Excluding servants, Dubliners accounted for only 47.8% of the total population, substantially lower than in Rathmines as a whole, but suggesting a migrant predominance in higher status housing. Migrants in Dublin, in marked contrast to emigrants tended to come from the more prosperous parts of Ireland, the counties adjoining Dublin, with a substantial number coming from England, no doubt reflecting the substantial movement of military and civil service personnel. In 1911, 20.14% came from the counties of Meath, Kildare and Wicklow and a further 18.8% came from the eight next closest counties. Natives of England and Wales accounted for a further 18.6%. Only 6.8% came from the province of Connacht. The fact that most came from the more prosperous areas may partly account for their seemingly favourable careers in the city. Many obtained either lodging or employment, frequently both, with relatives and neighbours who had already settled in the city. In 1901 Clery's department store had a resident population of staff who were 95% non-Dubliners and 44% of those in the best positions were natives of Munster no doubt reflecting the fact that Mr. Clery who had purchased the store in the 1880s was a native of that province. In Talbot St. most of the shop assistants in the stores and public houses in 1911 were natives of the same county as the proprietor.

C.S. Andrews' grandmother kept an unending series of lodgers but all were invariably[39]

> uncles or cousins or aunts from Wicklow or Wexford, or, from time to time, nieces and nephews from Longford where her only sister had married and produced a large family.

Michael Anderson noted similar patterns of migrants being assisted by family connections in his study of Preston.[40] The apparent infrequency of upward social mobility for much of the population; the fact that many groups of non-manual workers and some manual workers in secure employment came from beyond the city, coupled with the fact that

Table XIII

Percentage of daughters of a socio-economic group marrying sons of a socio-economic group

1871

	I	II	IIIa	III	IV	V	Farm	Total	N
	Father of groom								
Father of bride									
I	72.16	14.43	5.15	1.03	1.03	–	6.18	100	97
II	8.86	32.91	1.26	24.05	6.32	6.32	20.25	100	79
IIIa	9.09	13.63	9.09	36.36	4.54	9.09	18.18	100	22
III	3.01	11.2	3.87	45.68	14.22	14.65	7.32	100	232
IV	–	5	2.5	35	17.5	25	15	100	80
V	0.59	1.19	0.59	23.8	7.73	61.3	4.76	100	168
Farm	–	–	1.2	25.3	9.63	14.45	49.39	100	83
N	87	75	21	223	75	176	104	–	761

1911

	I	II	IIIa	III	IV	V	Farm	Total	N
	Father of groom								
Father of bride									
I	62.5	29.68	1.56	1.56	–	–	4.68	100	64
II	11.76	36.47	8.23	11.76	8.23	8.23	15.29	100	85
IIIa	11.4	31.4	5.7	31.4	5.7	5.7	8.57	100	35
III	2.36	8.05	6.16	45.02	9.95	21.8	6.63	100	211
IV	–	7.4	4.93	29.62	19.75	30.86	7.4	100	81
V	0.42	2.59	0.86	22.07	9.09	60.6	4.32	100	231
Farm	3.03	13.13	1.01	14.14	10.1	4.04	54.54	100	99
N	63	103	30	206	77	224	103	–	806

the professions and leading commercial occupations continued to be dominated by Protestants all contributed to considerable social fragmentation within the city's population. This was also increased by social divisions which operated between city and suburbs. The fragmentation is further confirmed if we investigate the social backgrounds of both parties in a marriage. For this purpose we have examined the occupations of both fathers as a measure of social distance. The alternative would have been to examine

143

Table XIV
Percentage of sons of a socio-economic group marrying daughters belonging to a socio-economic group
1871

	I	II	IIIa	III	IV	V	Farm	Total	N
	Father of bride								
Father of groom									
I	80.45%	8.04	2.29	8.04	–	1.14	–	100	87
II	18.66	34.66	4	34.66	5.33	2.66	–	100	75
IIIa	23.8	4.76	9.52	42.85	9.52	4.76	4.76	100	21
III	0.44	8.52	3.53	47.53	12.55	17.93	9.41	100	223
IV	1.33	6.66	1.33	44	18.66	17.33	10.66	100	75
V	–	2.84	1.13	19.31	11.36	58.52	6.81	100	176
Farm	5.76	15.38	3.84	16.34	11.53	7.69	39.42	100	104
N	97	79	22	232	80	168	83	–	761

1911

	I	II	IIIa	III	IV	V	Farm	Total	N
	Father of bride								
Father of groom									
I	63.49	15.87	6.34	7.93	–	1.58	4.76	100	63
II	18.44	30.09	10.67	16.5	5.82	5.82	12.62	100	103
IIIa	3.33	23.22	6.66	43.33	13.33	6.66	3.33	100	30
III	0.48	4.85	5.33	46.1	11.65	24.76	6.79	100	206
IV	–	9.09	2.59	27.27	20.77	27.27	12.98	100	77
V	–	3.1	0.89	20.53	11.16	62.5	1.78	100	224
Farm	2.9	12.62	2.9	13.59	5.82	9.7	52.4	100	103
N	64	85	35	211	81	231	99	–	806

the occupations of grooms' and that of the father of the bride, as a majority of brides list no occupation. The figures which emerge show somewhat greater openness in terms of choice of marriage partner than was evident in terms of social mobility, but the existence of strong class dividing lines is also apparent. A total of 47.5% of those marrying in 1871 and a virtually identical 46.89% of those marrying in 1911 came from the same social class. As in the case of social mobility, the most closed groups were at both extremes: 80.45% of sons of professional families in 1871 married daughters of similar backgrounds, while 58.62% of sons of unskilled workers married daughters of unskilled workers. The corresponding figures for 1911 were 53.49% and 54.54%. The figures appear to have been higher than those found in the London area by Crossick where in 1873-5, 65.5% of sons of professional, large business and financial households married daughters of men with non-manual occupations and 58.9% of labourers sons married daughters of labourers or servants.[41] The combination of religion with class divisions would have increased barriers to marriage. The registration returns do not identify religiously-mixed marriages but it seems probable that they were infrequent.

There was a decided tendency for farmers' sons and farmers' daughters to intermarry, a tendency which had increased by 1911, probably because there were more farmers' daughters resident in the city. This suggests that migrants tended to some extent to form a separate social grouping.

There was also a tendency among the working classes to choose marriage partners from the same residential area. In 1871, 21.3% of couples marrying gave the same address;[42] 7.9% lived in the same street and 39.3% in a different street but within a mile of each other. Only 22.9% lived in a different area of Dublin, while in 8.5% of marriages, one or both came from outside Dublin. The middle classes show a decidedly more scattered residential pattern.

The overall impression is of a very slow erosion of Protestant dominance in the higher status occupations and of no dramatic increase in the extent of inter-generational social mobility. The group which would seem to have advanced to the greatest extent were farmers' sons migrating to the city. The relative lack of change is not surprising given the unfavourable state of the city's economy and the absence of expanding opportunities. However it is of considerable significance. Dublin throughout this period emerges as a city seriously divided by both religion and class, a distinction increased by the religious and social gulf existing between city and suburbs. Not only were the suburbs predominantly middle-class, but they were also to a considerable extent Protestant, though by 1911, an increasing proportion of Catholics, particularly those with non-manual occupations were listing suburban addresses.

The social bias remained strong and even increased, as the locational pattern for certain occupational groups in 1881 and 1911 indicates. The fact that civil service clerks showed a greater tendency to reside in the city in 1911 merely reflects the boundary change in 1900 which brought Drumcondra, a favourite residence of this group within the city boundaries. The growing fashion for medical practices to be situated in the city's southern Georgian Squares may also be responsible for the shift city-wards of doctors.[43]

Table XV Index of residential location for various occupations 1881 and 1911

	1881 City	1881 Suburbs	1911 City	1911 Suburbs
Doctors	88.4	130.3	93.46	120.0
Barristers	101.24	96.75	67.9	198.1
Solicitors	81.1	149.5	41.98	277.4
Gentlemen	45.8	241.7	33.4	303.7
Bank clerks	56.4	214.2	34.4	300.5
Civil service	79.4	153.9	87.8	137.3

The individual suburbs were by no means uniform in their social composition. This was determined by a variety of forces, some partly within the control of the developers, such as the type of housing to be built, but many determined by long-term geographical and social circumstances. By the end of the eighteenth century the Duke of Leinster had decreed that the south-eastern quadrant of the city was the fashionable area and this trend continued with the establishment of the southern suburbs such as Pembroke and Rathmines. A protracted law suit concerning the land of the Blessington estate, a major landowner to the north of the city delayed development in this area, while the fact that until the late 1850s the major roads leading northwards out of the city were burdened with tolls, while those to the southern suburbs were free, is also important. One builder believed[44]

> that if the toll gates had been removed from the north
> side years ago, the southern suburban districts would

not have been so prosperous, but that the northern would have been equally built upon.

In the years 1848-54 a total of 421 houses had been built in the toll-free suburban area (approximately one-quarter of the area adjoining the city), compared with only 57 houses in the area subject to tolls.[45] As a result of turnpikes it was alleged that land to the north of the city had become depreciated in value and was in demand only for cemetries, prisons or lunatic asyslums.[46] In turn the existence of these establishments deterred subsequent house building.

Fashion and health also played a part. Low-lying land was unpopular because it was held to harbour fever and this militated against Clontarf, while part of the drift to the outlying seaside areas such as Kingstown and Killiney was prompted by a belief in the health-giving properties of sea-air. The railway line was also a factor, though a more limited influence than is generally supposed.

The timing of suburban expansion also influenced the character of an area. The professional and rentier class initiated the move to the suburbs, thus areas such as Rathmines and Pembroke which expanded rapidly during the 1860s catered for this class. By the mid to late 1870s the newer suburban residents tended to come to an increasing extent from the clerical, small business and perhaps artisan classes. Apart from considerations of fashion therefore, Drumcondra which only developed in the late 1870s would have been unlikely to house a substantial proportion of professional families.

The final factor was the pre-suburban population. Suburban expansion did not take place on virgin soil, but rather was superimposed on existing villages or countryside. Thus fishing villages such as Clontarf, Blackrock or Ringsend were swallowed up by the new townships. So too were existing industrial areas, particularly Ringsend and Irishtown which contained glassworks, boat building and a seafaring population which contrasted sharply with the new residents of Pembroke township.

The importance of professional and public service residents emerges from all townships from Table XVI. In Kilmainham, the absence of professional residents is compensated by a strong military presence. Drumcondra's high professional

147

percentage is achieved by a strong representation of clergy-men, theology students and monks, amounting to almost 8% of the overall occupied males. The social preeminance of Blackrock township is reflected in the high percentage of male domestic servants.

Table XVI Employment pattern occupied males 1891 (%)

	Pemb.	R&R	Kilm	Clon	Drum	Bl	Kings
MF	14.0	10.5	15.6	8.2	14.5	6.9	7.4
D	10.9	11.5	2.75	11.7	8.5	12.8	13.8
DS	5.8	5.3	1.8	7.8	4.7	13.8	7.3
PP	31.6	37.0	47.2	32.0	36.4	38.0	20.4
(Soldier	14.4	4.0	41.2	4.4	—	2.7	1.7)
T	8.1	6.4	12.5	5.3	4.8	8.6	18.2
B	5.4	6.2	5.8	3.7	6.1	6.2	8.5
ISI	8.3	15.4	2.4	15.4	14.1	8.4	5.3
Lab.	9.7	6.4	10.5	9.1	6.1	8.4	14.9

Pemb–Pembroke, R&R–Rathmines, Kilm–Kilmainham, Clon–Clon-tarf, Bl–Blackrock, Kings–Kingstown, Drum–Drumcondra.

Both Pembroke and Kilmainham register a strong indus-trial presence, so to a lesser extent does Drumcondra, though some of these manufacturing workers may have been em-ployed in the city. Rathmines, Drumcondra and Clontarf emerge as the most common residences for banking and com-mercial clerks, while Kingstown had the least 'suburban' profile, with a low proportion in professional and public employment but a very strong transport sector, many sea-men, and a significant number of general labourers — a pattern strongly resembling Dublin city.

Excluding the indigenous residents, the appeal of the sub-urbs was primarily to professional and public servants and to white-collar workers. Given the preponderance of Protes-tants in these occupations it is not surprising that virtually all the suburbs contained a substantially greater proportion of Protestant residents than the city. There is a remarkable divergence in the Protestant share of the population. The Monkstown Ward of Blackrock township emerges as unique in having a minority Catholic population as late as 1911.

Table XVII Religious composition of suburban population

	1871 RC	1871 CoI	1871 Pres	1891 RC	1891 CoI	1891 Pres	1911 RC	1911 CoI	1911 Pres
City	79.2	16.2	1.8	82.2	14.3	1.4	83.1	12.9	1.4
Bl W.	68.0	24.9	1.3	66.3	27.2	1.3	73.7	23.1	2.2
Boot W.	69.9	25.3	1.1	74.3	19.4	1.3	73.7	20.6	2.1
Monks. W.	35.6	57.3	2.7	45.0	45.8	1.9	49.3	42.1	1.9
Blackrock	61.4	32.2	1.6	64.1	28.9	2.2	67.4	26.1	2.1
Monks W	53.3	27.4	3.4	50.4	45.2	2.1	61.2	34.9	2.1
Kings E	58.0	35.9	1.4	63.9	31.0	1.4	61.4	32.3	2.5
Kings W	68.2	26.2	1.2	77.2	19.6	1.5	78.6	17.3	1.4
Glasthule	67.0	30.3	0.8	63.1	31.3	1.5	66.7	27.6	2.8
Kingstown	63.4	31.5	1.5	67.6	18.4	1.6	69.4	25.5	2.1
Pembroke	56.2	36.3	3.6	59.8	30.8	5.1	66.7	27.6	2.8
Rathgar	43.8	45.3	5.9						
Rath E.				47.6	40.8	3.8	54.2	34.6	3.7
Rath W.				52.5	36.5	3.9	53.9	33.6	5.1
Rathmines	47.8	42.3	3.6	49.9	38.7	3.9	54.1	34.1	4.4
Clontarf	61.3	31.8	2.9	55.5	32.0	5.5 (n.a. after 1900 due			
Clonliffe				67.0	22.1	4.4 to boundary			
Glasnevin				75.4	21.2	1.7 changes)			
Drumcondra W				82.7	12.7	2.0			
Drumcondra				72.3	19.8	3.3			
Kilmainham	65.3	28.6	2.3	67.6	28.8	0.7			

Monks W. —Monkstown Ward, Boot—Booterstown Ward, Kings E. and W— Kingstown East and West Wards, do. for Rathmines.

Rathmines records a substantially lower Catholic population than neighbouring Pembroke, due to the absence of an indigenous working class. Drumcondra was the most Catholic of all suburbs partly due to the concentration of religious houses, but also, one suspects due to the character of its development.

There are some interesting, though inexplicable variations in the percentage of Presbyterians and Methodists in various areas. In 1871 Presbyterians amounted to over 3% of the population in both Monkstown Wards and 2.9% in Clontarf. By 1891 they had left Monkstown but are very strongly represented in Clontarf, 5.3%, the neighbouring Clonliffe Ward, 4.43%, Pembroke 5.1% and at Rathmines 3.9%. Methodists tended to be found in the same areas, notably Clontarf where they accounted for 4.2% of the population. In 1891, Presbyterians and Methodists combined accounted for almost one-tenth of Clontarf's population. The concentrations of 1891 tended to survive in 1911.

Table XVIII Religious composition of occupations, city and county, 1881 %

	City RC	City CoI	City Pres	County RC	Co. CoI	Co. Pres
MF	81.71	14.09	2.6	73.6	19.96	2.89
PP	53.6	37.25	6.67	45.64	46.94	4.16
B	85.27	12.23	1.68	80.95	16.43	1.37
ISI	63.73	28.59	4.35	36.2	51.3	5.69
T	85.63	10.4	1.71	79.3	13.25	0.78
D	87.24	9.01	1.85	70.07	22.08	1.29
Lab.	95.77	3.98	0.21	94.85	4.93	0.21
DSM	75.92	18.92	1.21	76.03	22.08	1.29
Prod. M.	80.8	15.21	2.47	73.5	21.69	2.21

Table XIX Residential bias in occupations by religion, 1881

(%)	All City	All Co.	R.C. City	R.C. Co.	CoI City	CoI Co.
Barr/Sol	55.9	44.02	64.98	35.02	49.46	50.54
Teacher	48.18	51.81	50.14	49.86	43.98	56.02
Civil Ser	51.76	48.23	63.8	36.2	39.5	60.5
Printer	87.52	12.48	91.79	8.21	84.05	15.95
Carpenter	72.59	37.75	72.92	27.07	70.73	29.27

Most of the religious imbalance can be attributed to the middle class composition of the suburban population. However there is some evidence that Protestants, of all occupational classes, may have shown a greater tendency to live in the suburbs. Unfortunately the data on suburban occupations is not broken down by religion but we can examine the county occupations on a religious basis. Given that the number of clerical, professional and shopkeeping workers resident outside the suburban areas was insignificant, their religious composition should reflect that of the suburban population. Table XVIII reveals a consistently higher percentage of Protestants of all occupations residing in the county. This partly reflects the diverging occupations of the different religions, for example, Catholics engaged in 'dealing' were more likely to be hucksters, Protestants to own sizeable businesses. Taking individual occupations on a random basis, there is a reasonably consistent pattern of Catholics living in the city to a greater extent than Protestants. Making full allowance for the fact that Protestant civil servants may have been senior to Catholics and able to afford larger suburban homes there remains an apparent Protestant bias in favour of suburban residence. This is undoubtedly stronger among those in middle class occupations where they were less tied by work to a city centre home and less financially constrained. A Protestant dock worker, for example, might find it difficult to live in Rathmines, regardless of his personal wishes.

We have already noted a tendency on the part of minority Protestant religions to cluster in certain areas, presumably close to churches and schools of their own denomination. A similar tendency would seem to have existed for the Protestant community as a whole. The factors which prompted this are complex and not easy to document. There is little doubt that religion operated in combination with social preferences and a growing feeling of political isolation to drive many families into the suburbs. Clear-cut religious hostility was rarely overtly expressed, in contrast to Belfast. In public utterances it generally emerged as political antagonism. That it occupied a strong place in individual consciousness is obvious from some of the blunt statements of C.S. Andrews[47]

> From childhood, I was aware that there were two separate and immiscible kinds of citizens: the Catholics, of whom I was one, and the Protestants who were as remote and different from us as if they had been blacks and we whites. We were not acquainted with Protestants but we knew that they were there — a hostile element in the community, vaguely menacing us with horrors as Mrs Smylie's homes for orphans where children might be brought and turned into Protestants. We Catholics varied socially among ourselves but we all had the most common bond, whatever our economic condition of being second class citizens.

Chapter VI

SUBURBAN GROWTH: SIMILARITY AND DIVERSITY

A comparative examination of the various suburbs reveals a diversity of religious and occupational patterns which was the outcome of location, the indigenous population of that area and the development policies favoured by its landowners and builders.

These factors determined its character and strongly influenced its relationship with the city and its government. To understand these issues requires some knowledge of each individual suburb and the manner of its development.

Dublin suburbs may be divided into several categories. Some adjoined the city, whereas the railway suburbs of Blackrock, Kingstown, Dalkey and Killiney were separated by a substantial quantity of undeveloped land. There is a crucial distinction between those situated to the north and those to the south of the city. Over 50% of all suburban residents lived in the two neighbouring suburbs Rathmines and Pembroke; a mere 12.4% in the comparable northern suburbs of Clontarf and Drumcondra; 30.7% lived in the more distant railway suburbs and the remaining 6.3% in the working class township of Kilmainham. Another major distinction relates to landownership. In both Rathmines and Drumcondra development was controlled by private businessmen apparently concerned to maximise their short-term profits. In contrast, Pembroke and Clontarf were each dominated by one large land-owner who appears to have restricted development in both instances. Kingstown also experienced the impact of a large landed estate, while development in Killiney was determined by the decision of individuals to build a private residence.

All these factors combined to give each suburb a distinct character. While Rathmines and Pembroke are both situated to the south of the city, both appealing to a broadly similar market, the long-term evolution varied considerably. Of the two, Rathmines was the more successful. In 1847 when the township was formed it already had a population of ten thousand. The boundaries were extended twice in the 1860s to include Rathgar, and Harold's Cross. Milltown was incorporated in 1880 and by the early twentieth century house building had spread into neighbouring Terenure. By 1911 it had a population of 38,000. Despite short-term slumps Rathmines never ceased to grow. More remarkably, growth was achieved without any dramatic decline in the area's status. The expansion from the late 1870s was mainly contributed by clerical workers on modest incomes, but the area consistently retained a high proportion of professional and white collar workers.

Unlike Pembroke, the area was not dominated by any one landowner, though the Earl of Palmerstown, Earl of Meath and Lord Longford were among the ground landlords. None was actively involved in township affairs. The strongest influence on Rathmines was Frederick Stokes an English property developer, the township's founder and its chairman for thirty years.[1] He was a major house builder primarily in the Leeson Park area,[2] while in the city he built more modest housing at Portobello, originally called Kingsland Park but subsequently renamed Victoria St.[3] Other commissioners mirrored Stokes' interests. In 1871, twelve of the twenty commissioners are known to have owned property in the area and there was a policy of inviting property owners to become commissioners. In 1871 the township minutes noted that Brian G. Edward Fottrell had lately become a property owner and would be a very desirable candidate for the next vacancy.[4] Mark Bentley, who developed Brighton Square and Brighton Road received a letter from Frederick Stokes indicating that a vacancy was about to occur and as a large property owner he was entitled to a seat.[5] Elections in the early decades were extremely rare and the commissioners operated in a manner akin to the directors of a private company with large shareholders — i.e. property owners — being co-opted and commercial profit, symbolised by a rising valuation, an active building programme and few unoccupied houses being the principal ambitions. Frederick Stokes would appear to have been the dominant personality. A disgruntled ex-commissioner claimed that motions were rarely put to a vote and he had no recollection of any decision being taken contrary to Stokes' wishes. Attendance was poor, averaging six of a total of twenty members at the township's annual meeting.[6] To encourage people to move to Rathmines rates were kept as low as possible. In 1864 the commissioners resolved[7]

> That it is undesirable in the highest degree to raise the rate beyond 2/- in the £, but in preference to economise where possible.

Low rates were in the interests of property owners and also of their tenants. The typical pattern of development involved one individual laying out roads and preparing sites. These were leased in small units though the developer might undertake some building to generate interest. In 1868 an *Irish Times* advertisement stated[8]

> Building ground to be let at Brighton Square, Roundtown Road and Garville Ave. 2/6, 3/- and 4/- per foot frontage, lease for ever.
> Twelve months rent free. A number of houses are at present erected, others in course. Owner M.C. Bentley solr. Mr. Wilson's omnibuses pass hourly south of Brighton Sq.

Such sites were bought by business and professional men. Many built their private residence but it was by no means uncommon to build two or more houses as a secure investment. Many city businessmen did so. Among those building houses in Leeson Park were a Captain W.W. Hacket who built four houses, Rev. John Boyce, Dean of Ardagh who built two and Rev. F.C. Hayes who built three houses.[9] A more extensive builder in nearby Appian Way was Mr. Wight a city merchant and commission agent who was also responsible for Warwick Terrace in Leeson Park. Even full-time builders operated on a relatively small scale, building three or four houses at one time. In 1863 a local builder J. McGowan gave notice of building three houses in Ranelagh Rd. In later years he

154

gradually built substantially more houses in adjoining areas on a similarly small scale. An advertisement for sites in Grosvernor Sq. noted that[10]

> Proposals will be accepted from builders or other for one or any of the Building Lots.

Low rates were an essential element in any development programme. Rates were the responsibility of the house-builder or his tenant, not the site landlord, but they were an important inducement which would minimise living costs and maximise the return from renting property. An advertisement for sites in Dunville Ave. and Palmerston Rd. developed by E.H. Carson, father of Ulster Unionist, Sir Edward, began by stating 'lowest township rate'.[11] Rates could account for more than 25% of the rent in the case of some city properties. In 1873, 22 Gardiner Place was for rent at an annual charge of £60 plus £17-16-3 in local taxes. High rates reduced the potential rent. In contrast the burden on Rathmines properties was low. A cottage in Appian Way for example, could be rented for £38 plus £5 rates, approximately half the burden on the Gardiner Place property.[12]

Rathmines developers therefore clung to 2/- in the £ rates as long as possible. Many Rathmines houseowners would appear to have absorbed their tenants' rates. Given their extensive house ownership commissioners would suffer direct financial losses from increased rates. In 1880, ten paid rates amounting to £448-8-4.[13] Low rates appear to have stimulated the area's growth. In 1870 the commissioners noted that in the previous five years Rathmines' valuation had risen by 14.1%, Pembroke's by 11%, Kingstown's by 5.3% and Blackrock's by 7.3%.[14] Ten years later when there was a threat of annexation to the highly-rated city, one witness testified that he had spent £4,000 on housing in Rathmines and would not have done so if the area was under city control. Others gave evidence in a similar vein.[15]

Low rates were maintained by economising on public services. All curbing, flagging of streets and the provision of mud-free crossing points (essential in the days of long skirts) were suspended except where the applicant paid the entire

155

cost.[16] Dublin Corporation's Vartry water was rejected as too expensive, instead Rathmines took a supply from the canal company at a capital cost of only £15,000.[17] This left the inhabitants with polluted water and a supply that proved seriously inadequate for the rapidly growing population. There were allegations that canal water was chosen because several commissioners were canal company shareholders to the tune of £600,000.[18] Water pressure was inadequate in higher lying areas such as Rathgar and by the late 1870s water was turned off from extensive areas every night.[19]

The only sanitary officer was the township porter and messenger who was obliged to be in attendance at the Town Hall from 10-4. The surveyor was forced to build houses for Michael Murphy, one of the commissioners, and to work as a market gardener in order to supplement an inadequate income.[20] As a result of such laxity Rathmines contained innumerable cesspools and lanes deep in mud and refuse.[21] The drainage was completely uninspected and in the case of 2,300 houses it was unknown 'whether they drained into cesspools, or what'.[22] It is therefore not surprising that the *royal commission on municipal boundaries* concluded that[23]

> sanitary matters appear to have been totally neglected until the spring of 1879. Previously there was not the slightest real compliance with the Public Health Acts of 1866 or 1874.

These economies inevitably aroused some opposition. In 1873 the annual meeting was an acrimonious occasion when some ratepayers protested at the lack of horses for watering dusty streets, the quantity of mud, absence of public lighting and inadequate refuse collection.[24]

The supply of Vartry water became the central issue. In 1877 a deputation of residents including Mark Bentley, a commissioner and house developer who had broken with the official commissioners' policy, demanded that Vartry water be introduced.[25] Negotiations with Dublin Corporation were re-opened[26] and it was agreed to accept Vartry water at an extremely favourable price to the township.[27] This decision would appear to mark the first time that Frederick

156

Stokes was overruled and it led to his protest that 'the health and independence of the township would be damaged by Vartry water'.[28] Following this victory the opposition contested the township elections only to suffer defeat[29] though in the following year they successfully ousted several established members, a victory welcomed by the *Irish Times*[30]

> the sooner the board now begin to drop its establishment exclusiveness to allow new ideas to develop themselves in accordance with the infusion of new blood which yesterday's proceedings made, the better.

The opposition movement, with the exception of Mark Bentley, consisted of less prosperous citizens. In 1877 the rateable value of property owned by opposition candidates amounted to £46-13-4 in contrast to £326-5-2 held by outgoing commissioners.[31] It is perhaps significant that the emergence of an opposition party was delayed until the final months of Frederick Stokes' chairmanship and that their electoral victory followed his resignation. While they achieved some short-term improvements in sanitary matters and a commitment to Vartry water the Rathmines instinct for independence and economy soon reasserted itself. The agreement for a supply of Vartry water was broken and in 1880 the commissioners promoted a Bill to take water from the river Dodder. An alternative scheme for Vartry water promoted by the ubiquitous Mark Bentley and others was thrown out.[32] The Glenasmole scheme ultimately cost Rathmines considerably more than a Vartry supply[33] but it did ensure their independence, a matter which received urgent attention when the *royal commission on municipal boundaries* reported in favour of its annexation. This seems to have caused a closing of ranks. Whatever support opposition candidates had previously gained disappeared and local politicians presented a remarkable determination to preserve the area's independence. Even the increase in the electorate in 1899 from 1900 to 6,000 voters did not significantly alter the composition of the council. The fact that 1,400 of the new voters were propertied women undoubtedly acted as a conservative influence.[34] As late as 1910 Rathmines urban district council was dominated by prosperous businessmen, many with property interests. Three were large builders, two were plumbing and engineering contractors, one an architect and another an estate agent. The remainder included a barrister, a solicitor, a drug merchant, sack merchant and an insurance director. Another was Robert Booth owner of an engineering works situated in the township.

The comparative stability in the composition of local representatives reflects the continued dominance of white-collar workers in Rathmines. From the mid 1870s new housing tended to cater for more modest incomes than the earlier schemes. Thus Arthur Percy Stokes whose family had previously built substantial houses in Leeson Park developed five-roomed houses in Oxford Rd. From this period there was a switch to smaller terraced houses with a greater density per acre. The only significant exception was the Cowper Garden estate, developed by William Pickering during the early years of the twentieth century and glowingly advertised complete with an outline sketch[35]

> YOU COULD SETTLE DOWN in one of these charming villas with the knowledge that a better choice of a home in the Dublin district is impossible. On the outskirts of Dublin — in country surroundings — viewing the Dublin mountains with the new Golf Links nearby the COWPER GARDENS BUILDING ESTATE possesses in addition all town advantages. By train or tram you can reach central Dublin in a few minutes. Villas of attractive architecture with the modern fittings which constitute the desirability of a home have been built on this salubrious site.

The shift to smaller houses reflects the recognition that the expanding suburban demand came from the lower middle classes. This change with the continuing population expansion is in marked contrast to Pembroke. In equal contrast, working class residents remained few. Some working class cottages were provided by the commissioners in 1894[36] and subsequently the block buildings at Mountpleasant were erected, however this would not have compensated for the cottages apparently demolished by the developers in earlier

158

decades.

For many residents the lack of a substantial labouring class, close proximity to the city and economical administration must have been among the major attractions. New residents could also, particularly in the early decades, feel assured that the area would not be permitted to decay. A 'house of doubtful character', at 2 Ranelagh Rd. was refused a water supply, because of its occupants, while the police were instructed to prosecute.[37] Similar houses in Mount-pleasant were also prosecuted, while commissioners made incessant efforts at Kilmainham Assizes with some success to reduce the number of licensed premises in their area. In his letter of resignation from Rathmines commissioners, Frederick Stokes concluded that[38]

> last but not least we have fewer public houses now than then (1847), a very material ingredient in our prosperity.

Finally the township's strong sense of independence and its unashamed hostility to the city and its administration must have provided a congenial atmosphere for many Protestant families increasingly alienated from Dublin's catholicism and nationalism.

At no stage were Catholics prominent in the life of Rathmines. They fell from 52% of the population in 1861 to 48% in the following decade and only recovered to 50% in 1891. Frederick Stokes claimed that he had endeavoured to reserve two or three positions as commissioners for Catholics but they invariably had to be co-opted and generally lost their seats on re-election. He claimed that no Catholic could achieve membership if not supported by the board.[39] The Catholic electorate was undoubtedly small as a substantial proportion of the Catholic population were non-voting domestic servants.

In contrast to the free enterprise business mentality of Rathmines Pembroke was the paternalistic venture of an absentee landlord. The Earl of Pembroke owned over seven-ninths of the township and one-sixth of the south city area.[40] The Pembroke estate personnel responded somewhat cautiously to house building proposals. There is no evidence that they ever advertised building sites or actively encouraged developers. John Vernon, agent from 1835 told the *royal commission on municipal boundaries* that 'If builders tell me they will build, I will lay out the roads, but not until then'.[41]

The expansion of housing in Pembroke followed almost inevitably from the late eighteenth century upsurge of interest in the Merrion Sq. area. Development flowed beyond the canal when further vacant land in the city proved unsuitable. Leases in Upper Leeson St. were issued as early as 1833, though many date from 1845. Those in Pembroke Road date mainly from the 1830s; Wellington Place, 1834-43; Waterloo Road, 1845-55; Wellington Road 1844-55. Much development therefore predated the establishment of a township in 1863.[42] The Pembroke estate would appear to have been primarily concerned to safeguard the long-term value of their property, perhaps at the expense of short-term profits, a characteristic of aristocratic estates.[43] The estate rental rose from £11,719 in 1885[44] to £14,000 by 1902[45] but a substantial proportion of this was reinvested in roads and sewers. It was estimated that the average ground rent per house was £9, but sewers and related expenses imposed an annual cost of £4-17-0.[46]

There was a strong determination to retain maximum control in the estate's hands. Leases issued during the Earl's minority were limited to ninety-nine years, but were subsequently extended to 150 years,[47] a term which the *Irish Builder* deemed too short.[48] In Rathmines, in contrast, leases of 999 years were common,[49] while freehold sites were also available.[50] Efforts were made to discourage sub-letting of sites[51] while all prospective builders were subjected to stringent controls.[52] A standard lease issued by the Pembroke estate required a tenant to build

> two good and substantial dwelling houses and that the area of space of ground in front of the said house shall be enclosed with a stout kerb, with iron pallisades on the top ranging uniformly along the said road or street and that the front of the said house shall be built of stone or the best stock bricks, according to ground plan and elevation, particularly delineated on the plan approved of by the Agent for the time being of the Estate and if the said house or houses shall not be built up and made in the manner aforesaid within the

first year he shall pay an additional £40.

The completed house was to be insured for £500 and kept in 'good and substantial repair' while its use for a wide variety of activities such as unpleasant trades, e.g. butchery, or more innocuous purposes such as a school, was forbidden.[53] The short lease, tight building time-scale and stringent clauses on materials and finish may have deterred many builders. This might not have concerned builders of first class houses. However builders of small houses would have felt constrained, while it seems probable that the Pembroke estate would have discouraged high density developments. The area never attracted the volume of clerical residents found in Rathmines and Drumcondra.

The township strongly reflected the Pembroke estate's development policy. The initiative for its establishment came, not from the estate, but from local residents though the Earl, who was still a minor, or his agent did not object.[54] The township could have reduced the estate's authority by establishing an alternative source of power and this may have been the purpose behind its formation. The fifteen founder commissioners did not differ markedly from their Rathmines counterparts. At least seven had interests in building, either as builders or architects, men such as John Hawkins Askin, Patrick Leahy, a major developer in Sandymount or Edward H. Carson. Both Carson and another founder commissioner, Michael Murphy had substantial interests in Rathmines and there would seem little reason to presume that Pembroke would not follow the firmly established practices of Rathmines. Clause fifteen of the Pembroke township act[55] stated that the first meeting of the commissioners should be held at the Pembroke estate office in Wilton Place, which was in fact outside the township. John Vernon, ex-officio commissioner became chairman, a post he held until his death in 1887 when he was succeeded by his son, and he dominated Pembroke township in the interests of the Pembroke estate as thoroughly as Frederick Stokes controlled neighbouring Rathmines. Possible criticism of the Pembroke estate's authority was reduced by the considerable financial benefits which it conveyed on the township, such as a free site and two-thirds of the cost of their town hall,[56] a subsidy amounting to

20% of the cost of the main drainage system,[57] a technical school at Ringsend[58] and the free gift of Herbert Park.[59] The fact that Pembroke estate so thoroughly paved and sewered its roads also reduced the burden on the township.[60]

Despite these financial benefits the rates burden in Pembroke was consistently above that in Rathmines. This partly reflected the township's higher standards. Unlike Rathmines, Pembroke adopted the costlier Vartry water from its inception and implemented the 1874 Public Health Act. By 1875 its sanitary expenditure had risen to £1,000 and they employed a sanitary staff of ten in contrast to the lone Rathmines part-timer.[61] The *royal commission on municipal boundaries* noted that the contrast in sanitary staffing levels between the two neighbouring townships was remarkable. Evidence suggests that Pembroke had serious need of a large sanitary staff and had only employed them as a result of official pressure. Unlike Rathmines it had had a substantial indigenous working class population concentrated in the industrial villages of Ringsend and Irishtown. These brought in their train the familiar problems of poor-quality housing and fever.

The township minutes of 1866 contain a letter from the Under-Secretary Sir Thomas Larcom concerning numerous sanitary defects in Pembroke housing.[62] In 1869 an outbreak of fever in the Ringsend Irishtown area focussed attention on sanitary conditions, revealing in the report of the poor law commissioners severe overcrowding and minimal sanitation.[63]

> Whiskey Row is a narrow lane leading down to the Dodder at Ringsend. Whiskey Row is tolerably clean and all the houses are provided with privies and ash-pits in small yards in front of some and at the sides of others. The houses are let in tenements, each room occupied by a family. The rooms are small, insufficiently ventilated and over-crowded with furniture and inmates. In one house there are seven cases of fever, four in one family, three in another, the latter sleeping in *one* bed. In another house in the same land there are six cases in one family, a woman Nally and five children all in *one* bed.
>
> In Cambridge Road a man named Bird, wife and

three children attacked by fever live in the innermost room, the other two are full of potatoes and vegetables, in which the Birds' deal. Adjoining is a yard which used to be kept in a disgraceful condition until compelled to clean. The woman next door who lived in a *clean* house died. Another fatal case: a man Waters lived in a clean house but at the back a yard common to two, three or four houses was in a scandalous state. Pembroke St. Irishtown: four cases in 5 Pembroke St., three cases in a family named Doyle. This house is in tenements. On the ground floor there are two rooms: the front clean the back very dark and badly ventilated suggesting neglect and dirt. This is tenanted by a man Redmond who keeps an ass at the foot of his bed.

This report brought a personal complaint from the Lord Lieutenant to which the commissioners replied citing legal difficulties in bringing a prosecution.[64] Another medical officer contacted the poor law board concerning further cases of typhus claiming that 'there do not appear to have been any steps taken by the Pembroke commissioners to abate the nuisance',[65] while a local doctor protested about the lack of drainage at cottages adjoining the River Dodder, which apparently acted as a focal point for fever.[66] This brought a further appeal by the poor law board to the Lord Lieutenant explicitly criticising Pembroke's sanitary administration[67] and though this particular nuisance was remedied the poor law board served subsequent notice on the township for failure to comply with provisions concerning sewers.[68]

The volume of official material concerning Pembroke sanitary defects is almost as great as that dealing with the city. There is no analagous material concerning Rathmines suggesting that despite its neglect of mundane sanitary matters it was the healthier area. The reported cases of fever in Pembroke must have damaged the area's growth. An outbreak of typhoid in the premier residential area of Raglan, Clyde and Elgin Roads brought deputations from concerned householders, resolutions from Pembroke commissioners, a report from the medical officer of health and the predictable intervention of Dublin Castle.[69] The fact that so many senior civil servants and army officers lived in

Pembroke may account for the disproportionate attention given to its sanitary problems in contrast to the city.

Pembroke was also saddled with considerable responsibility for working class housing. In 1884 it contained 672 houses in weekly tenancies inhabited by 5,506 persons approximately 23% of the township population. Of these, 684 lived at a density of five or more families per house, and 923 in units of four families per house.[70] Many families inhabiting individual houses lived in tiny overcrowded cottages. These conditions contrasted dramatically with the high standards imposed by the Pembroke estate on prospective builders, causing the *Irish Times* to describe Pembroke as a miniature reproduction of London's East and West Ends containing the stateliest mansions and the most wretched hovels, adding 'not even on the west coast of Africa are the natives worse housed than are the humble residents of Irishtown, Ringsend and Ballsbridge.'[71]

Many such houses were demolished, some to make way for suburban villas,[72] but few efforts were made to rehouse the labouring classes until 1894 when forty artisans dwellings were completed at Ringsend.[73] By 1914 Pembroke had completed six schemes providing a total of 354 houses; of these 59 accommodated artisans and 295 labourers.[74] In addition local employees such as builder James Beckett, Joseph Mulholland a Ringsend rope manufacturer, the Dublin and South Eastern Railway and the Earl of Pembroke built working class accommodation.[75]

Pembroke failed to cater for lower middle class residents. In consequence its growth tailed off sharply after 1881. While Rathmines grew steadily leaving little undeveloped land within its boundaries by 1914, large tracts of Pembroke remained untouched.

Pembroke's stagnation from the 1880s contributed to a financial crisis as did excessive dependence on Pembroke estate agent John Vernon. He died in 1887, by 1892 the township faced considerable debt and had apparently been in that state for some years.[76] Matters further deteriorated when the township secretary disappeared with official funds. The Pembroke Ratepayers Association demanded unsuccessfully that Dublin Castle should undertake an inquiry into local administration[77] and ran a number of candidates in local elections. However there is no evidence of greater administrative efficiency. By 1901 Pembroke Urban District Council was incurring the wrath of the Local Government Board auditor in a manner generally reserved for Dublin Corporation.[78] A sum of £19,000 which should have been charged to current expenditure had been met by debentures and the Council was forced to introduce savage rate increases.[79] An appeal to their constant benefactor, the Earl of Pembroke for assistance was rejected and he suggested that 'others peculiarly interested in the township should co-operate in the matter'.[80] There was no alternative but to levy rates of 11/- in the £, more than double those in Rathmines.[81] The crisis had resulted from the 'unbusinesslike management' of the council,[82] in particular from the desire to hold rates down despite the considerable burden resulting from working class housing and from the belief that in a crisis the Earl would defray exceptional expenses.

The disengagement by the Earl may be the result of the 1898 Local Government Act which extended the electorate from 1,800 to 4,750 voters, eight hundred of these were women, but the remainder were working class men. In 1902 nationalists gained temporary control of the urban council, and in 1911 a nationalist chairman was appointed.[83] The growing nationalist representation was probably distasteful to the Earl and may have prompted his financial withdrawal. The Dublin nationlist M.P. John Joseph Clancy discovered that Pembroke had survived previous crises because of bank overdrafts unauthorised by Parliament but guaranteed by the Earl and wealthy residents. The withdrawal of these guarantees had precipitated the financial crisis.[84] By the early twentieth century Pembroke faced seemingly irreconcilable conflicts between its established role as a paternalistic Unionist township housing professional and business families, and its responsibility towards its nationalist working class residents, a group increasingly asserting their democratic rights.

Our knowledge of the northern suburbs is much less complete than in the case of Rathmines and Pembroke whose local authority records have survived. Both Clontarf and Drumcondra were considerably less significant than their south-side counterparts. Clontarf's prospects were un-

165

doubtedly hindered by its location adjoining the increasingly unfashionable north-eastern quadrant of the city. A journey to Clontarf entailed braving an area of tenement housing which contained a substantial proportion of the city's prostitutes, the urban blight associated with the expanding docks and railway stations plus the malodorous Dublin and Wicklow Manure Works and finally a tract of undeveloped slobland commonly used as a refuse dump. The land in Clontarf itself was low-lying and poorly drained and houses along the seafront suffered periodic flooding.[85] These were not merely inconveniences. To those who believed in the miasmic theory of disease, low-lying swampy ground was synonymous with fever, just as higher ground and gravel soil guaranteed health. The long unsettled question of Dublin's main drainage with the prospect of city sewerage being deposited near Clontarf was a further deterrent to development.

Clontarf's image was also a handicap. The *Dublin Builder*, a newspaper generally unduly enthusiastic about suburbs and their potential was uncharacteristically critical in the case of Clontarf, describing it as 'a scene of dilapidation' and noting the prevalence of 'ruins and cabins'.[86] In an effort to enhance development prospects cabins were demolished during the 1860s[87] but suburban expansion remained slow.

The Clontarf area was dominated by large landowners. The most prominent was the Vernon estate, though the Howth estate and the property of Arthur Edward Guinness (Lord Ardilaun) was also important.

The attitude of the Vernon estate towards suburban growth is unclear, but many categories regarded it as unhelpful. The *Dublin Builder* alleged that they offered very limited leases and charged excessive ground rents while providing no facilities.[88] However the agent claimed that leases for 150 years were available for those prepared to spend £4-500 on building a house.[89] During the 1860s, a decade of record growth in south-side suburbs, Clontarf's population declined. Many prospective developers attributed this to the lack of public lighting, absence of water supply and the inadequate state of roads.[90] To rectify this a bill was promoted in 1869 creating a Clontarf township. The Vernon estate opposed the original legislation and the

166

eventual Act was forced to constitute John Edward Venables Vernon chairman for life giving him a veto over all policy.[91]

The original commissioners also included Sir Arthur Edward Cecil Guinness and local landowner John Calvert Stronge. The remainder were businessmen, many engaged in local property development, and a solicitor. The most prominent was George Tickell, owner of a furniture warehouse and a persistent house-builder for many decades. Three were house agents, one, Graham Lemon, an extensive owner of poor quality tenement property in the city. Another was a pawnbroker, a man who would not have been out of place on Dublin Corporation. On the whole they did not have the social or economic status of the Rathmines and Pembroke commissioners. Local government brought no obvious change, either in the level of amenities or in house building prospects. By 1880 Clontarf still lacked public lighting, police, adequate roads, sewerage and a fire brigade.[92] It is perhaps not surprising that a group of property owners petitioned Dublin Corporation requesting annexation,[93] though one Clontarf witness claimed that this petition was masterminded by the local publicans anxious to benefit from the more liberal licensing laws in the city.[94] It is a measure of the area's problems and lack of income that even the expansion minded Dublin Corporation refused to annexe Clontarf, arguing that it was separated from the city by one mile of agricultural land and therefore not a valid case for boundary extension.[95]

In 1900 Clontarf was absorbed into the city. By the 1890s the area was growing more rapidly than in earlier decades and the early years of the twentieth century were a time of rapid growth the population rising from 6,930 in 1901 to 8,965 in 1911. This later expansion took the form of modest terraced housing catering for clerical workers. In 1891 Clontarf shared with Rathmines the distinction of having the highest proportion of its workforce in banking and clerical employment. Like Rathmines, Clontarf retained its strong Unionist complexion until the early twentieth century and the 1898 Local Government Act made no material difference. Two of the founding commissioners, Lord Ardilaun and George Tickell still retained their place in 1899, as did two descendents of other founders, Col. Vernon and

T.O. Lemon.[96]

Despite returning the highest proportion of Unionists in any of the Dublin local authorities, Clontarf lost its independence. This was attributable to the lack of a main drainage system. Clontarf was regarded as too small and too poor to undertake an independent scheme and the Joint Committee of the British Parliament recommended annexation by the city.[97] Size therefore contributed to ultimate extinction, as did location. Whereas Rathmines and Pembroke, each considerably larger, stood side by side, Clontarf stood next to the consistently nationalist suburb of Drumcondra. By 1900 housing from both the city and Drumcondra was tending to spill over into Clontarf dwarfing the area's individuality.

Drumcondra is unique among Dublin suburbs in several respects. It is the only suburb which from the beginning set out to cater for clerical and skilled working class residents and it is also the only suburb with a generally nationalist orientation. The development of Drumcondra was strongly influenced by two men: J.F. Lombard, a director of Arnott's drapery company and Edward McMahon, a Home Rule M.P. In the early 1870s they exploited the vacant land which was available to the north of Sackville St. where they built innumerable streets of modest terraced housing. By 1875 their activities had spread beyond the city boundaries. Though vacant sites were plentiful and houses were within walking distance of the city centre, development was handicapped by a lack of water, sewerage and roads.[98] The condition of the river Tolka, 'a nuisance rivalling on a small scale that of the Liffey' was a further deterrent.[99] Various efforts were made to overcome these handicaps. At one point the annexation of Drumcondra to Clontarf was suggested[100] but this was not seriously pursued. A drainage scheme was organised to deal with the area, but this was rejected by the local government board.[101] Efforts to obtain water under the auspices of the north Dublin rural sanitary union also proved unavailing,[102] leaving the developers with no alternative save to establish an independent township.

The proposal to establish a township, with the presumption that further development would follow did not meet with universal approval. It was proposed to include the

168

largely undeveloped area of Glasnevin and its residents, many living in large houses objected, arguing that the area was a 'pastoral district', fearing that they would be faced with higher taxes to meet the costs of suburban development.[103] The vigorous opposition proved unavailing and the bill, promoted among others by Cardinal Paul Cullen, became law in 1878.

Drumcondra commissioners included two distinct and hostile groups. The local landowners and settled residents were represented by men such as Henry Gore Lindsay, Glasnevin estate owner, Henry Joseph Gogarty father of the well-known doctor and literary personality Oliver St. John Gogarty and Stephen McCarthy, agent of the Lynch estate. This element dominated Glasnevin Ward. In contrast the two remaining wards were controlled by property developers who held a majority of all seats. From the beginning Drumcondra set out to encourage builders of small houses. The franchise was the most democratic in the Dublin area, with a voter qualifying if a tenant of a house valued in excess of £5 — a very modest dwelling — or owner of a property valued at £25.[104] In contrast to the other townships, the 1898 Local Government Act brought a relatively small expansion in the electorate, from 1,127 to 1,404 voters. Most of the new voters were women.

In 1884, perhaps as a result of slow growth in valuation in the previous year, it was proposed to obtain parliamentary approval to remit 50% of rates on houses valued at less than £12.[105] By 1884 over 200 houses of this scale had already been built, sixty apparently by persons expecting this remission. Among the major beneficiaries were several local commissioners such as Mr. Butterly whose houses 'let as fast as they could be built',[106] while Edward McMahon had built 200 houses of the artisan type, valued at £8 with money borrowed under the 1866 Shaftsbury Act.[107] Many Drumcondra houses were built by small builders with money advanced by Edward McMahon[108]

When they have a little money they come to me and get a plot of ground, and I get them a loan of money; and they build houses and sell to small capitalists — men of £4-500, grocers etc.

Small builders and grocers were not among the most strin-

169

gent builders. A meeting of commissioners in 1894 ordered one builder to demolish five houses which he had built of breeze. One commissioner claimed that 'the way in which houses were built in the township is disgraceful and is talked about all over Dublin'. Breeze block, made from cinders and gas works refuse were commonly used and some houses in Carlingford Road apparently consisted of brick facing, a mere 4½ inches thick disguising breeze blocks.[109]

Not all Drumcondra houses were of such quality. Towards the end of the century, and in the years prior to 1914, there would appear to have been greater emphasis on 'well to do middle class residences'. Some of these were built by Edward McMahon, particularly in the area known as the 'Bishop's field'[110] where St. Brigid's and St. Alphonsus Road subsequently emerged. Quality housing also dominated Glasnevin, which the builders were coming to exploit around 1914 when the Carroll estate adjoining Botanic Road was opened up.[111]

The final suburb adjacent to the city, New Kilmainham, was in fact a self-contained village, most of those residents were either soldiers, employees of the Great Southern and Western Co. engineering works, or some smaller factories, or warders at Kilmainham jail. In addition the area contained a large reformatory and a Catholic religious house.[112] The residents were almost exclusively working class. In 1868 only sixteen houses were valued at more than £20.[113]

Kilmainham's largest employer, the Great Southern and Western Railway Co. opposed the establishment of a township and failing this, sought to control the commissioners. Two of their staff were among those initially elected, while the election of a third was declared invalid.[114] The initiative for the establishment of a township came from a number of other industrialists such as Francis Moore Scott, owner of a woollen business, David McBirney a prominent city draper and textile producer and Samuel Shelly a flour miller.[115] The prime motivation was the need for water and sanitary facilities.[116] The development of Kilmainham owed more to the state of local industry than to suburban expansion. The area remained overwhelmingly working class and sprouted few related service jobs, either in dealing or domestic service. Such housing as was built catered for local residents and

170

the area remained distinct from the city.

Kilmainham's working class also differed somewhat from the city workers. The majority were in relatively secure employment connected with the railways or local industry or the prison service. The population contained an unexpectedly high number of Protestants and a seemingly disproportionate number of migrants many from England or Scotland, reflecting the recruitment preferences of the area's major employers.

Our account of the neighbouring suburbs has been written without reference to transport services. The main forms of transport in the area close to the city in the 1860s were licensed cars, cabs, private carriages and omnibuses. In 1871 there were a total of 1,750 licensed cars and 1,171 cabs in Dublin,[117] in addition to an unknown number of private carriages. These services were relatively expensive. Regulated charges for carriages in 1860 amounted to 1/- for a single trip to Rathmines, 1/6 to Rathgar Road and 1/- to Clontarf or Drumcondra.[118] Omnibuses were considerably cheaper but the service was limited. In the 1860s, Rathmines was served by a total of seven cars providing an average frequency of one car every ten minutes.[119] The fare per journey was 4d.[120] Sandford and Ranelagh had one omnibus every 45 minutes, Donnybrook — in Pembroke, one every 30 minutes,[121] while with the exception of a limited service to Glasnevin there was apparently no line north of the river Liffey.[122] We can only presume that the majority walked regularly to work, while a substantial proportion of suburban residents spent most of their time within the suburb itself.[123] The major transport revolution came with the introduction of street trams. These were first proposed by an American gentleman with the appropriate name of George Francis Train in 1861.[124] His plans to build a line from the city to the extreme boundary of Rathmines and a second line to the northern suburb of Dollymount (Clontarf) were supported by Rathmines commissioners.[125] This scheme was never implemented and an experimental line laid in 1866 from Kingsbridge station to the exhibition hall at Earlsfort Terrace[126] was not successful and the lines were lifted. In 1870 the firm of Barrington and Jeffars who had previously been interested in various cross city railways and had also dabbled in sewerage farming (Barrington was a member of a prominent Dublin business family engaged in soap manufacture) proposed to run lines to Rathmines, Donnybrook, Sandymount, Clontarf, plus a route from Kingsbridge Station to the North Wall.[127] Their proposals received parliamentary approval in 1871[128] and on 1 Feb. 1872 the first tram ran from the city to Rathmines at a fare of 3d. In retaliation the omnibus company cut their fare to 1d[129] but by August they had been bought out by the tram company giving the latter a public transport monopoly.[130] The initial plans proved unduly ambitious. Extravagant spending was alleged and Mr. Barrington resigned[131] to be replaced, somewhat ironically, by Mr. Wilson the former omnibus proprietor.[132] The main problem was the limited demand for tram services. Of the four lines in operation in 1874 the Rathmines route was 'highly successful', the Sandymount and Donnybrook routes were described as 'fairly successful', while the route to Clontarf was termed a 'disappointment' and was blamed on Mr. Barrington's extravagant plans.[133] His reaction had been to urge more aggressive marketing and proposed that the company 'should get up some entertainment at the end of the line to encourage the public to travel',[134] the company, without his direction adopted a more conservative policy and further extensions of the service, particularly to the north of the city were ruled out.[135] In 1875, the rival North Dublin Tramway Co. directed by William Barrington received parliamentary permission to run trams to Drumcondra, Glasnevin and the Phoenix Park[136] As an economy measure trams were to run without conductors.[137] In 1876 they extended their plans to include lines through much of the central city reaching Kilmainham.[138] By 1877 however the company faced a familiar financial crisis with shares at a considerable discount and William Barrington became involved in further disagreements with major shareholders.[139] In the meantime a third tram company, the Dublin Central Tram Company, whose directors were James Fitzgerald Lombard and William Martin Murphy — already an experienced tram builder — proposed to build various lines, several in competition with the Dublin Tramway Co.[140] This threat forced the latter to reduce its fares to outside passengers amid allegations that they failed to cater for the working class[141] while the economic recession of 1879 reduced their receipts for the first time.[142] It is therefore not surprising that in 1880 all tramways were amalgamated under a board which came to be dominated by William Martin Murphy.[143] William Barrington had emigrated to the United States in 1879.[144]

The role of trams in suburban development has received relatively little attention, though it was a much more common form of short-distance transport than railways. In the year 1884-5, the Dublin United Tram Co. carried 18.3m. passengers.[145] On the whole trams followed housing development, rather than instituting it. The greatest frequency of service in the Dublin area was from Rathmines. By 1879 there were two lines from the city each with a frequency of one car every 3½ minutes at peak hours. In contrast the service from Drumcondra operated every twenty minutes; from Clontarf every fifteen minutes, and from Sandymount and Donnybrook every ten minutes.[146]

The only possible area of Dublin where trams may have contributed to suburban growth was Drumcondra. James Fitzgerald Lombard was a director of the tram company and a Drumcondra commissioner and housing developer. Like Rathmines however Drumcondra was within walking distance of the city centre. Tram lines expanded their services, but one suspects this happened in response to housing development rather than in anticipation. In 1894 a line was provided to the expanding district of Dolphins Barn;[147] four years later it was proposed to extend this to Rialto,[148] however this was not done until 1905.[149]

There remains the question of whether trams catered for the working class. The limited evidence available suggests that they did not. As early as 1878 Maurice Brooks, a Dublin employer and M.P. stated that[150]

> The Dublin Tram Company has turned out very renumerative and in some respects a useful institution, excellent returns to its proprietors, and proving of great convenience to passengers of the genteel and well to do class.
>
> The company has however failed to confer equal advantages on the working or labouring class. There is a sole provision of one car each way before 7 a.m. and

one after 6 p.m. at 1d per mile.

Dublin fares were higher than those in London where the general charge was 1d per mile. In response to criticism the fares for outside passengers were reduced, while those of inside passengers remained constant.[151] The Dublin United Tram Co. introduced penny fares for short distances and noted by 1884 that an increasing amount of revenue came from this source.[152] However the concentration of services on predominantly middle class routes, coupled with their frequency pattern suggests that the working class was a small minority of passengers, more likely to travel to the Phoenix Park on Sunday, than on regular week day journeys. The Rathmines line only offered four trams leaving Terenure prior to 8.30 a.m., while the peak service operated from 8.30 until 9.42. The working class area of Inchicore had a mere six trams leaving before 9 a.m. By 1886 the peak service on the Terenure line was delayed until 9 a.m. The usage of trams expanded continuously, except in years of major recession such as 1879.[153] Dividends remained satisfactory, generally ranging from 4-6%. This reflects the expanding white collar population, the benefits of reduced fares — the journey from Terenure to city centre which cost 3d in the 1870s had been reduced to 2d by 1910 — and the long-term rise in real incomes. There is no indication of active promotional efforts by the tram company, nor of any collaboration with suburban developers, with the possible exception of Drumcondra.

Railways cannot be said to have impinged on the development of the suburbs immediately adjoining the city, except indirectly in the case of Kilmainham where the railway engineering works was a major employer. The Dublin Kingstown railway ran through Pembroke but only in the late 1860s does the question of building stations there arise.[154] Stations were eventually built at Sydney Parade and Lansdowne Road but they seem to have been used mainly for the Dublin Horse Show, not regular commuter traffic. Rathmines was skirted by the line which ran from Bray to Harcourt St. but it made no apparent impression. An attempt in 1864 to promote a line through Rathmines to the city, the Dublin Rathmines, Rathfarnham and Rathcoole line[155] which would run underground through the township pro-

174

viding three stations was opposed by the commissioners.[156] This projected line never materialised: in 1865 it was provisionally extended to Poulaphouca[157] a remote part of Co. Wicklow, postponed due to the financial panic of 1866 and when the directors prepared to recommence in 1871 a tram line had been proposed which would run 'parallel with points on which the Rathmines Railway Co. propose to construct the most valuable part of their undertaking'.[158] No railway station was built in Drumcondra until 1897[159] although a railway line ran through the township, and this station closed in 1911.[160]

If railways were of no importance in the neighbouring suburbs their impact on distant suburbs such as Kingstown is more complex. The Dublin Kingstown line opened in 1834 was the first Irish railway and a key element in its development was the prospect of suburban commuter fares. The report of the commission in connection with the Kingstown railway stated[161]

> When this accommodation is considered in connection with the dense and rapidly increasing population of the several avenues leading from the present line of road (which are beginning to assume the character of streets) and of the district between Kingstown and the foot of the Killiney Hills — a large part of which is now laid out for building — it must be looked upon as a great public accommodation, and one which must secure to the railway a decided preference over every other mode of conveyance for time.

Suburban development had obviously preceded the railway but the Dublin and Kingstown Co. encouraged further development to increase their potential market. The company, under its chairman James Pim Jnr. offered a wide variety of commuter tickets at reduced prices. Weekly, annual, monthly or quarterly tickets gave the owner free bathing rights in the railway company's sea baths, while there were special discounts for students, governesses and families — all calculated to achieve 'the all important object of promoting permanent residence in the neighbourhood of the railway'.[162] A further encouragement was offered by the policy of running trains each half hour from 6 a.m. to 11 p.m. by 1842.[163]

The coming of the railways brought significant population expansion. In the decade 1841-51 the population rose by a spectacular 43%, and growth remained steady, though at a slower pace throughout the 1850s and 60s. In 1860, while urging Kingstown's claim to be a borough, the chairman of the town commissioners remarked that in the previous three years, a total of 370 houses had been built and a further 80 were on stocks, while the valuation of the electoral division had increased by £10,000 since 1857. By this stage Kingstown contained seven churches and one bank, while the etablishment of a second bank was rumoured. House rents had almost doubled in the previous ten years.[164] In 1863, at the peak of euphoria the Royal Marine Hotel Co. was floated by Chairman William Dargan with a proposed capital of £100,000.[165] This proved a victim of the 1866-7 recession and in 1867 the company was wound up, and a more modest venture, at one-quarter the initial costs was planned.[166] The growth of Kingstown tailed off sharply after 1881, as the number of houses indicates. By 1891 a total of 359 houses was vacant, in contrast to 186 in 1871. During the 1880s, a depressed decade in the Dublin area, it was believed that conditions were worse in Kingstown than elsewhere,[167] while the rents of properties on house agents' books showed a reduction of between 15 and 30%.[168] By 1911 Kingstown contained fewer houses than in 1881.

Houses in Kingstown 1841-1911

1841	1,394
1851	2,119
1861	2,448
1871	2,964
1881	3,388
1891	3,493
1901	3,582
1911	3,371

Kingstown's problems were caused by the limited numbers who could afford to pay railway fares as a normal commuting expense. The market was reduced when the railway company reversed its pursuit of what Joe Lee has termed

Grafton Street. (Lawrence Collection, NLI)

South Great George's Street 1879; note absence of tramlines. (Irish Architectural Archive)

Guinness workers and their families returning from brewery fete at the R.D.S. 1904. (Guinness Museum)

Shoemakers of the Third Battalion Grenadier Guards at Beggars' Bush Barracks 1868. (Irish Architectural Archive)

Labourers working in Cooke's Lane maltings of Guinness' brewery. (Guinness Museum)

Guinness transport workers: a new steam lorry in 1901 and drayman 1906. (Guinness Museum)

Guinness' brewery, racking machines 1889. Processes were mechanised as far as possible. (Guinness Museum)

The visitors sample room. (Guinness Museum)

Rathmines Road. (Lawrence Collection, NLI)

Elgin Road, Ballsbridge. (Lawrence Collection, NLI)

THE PARK KINGSTOWN 3988 W.L.

Kingstown in the early twentieth century. (Lawrence Collection NLI)

KINGSTOWN 689 W.L.

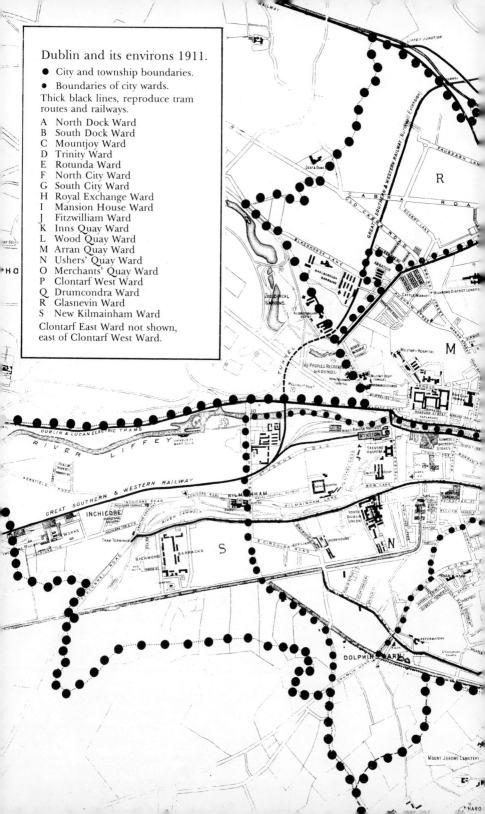

Dublin and its environs 1911.

● City and township boundaries.
● Boundaries of city wards.

Thick black lines, reproduce tram
routes and railways.

A North Dock Ward
B South Dock Ward
C Mountjoy Ward
D Trinity Ward
E Rotunda Ward
F North City Ward
G South City Ward
H Royal Exchange Ward
I Mansion House Ward
J Fitzwilliam Ward
K Inns Quay Ward
L Wood Quay Ward
M Arran Quay Ward
N Ushers' Quay Ward
O Merchants' Quay Ward
P Clontarf West Ward
Q Drumcondra Ward
R Glasnevin Ward
S New Kilmainham Ward

Clontarf East Ward not shown,
east of Clontarf West Ward.

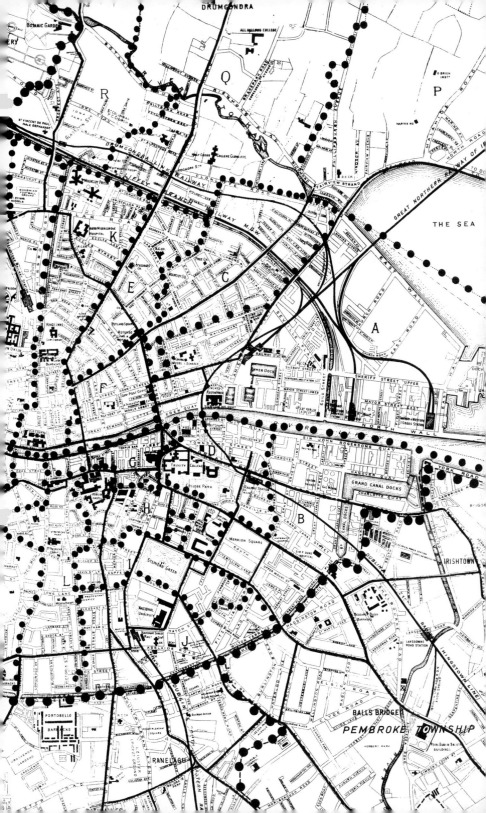

A lane off Townsend Street.

Ryan's yard, rere 68½ Church Street is an almost rural scene. Its owner was the same Mrs. Ryan, landlord of two tenement houses in Church Street which collapsed causing fatalities in 1913. (See p. 293)

Rialto buildings 1880's were mostly inhabitated by Guinness workers. Note plough in foreground. (Guinness Museum)

Cumberland Street (Below)

These photographs show the extent of dilapidated and derelict property in the city by the early twentieth century. (Darkest Dublin Collection, Royal Society of Antiquaries of Ireland)

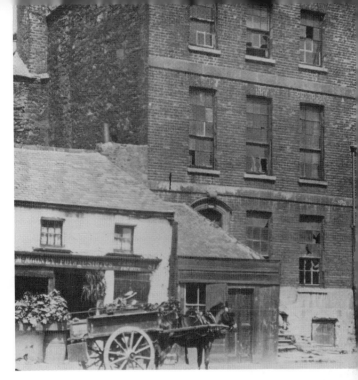

Dereliction even extended to major streets as this tenement in Dorset Street shows. (Architectural Archive)

Aungier Place, off Aungier Street. (Darkest Dublin Collection, Royal Society of Antiquaries of Ireland)

Morgan's Cottages. Note hens, pump - often the only water supply.

Tenement interiors. These show the decrepit state of buildings, ragged wallpaper, holes in ceilings and walls, and the poverty of material possesions. Religious pictures and advertising posters form virtually the only decorations. (Darkest Dublin Collection, Royal Society of Antiquaries of Ireland)

'A cautiously expansionist policy'.[169] James Pim was virtually unique among Irish railway magnates in seeking to actively promote a market for his company. In 1856 the Dublin and Kingstown line was leased by the Dublin Wicklow and Wexford Railway Co. who would appear to have adopted a more restrictive policy favouring higher fares. Worker's fares which had operated before 7 a.m were abolished.[170] The Dublin Wicklow and Wexford Co. owned an alternative route to Dublin which ran overland from Bray through Foxrock and Dundrum. They also ran lines to Wexford. Unlike the Dublin and Kingstown Co. their primary interest was not in suburban traffic from Kingstown. In 1861 the *Daily Express* alleged that the company discriminated in its season ticket charges against Kingstown charging rates almost double those for season tickets on the Bray line, 'because some of the directors have property in Bray whose value they wish to increase'.[171]

There is substantial evidence that they pursued a policy of neglect on the Dublin-Kingstown line, combined with charging very high fares. In 1867 the fare for a second class season ticket of three months was increased by 20% to £3-10-0, or approximately 5/6 per week.[172] In 1869 fares were once again increased substantially and in 1872 the Kingstown commissioners registered a protest against high fares which they regarded as 'most prejudicial to Kingstown and adjoining townships'. A Board of Trade inquiry which investigated a host of complaints concerning the Kingstown line agreed that protests of dilapidated rolling stock and lack of waiting rooms were substantially true. On the question of fares they reported that[173]

> having regard to lines of somewhat analagous character and having regard to the terms of the 1856 Act by which the present company were empowered to lease the Dublin and Kingstown line and work it 'more efficiently and beneficially for the public', and having regard to fares on the Harcourt St. line the fares (especially season tickets) are unreasonably high.

The report had immediate results. All fares were reduced by one-third and stations were improved.[174]

This discrimination against Dublin-Kingstown commuters obviously hindered suburban expansion, but one doubts

193

whether it was of long-term significance. There is no evidence that the discrimination in favour of Bray contributed to substantial growth there. Regular rail transport was within the reach of only a limited social group and from the 1870s most suburban expansion catered for the lower middle class who could not afford regular rail fares. The appeal of the railways was strictly limited, not just in Dublin. Kellett in his study of the impact of railways on the development of five major British cities concludes that in the case of Birmingham 'the railways played virtually no part in the suburban extension'[175] and this is also true of the other cities, with the exception of London. Even in London he argues that trams were of considerably greater significance, while the only case where suburban growth may have been 'prompted and sustained by railway services', was to the north-east of the city, along the route of the Great Eastern Railway.[176]

Kingstown's problems may have been compounded by the policies of local landowners and by the strategy of its commissioners. The major landowners were Lords Longford and de Vesci, joint owners of 1,200 acres. They would appear to have favoured the railway line and three stations were built on their estate.[177]

Much of the estate had been leased in the early decades of the nineteenth century, prior to the coming of the railways, at low rents based on agricultural usage. In 1837 the landlords bought back the leases of large tracts of Monkstown and undertook the orderly and harmonious development of Longford and De Vesci Terraces, the Hill and Crescent.[178] Much of the remainder of the estate had been sublet to speculative builders at sums occasionally amounting to 'ten times the original lease'.[179] The profits of suburban development were lost to the estate and accrued to speculative builders while their control over development, in contrast to Pembroke, was nil. The total estate income from the large suburban area stretching from Tivoli Road to the sea, and from York Road to Glenageary Rd. was a mere £730 per annum, yet its rateable valuation amounted to £35,000.[180] Many builders subdivided plots and built houses in gardens, matters which the early leases did nothing to prevent.[181]

These leases began to expire in the early twentieth cen-

194

tury and this provided the ground landlords with opportunities to increase rents to take account of the commercial development which had taken place, while recovering some control over estate property.

The threatened expiry date of leases acted as a severe blight on the Kingstown property market during the closing years of the century. In the case of commercial property lease renewal was contingent on complete rebuilding to the specifications of the estate, no doubt in a belated attempt to recapture a Pembroke-type control. The Nationalist, *Freeman's Journal*, reflecting the fact that many of the affected merchants were nationalists, bitterly noted that 'The Kingstown man of today is as much at the mercy of a ground landlord as was the peasant tenant at will', and they criticised Lords Longford and de Vesci for having 'done little to help Kingstown'.[182]

Kingstown politics were more strongly influenced by local businessmen, particularly coal merchants and property investors than by ground landlords. John Crosthwaite, chairman for many years was described by the de Vesci estate agent as having 'speculated very largely in property'. In 1867 a ratepayers' meeting, urging that 'new blood be infused into the commissioners' requested Mr. Kincaid, agent to the de Vesci estate to become a member.

Unlike the Pembroke estate, which at this stage was being administered in trust for the young Earl, by Viscount de Vesci, the Kingstown ground landlords were unwilling to assume active responsibility for township business, as, unlike the Pembroke estate, they had lost a considerable measure of control over their property. The cause of the 1867 ratepayers meeting was the poor sanitary state of the area and the fact that, in contrast to Blackrock and Pembroke, there was no proper water supply.[183] Sanitary matters were apparently of limited interest to many of the area's property developers. In 1873 a proposed sewerage and improvement bill, supported by the ground landlords, but opposed by their lessees was rejected.[184] Rathmines township gave a similarly low priority to sanitary matters, with no apparent adverse consequences. Kingstown had a much less favourable social structure with a high proportion of the population concentrated in transport and in general labouring.

This reflects the area's dual characteristics, a suburban residential area and seaside resort, and a port. The building of the harbour was regarded by at least one local developer, John McEvoy, as 'not an unmixed blessing' because it attracted many unskilled labourers to the area. Squalid cramped houses emerged convenient to the harbour, while the building of the railway attracted labourers.[185] The employment provided by both port and railway was inadequate for the labouring population while the depressed state of the local building trade from the late 1870s removed another source of casual employment. In a paper read to the 1884 congress it was noted that[186]

> Kingstown presents some of the worst features of a town of decaying industry, crumbling hovels and an undue proportion of perhaps the most helpless class in the community, worn out workmen too old to seek employment elsewhere and clinging to the spot which once afforded them the means of comfortable existence.

By this stage Kingstown was characterised by a low birth rate, relatively high death rate and a high level of admissions to the workhouse. As in the city, the landlords of slum property tended to be small businessmen and tradesmen.[187] In 1887 Kingstown commissioners applied to the Local Government Board for power to demolish some of the most insanitary housing. This scheme was about to go ahead when the commissioners moved its postponement 'because the depressed state of the times is innopportune for carrying out any expensive schemes'.[188] The Local Government Board noted that the postponement was due to electoral change. Kingstown, which in its earlier years had been controlled by representatives of the 'upper third',[189] had by the 1880s reached the point where unionist and nationalist interests were finely balanced. The rejection of the slum clearance scheme occurred when local elections gave the nationalists, many of them small businessmen similar in background to the majority of tenement owners, a majority of one.[190] The houses which were proposed for demolition in 1887 still stood in 1903, when they were described as 'the worst of the township slums'.[191] No further action on slum clearance was taken until that year when the local parish priest estimated that 687 labouring families required housing adding that 'nothing in the Dublin slums would compare to this'.[192] By 1903 Kingstown was forced to undertake artisans dwelling schemes costing £58,000,[193] a considerable burden for a township of only 17,000 people when one recalls that Dublin Corporation's total commitments by 1914 amounted to £300,000. The intertia of local politicians had served to postpone action, as had the vexed question of ground leases. The scheme commenced in 1903, precisely the time when the leases of the area to be rebuilt, fell in.

The problems posed by Kingstown's labouring population were undoubtedly severe. In 1910, 200 labourers applied for work under the Relief of Distress Act,[194] but they were not the dominant group in the township. The Kingstown of 1911 was a failed holiday resort, a mere 82 females and 25 males were listed as employed in hotels and lodging houses, however it had acquired a new function in housing the elderly. The Kingstown climate was claimed to promote longevity and the proportion of the population aged over 45 rose steadily.

Kingstown has been examined at some length because it is the largest of the 'railway suburbs' and because the port complicates the picture. The more distant areas of Killiney and Dalkey were much less densely populated. They were linked to Dublin by the Kingstown-Bray line which opened in 1856. In 1861 the population of Dalkey amounted to 2,187, that of Killiney to a mere 1,232. By 1911, Dalkey's population had risen to 3,536, while Killiney's had doubled to 2,721. Dalkey became a township in 1867, having adopted the 1854 Act in 1863.[195] The establishment of any form of municipal organisation was opposed by a number of inhabitants who claimed that the whole area was too scattered. At this stage much property in both Dalkey and Killiney was only occupied during the summer months. Recalling Killiney, Page Dickinson wrote[196]

> In the early days of its rise to fame, about the middle of the 19th century it became popular as a summer resort for the well-to-do Dublin families. It was not really residential until the last quarter of the century. It had no cohesion, no collective social life and its hill side

was dotted with the houses of rich families who spent their summer there.

The summer residents were not wholeheartedly welcomed by the permanent Dalkey population. They argued that unoccupied houses should be charged full rates because under the present system permanent residents bore an undue proportion of the taxes in contrast to 'persons who furnish houses for letting which are only occupied for a portion of the year'.[197] The interests of the latter group would appear to have been dominant and unoccupied houses were not rated.[198]

The main impetus to establish local government in Dalkey came from the desire to encourage its holiday trade rather than suburban residence. Its chief promoter was James Milo Burke, proprietor of Dublin's Shelbourne Hotel[199] and three of the twelve initial commissioners were hoteliers.

Insofar as permanent housing developed, it did so on the basis of individual villas with a considerable premium being placed on locations beside the sea. By 1869 it was stated that there was a 'want of sites for marine villas'.[200] With most coastal sites already developed the most obvious attractions had been exhausted, while the hilly terrain made other sites both difficult and less attractive. Given the relatively limited demand for residences in Kingstown it would be unrealistic to have expected mass development in either Dalkey or Killiney. Blackrock on the other hand should have benefitted from being closer to the city and possessing a less difficult terrain. In fact growth in Blackrock was rather sedate reaching its peak in the 1860s.

Housing in Blackrock 1841-1911

	Total	Blackrock	Booterstown	Monkstown
1841	1,045	—	—	—
1851	1,184	—	—	—
1861	1,257	—	—	—
1871	1,588	798	402	388
1881	1,608	861	409	338
1891	1,587	853	380	354
1901	1,648	856	415	377
1911	1,795	980	416	399

Blackrock township, like Pembroke contained a somewhat varied population. Blackrock village was an old fishing village which owed its prosperity to being a popular seaside resort for Dubliners. This encouraged a substantial concentration of public-houses, though marine residences such as that of Lord Cloncurry at Maretimo, or Lord Edward Fitzgerald at Frascati attracted a more exclusive population. In 1860 Blackrock village and a surrounding area became a township, mainly on the initiative of the village businessmen. Of the thirty-five who signed the requisition to the Lord Lieutenant, twenty were local shopkeepers or others residing on the main street.[201] The legislation was opposed both by the impoverished inhabitants of Williamstown, who feared that it would result in increased taxes which would be passed on by their landlords in higher rents, and by the inhabitants of the area's avenues and rural district. At this stage the valuation office did not favour including the Temple Hill, Seapoint and Montpelier sections of Monkstown arguing that[202]

> It would be somewhat premature to include this district within the limits of the proposed district as the streets and avenues are only now being laid out and formed and although there are many houses in progress I (Richard Griffith, valuation commissioners) consider the district should be omitted for the present.

Control in the new township rested in the hands of local shopkeepers, a factor which was helped by the low voting qualification of £4. During 1861 and 1862 memorials were sent to Dublin Castle by Monkstown property owners, many of whom had recently built houses requesting that they be annexed, either to Blackrock or Kingstown. This request was supported by the owners of over half the property but opposed by the residents of cottages or weekly tenements.[203] To the city-side of Blackrock, residents of Booterstown, among them Lord Gough, also requested annexation.[204]

The extension of Blackrock in 1863 brought a considerable change in its character. The franchise was increased to £8 and the area was divided into three wards. Political power had previously rested in liberal/catholic hands. A disgruntled pamphleteer of this persuasion regarded the boundary extension as 'successful activity to obtain local power, position, influence and patronage for the exclusive benefit of the ascendancy faction' and argued that Monkstown was included as a separate ward to secure a majority for 'the Ascendancy party' on the board.[205]

Monkstown Ward was the most socially exclusive suburb of Dublin boasting the highest proportion of male servants and a Protestant majority as late as 1911. The number of houses actually fell until 1881 as cabins and cottages were demolished to make way for suburban villas.

Those displaced crowded into Blackrock village. In 1884 one road, Chapel Lane contained 'miserly mud cabins' rented at 1/6 per week for one room, and 2/6 for two rooms with local shopkeepers acting as landlords.[206] They were inhabited by labourers, gardeners or washerwomen many of them employed in large houses in the vicinity.

The segregation of the working class in Blackrock village and in the coastal village of Williamstown produced clear electoral consequences in the 1899 local elections. In both Booterstown and Blackrock Wards, all but two of those elected, one in each ward, were nationalists. Some were professional men, but they included William Field, butcher and nationalist M.P. plus a local cowkeeper. In contrast those elected for Monkstown Ward were exclusively unionists, all gentlemen and professional men, with one exception, Mrs. Dockrell, wife of a prominent businessman and the first woman local representative in the Dublin area. Blackrock therefore represented a somewhat uneasy co-existence of classes and political allegiances.

Other than Kingstown railways had little impact on suburban growth and even there its impact tailed off sharply after 1871. However Kingstown and its neighbouring villages had the advantage of a fashionable seaside location, and in Kingstown, a well-established town. The effort to establish an isolated suburb in Foxrock where none had previously existed and without the benefit of a seaside location proved a singular failure. The sites were developed by Bentley estate agents — who developed Brighton Square Rathmines, and were within three minutes walk of Carrickmines and Stillorgan stations.[207] A further station was actually opened on the estate, on land provided by Messers. Bentley and first and second class tickets were provided at concessionary rates. They also arranged an omnibus service to Kingstown and granted a free site for a Church of Ireland church to act as a focal point for the development. By 1865 Mark Bentley had spent £40-50,000 on roads and site development and he estimated that his tenants had spent a similar amount in building houses. These were valued at from £500-£3,000 and occupied sites of from one to ten acres. By 1865 a business rival claimed that the scheme was a failure.[208] In the following year Messrs. Bentley abandoned their building agency to concentrate, it was claimed, on other business[209] and in 1870 the Foxrock estate, consisting of 505 acres extending along the Dublin Wicklow and Wexford railway with an average breadth of three furlongs was sold to the Royal Exchange Assurance Co.[210] As late as 1906 the latter described the land as 'capable of development'.[211] Census figures show that there was slow growth in the 1860s and 1870s, but not until the first decade of the twentieth century did expansion resume. The majority of the area's residents, numbering a mere 824 by 1911, were not suburban dwellers.

The story of Dublin's suburban development is of the failure of many high-flown ambitions. While an undoubted market for suburban housing existed it was a limited one: a consequence of the economic limitations of the nineteenth century city. In this development, transport, particularly the railways played a limited part. The role of the landowners was more evident, but the key factors were the area's location and its existing population. The suburbs of Dublin repeated the social pattern prevailing in the city and reinforced the social domination of the area south of the river Liffey, somewhat distant from the river itself and its related dockland. This ensured the social pre-eminence of Rathmines and Pembroke, though in the latter case the matter was complicated by the working class dock areas of Irishtown and Ringsend. In summarising the suburban development of London, Kellett noted[212]

> where clear distinctions of social status existed between the different areas of Victorian London, they have tended simply to be perpetuated and extended further outwards into adjacent suburbs as if all social classes were castes and all travel were pedestrian.

This is broadly correct for Dublin. However in Dublin suburban migration had political and religious significance. Many escaped from a city whose political tone was becoming increasingly unpalatable to live in to a more congenial atmosphere where the Protestant conservative ascendancy had not yet been challenged.

Chapter VII

DUBLIN MUNICIPAL POLITICS

The political and social background to the city's municipal politics provides an essential key to understanding attitudes towards health, housing and other municipal matters. It also highlights the problems of religious and political controversy which served to alienate the Protestant ascendancy. This chapter does not attempt to provide a detailed account of city politics, rather to sketch its main dimensions and the major changes which took place.

Dublin, in common with other British and Irish cities underwent a revolution in its municipal government in the mid nineteenth century. Prior to the 1840 *Municipal Corporations Ireland Act* city government had been controlled by a small and largely self-perpetuating body. Freeman, either hereditary members of city guilds, or men elected by the common council, elected the common council which in turn elected the sheriffs. From these the aldermen were chosen and one of these became Lord Mayor, elected by the common council.[1]

By the 1830s those bodies were highly unrepresentative both of the city's population, and of its business and professinal elite. The report on the Municipal Corporations noted[2]

the commons are totally distinct from the mercantile body of the city and nothing can more clearly illustrate the position in which the corporation and the citizens at large at present stand, than the facts that the Council of the Chamber of Commerce, the Committee of the Commercial Buildings, the Directors of the Corn Exchange and the Committee of the Linen Hall — the principal commercial institutions of the city do not

203

contain a single alderman, sheriff's peer or member of the commons.

Catholics had been permitted to become freemen from 1793 but none had been elected while liberal Protestants who favoured emancipation were also excluded from becoming either freemen or members of the common council.[3]

This system was replaced by a straightforward property qualification in 1840. Future members were required to be burgesses, resident within seven miles of the city, holding city property valued at £1,000, or the rated occupier for one year of a house valued at £25. Electors were also required to occupy a house, or to reside within seven miles, and, most importantly to be separately rated. This requirement acted as a major limitation on the franchise, as those occupying houses of less than £8 valuation were not separately rated, nor were those occupying property let in monthly tenancies. Electors had to be resident and paying rates at the same address for almost three years, further reducing the electorate. In the mid 1890s there were approximately 8,000 municipal voters, compared with 37,000 for parliamentary elections.[4]

Such reforms were designed to give adequate representation to property. In Dublin they were marked by the participation in municipal government of many of the city's premier businessmen. Lord Mayors in the following twenty years included Benjamin Lee Guinness, another leading brewer John D'Arcy, distiller George Roe, paper manufacturer and chairman of the Great Southern and Western Railway Company, Sir Edward McDonnell, poplin manufacturer Richard Atkinson and several of the city's leading merchants. In 1851, in marked contrast to the unreformed corporation, fourteen members of Dublin corporation were also bank or railway directors, or members of the Dublin Chamber of Commerce.

This participation by the city's business elite proved a short-term phenomenon. Small manufacturers tended to replace the large, while the representation of grocers and publicans began its inexorable increase. By 1876 only two corporation members were numbered among the banking and railway directors.[5] This transformation was the almost inevitable outcome of the shifts which were taking place

204

Table I. Occupations of Dublin Corporation members 1850-1910

	1850	1860	1870	1880	1890	1900	1910
Merchant	25	20	21	21	18	12	21
(small)	(2)	(3)	(5)	(3)	(1)	(2)	(10)
Publican/grocer	4	7	12	9	16	19	19
Brewer/distiller	7	4	1	–	–	–	–
Other manuf.	4	8	6	13	7	4	5
(small)	–	(6)	(2)	(5)	(2)	(1)	–
Profession	13	13	10	5	6	7	6
Tradesman	–	–	–	2	2	7	7
Hotelier	–	3	2	2	–	–	3
Builder	–	–	2	2	4	–	–
Publisher/news proprietor	1	1	2	2	3	–	–
Clerical/shop assistant	–	–	–	–	–	2	5
Unknown	6	5	6	4	3	9	13
Big Bus.	(23)	(13)	(15)	(11)	(1)	(3)	(7)
Total	60	60	60	60	60	60	80

in the social and religious composition of the city's population. The Protestant big business elite were a minority of corporation members even in the 1840s, but they diminished in subsequent decades. Many drift out of municipal politics from a sense of disillusionment, alienation and increasing awareness of their impotence, diverting their energy to township politics or to voluntary organisations. The decline in social composition of city councillors also reflects the composition of the Catholics middle-class. With some exceptions, such as Sir Alexander McDonnell, or Peter Paul McSwiney, twice Lord Mayor and owner of the city's largest drapery business, the majority tended to be found in small scale retail trade, notably the grocery and drink trades. A list exists in 1860 of those contributing to a fund to assist Pope Pius IX in his political and military difficulties resulting from the Italian unification campaign. Of the small minority who contributed £10 or more, and excluding the clergy, the largest single block were publicans and grocers, a total of twenty-two. A further eight subscribers were brewers or rectifying distillers, fourteen were merchants of a miscellaneous variety, nine were professional men, six

205

manufacturers, all small scale, four were builders, four engaged in trades such as baker or tailor, while there was one pawnbroker, one bookseller and one journalist.[7]

The pattern emerging from this somewhat imperfect picture of the Catholic middle class in 1860 prefigures the elements who dominated municipal politics in the subsequent decades. Distribution, particularly of food and drink, or related to agriculture predominated, while manufacturing and the professions had a distinctly lower profile.

A significant omission from the ranks of corporation members is any major concentration of builders, estate agents or property developers, if we exclude tenement owners. This is in marked contrast to the townships where such elements formed a readily identifiable block.

The changing social composition of Dublin Corporation inevitably aroused comment and concern. As early as 1860 one correspondent spoke in terms of[8]

> a cabal of pork butchers and potato factors, of pawnbrokers and publicans, or pettifogging attorneys and mendicant patriotic men who derive a sordid livelihood by ministering to the meanest wants of mankind.

By 1876, J.T. Pim, a leading city businessman remarked that[9]

> Men who would make more suitable members of the Corporation cannot be induced to come forward — abstention from participation in municipal affairs is now in fact just as common among the more extensive mercantile men as in the U.S.

Pim, and the Dublin Chamber of Commerce lobbied for a reform of the municipal electorate to give greater representation to property owners, noting that[10]

> those who pay the major portion of rating are outvoted by those who pay the lesser portion.

The allegations of a takeover by men of no property were somewhat excessive. Though not competing in wealth with the men of 1851, corporation members in 1875 owned property with an average per capita rateable value in the city of £167, though this concealed dramatic differences between the £755 valuation on the drapery store of Peter Paul McSwiney, or the £569 accounted for by hardware merchant Hugh O Rorke and the £38 valuation of publican

206

Philip Redmond.[11]

The 1880s and 1890s brought a marked decline in average wealth levels. This began with the sweeping nationalist victories in the 1880s and was reinforced by the local government reform of 1898 which increased the electorate to that of the parliamentary franchise, plus propertied women, while removing property qualifications for corporation membership. Both these moves resulted in the removal of further Protestant, Unionist representatives, and, despite the expansion in the proportion of Catholic professional and business men within the city, the Protestants were consistently replaced by men of limited wealth and standing, many of them publicans and grocers. Even the status of Catholic representatives would seem to have undergone a similar decline. The predominance of local publicans and grocers among municipal representatives was greatest in the poorest city areas. By 1871, all three representatives from Wood Quay Ward were either grocers or vintners, reflecting the fact that these were among the few thriving businesses in such an area.

Until 1898 all Corporation members held some property, however modest. The removal of the property qualification in 1898 brought about the emergence of a small, virtually propertyless, element. Many, in the initial electoral enthusiasm which followed municipal reform were tradesmen or proprietors of small businesses who ostensibly represented trade union interests. However the dominance of grocers and publicans survived, probably because the new electorate were even more dependent on such men for credit, housing and other local services than the previous electorate. The professional representation after 1900 is virtually confined to the suburban wards of Drumcondra and Clontarf, indicating that the professional class, both Catholic and Protestant had largely left the central city area. The relative scarcity of Catholic professional candidates also raises the question as to whether they, like their Protestant counterparts, consciously stood aloof from the rather robust nature of Dublin city politics, leaving control to the petty business class.

The reform of Dublin Corporation in 1840 had implications much wider than giving adequate representation to property and commercial interests. The municipal reform movement in Ireland had been in existence from approximately 1810, but in the 1820s it was largely taken over by the O Connellite momentum for Catholic Emancipation.[12] The success of this campaign brought political polarization on denominational lines.[13] The old corporations were condemned as bastions of the Protestant ascendancy, a charge irrefutable in Dublin where no Catholic or Catholic sympathizer could either vote or become a member. The unreformed Dublin Corporation stated its case for survival unashamedly in terms of preserving the Protestant ascendancy. In their petition against municipal reform they noted[14]

> we feel that the question now at issue involves the peace of Ireland and the interest of Irish Protestants even more nearly and practically than the Bill of 1829.

They regarded Irish municipal corporations as inherently Protestant institutions. In a further plea for support to the Protestants of the United Kingdom they stated that in the event of reform[15]

> The Lord Mayor of Dublin will then be President of the *Popish* schools — will be Chairman at the meeting of *Popish* religious societies — will lay the first stone of *Popish* chapels — will throw the weight of his influence — that is to say the weight of the influence of a British Magistrate into the scale with whatever is *Popish* and therefore idolatrous and damnable.

Unlike the English municipal reform movement that in Ireland did not concern itself with 'the gas and water question in the towns'[16] but rather with achieving municipal reform as part of the wider battle for Catholic democratic rights and repeal of the Act of Union. This was highlighted in 1841 when Daniel O Connell became the first Catholic Lord Mayor of Dublin since reformation times and used his position to launch a full-scale campaign for Repeal. One of the high points was a formal debate within Dublin Corporation on the repeal question, when the unionist position was defended by Isaac Butt, subsequently founder of the movement for Home Rule.[17] This firmly established Dublin Corporation as a body with wider political interests, a type of substitute for the lost Parliament of College Green. Throughout the remainder of the century many issues of little municipal significance but of great political and religious controversy were debated in its chamber.

Catholic numerical dominance within the the corporation followed immediately on the introduction of the reformed electorate. By 1866 Catholics accounted for 43 of the 60 members[18] and this proportion rose in the 1880s and once again following the reforms of 1898. Although he had almost certainly irrevocably polarized the two religious communities,[19] O Connell urged the Catholic representatives 'not to use this power with sectarian exclusiveness'.[20] He suggested a power-sharing arrangement whereby one-third of all wards, and one-third of seats would be taken uncontested by the minority, but this offer was rejected.[21] However O Connell was succeeded by a Protestant Liberal — an increasingly rare breed — elected by the Catholic majority[22] and from 1840 to 1851 one Lord Mayor in three was a Protestant, though generally a member of the Liberal political majority. In 1850 an arrangement was apparently made to alternate the office of Lord Mayor between the majority and the minority and this practice continued with no apparent acrimony until 1858 when the Protestant candidate, Mr. Wilson was vetoed by the Catholics.[23] However another minority, i.e. Protestant Conservative candidate, Mr. Lambert was then proposed and accepted. Similarly in 1860 and in 1862 the first choice Conservative candidates were vetoed and eventually replaced by more acceptable candidates of the same political and religious persuasion.

This practice of alternating the office of Lord Mayor was apparently the result of a verbal agreement made in 1850. However a committee of Dublin Corporation, set up in 1864 to investigate its existence concluded that no such agreement existed, nor was such a compact found in any other Irish city.[24] All evidence suggests the agreement's existence — many of the confusing statements in the corporation report suggest that the committee privately accept this, but no written proof existed. There was also considerable confusion as to whether it provided for alternative Liberal and Conservative Lord Mayors, or for alternative Catholic and Protestant candidates. Alderman Roe, who as a Protestant Liberal would have had some vested interest in the matter believed that it was an agreement to alternate Catholics and Protestants.[25] The most obvious proof that the practice had some moral sanction is the fact that it survived though not without considerable strain, until the heady conflicts engendered by Parnellite Home Rule and the Land League. That certain Catholic elements believed such a power-sharing arrangement to be desirable is confirmed by the rather pious urging of the committee which inquired into its existence that[26]

> This tolerance (conferring high office on the minority) your Committee strongly recommend your Council to adopt and act upon.

They claimed that the moral value of such a practice would be destroyed if it were controlled by a compact.[27]

The survival of such an arrangement without friction would have been virtually unimaginable in the heavily-sectarian climate of nineteenth century Dublin. Following in O Connell's train the majority of Catholics members were Liberals, though a small Protestant Liberal minority also existed. During the late 'forties and 'fifties the city's parliamentary representation was exclusively conservative. Catholic municipal representatives frequently found themselves at odds with mainstream liberalism on issues such as Italian unification which severely curtailed the power and possessions of the papacy. Local politics, in the absence of clear-cut national issues tended to concentrate on sectarian questions. This in turn reflected the growing influence of the Catholic Archbishop of Dublin, Paul Cullen. In 1860 the virtual imprisonment of the pope in the Vatican brought several large Catholic demonstrations, such as the gathering of signatures and the passing of a formal vote of sympathy in a mass ceremony in the Pro-Cathedral. The resolution confirming the 'unshaken attachment of the Catholics of Ireland to the Pope' was proposed by the Lord Mayor and seconded by Alderman Reynolds while a second resolution was seconded by Alderman Martin.[28]

A more immediate local issue — the refusal of the British Government to grant a charter to the Catholic University was the occasion of a corporation debate. This event prompted the protest of Councillor Bonsall (Protestant Conservative) that it 'was a purely Catholic question which ought never to have been introduced there'.[29] Another burning issue was the survival of a freeman franchise. All freemen were Protestant, but those eligible by birth had to be admitted by the Lord Mayor. Catholic Lord Mayors refused to admit freemen and Catholics used their veto to prevent the appointment of any Protestant Lord Mayor who would do so. This occasioned many of the disputes relating to the alternating of the Lord Mayor's office. In 1862 the dispute over the choice of Lord Mayor for the following year lasted from July to November before being resolved.[30]

With the growing emphasis on Catholic rights and the increasing friction with orthodox liberalism the way was open for the emergence of a new political grouping which would give priority to Catholic interests. The National Association eventually emerged from the committee which organised the laying of the foundation stone for the O Connell memorial in Sackville St., an event over which Peter Paul McSwiney, the then Lord Mayor presided.[31] The original National Association had several members of Dublin Corporation, in addition to Catholic clergy as its nucleus[32] and it soon became a force within the council chamber, continuing the well-established practice of debating religious issues. When MacSwiney's term of office ended on 1 January 1865 and he handed office to John Barrington, a Quaker Conservative, the vote of thanks to the outgoing Lord Mayor, moved by Sir John Gray (M.P. Kilkenny and member of the National Association) which was generally passed unanimously was opposed by Messrs. Bonsall and Norwood who criticised MacSwiney's lack of impartiality.[33]

A further controversy arose when Sir John Gray brought forward a motion condemning the oath which all Catholic elected representatives were forced to take disclaiming the right of the pope to absolve subjects from their political allegiance and binding Catholics to 'abjure any intention to subvert the present Church Establishment as settled by law within this Realm'.[34] This had been a matter of some controversy since 1862 when A.M. Sullivan, a journalist refused to take this oath and was disqualified from membership of the corporation. The resolution led to a Conservative walk out and it was passed by the remaining Catholic and Liberal members.[35] In 1866 and 1868 motions favouring the disestablishment and disendowment of the Church of Ireland were carried.[36] These tensions turned

the alternating Lord Mayorship into a battlefield. Given
Liberal support for disestablishment the outcome was a
strengthened Catholic-Liberal alliance and reflecting this,
in 1867, W. Lane Joynt a Protestant Liberal became Lord
Mayor. This was the 'minority's' turn to hold office, but
his appointment was condemned by the Conservatives, who
argued that one of their members should have been appointed.

The mayoralty for the year 1869 — the peak of the disestablishment agitation — was another occasion for conflict.
In July 1868 James Vokes Mackey was nominated to take
office in the following January, though not without a
division.[37] Moves to rescind this, led by Peter Paul McSwiney
followed and proved successful. One Liberal member,
however, Philip Redmond resigned his seat rather than with-
draw his vote in favour of Mackay.[38] Sir William Carroll,
a Catholic who had been Lord Mayor for 1868 continued in
office.

The relationship between disestablishment and political
conflict is evident from the nomination of a Lord Mayor
for the year 1870. When the matter was raised in July 1869
— the usual date, Councillor Dennehy announced that he
felt that they should nominate 'a member of the opposite
religion and politics', but that they could not do so, nor were
they in a position to do so the previous year. He proposed
that nominations be deferred for a month pending the
settlement of the disestablishment question[39] and at the
following meeting, Councillor Purdon, a Protestant Conservative was nominated without challenge.[40]

With the passing of disestablishment, sectarian questions
lost their urgency though matters such as denominational
education remained unresolved. For the remainder of the
decade the office of Lord Mayor alternated without controversy.

Disestablishment meant a new political alignment on the
part of some Dublin Conservatives who flirted with some
form of self-government as an alternative to unpalatable
government from Westminster. These frustrations were a
factor in the establishment in 1870 of the Home Government
Association, an alliance of frustrated conservatives and frustrated nationalists led by Isaac Butt, erstwhile defender of

212

the Union in the debate with O Connell. The founding meeting was attended by a total of 61 members, including Edward Purdon, Conservative Lord Mayor and a former Lord Mayor, Alderman John Barrington who was a Quaker. The Protestants were in a majority, while with 28 members, the Conservatives were the largest single group.[41]

In July 1871 the Home Rule case was presented before Dublin Corporation with McSwiney opposing its being debated without success.[42] However this early conservative phase of Home Rule proved short lived and of little long-term significance in local politics. The alignment of the Liberal Catholic majority versus a Protestant Conservative minority — the latter of superior social standing, remained. In later years Sir John Barrington explained his initial support for Home Rule as follows[43]

> They, as honest Irishmen, and wishing for the benefit of the city of Dublin, and Ireland generally, thought that if there was a combined movement made at the time — combining parties of all politics, going for one common object — to check the great expenditure of money that took place in London, dragging their aristocracy over there, and their lawyers over there to carry bills, and, as it were, dragging the vitals out of the country and if they could manage by any effort of theirs to induce any representative of the royal family to come over, and occupy a residence in Ireland, they thought they would be achieving a great object.

The Protestant Home Rule movement scored one decisive victory in the 1874 general election when the city's sitting Liberal M.P., Jonathan Pim, a Quaker who had been elected with clerical support, was defeated by Lord Mayor, Maurice Brooks, a Protestant Home Ruler. This was virtually the last manifestation of conservative nationalism. Catholic triumphalism raised its head again in 1875, when Peter Paul Mc Swiney the Lord Mayor led the celebrations for the centenary of the birth of Daniel O Connell, placing his main emphasis on the victory of catholic emancipation rather than on the later repeal movement. Conservative representation continued to dwindle, as did the number of Protestant Liberals. A lackluster campaign was initiated by the Chamber of Commerce to reform the electorate in order to give greater weight to property and presumably in the process to shore up Conservative representation. By the late 1870s conservatives numbered approximately one-third of all members with the practice of alternating Lord Mayors still surviving. However the *Irish Times* remarked that 'In years when it is the Conservatives turn for office the Lord Mayor's post is literally going a begging'.[44]

The land war and the new militancy of the Home Rule campaign brought an end to this pact and led to a further depletion in Conservative ranks. In 1876 the *Municipal Privileges (Ireland) Act* gave Irish corporations the power to confer the freedom of boroughs and the decision to confer or withold this privilege soon became a new political battleground. In 1881 nationalists proposed to confer the freedom of the city on Parnell and John Dillon, then imprisoned in Kilmainham, but the proposal was defeated by the casting vote of the Conservative Lord Mayor, Alderman Moyers.[45] The defeat of this motion despite conservatives being in a one-third minority indicates that many of the liberal representatives were by no means committed to the Home Rule camp. The 1881 local elections brought an increase in nationalist strength and in 1882 under a Home Rule Lord Mayor the freedom was conferred.[46] The use of the freedom of the city to emphasise a political stance was not new. The old corporation, in its dying months conferred the freedom of the city on the Reverend Dr. Cook, the militant Ulster Presbyterian leader, on the Rev. Hugh McNeill and Rev. Mortimer O Sullivan, in all cases[47]

> in consideration of the zeal which he has long manifested in the support of our pure religion.

Under the new regime freedom of the city was limited to those receiving nationalist approval. An attempt in 1882 to confer the freedom on General Sir Garret Wolseley who had successfully commanded the British army, including many Irish troops in Egypt, was defeated by 27 votes to 21.[48] Increased tensions over such issues, coupled with growing Home Rule strength at the polls, brought an end to Conservative Lord Mayors being appointed. Sir George Moyer, who held the position in 1881, was in the words of nationalist journalist, T.D. Sullivan 'the last of the Mohicans'.[49]

The elections of 1883 brought a sweeping victory for Parnellites, mainly due to greater efforts to register nationalist voters. The results were described by the *Irish Times* as 'alarming'. Overwhelming nationalist control, coupled with the rising tensions over Home Rule brought further defiant gestures designed to alienate remaining Protestant councillors. An address of welcome to the Prince of Wales was refused in 1885,[50] a new street which had been cleared in the vicinity of the City Hall was named Lord Edward Street in honour of the leader of the 1798 rebellion (this may have contributed to its commercial failure) and the sinecures of City Marshal and Sword-Bearer were conferred on Thomas Sexton, impoverished Home Rule M.P. and James Egan, a recently released Fenian ex-prisoner. When in 1887 the then Lord Mayor T.D. Sullivan was arrested for publishing the proceedings of the National League in his newspaper *The Nation*, he was accompanied to court by the corporation members in their robes of office, preceded by the city sword and mace. While he was in jail the corporation voted him the freedom of the city.[51]

Dublin politicians overwhelmingly supported Parnell in the split of 1890, however deprived of the cohesion afforded by the urgent national issues of the 'eighties and with a secure majority, fragmentation emerged within the nationalist ranks. A majority voted to receive Queen Victoria in 1901. By 1896 Conservative representation had shrunk to a mere eleven representatives.[52] The city's trade unionists (mostly skilled workers) were becoming increasingly frustrated at their lack of representation and the Irish Trades Union Congress passed a resolution in 1894 demanding an extension of the municipal franchise.[53] In 1895 they urged that a clause extending the franchise be included in a municipal improvement bill and a resolution favouring such a move was introduced by Thomas Lenehan, councillor for Inns Quay Ward and a local hardware merchant, but it was defeated for want of a quorum, mainly because of the opposition of the Lord Mayor.[54]

The trades council continued their campaign with a deputation to the Chief Secretary[55] and in 1896 Dublin Corporation voted in favour of extending the franchise.[56] This bill, introduced by Tim Healy was defeated by the

House of Lords and Dublin Corporation accepted the loss of the franchise clauses without opposition.[57]

The battle for an extended franchise shifted to the level of individual wards. In Wood Quay Ward over 1,100 claims for a vote were served — double the usual electorate. The senior assessor to the Lord Mayor, Mr. Macinerney, Q.C. stated that the normal electorate only amounted to one-third of those entitled, as the lists only included those rated individually. Others wishing to vote had to pay their rates separately and then claim their franchise.[58] In 1897 this method of extending the franchise was adopted and a clause in the city's improvement bill proposed to make registration of voters more automatic. This was opposed in the Commons by the Unionist leader Sir Edward Carson who claimed that it 'would practically destroy altogether the small Unionist minority'.[59] This provision was defeated by the House of Lords.

The municipal franchise was not extended until the 1898 Local Government Act when the electorate increased from approximately 8,000 to almost 38,000.[60] Some of this increase was accounted for by women. Their share of the electorate ranged from 8.6% in South City Ward to 19.7% in Fitzwilliam Ward and an amazing 23.88% in Inns Quay Ward, but the majority of new voters were working class.

Until 1898 the prospects of labour representation within the corporation was limited. In 1894 only W.J. Leahy, a cooper could be viewed as a labour supporter, but he owed his position more to his nationalist credentials.[61] When John Simmons a trade union candidate stood in a by-election in Fitzwilliam Ward in 1895 he succeeded only in splitting the Nationalist vote and securing a Unionist victory.[62] However the 1898 elections on the unreformed register returned two labour candidates, Richardson, President of the Trades Council and Nanetti a printer, unopposed.[63] They displayed their independence of the nationalist block by voting for Sir Robert Sexton, a Conservative as Lord Mayor.[64] This was not a reflection of their political allegiance but was due to trade union hostility to any Lord Mayor continuing in office for a second term and depriving the city trades of some business.[65]

The elections of 1899 on the new electorate brought the

prospect of significant labour gains. The trades council endorsed a total of eleven candidates of whom seven were elected while five other candidates standing as nationalists but with close trade union affiliations were also returned.[66] This was the peak of labour's electoral influence. All but two of the labour councillors immediately attended a meeting of newly-elected Parnellite members of the corporation and voted in support of the re-election of Daniel Tallon as Lord Mayor.[67] The weakness of the labour block was further demonstrated in the following year when the election of Dowd as the first trade unionist Lord Mayor with Parnellite support was defeated by the vote of another trade unionist E.L. Richardson who ensured the election of Sir Thomas Pile.[68] From this point labour strength declines because of the failure to retain an independent identity. J.W. Boyle has noted[69]

> Most of the labour group identified themselves with their fellow corporators and rose out of their class rather than with it.

A more recent analysis, by Brendan McDonnell endorses this view.[70]

> Because of the very close connection between the labour members and nationalist groups, the separate existence of a corporation labour party must be doubted; more accurately the labour members formed a distinguishable group among the nationalists.

Their almost total integration is shown by the election of the printer and former trades council president, J.P. Nanetti, as Lord Mayor in 1906 and 1907.

Labour failed to provide a viable alternative opposition to replace the declining Unionist representation. After 1899 Unionists were limited to seven seats in three wards: South City, Fitzwilliam, and Royal Exchange[71] and although the boundary extension of 1900 increased their numbers slightly their power had collapsed. In consequence no effective opposition existed and no group put forward coherent criticism or alternative municipal policies. There was some limited opposition, notably the unsuccessful candidature of socialist James Connolly in Wood Quay Ward in 1903,[72] or the criticisms voiced by Sinn Fein leader Arthur Griffith. Those who voiced opposition within the corporation such as

P.T. Daly who combined Sinn Fein and labour allegiance were in a small minority. Connolly and Griffith focussed primarily on corruption, maladministration and jobbery and the close association which existed between local politicians and the perpetuation of the tenement housing system. Speaking of John Scully, High Sheriff of Dublin, Connolly wrote[73]

> Scully is running in the interests of the United Irish League, and high rents, slum tenements, rotten staircases, stinking yards, high death-rates, low wages, Corporation jobbery and margarine wrapped in butter paper.

The lack of a coherent opposition, given the social problems in the city is of interest. Connolly tended to attribute the continuing success of nationalist candidates to free drink and the power which local shopkeepers and tenement owners could exercise over the electorate. In his 1903 address to the Wood Quay Ward electors he wrote[74]

> Let us take lesson by the municipal election of last year. Let us remember how the drink sellers of the Wood Quay Ward combined with the slum owners and the house jobbers; let us remember how Alderman Davin, Councillor McCall and all their fellow publicans issued free drinks to whoever would accept . . . . Let us remember the threats and the bribery, how Mr. Byrne of Wood Quay told the surrounding tenants that if 'Mr Connolly was elected their rents would be raised' . . . . You will understand that there can never be either clean, healthy or honest politics in the City of Dublin, until the power of the drink sellers is absolutely broken — they are positively the meanest and most degraded section that ever attempted to rule a city.

The role of free drink in local elections was signficant. One working class autobiography recalls[75]

> We remember living in Lower Gloucester St. and hearing that in Johnny P's public house free beer was to be got by promising to vote and work for Johnnie in the elections.

To attribute nationalist success solely to the value of free drink and control of tenement property is somewhat naive. Elections provided the working class with some ex-

218

citement and a rare opportunity for free indulgence, but we must not ignore the role of Irish nationalism, and in particular the all-embracing Irish Parliamentary Party, in curbing any effective opposition. The Irish Parliamentary Party sold itself very effectively as the Irish labour party, with men such as J.J. Clancy promoting legislation for improved financial terms for municipal housing[76] and the party invariably supporting virtually all social legislation at Westminster. Instead of regarding the trades council candidates with hostility they sought to include them within the mainstream parliamentary party to the extent that the trade unionist J.P. Nanetti was returned as M.P. for the College Green division of the city in 1900. Given the belief that the Act of Union was the major cause of all Irish ills — a belief shared by most trade unionists, any serious deviation from supporting the nationalist party smacked of treason. The result was a corporation whose actions were unchecked by any viable political alternative and a body whose dominance by drink sellers and tenement landlords did little to articulate any broader goals for municipal government, other than narrow political gain and survival in office.

E.P. Hennock, in his work on nineteenth century English local government and on the ideological motivations of different groups has distinguished between the expansion-minded and reformist mentality of large businessmen and the obsession with economy shown by small businessmen.[77] His work also demonstrates, particularly in the case of Birmingham, the strength of the commitment made by many large businessmen towards civic service.[78] The Hennock analysis fits rather uneasily in the Dublin context. True, there was a supplanting of Protestants by Catholics. Dublin's small businessmen were not particularly concerned with economy. The only groups advocating control on expenditure were invariably, as in the case of John McEvoy and the Dublin Ratepayers' Association, Protestants, who would have included more large businessmen than their corporation counterparts. The Dublin city water scheme was largely disputed on sectarian lines, 'a battle of the Boyne and Blackwater',[79] though it is perhaps significant that the scheme was supported by Benjamin Lee Guinness, one of the largest Conservative businessmen, though opposed by the Conservatives as a whole. Where Dublin's small businessmen parallel their English counterparts is in lack of broader municipal concern, and tolerance of sanitary breaches, mainly because they and their allies tended to be tenement landlords or proprietors of slaughter houses or dairy yards. Despite the similarities in legislation and administration, Anglo-Saxon parallels sit uneasily on Dublin's municipal history. A more valid analogy would seem to be that mentioned by Hennock when he refers to the American historian Richard Hofstadter's contrast between the Anglo-Saxon tradition of public service and the boss system which prevailed in the United States.[80] Dublin would seem to have been closer to Tamanny Hall than to Birmingham, or Leeds Town Hall. Religion and politics were undoubtedly a factor in this seeming lack of municipal pride. Belfast, though operating a system of municipal government which excluded a substantial minority of its citizens, the Catholics, still managed apparently to operate with a considerable level of administrative efficiency.[81]

It should be borne in mind that no British city, nor indeed Belfast, operated within such tight financial limits as did Dublin. The 1847 valuation of £663,768 was substantially reduced in 1854[82] and was not again achieved until the late 1880s. Revenue was not augmented by income from a city estate, or from municipal utilities, as a result there was little scope for municipal largesse or civic pride in contrast to English cities whose rapidly increasing revenues gave considerable financial leeway, as Asa Briggs has noted[83]

> Although the total rates expenditure of England and Wales increased from £10-£16½m. in 1868, £28m. in 1890 and £56m. by the middle of the first decade of the twentieth century the average rate poundage changed little until the 'explosion' of the 1890s. Rateable valuation rose more rapidly than population and corporations could spend more without increasing the rates.

Dublin Corporation's political allegiance served to alienate the British administration in Ireland and much of the city's commercial elite. The attitude adopted towards Dublin Castle was generally distant. Official functions were boycotted from 1880 until the arrival of the pro-Home Rule

220

Viceroy, Viscount Aberdeen in 1886 when there was a temporary thaw.[84] With their departure relations again ceased until the return of the Aberdeen's for a second term over twenty years later, at which point the regular Dublin Castle guests vanished. One Dubliner recalls that[85]

> Social amenities were flung to the winds and the ragtag and bobtail of Dublin went to Court. After a few years of the Aberdeens' term of office many people of breeding gave up all idea of going to the Castle and social life in Dublin underwent an amazingly rapid decline. Man after man of my own generation who formerly would as a matter of course have gone to court functions avoided them and laughed when the Castle was mentioned. Without being a snob it was no pleasure and rather embarrassing to meet the lady at dinner who had measured you for your shirts the week before. As a result of the upsetting of values, social life in Dublin, from the point of view of good breeding, rapidly declined.

This Unionist boycott is confirmed by Ishbel, Countess of Aberdeen.[86]

> As time went on the Unionist landlords and their families absented themselves from the Viceregal Court, when it was perceived that the Home Rule Bill would be passed through.

The temporary friendship did little to reduce the underlying tensions which existed between Dublin Corporation and the Irish civil service. Regular altercations took place with the Local Government Board over the level of city rates, excessive municipal borrowing or the enforcement of public health regulations. Expenditure proposals were regularly vetoed, borrowing requests rejected, while the report on the city's death rate by Surgeon Colonel Flinn on behalf of the Local Government Board in 1908, was highly critical of the municipal administration.[87]

The principal body representing the city's business interests was the Dublin Chamber of Commerce, a group which was primarily mercantile in its interests. Their attitude towards the reformed corporation underwent modifications. Initially in 1849 there was great concern to ensure a strong mercantile representation in Dublin Corporation[88] a movement has been organised to deter the moderate and the unoffending and the respectable members of every class and party from connecting themselves with the new corporation.

It is well understood that these, the most useful portion of community, the persons most qualified to conduct the municipal affairs of a great city, the persons really interested in their proper and judicious management, because they are the possessors or producers of property which such management is to protect and foster as well as to tax it as may well understand that men such as these engaged in the peaceful pursuit of industry are by character, habit and industry averse to scenes of violence or disorder and peculiarly sensitive to personal allusions.

They called on members to declare themselves as municipal candidates. Following this unsuccessful intervention the Chamber of Commerce apparently adopted a less active role. In reply to a letter from the North Dublin Union seeking reform in the system of rates collection they noted their previous interest and continued[89]

the whole subject engrossed so much of their time, and moreover the interference exposed their motives to so much misconstruction that they felt it necessary to record their deliberate opinion that affairs of this or any other analagous character should never be undertaken by this Body, but with complete reluctance and in obedience to an imperative public exigency.

Thereafter they played no active role in municipal elections, though they repeatedly lobbied against various corporation expenditure proposals and opposed a continuing stream of municipal legislation. Legislation which would interfere either with city business or property was opposed and their opposition frequently related to highly technical clauses. In 1868 they opposed greater corporation control of city markets on the basis of interference with the cattle grain and coal trades, and the petition of opposition was signed exclusively by members of the interested trades.[90] In 1877 clauses in a proposed bill which would give greater control over buildings and the power to close slaughter houses were opposed on the grounds that they would jeopardise commercial interests.[91] Their opposition was not unavailing. The proposed 1877 bill was withdrawn.[92] In 1890, partly as a result of Chamber opposition the House of Lords struck out clauses giving Dublin Corporation power to collect rates.[93] In some respects the Chamber of Commerce acted as a more effective opposition than the Unionist minority who sat in City Hall. They were not unconscious of holding this role. There was considerable uncertainty as to the merits of opposing the 1890 Dublin Corporation Bill as it had been approved by a large majority of rate-prayers, however the representatives of the Chamber of Commerce at Westminster noted[94]

> that the representatives of the Port and Docks Board with whom I was desired by the Council to act, unite with me in the opinion that although we did not carry our point, yet the action we took is calculated to be of use in showing the Government that there are public bodies in Dublin other than the Corporation who desire to be consulted when important public changes are being introduced.

The opposition of the Chamber of Commerce which was based on commercial principles frequently had strong political undertones. In 1886, welcoming the Conservative Lord Lieutenant, Lord Caernarvon, a man believed to hold Home Rule sympathies, they emphasised that[95]

> the mercantile community which we represent feel that it is only under the security of the Constitution and surrounded by the assuring influence of peer and order that trade and commerce can flourish.

His successor the Liberal Home Ruler, Earl of Aberdeen received no official welcome, though his successor, the Unionist Marquis of Londonderry was greeted with enthusiasm.[96] In 1892 the secretary of the Chamber of Commerce was delegated to attend the Dublin Unionist Convention and read a statement to the effect that the body's politics were[97]

> strictly confined to matters affecting trade and commerce. As a corporate body we have no politics yet we are essentially a Unionist Chamber, not for any political end, nor for any part purpose, but solely and simply

223

because in defending the Union we are defending the commercial interests with which we are identified. Such views were unlikely to endear them to Dublin Corporation, yet hostility between the two bodies remained muted, though E. Dwyer Gray criticised their interference in municipal affairs.[98]

> Whenever the Corporation proposes any large scheme, there starts up an amount of opposition to it which very frequently paralyses to a considerable extent the power of the Corporation. The Chamber of Commerce and amateur bodies which call themselves Citizens Committees, and so on, start up and represent themselves as citizens of Dublin. This section is an influential section, as regards the social standing and position of its members.

For the Chamber of Commerce however commercial interests took priority. In choosing William Martin Murphy, leading Catholic businessmen and prominent Home Ruler as President in the admittedly fateful year of 1913, they showed a considerable measure of pragmatism and an ability to adapt to changing political circumstances.

Dublin Corporation's relations with the Port and Docks Board were more contentious, because there were apparently more areas of competing interests. The board, and corporation came into direct conflict over matters such as maintenance of the quays, river walls and city bridges and responsibility for the state of the river Liffey. When the question of a revised electoral system for the then Ballast Board was being considered, the Lord Mayor demanded an electorate which would 'provide for the representation of the great body of consumers'[99] by including members of Dublin Corporation. They were given four representatives on the newly constituted Port and Docks Board, however this was insignificant in a body largely dominated by steamship owners and they were generally to be found holding minority opinions. Conflict between both bodies flared on several occasions during the 1870s as Dublin Corporation attempted to offload responsibility for cleansing the river Liffey. A demand by Dublin Corporation in 1874 that the Port and Docks Board 'abate or remove the Liffey nuisance'[100] eventually led to a court summons of the Board,[101] but a complete dismissal of the charges with costs in favour of the Board.[102] Hostility was not limited to questions of jurisdition. In 1880, while in the throes of nationalist fervour Dublin Corporation proposed to change the name of Carlisle Bridge to O Connell Bridge and demanded that the Port and Docks Board change the tablets on the bridge accordingly; this the Board repeatedly refused to do,[103] and although it ultimately capitulated, name changes on other city bridges were productive of similar friction.

The exhaustion of borrowing powers and growing dissatisfaction with port management permitted Dublin Corporation to exert pressure for electoral reform within the Port and Docks Board. In 1897 a meeting of the Lord Mayor, the Dublin Mercantile Association — a group representing businessmen, and Messrs. Guinness, met to plan reforming legislation.[104] However a cheque sent by the corporation Law Agent to defray the costs of the measure was declined. Ultimately the reforming initiative fell to the Dublin Chamber of Commerce, a body equally critical of the Port and Docks Board, but motivated by commercial rather than political concern. The resulting franchise increased corporation representation to six, though the greatest gains were recorded by the trading and shipping representatives.

The reforming legislation received a measure of welcome from nationalist circles, primarily on political grounds. Commenting on the measure the *Freeman's Journal* noted[105]

> The Port and Docks Board has hitherto been one of the most exclusive Boards in existence in Ireland. No Nationalist no matter what his business capacity had the slightest chance of a seat on it except as a member of the Corporation. Moreover of all the members elected as traders representatives on the old franchise, one is a Catholic.

A meeting was organised by the Lord Mayor to choose other shipping and trading candidates who would stand as reform candidates for the new Board and ultimately twelve of the candidates which they endorsed were returned, including the cattle dealer William Field, a member of Dublin Corporation and M.P. for the St. Patrick's Division of Dublin City.[106] The harmonious relationship between Dublin Corporation and some sections of the Board proved only

225

temporary. By 1901 when further legislation was necessary to increase the Board's borrowing power, Dublin Corporation sought yet a further reform of the electorate.[107] Another attempt by Dublin Corporation to annexe control of the Board by means of port franchise clauses in a corporation omnibus bill in 1908 had to be abandoned in the face of opposition from the Chamber of Commerce, the Port and Docks Board and many ratepayers.[108]

A desire to control the port was not surprising given its importance in the city's economy and the fact that the port of Liverpool was under municipal control. The year 1898 marked a limited victory when an alliance was forged with trading interests. However they were primarily concerned with commercial issues, Dublin Corporation with political status. The dominance of the port authority by a group politically hostile to the corporation was not unique to Dublin. Belfast port was largely controlled by Liberals who had found themselves increasingly isolated in the City Hall.[109] Dublin Corporation's relations with the Port and Docks Board primarily reflect their attitude to all hostile bodies outside their immediate control: to actively attempt a takeover. As such it may have intensified the siege mentality which developed among the city's business and professional classes, particularly those of the Protestant persuasion.

City-Suburban Relations

Dublin city boundaries were limited to an area which was largely developed by 1840, condemning it to slow population growth and relatively stagnant valuation. Middle class residents moving to healthier surroundings left the city for independently governed townships. In the process they successfully avoided, not just the poverty and squalor of much of the centre city but also the financial costs which this imposed. The city's workhouse inmates were a burden on city ratepayers, the suburbs were only responsible for the proportionately smaller number of suburban inmates, while the costs of hospitals and police were disproportionately allocated to the city rates.

Financial problems were compounded by rates revaluation which reduced the 1847 valuation of £663,768 to

226

£541,377 in 1854.[110] This reduction which was not matched by reduced expenditure needs inevitably meant steeply rising levels of rates. The total rates in the city of 6/8 in the £ in 1859 rose to 8/- in 1866 and a record 9/8 by 1873. The improvement rate had been limited by the 1849 legislation to 2/-, a figure based on the higher 1847 valuations. By 1863 it had reached its maximum level[111] and was striving with little success to meet the city's needs.

In 1865 Dublin Corporation demanded an adjustment of the city's valuation 'to secure a just and proportionate valuation of all property within the city and a consequent equitable apportionment of the present heavy taxation of the ratepayers',[112] but though this request was supported by Richard Griffiths, Commissioner for Valuation,[113] Dublin Castle's legal opinion was that no power existed for a general valuation of towns, as opposed to revaluing the country as a whole.[114]

In the absence of revaluation city rates mounted as did the discrepancy with the suburban rates. In 1874 total rates (municipal plus poor law, grand jury and police rates) in the north city area were 9/3 in the £, more than twice the levels in the suburbs: 4/6 in Clontarf and Pembroke and 4/- in Rathmines.[115]

The initial pressure to remove this anomaly came from the North Dublin Union and in 1872 one member, a Mr. Arkins gave notice of a motion to extend the city boundaries to those of the Dublin Metropolitan Police district.[116] A similar resolution was passed in December 1874. This drew attention to the inequitable poor law burdens and noted that whereas the city side of the North Circular Road paid '10/- in the £ in taxes . . . the other side of the road only pays 3/.[117] In 1876 Dublin Corporation decided to devise an improvement bill which would extend the city boundaries.[118]

Pressure for extension resulted from straitened financial circumstances. By 1877 the city was virtually bankrupt and an economy committee was established which was forced to consider the dismissal of the sanitary policemen.[119] To avoid this drastic step attempts were made to levy an extra borough rate of 4d in th £, as the general improvement rate was already at the maximum level.

A ratepayers association obtained a writ preventing this

action.[120] As a result, all unnecessary expenditure was halted. On the capital front the limitation on total borrowing to twice the city's valuation meant that there were not sufficient borrowing powers to carry out a main drainage scheme.[121] The extension of municipal boundaries appeared a possible solution to both current and capital financial pressures.

Such an extension was unlikely to occur voluntarily. The suburbs, particularly Rathmines, boasted of their independence and were unwilling to relinquish low rates. Although suburban politics does not merit being described in party-political terms there is little doubt that in the 1860s and 1870s all the Dublin suburbs were dominated by Conservatives. Many of the city's Conservative councillors were suburban residents, a few were also suburban representatives, such as E.H. Carson. Given the social composition of the suburbs and their religious breakdown it seems valid to suppose that a contributory factor to the suburban exodus was a desire to escape from the alien rule of Dublin Corporation into a more congenial atmosphere. Membership of Rathmines or Pembroke commissioners emerged as an alternative for many prominent business or professional men who found that Dublin Corporation had lost its attractions. In such circumstances suburban resistance to corporation annexation was not surprising and almost certainly reflected the wishes of the inhabitants.

The various contacts which had occurred between the city and the townships during the 1860s and 1870s gave firm indication of the suburban desire for independence and the seeming inability of city and suburbs in reaching amicable agreement. The proposed supply of Vartry water in the 1860s had led to a considerable degree of verbal sparring between Rathmines and Dublin Corporation. Relations with the more patrician Pembroke township were more amicable and while Rathmines pursued an independent water policy Pembroke and the city agreed terms, which were highly favourable to the latter. The effort to mount a main drainage scheme proved much more contentious, because Dublin Corporation had become more agressive by the 1870s and had lost the considerable diplomatic skills of Sir John Gray who organised the water scheme. An attempt by Dublin Corporation to undertake single-handedly a main drainage scheme for the greater Dublin area and to tax the suburbs without conceding any administrative control, not surprisingly aroused suburban hostility. Ultimately a main drainage committee, representative of both city and suburbs, and chaired by a Conservative Councillor Norwood — in a remarkable gesture of conciliation, was established. This faced a number of difficulties. The key problems were financial, but mutual distrust caused some of the committee members, including the suburban representatives, to appeal that the question be removed from corporation control[122]

> such works cannot satisfactorily be carried to their completion by a fluctuating and capricious body subject to popular influence and should be entrusted to a permanent body of commissioners subject to the Local Government Board.

Ultimately the joint drainage proposals collapsed and Rathmines and Pembroke promoted their own bill in 1877.[123] By the late 1870s therefore mutual distrust between city and suburbs had been sown, while Frederick Stokes' announcement of an independent suburban drainage scheme under the stirring slogan, 'Rathmines will drain alone'[124] suggested an unwillingness to acquiesce peacefully in annexation.

In fact there is no evidence of any direct communication from Dublin Corporation to the suburbs on the question of boundary extension. Preliminary negotiation, or informal diplomacy was not the corporation's strongest point. The 1876 resolution proposed that the matter be approached by a Dublin Corporation improvement bill — there was no question of a joint city-suburban approach to Parliament. It rapidly emerged that Dublin Corporation could not promote such a bill, but must rely on a measure being promoted either by the inhabitants or by the government.[125] There is no evidence of efforts being made to encourage a citizens bill for this purpose. At this stage all ratepayers, or citizens bodies which had emerged in the city had been decidely opposed to Dublin Corporation.

The initiative was left with the Irish administration. The then Chief Secretary, Sir Michael Hicks Beach, who emerges as having more sympathy with the city's problems than virtually any of his successors, decided to defer action pending the report of the *select committee on taxation of towns*. This reported in July 1876 that a local investigation of all circumstances would prove necessary.[126] The committee was reappointed in 1877 but its second report temporised, claiming the need for a detailed report by a local government board inspector. Ultimately they recommended that the boundaries of Dublin merited extending, but that a general inquiry was necessary to determine the exact limits.[127]

This function was served by the *royal commission on municipal boundaries* which visited Dublin in 1879. Dublin Corporation laid claim to extend their boundaries to include the townships of Pembroke, Rathmines and Rathgar, Kilmainham, Drumcondra, Clonliffe and Glasnevin, and certain parts of Co. Dublin.[128] The only adjoining suburb excluded from this claim was the northern suburb of Clontarf on the grounds that it was separated from the city by an agricultural district of one mile.

The case presented by Dublin Corporation rested primarily on the decay and consequent falling valuation of many central city areas, the departure of middle class residents to the suburbs, and the disproportionate burdens which the city bore in terms of hospitals, workhouses, improvement of tenements and city roads.[129] The evidence given to the commission showed mutual hostility on the part of both suburban and city witnesses. The commissioners heard innumerable allegations of corporation insolvency on the one hand, and of the total inattention to sanitary matters of township authorities on the other.

Their conclusion in fact was decidedly favourable to Dublin Corporation. They recommended the extension of the city boundaries on the lines requested, but including Clontarf and the county districts of Dolphins' Barn and Grangegorman.[130] In their report they noted that[131]

> the area of Dublin is practically built on and cannot be extended otherwise than by including the townships within the city area and with them a certain portion of the county district.

They also determined that the townships fulfilled all the conditions in which extensions of towns have taken place in

230

England 'namely (that they) are in fact suburbs, or rather a part of a city'. It was also felt that sanitary administration was better carried out by 'centralised management',[132] while any doubts as to corporation solvency were dismissed,[133] though they recommended a revaluation of the city.[134]

They emerge as strongly favouring centralised administration; they recommended the unification of the Kingstown, Blackrock and Dalkey suburbs[135] and the establishment of a metropolitan fire brigade which would operate over an area which included the extended Kingstown township.[136]

With the publication of this report, opposition to extending the city limits gathered pace. When the commission was sitting, the conservative newspaper, the *Irish Times* had expressed opinions strongly in favour of extension, seeing the problems as[137]

> whether a very large number of persons who are to all intents and purposes citizens of the metropolis shall be allowed to evade a great proportion of their obligations because they live beyond the Municipal Boundary.

When the report was published in 1881 they had somewhat modified their position.[138]

> As the real question in the case is not one of the desirability of extending the boundaries, but of the method of doing it in a manner so conspicuously just as to reconcile the township owners, and residents to the change.

Some days later the paper's position had become more hostile to annexation, not on grounds of principle but for apparently pragmatic reasons[139]

> Who does not see if they (suburban residents) were to be compelled to pay city rates on one side and again on the other side of the Canal Bridges, paying twice to the City, they would simply in days of tramways seek a residence further out beyond Mr. Exham's yellow lines, and add to the area of City desolation and impoverishment, house waste, without inhabitants. We should have a new Rathmines at Terenure, a new Pembroke beyond Donnybrook . . .

The Exham recommendations remained a dead letter. Dublin Corporation apparently lacked the powers to promote an annexation bill[140] and Dublin Castle was unwilling to do so. Matters cannot have been helped by the fact that by 1881 Dublin Corporation had shown growing nationalist militancy. In the process relations with Dublin Castle had suffered while the breaking of the traditional custom of alternating the office of Lord Mayor was unlikely to reassure suburban residents. A further memorial by the corporation to the Lord Lieutenant in 1883[141] provoked a statement from solicitors representing Rathmines and Pembroke demonstrating that there was no precedent for annexing townships which had been constituted by special act of Parliament, to other corporate bodies against the wishes of the ratepayers.[142] In response to yet a further memorial by Dublin Corporation,[143] the Lord Lieutenant took refuge in the excuse that the boundaries could not be enlarged until the city's rating system was overhauled.[144] The city case was given further support with the publication of the report of the *royal commission on the housing of the working classes* which recommended the extension of the city boundaries,[145] and a general revaluation of the city. These recommendations were regarded favourably by the Under-secretary of the local government board, Sir Henry Robinson who felt that the necessity for revaluation was 'obvious', and on annexation noted that he[146]

> see(s) no reason whatever to question the view expressed both by the municipal boundaries commission and the commission on the housing of the working classes concerning the extension of boundaries, but there are many details in the scheme which require careful consideration.

The principal private bill clerk in the House of Lords reported that there was no precedent for abolishing an existing municipal body except by consent. However the recommendations of the *royal commission on the housing of the working classes* guaranteed the support of Sir Charles Dilke and other radicals for the cause of annexation.[147]

The flurry of interest in annexation provoked Rathmines commissioners to address the Lord Lieutenant and their letter is notable in being the first occasion when they

232

play the loyalist card as a defense of their autonomy.[148]
It would be neither just nor politic that the Government
should take up and lend their powerful assistance
to pass a bill of compulsory annexation which necessarily would prove an Act of spoilation and subjection
of a township . . . which has always been loyal and law-
abiding, and thus assist in furthering the designs of a
body such as the Corporation of Dublin, the majority
of whose members have so recently done all they
could or dare venture, to parade their disloyalty to
Crown and Constitution.

The following year was marked by the first legislative
attempt to annexe the suburbs, — a private bill, backed by
Nationalist M.P.s, many of them with Dublin Corporation
connections.[149] It failed, as did its successor in 1888,[150]
but with the seeming prospect of Home Rule the matter
did not appear unduly urgent.

The subordinate issue of revaluation also aroused regular
responses from Dublin Corporation, partly because Dublin
Castle used it as a device to stall calls for annexation. By
1889 suburban rates had risen considerably so that the
effective gap between the city and Rathmines, allowing
for the fact that households in Rathmines paid directly
for refuse collection — had fallen to 1/6 in the £ and Dublin Corporation felt that a revaluation which would lower
city rates would weaken the case against annexation.[151] In
addition to raising the overall valuation of the city and so
increasing borrowing powers, revaluation would take account of the rise in the rental of properties in the south-
eastern axis i.e. Grafton St. and the sharp decline in valuations in the north city area. The valuation problem was not
unique to Dublin. Belfast, Cork and Limerick had all sought
readjustments[152] and in 1891 Belfast actively pursued,
the possibility of obtaining legislative power for revaluation.[153] The commissioner of valuation felt that there was
'no doubt of the irrelativities of valuations in Belfast'. He
also noted that 'the same state of things existed in Dublin
and to a lesser degree in other towns throughout Ireland'.[154]
Though admitting anomalies, the valuations office, which
was under the authority of Dublin Castle did nothing to

remedy the situation. This may be partly attributable to bureaucratic delays, but a further motive is equally possible. In a memorandum in 1897 following a demand from Dublin Corporation that provisions, both for revaluation and for boundary extension be included in the forthcoming Irish local government bill, the commissioner of valuation noted that the kernel of the Dublin Corporation argument was the degree to which the low valuation crippled their borrowing powers. He felt that it was 'open to question' whether the corporation should be granted a higher valuation and consequently increased borrowing powers. Given the suspicion with which the local government board regarded Dublin Corporation it is not implausible to see the failure to re-value the city, and perhaps the failure to extend boundaries as a means of keeping corporation extravagance in check.[155]

The prospect of a major overhaul of Irish local government gave renewed pressure to Dublin Corporations's demands for boundary extension. They argued their case, partly in demographic terms, 'There is not an important city in the United Kingdom which has so dense a population', and on nationalist grounds[156]

> The extension (of boundaries) by increasing the valuation and population of the city would raise larger Dublin to a position worthy of a capital of Ireland and prevent the not improbable contingency of its drifting into a secondary position.

Dublin's boundary extension had been given greater urgency by the fact that in 1896 the area of Belfast was doubled resulting in a population greater than that of Dublin.[157] The case was put with considerable force by a leader in the *Daily Independent*[158]

> to expect that the capital city of Ireland, should, of all the great cities on the earth, be the only one denied the natural course of municipal expansion is to expect the impossible.

The question of Dublin's boundaries was not included in the 1898 local government act, however John Redmond introduced an amendment providing for an extension of the city's boundaries.[159] When this failed, Dublin Corporation belatedly introduced its own bill[160] and the Solicitor General

234

decided that they had full power to do so.[161] The measure was opposed by the townships, no longer on financial grounds, but almost exclusively for political reasons, as Col. Saunderson, the Ulster Unionist, who with Sir Edward Carson led the opposition, admitted[162]

> the objections obtained by the townships to becoming incorporated into the Corporation of Dublin had to a considerable extent been affected by political considerations.

He described Dublin Corporation as 'a sort of Greenwich Hospital for Nationalist wrecks'. From this point of view the timing of the annexation bill was bound to generate even greater fears than in the past. The democratization of the municipal franchise had reduced Unionist representation to a mere seven members. Pembroke was finely balanced between Unionists and a Nationalist majority. Only Clontarf and Rathmines held firm, thus within an enlarged corporation Unionist strength would have been minimal. On the boundaries question the *Irish Times* voiced the[163]

> Fear that this (extension) would lead to the establishment of secure control over us of a Tamanny as powerful as . . . but it was admitted that the political influences paramount in the city were exactly those the existence of which the Townships deplore. To the extent of their opportunities the Municipalities about us show that they will have none such intruders within their bounds. They fear and not without reason that if the greater Dublin conception were realized the results would be to raise amongst us a sort of metropolitan centralized and pretentious party institution which would have all the sway and might be position of a Parliament.

The Dublin municipal boundaries bill passed the House of Commons — a Commons it must be noted which was under Conservative control.

The House of Lords committee rejected the measure, seeing the preamble as not proven, though they did consent to extend the city boundaries to include the working class township of Kilmainham, the township which had least contact with the city, and one whose independent identity could have been validly defended. Kilmainham, the Lords argued, would provide ample space for the city's artisan dwellings.[164] This ruling was designed to perpetuate the social, political and religious divisions which existed in the Dublin area. One of the most emotive fears expressed by Pembroke commissioners was that Dublin 'corporation wanted Pembroke merely to put artisans dwellings among the best houses in the township'.[165]

When the Lords decision returned to the Commons, it was reversed,[166] but the Lords in turn rejected the Commons amendment, claiming that if they reversed their previous decision, 'they would deliver a very serious blow at the independence of their house'.[167]

The Dublin boundaries bill was re-introduced in the following session and to avoid an impasse was referred to a joint committee of Lords and Commons,[168] despite Carson's objections. The committee recommended the inclusion within the city of Clontarf, Drumcondra and Kilmainham plus a section of Co. Dublin including purely rural parts which would give a 'reasonable margin' for building land.[169] Clontarf was to be included mainly because the cost of an independent main drainage scheme for the township would prove too great a burden. Rathmines and Pembroke, though retaining their independence did so at some financial cost as the committee drew attention[170]

> to the heavy burdens falling on the City of Dublin ratepayers for objects to which the two townships of Rathmines and Pembroke do not adequately contribute.

They recommended the implementation of legislation similar to the London *equalization of rates act*, by which the townships would make a financial contribution to the city for matters which were regarded as a joint financial responsibility.

The Dublin boundaries bill became law on 6 August 1900 when it received the Royal Assent.[171] This increased the city's area by 4,125 acres, its valuation by £100,000 and its population by 26,000.[172] By this stage the city had already come to an agreement with Kilmainham to build artisans dwellings in the event of annexation[173] and Drumcondra had also acquiesed in annexation.[174] A petition of approximately 400 signatures in favour of Clontarf being annexed had been collected but they consisted largely of the smaller occupiers and, according to the *Irish Times* constituted only one-fifth of the area's property valuation.[175] Many of the larger property owners threatened to leave as a result of annexation.[176] Meanwhile the Lord Mayor of Dublin reopened negotiations with Pembroke on possible unification,[177] using the promise of favourable electoral representation plus the threat of a greater rates burden from the equalization of rates bill.[178] These talks proved unsuccessful and Rathmines and Pembroke retained their autonomy though they gradually bore a greater financial burden than in the past.

The first steps towards equalising the financial burden came in 1898 when union rating, which had existed in England for thirty-three years was introduced into Ireland.[179] This spread the burden of poor relief over the entire poor law union, instead of the previous arrangement whereby each electoral district was responsible for its own poor relief. This transferred part of the cost from the city to the suburbs, though at a time of an overall rising poor law the relief to the city was slight. The *1901 equalization of rates act*[180] was designed by the local government board to continue this process[181]

> the townships will to a very great extent have to bear the very same burdens of taxation as if they had been included (in the city).

The House of Lords defended Pembroke and Rathmines interests once more, amending the bill to limit the increased burden on the townships to 6d in the £, and postponing its operation until 1907.[182] However the government stood firm emphasising that the measure was based on the recommendations of the 1900 joint committee and had to be accepted.[183]

Under the act, the local government board was to determine the average annual expenditure for the previous five years and to decide the relative benefits which accrued to the various local authorities. Spending under various headings such as public health, lighting, streets, markets, reformatories and asylums was examined and as a result of the inquiry, Rathmines was ordered to pay £4,500 per annum to Dublin Corporation, with Pembroke paying £2,240. In 1911 payments were increased to an annual £6,800 from Rathmines and £3,750 from Pembroke.[184] The relief in 1912 amounted to a reduction of 6d in the £ on city rates, while posing a burden of less than 9½d on Rathmines.

Meanwhile another long-standing corporation grievance, the need for general revaluation was being remedied, though by this stage in the teeth of corporation opposition. A general revaluation was provided for in the 1900 *Dublin corporation act*.[185]

The progress of Belfast's revaluation, which brought increases averaging 25%, but ranging as high as 100-500% caused many Dubliners to take fright.[186] The *Freeman's Journal* announced its opposition to revaluation[187] as did a majority of members of Dublin Corporation,[188] though the *Irish Times* was in favour,[189] as were many large property holders. A writ forcing the valuation office to proceed with revaluation was brought by T. Picton Bradshaw, a large Clontarf ratepayer.[190] Efforts by Dublin Corporation to counter this with a partial revaluation, beginning with Grafton St. were rejected by the valuations office as inequitable.[191]

Dublin Corporation's reluctance to proceed with a general revaluation stemmed from the fear that public houses would be subject to substantial increases, as had happened in Belfast.[192] According to the valuation office, few public houses had been valued by Sir Richard Griffiths and it was felt that their valuations were 'much below the statutory amount'. In addition, unlike the practice in England, the value of the publican's licence had not been taken into account for rating purposes, though it had been included in the recent Belfast revaluation. The strong publican lobby in Dublin Corporation inevitably feared a massive increase in their rates bills, as in fact happened. The aggregate valuation of licenced premises increased from £24,659 to £36,154, an increase of almost 50%,[193] whereas the total city valuation only rose from £1,001,640 to £1,177,940, a rise of 17.57%, less than had been expected. The increase rectified inequities between the central city area and the newly annexed suburbs. The valuation of suburban property rose by an average of 8%,[194] the increase in the central business district was much greater.

The annexation of some suburbs, the more equitable

238

financial burden on those remaining and the revaluation of the city were measures which had been urged by Dublin Corporation for many decades as a magic solution to financial difficulties. In the event their financial significance proved somewhat disappointing. The problem of inadequate finances remained critical, at which point, in 1914 Dublin Corporation sought a new scapegoat in the form of Dublin Castle which was increasingly urged to bear a greater proportion of the city's financial burden.

By 1900 it is increasingly obvious that financial matters were no longer a priority in city-suburban relations. One feels that Rathmines and Pembroke would willingly pay a substantial sum to maintain local autonomy. Dublin Corporation, faced with the choice between revaluation to improve its overall finances, and alienating the politically important publicans, twice rejected motions in favour of revaluation. At base therefore Dublin local politics was grounded in sectional interests. Loyalty to either nationalism or unionism, class or creed took priority over the welfare of the city or its people. In this respect the most obvious offender was Dublin Corporation, but the city's prosperous classes, securely cocooned in their independent suburbs are equally guilty. This political context must be borne in mind in any detailed assessment of social policies, particularly those pertaining to housing and public health.

Chapter VIII

MORTALITY AND PUBLIC HEALTH

Public health, mortality and disease were among the major social issues facing nineteenth-century cities. The problems posed by rapidly increasing urban populations aroused concern as did the waves of epidemic disease, particularly the terrifying cholera epidemics of 1831-2, 1848-9, 1853-4 and 1866. Dublin shared many of the problems common to U.K. cities. As a port in regular contact with Liverpool it was vulnerable to British epidemics. Filth, inadequate water supplies and other environmental hazards were major problems. General trends in disease and mortality were broadly in line with British patterns, though with some significant differences. Public health legislation was broadly similar to England and Wales, with a short time lag.

Compulsory registration of births and deaths introduced into Britain in 1847, was not established in Ireland until 1863.[1] However mortality statistics were collected in the Censuses of 1841, 51 and '61 and these three volumes carry pioneering reports on the sanitary conditions of the city of Dublin, the first two by Sir William Wilde.[2] The primary source of information at their disposal was the Census returns where householders listed the members of their family who had died in the previous decade, their age and cause of death. These returns are somewhat hazardous: human memory is fallible, families could move from the city, recollection, particularly of deaths of infants may have been faint. It would seem probable that deaths in years immediately prior to the census would be recalled to a greater degree than those eight or nine years previously. However Wilde also collected returns in 1841 from city and suburban cemetries for a two-year period June 1839–June 1841. Based on this experience detailed burial statistics were presented in the subsequent censuses. On the assumption that 12% of those buried lived outside the city area (a figure based on detailed analysis of the 1841-51 burials) these figures permit us to calculate average mortality levels from 1839.

The pre-registration returns provided information also on deaths and burials by age and by disease, plus voluminous statistics on the incidence of death by locality and occupation. First Class Private streets on the south side of the river Liffey emerge as having the lowest mortality levels at 0.81% over the decade 1841-51, compared with 2.64% in overcrowded St. Paul's Ward. The latter figures, Wilde noted, was an underestimate; most of the inhabitants of prosperous localities died at home while those from poor areas frequently died in hospital and were excluded from ward statistics. The differential incidence of disease between different localities was also obvious from Wilde's analysis. In the decade 1841-51 the incidence of smallpox in First Class Private streets was 1 in 1,646 of the population, while in Merchant's Quay Ward it was 1 in 113.

The returns were also analysed by occupation. The average age at death of merchants and prosperous businessmen in 1831-41 was 55-60, compared with 35-40 in the case of tailors and 30 for dressmakers. Over 40% of washerwomen died of respiratory disease and a further 23% from epidemics, in contrast to the mercantile class where 25% died of respiratory ailments and less than 10% of epidemic diseases. Of the 450 deaths among those of private means, 100 were certified as being due to 'old age', a category in little use among the poorer classes.

These reports, written many years before the introduction of comprehensive registration and before the appointment of a medical officer of health, and many years before Greenhow's pioneering reports on the distribution of death and disease in England and Wales[3] isolate the main characteristics of Dublin mortality as they would remain for many decades: the concentration of high mortality in overcrowded working class areas, the differences in the incidence of death between social groups and the importance of zymotic (epidemic) diseases and respiratory ailments, particularly consumption. The 1861 census recorded that more than one third of all deaths among clerks and tailors in the previous ten years were attributable to consumption.

The compulsory registration of births and deaths should have ushered in a new era in mortality statistics. In fact statistics for the 1860s are not noticeably better than those obtained for the 1850s. Although class 60 of the registration act laid down a penalty of 20/- for failing to give notice of births or deaths, the 1871 census revealed that numbers buried in the city and vicinity consistently exceeded the number of registered deaths by an average of 9.7%.[4] It would appear from contemporary statements that this level of deficiency continued until 1879 when an amendment to the 1878 *public health (Ireland) act* required all burial returns to be forwarded to the registrar.[5]

Table I Dublin city death rates 1831-1914

	Deaths per 1000	Burials per 1000 of population
1831-40	28.6	29.04*
1841-50	30.13	33.4
1851-60	25.01	29.38
1864-70	27.45	30.36
1871-80	30.62	32.73**
1881-90	29.5	
1891-1900	29.65	
1901-10	23.92	
1911-14	22.15	

* June 1839-June 1841 only.
** Calculation based on contemporary statements of a 9.7% deficiency in death registrations compared to burials.

Combining figures from the census, burials and registration returns enables us to examine the long-term mortality trends, bearing in mind the possible inaccuracy of the earlier statistics. One conclusion is inescapable from Table I, despite possible statistical hazards: there was no significant decline in the city's death rate until the early twentieth century.

The trend in the earlier years was not radically different from that in Britain, where overall mortality levels remained constant from the 1840s until the 1870s, but then began to decline. Dublin therefore lagged behind Britain in its overall improvement in mortality. However, even at a time when English mortality figures had yet to show signs of improvement, Dublin's death rate seems to have been considerably higher than the English average. The years 1864-80 record an average death rate of 29.31, or 31.6 if adjusted for burials. Even the lower figure was considerably above English levels. London's death rate for the twenty years before 1880 averaged 23.4, Birmingham's was somewhat higher. The closest comparable English city was Liverpool with a death rate of 29.3.[6] English death rates fell steadily from the late 1870s and at an increasing rate from the mid 1890s. By the decade 1895-1904, London's death rate averaged 18.2, a decline of 5.2 points from the pre-1880 level. The Birmingham average had fallen to 20.2, while Liverpool, the city with the highest pre-1880 figures had reduced its death rate to an average of 23.2, a fall of over 6 points. In contrast, Dublin city's death rate had fallen by a mere 3.4 per thousand. In 1905 London had a death rate of 15.6, Liverpool 19.6, Birmingham 16.2, compared with Dublin's 22.3.[7] Over time therefore the gap between Dublin and the English cities had actually widened, though the disparity in mortality levels between different English cities had declined.

The first improvement came in the incidence and mortality of zymotic or epidemic diseases. Dublin was no exception. The mortality from such diseases, according to the census returns, was as high as 11.24 per thousand in the decade prior to 1841, but in the years 1851-61 had declined to 5.77 per thousand. These figures, based on the census are almost certainly too low, but give some indication of the magnitudes involved. The first twenty years after registration show little improvement. Mortality from zymotic diseases in the years 1864-70 was 5.64 per thousand for the Dublin registration district (city plus southern suburbs), and for 1871-80 reached 5.74 per thousand. From 1880 it fell sharply to 3.25 per thousand for the years 1881-90 and the downward trend continued thereafter.

The trend in the case of phthisis, or pulmonary tuber-

243

Table II Mortality from phthisis Dublin 1831-1914

	City	Registration District
1831-41	3.03	
1841-50	3.61	
1851-60	3.84	
1864-70		3.2
1871-80		3.15
1881-90	3.72	3.49
1891-1900	3.67	3.32
1901-10	3.27	2.91
1911-14	2.81	2.47

Table III Deaths of infants under 1 year per 1000 live births [10]

	Dublin	London	England and Wales	Major towns excluding London
1890	163	163	151	172
1890-99	171.8	159.9	153.3	172.1
1900-9	156	132.4	132.5	148.2
1910-14	147.4	106	109	121.1

culosis in the early decades is not very accurate and under-estimates its incidence. The English statistics indicate a halving of all tubercular deaths from 3.8 per thousand in 1838 to 1.83 by 1894.[8] The decline was steady from the 1850s and by 1901-5 the English death rate was only 1.21 per thousand.[9]

The remaining general point concerns mortality by age. Infant mortality in England and Wales does not seem to have declined before the final decade of the nineteenth century. Detailed figures for Dublin are not available before this period but there is little reason to suppose that it proved an exception to the English trend. While infant mortality rates in Dublin were not noticeably dissimilar to the English figure in 1890, Dublin's subsequent improvement was much less dramatic.

244

Table IV Deaths per 1000 by age
a) Dublin and London 1877[12]

	Dublin	London
All ages	28.2	21.9
less 5	82.5	69.7
20-25	9.1	6.5
25-34	14.0	9.1
35-44	20.8	14.4
45-54	29.3	20.4

b. England, Scotland, Wales and Dublin 1872-1912[13]

	England and Wales						Scotland					
	20-24		25-34		35-44		15-24		25-34		35-44	
	M	F	M	F	M	F	M	F	M	F	M	F
1872	8.7	7.6	10.3	9.3	14.0	11.8	9.3	8.5	11.2	10.4	14.0	12.0
1882	5.9	5.9	8.2	7.9	12.6	11.0	7.1	7.0	8.9	9.2	12.5	11.0
1892	5.2	4.7	7.3	7.0	11.9	10.3	6.5	6.2	8.3	8.8	12.2	11.6
1902	4.6	3.9	6.2	5.3	10.4	8.4	5.0	5.1	7.5	7.1	11.7	10.0
1912	3.4	3.2	4.8	4.0	7.9	6.3	4.0	3.9	5.6	5.3	8.7	8.2

c. Dublin Registration District 20-40

1872	16.9	1872-9	13.98
1882	12.7	1880-90	13.2
1892	12.9	1890-1900	12.96
1902	11.4	1900-9	10.69

Dublin Registration District 1912, deaths 15-24, 25-44

15-24	5.4
25-44	11.1

While the death rate of infants in 1890 was broadly comparable to figures in England and Wales, deaths among adults were significantly greater. In 1890 infant deaths only accounted for 166 per 1000 deaths in Dublin, compared with 233 in London, 233 in England and Wales and 241 in the largest towns. The proportion of total deaths among those aged over one year was considerably greater in Dublin. In 1901 the death rate for those aged from 1-60 in Dublin was 75% above the English level.[11]

Unfortunately it is not possible to make direct comparisons between Dublin mortality levels by age and those in Britain until 1912. Table IV however suggests that Dublin death rates were higher in the 1870s and declined more slowly than in England or Scotland for specific age groups. The presentation of Dublin's statistics was changed in the year 1911, so that for 1912 the Dublin and Scottish figures are directly comparable and they reveal a higher mortality rate for young adults than in Scotland. This apparently bore more heavily on men that on women. Figures for 1877 reveal a higher male death rate for all age groups from 20 to 54, with the gap widening considerably from 25 years of age.[14] A major factor in the high mortality of young adults was the incidence of tuberculosis. In the recent years 1912-14, over 50% of all notifications of tuberculosis concerned people in the age group 15-35.[15]

The following sections examine the detailed implementation of the city's public health policy.

Zymotic Disease

Infectious diseases were the primary focus of attentions for medical and sanitary reformers during the mid nineteenth century, reflecting the belief that such diseases could be prevented, but only by public intervention. As Finer states, 'the individual had no control over his conditions'.[16] The key influence on public policy was Sir Edwin Chadwick's *Report on the sanitary condition of the labouring population of Great Britain* (1842) and the subsequent *Royal commission on the health of towns* which echoed his opinions.

These focussed attention on the need for effective removal of all forms of waste. For domestic sewage it was felt that water carriage through drains was the most effective method. Chadwick urged the need for a widespread system of drains, sewers and scavenging designed to rid houses and streets of all evil smells which might act as a focus for disease. These reports ultimately resulted in legislative measures which were largely permissive in the initial years. The onus for sanitary reform fell on local authorities rather than central government and in many cities it led to considerable interest in sanitary matters, on the part of middle class pressure groups, though reform was frequently thwarted by the power of vested interests.

Interest in sanitary reform would appear to have developed somewhat belatedly in Dublin. The reports on city health in the census provided detailed data on the mortality from specific diseases. They also highlighted the differential mortality between various parts of the city and isolated the area with the greatest incidence of epidemic diseases. Wilde's reports are purely factual. They make no inferences as to the factors responsible for the differing incidence of disease, nor do they recommend any measures which might reduce mortality. There is no indication that this information was used as a basis for policy recommendations. As in British cities, the body with primary responsibility for public health was Dublin Corporation. The first responsibility was cast on the corporation by the 1848 public health act[17] which required the town council to act on the receipt of a report by any two inhabitants of the existence of a nuisance. Nuisances included offensive cesspools, drains, manure heaps, swine houses or filthy buildings which could be injurious to health. The Lord Lieutenant brought this Act to the notice of the corporation and at a special meeting it was resolved to form a Health of the City Preservation

Committee.[18] Initial activity was leisurely despite the fact that 1849 was a year of record mortality when the city was visited by cholera. The sanitary presence at this point was limited to four police sergeants, presumably without training. In 1851 however an inspector of nuisances was appointed and the first prosecutions were instituted.[19]

By emphasising the importance of drains, Chadwick afforded the major sanitary initiative, not to doctors, but to engineers. The most important, and virtually the sole sanitary official in the city in the 1850s was the city engineer, Parke Neville. His report for the year 1853 with its emphasis on the need to build new sewers and replace existing ones provided the main framework for sanitary activity for many years. The relationship between the lack of sewers and disease was emphasised[20]

> the fever sites and places where the population suffers most during visitations of cholera, or other epidemics being always situated in localities deficient in sewerage, ventilation and water supply and I submit that those three great requirements should first be provided for.

On this recommendation a general sewerage scheme, estimated to cost £74,283 was undertaken during the 1850s and continued at a steady pace during the 1860s. The corporation did not acquire the power however to compel house owners to install drains until 1861[21] and many houses still lacked connection with the sewers in 1880.

The emphasis on sewers raised two further problems: water supply and main drainage. Water carriage of sewerage required an adequate flow of water, while the growing volume of sewerage being channelled into the river Liffey increased the general offensiveness of the river.

Dublin's water supply
Dublin's water supply was already inadequate by the 1840s. It had come from the canals for several decades, though private wells were in common use in older parts of the city. An unsuccessful bill to improve the water supply was promoted in 1846.[22] When new water mains were laid in 1853-4 the inadequate water pressure became even more obvious. Negotiations with the canal company for an increased supply, plus provision for a supplementary 3m. gallons for business

use from the river Dodder seemed to provide a satisfactory outcome.[23] In the summer of 1859 the canal company withdrew its offer because they could not guarantee supply, while it was belatedly discovered that the canal water was polluted.[24] Water pollution at this stage was not of primary concern to public health experts. Finer summarised Chadwick's position on this as follows[25]

All smell is disease . . . relegated pure water supply to subsidiary importance. Bad water was only a 'predisposing' cause of fever: the smell caused it.

Pollution was detected either by smell or by colour. The methods of analysis devised by Pasteur were not widely known in England until 1863-4.[26]

With the abandonment of the canal plan, the consulting engineer Hawkseley proposed drawing water from the Liffey at Coyford.[27] A bill based on this proposal was introduced to parliament but withdrawn in the face of opposition and the canal companies responded by offering an improved supply at seemingly favourable terms.[28] A supply of canal water drawn from an unpolluted area some distance from the city would prove expensive, while the water was alleged to be impure and hard.[29] Given the degree of uncertainty the Lord Mayor requested the Chief Secretary to establish a royal commission.[30] The commission under John Hawkshaw opened on 21 August 1860 and reported two months later, proposing a supply from the river Vartry, which though more expensive than other options would provide ample colourless water.[31] This proposal was adopted and was completed by 1871[32] at a cost of £541,402.[33] Many areas of the city and adjoining suburbs such as Pembroke received supplies by 1867.[34]

The Vartry scheme, though criticised for its expense was the cheapest water scheme in the British Isles.[35] The doubling of cost which it experienced was by no means unique, particularly as the late 1860s were a time of rising prices. Liverpool's water supply increased in cost from an initial figure of £200,000 to over six times that amount.[36] The scheme was not without opponents. It is difficult in Dublin to pinpoint identifiable opposition to sanitary reform. There was no permanent 'dirty' party in city politics. Many opponents of the new water scheme were motivated by vested interests such as canal shareholders.[37] Others attempted to gain maximum compensation. The Earl of Meath who traditionally had the monopoly of water supply in the Liberties was paid £6,000, while Earl Fitzwilliam who owned land near the Vartry received £2,000 though no water was taken from his stream.[38] The opposition of a committee of citizens was motivated primarily by the rates burden.[39] On the whole nationalists favoured the measure while conservatives tended to be hostile. The chairman of the waterworks committee, Sir John Gray, pursued the scheme with passionate conviction, refuting all criticism.[40] The fact that he was strongly identified with Archbishop Cullen's National Association may have coloured attitudes both for and against the measure. When the scheme was officially completed, the waterworks committee's report (presumably written by Gray) declared that it has been 'fought out on religious divisions a battle of the Boyne and Blackwater'.[41] The provision of an adequate supply of pure water was an impressive achievement. London did not have a constant supply until 1891.[42] It brought the renewal of old water pipes and the introduction of water to areas previously without piped supply.

The other priority was the provision of an adequate sewerage system. With the increased emphasis on waterborne sewerage the need for disposal increased. By 1853 Parke Neville, the city engineer noted that the river Liffey was the principal sewerage outlet.[43] By 1869 a further fifty miles of sewer had been built discharging into the river in addition to several hospitals, six military barracks and other public institutions.[44] The result was significantly increased river pollution. An *Irish Times* leading article in 1864 noted. 'Every summer and autumn the citizens of Dublin suffer from the exhalations of the river Liffey'.[45] Concern with the Liffey smell was increased by the contemporary belief that many diseases such as cholera were caused by the noxious effluvia rising from smelly rivers or refuse heaps. In 1865 a memorial from the inhabitants of Lower Ormond Quay to Dublin corporation noted[46]

> the stench of the river Liffey opposite their doors and houses during the last summer and harvest has been intolerable, in fact destroying their health and

local interests, though compelled to pay exorbitant taxes and rates for premises they are thus unable to live in for fear of noise and disease even to the introduction of cholera.

Interest quickened with the cholera epidemic and the belief that this disease favoured riverside areas. The *Daily Express* noted: 'the disease raged all along the banks of the Dodder and Liffey with special violence'.[47]

As early as 1853 Parke Neville had outlined a proposed solution — the building of intercepting sewers along the river banks.[48] Chadwick's solution had been to make sewerage removal self-financing by piping it to the country for use as fertiliser. This had already been uneconomic by the 1840s with the emergence of cheaper fertilisers.[49] In 1864 the Sewage Utilization and Land Reclamation Co. made its first appearance.[50] This company was controlled by Dublin solicitors Barrington and Jeffars, (they were subsequently involved in Dublin's first tram lines) with some English involvement, proposed to build intercepting sewers to pipe the sewage to Clontarf, using it to reclaim the slobland from there to Malahide.[51] This company was to shoulder the construction costs and give one-half of their profits to the corporation. Not surprisingly the latter voted its approval.[52] However local landowners such as the Earl of Howth, Viscount St. Lawrence and the Vernon family were opposed.[53] The bill to launch this scheme was withdrawn shortly afterwards,[54] but re-emerged in 1868. A report by J.W. Bazalgette, the engineer responsible for London's main drainage concluded that[55]

> The scheme does not appear to be well devised and would not sufficiently effect the purification of the Liffey, would not be renumerative and if abandoned would cast on the corporation the pumping, the maintenance of an unnecessarily costly and very defective system of drainage.

As an alternative he proposed a more conventional system jointly financed by city and suburbs.

Dublin Corporation was unwilling to lose any possible financial benefits from sewerage disposal. Eventually after many delays a Liffey drainage act was passed in 1871.[56] This provided for a scheme controlled by a committee consisting of twelve representatives of the corporation and six from neighbouring suburbs. Sewerage was to be intercepted and piped to Ballybough where it would be taken by Barrington and Jeffars for use in reclaiming the estuaries of Baldoyle, Malahide and Rogerstown.[57] The corporation was to receive one-sixth of the company's profits. The chairman of the sewerage company was Sir Arthur Guinness, his interest the crown solicitor alleged, motivated by the desire to pipe sewerage to Malahide, away from his estate at St. Anne's.[58] When tenders for the sewerage scheme were opened they ranged from £775,314 to £968,646,[59] far in excess of the borrowing powers of £350,000. This reflected the rapid price inflation which followed the Franco-Prussian War and which was most marked in metals. The cost escalation ended the possibility of a main drainage scheme for more than twenty years. Dublin Corporation sought to shift some of the burden for cleaning the Liffey to the Port and Docks Board[60] and lobbied Dublin Castle for a grant or a loan with favourable interest and repayment terms. Even the minimum necessary loan of £500,000 would have been well in excess of their statutory borrowing limit.[61]

Dublin Castle was not unsympathetic. In a confidential memorandum to the Chief Secretary, Sir Michael Hicks-Beach, the Under Secretary proposed that the loan be granted and that the state would contribute to the cost of the city's pauper lunatics which would mean a relief of £6,000.[62] The Chief Secretary supported this application to the Treasury urging that

> the existing high rate of local taxation in Dublin may not unfairly be urged as a reason for special consideration being shown in this matter towards the ratepayers of the city.

The Treasury rejected the plea in somewhat intemperate terms.[63]

> surely it is quite time to say that the long-suffering English or Scottish taxpayers deserve some consideration when these incessant raids are made by Irish members on the Imperial Treasury.

In 1891 main drainage became feasible as a result of the conversion of existing loans and reduced repayments following the Dublin Corporation loans act.[64] Work was be-

252

gun in 1896 and completed ten years later.[65] The official opening of the scheme was marked by possibly the first public demonstration by the *Sinn Fein* party, when Alderman Tom Kelly climbed up the mast of the sewerage tug the 'Shamrock' and cut down the Royal Ensign.

Dublin Corporation's efforts to introduce a main drainage scheme suffered to some extent from opposition but primarily from financial constraints. By the mid 1870s borrowing powers had been virtually exhausted while rates were at record levels. Popular opinion was ambivalent, wishing to clean the river, but resenting the cost. In 1870 a ratepayers memorial demanded action,[66] in 1874 another ratepayers' group opposed the main drainage scheme, alleging that it would cost £1m., or 2/- on the rates.[67] The Under Secretary noted that the Lord Mayor had explained[68]

> that the real opposition was not factious nor arising from indifference to health but based on dread of taxation and poverty. Mr. Moylan the Collector-General of rates did not think that the poorer parts of the city could well bear any further taxation.

Pressure for the completion of the main drainage system was eased by the report of a royal commission to the effect 'that upon the evidence placed before us, we cannot hold the Liffey accountable for the high rate of mortality which has prevailed'.[69] With the declining belief in the miasmic theory of disease, malodorous smells lost much of their terror and protests concerning the Liffey dwindled. The only one to come to light post 1880 is an anonymous letter from a householder in Arran Quay to the Lord Lieutenant, dated 21 July 1887.[70]

The condition of house drainage was of greater concern. Many tenement houses lacked sanitation and cess pools in yards and courts abounded. A letter to the corporation from Sir Thomas Larcom noted that the area between the river Liffey and Great Brunswick St. consisted of[71]

> houses overcrowded confined and abounding in foetid yards, stinking cesspools.

Innumerable house sewers were installed yet in 1879 it was reported that 12,000 houses required immediate attention to drainage.[72] Where sewers existed their quality seems to have been poor and they posed considerable medical risks. The *royal commission on sewerage and drainage* reported that[73]

> Dublin is however only in a condition with respect to its main sewering similar to what London, Liverpool and other large towns were before the old and defectively designed and badly constructed great drains were improved to better fit their modern uses as main sewers.

They recommended spending £30,000 to build and ventilate main sewers. On the question of house sewerage they noted[74]

> The evidence laid before us leads to the conclusion that the house drainage in Dublin is extremely defective and we have reason to believe that this is the case in all classes of houses.

The basement sub-soil was frequently saturated with sewerage. Considerable money was spent on sewers, yet in 1894 a meeting organised to protest against the main drainage proposals (not perhaps an unbiased source) alleged that the condition of Dublin's cross drains was extremely bad and that sewerage continued to leak into the subsoil.[75]

Mortality statistics provide indirect evidence that the city's sewers may have posed a health problem. Although, the death rate from infectious diseases declined, a major factor was the ending of cholera epidemics and the declining incidence of smallpox due to increased vaccination. The vaccination of infants was made compulsory in 1864. There was no marked improvement in mortality from typhoid and diarrhoea until the early twentieth century. Grimshaw, the Registrar-General claimed that typhoid deaths were on the increase during the 1870s[76] and published statistics suggest that mortality rose during the 1890s.

Table V Mortality per thousand of population

	Dublin city Typhoid	Diarrhoea	England and Wales Typhoid[78]
1871-80	–	–	0.332
1881-90	0.405	0.88	0.190
1891-1900	0.487	1.05	0.174
1901-10	0.202	0.811	–
1911-14	0.153	1.48	–

The figures for London in the years 1871-80 were only 0.24, but in the mining areas was as high as 0.43 to 0.56 per thousand.[77] The improvement in typhoid mortality in English and Welsh cities was rapid following the building of sewers. By 1893 the death rate from typhoid was higher in Dublin than in any other U.K. city except Belfast.[79] Typhoid was a disease of dirt rather than poverty, a fact confirmed by the report that the typhoid mortality in Dublin's predominantly middle class suburbs was higher than in London and in many English towns.[80] The disease was spread by dirty water or by infected milk. More milk was drunk by Irish working class families than their English counterparts which may have increased the incidence.[81] An outbreak in 1879 which affected prosperous residential areas such as Fitzwilliam Square, Raglan Road, Elgin Road and Northumberland Road was traced to an infected milk supply.[82] The special report on typhoid in 1893 highlighted the existence of dairy yards within the city and their inadequate cleansing, plus the condition of subsoil drainage as the primary culprits.[83] A contributory factor may have been the eating of shellfish, especially cockles and mussels polluted by sewerage carried into Dublin bay.[84] The closure of cockle beds in the early twentieth century was followed by a significant reduction in typhoid mortality. Perhaps the ballad of Molly Malone, the cockels and mussels dealer, who 'died of the fever' contains a moral.

The elimination of typhoid would seem to have entailed the introduction and implementation of various cleansing procedures and controls on drains, cesspools and dairy yards. The extent to which Dublin corporation had adequate powers in this respect and the degree to which they enforced their powers are of interest.

Public health administration and legislation

Irish public health legislation was generally introduced at a somewhat later date than its English equivalent. Early legislation was almost entirely permissive and although it provided for the appointment of a medical officer of health from 1848, Dublin failed to do so until 1864 when Edward Dillon Mapother was given a part-time appointment at an annual salary of one hundred guineas.[85] Two years previously Dr. Charles Cameron had been appointed as city analyst with responsibility for the purity of food, drink, chemicals and water,[86] though the initiative for this measure would seem to have come from the South Dublin Union.[87] The initial powers of the medical officer of health were limited to informative and educative functions. His duties were defined as[88]

> (to) ascertain the existence of diseases within the limits of the Special Act especially epidemics and contagious diseases and to point out any Nuisances or other local causes likely to cause and continue such diseases, or otherwise to injure the health of the inhabitants and to point out the best means for checking or preventing the spread of such diseases within the limits aforesaid and also to show the best means for the ventilation of churches, chapels, schools and registered within the limits aforesaid and from time to time as required by the Commissioners to report to them.

There were a number of serious defects in the powers of the medical officer of health. As in England he was totally independent of the treatment systems available. Dublin had fourteen dispensary medical officers, two in each dispensary district who carried the major burden of caring for the city's poor and were obviously highly informed as to the health of the city and in particular about outbreaks of epidemic disease. They were under the authority of the poor law commissioners, while the medical officer of health reported to the corporation.[89] A further set of medical officers were attached to the dispensaries of thirteen city hospitals and they were independent both of the corporation and the poor law commissioners. No organisation existed to co-ordinate these various bodies.

Powers of initiative and enforcement in public health were significantly more limited than those operating in England, though Royston Lambert claims that Irish and Scottish legislation, which tended to lag behind English measures generally proved more effective.[90] There was provision under English legislation for instituting investigations into the health of any town on the petition of one-tenth of the inhabitants, *or* when the death-rate exceed 23 per thousands (as it constantly did in Dublin). It was

256

also possible to institute inquiries concerning the neglect of sewerage disposal, infant mortality, cattle disease and the supply of meat, or the control of offensive trades, pleasure grounds and morgues. Such powers were lacking in Dublin, though Mapother, the medical officer of health obviously felt that they were necessary. Dublin Corporation also lacked the power to erect and run lodging houses, to provide vehicles for bringing fever patients to hospital or licence cow houses.[91]

Some steps were taken in the field of sanitary reform following the appointment of a medical officer of health. Private legislation passed in 1864 gave powers for the establishment of a cattle market which would remove cattle from congested city areas, and the control of slaughter houses. It was also proposed to introduce bye-laws for lodging houses and also for houses let at less than 3/- per week in separate rooms and for periods of less than four weeks.[92] These controlled the structural condition of the buildings, required the provision of ashpits and privies and the enforcement of penalties for soiling the building. Provision was also made for inspection at night to control overcrowding.[93] These regulations were eventually confirmed, with some reservations by the Lord Lieutenant[94] and published in the *Dublin Gazette*. It remains doubtful whether they were enforced. A group calling themselves the anti-political ratepayers society claimed to represent 10,000 housholders claimed that they were 'not only stringent but oppressive'[95] and in response Dublin Corporation's sub-committee claimed that the bye-laws were[96]

> not more stringent than the evils of the city required . . . no measures would be adopted with respect to any individual without special direction guarding against unnecessary or avoidable hardship.

The abuses which the bye-laws were designed to control persisted for decades.

Local authority powers were substantially strengthened with the passing of the 1866 sanitary act. This extended to Ireland virtually all the powers of the 1855 nuisance removal act and gave power to enforce the drainage of houses into public drains.[97] Where a local authority seemed lax, the Irish administration could intervene. The Lord Lieutenant could enforce a time limit on local authority's performance of duties, the police could be ordered to enforce sanitary regulations, while the poor law commissioners had power to inquire into the sanitary state of any town. In September 1866 the under-secretary, Sir Thomas Larcom declared the act to be in force in Dublin[98] and some weeks later he submitted a list of 1,648 houses inhabited by 3,767 people which had no sanitation in default of the 1866 act.[99] This pressure from Dublin Castle had some effect: the newly formed public health committee listed spectacular numbers of privies built and repaired during 1867.

By the early 1870s the efficiency of Dublin Corporation's enforcement of public health measures was coming under suspicion. A bill, which in line with English procedure would place responsibility for prosecutions for food adulteration in the hands of the corporation met with numerous objections. A divisional magistrate replied that[100]

> no legislation could give us personally more satisfaction than transferring to some other tribunal the adjudication of cases connected with the sanitary laws: cases always troublesome and most repulsive in detail.

He instances a case where a man named John Daly, convicted of having a large quantity of diseased meat for sale was sentenced to three months in prison. A total of 38 members of the corporation had signed a memorial to the Lord Lieutenant urging his release. On more general sanitary matters he noted

> Tenement owners are a large and influential class in Dublin both in and out of the corporation. They are frequently prosecuted and it is in the public interest for them to be tried by magistrates free from civic and corporation influences.

These opinions were supported by Professor Ferguson of the local government board who also objected to entrusting administration of sanitary law to the Lord Mayor[101]

> The competition for civic honours is so very great and contests at municipal elections are of the keenest kind. At the Lord Mayor's Court frequently the trading interests of the justice are identified with those of the defendant.

Both reports suggest the corporation's unwillingness to

258

use members of the Dublin Metropolitan Police as sanitary officers because they were not totally under their control. The corporation decline to depute the police generally to assist in sanitary inspections which fully accounts for the great failure of the Sanitary Act within the city of Dublin.

Professor Ferguson felt that the powers of the Lord Mayor should be curbed. In fact the tendency was in the opposite direction. The 1874 public health act,[102] which was essentially an Irish version of the 1872 English act, transferred powers from the poor law commissioners to the corporation. The existing sanitary staff of twenty-one[103] was augmented by fifteen dispensary medical officers, previously under the poor law and the local government board was constituted the supreme public health authority with control over all sanitary authorities. A further public health act in 1878[104] consolidated the mass of existing legislation. Its most important clause removed the 2/- in the £ rates ceiling for sanitary purposes.[105] This removed a favourite corporation excuse of inadequate funds.

It is difficult to pinpoint the impact of the sanitary officials on the city's health. The public health reports, such as that for 1873-4 contain a seemingly impressive list of activities[106]

Report public health 1873-4

Drains and sewers built	256
Drains and sewers cleansed and repaired	757
Ashpits built	190
Privies and closets built	286
Privies and closets repaired	1,008
Ashpits cleansed	6,961
Dwellings cleansed and repaired	6,304
Dwellings condemned	65
Dwellings unsafe	33
Cellars closed	14
Yards cleansed	2,246
Lanes and alleys cleansed by private parties	146
Manure removed	840
Swine removed from houses	140
Other animals removed from houses	141
Smoke nuisances	2

Bone nuisances	1
Manure nuisances	1
Miscellaneous nuisances	53
Tenement houses inspected	35,038
Tenement rooms inspected	70,724
Lodging houses inspected	2,826
Bakeries	2,145
Slaughter houses	998
Dairy yards	149
Oral sanitary convictions	3,456
Notices served	8,946
Summoned	3,515

However the Dublin sanitary association who regularly reported nuisances complained of corporation inaction.[107] They failed to provide any regular system of scavenging or for removal of refuse from ashpits. Refuse was only removed and privies cleansed when they had been designated a nuisance and a court order approved ordering the removal of the nuisance,[108] while ashpits were only cleaned at a minimum charge of 6/-.[109] For a responsible tenement owner, or private householder who wanted refuse removed the position was extremely difficult. Private manure collectors existed in the city, but their yards were under threat of closure as nuisances and charges had more than doubled because of disposal difficulties. In the past it had been sold to farmers as fertiliser, but it was 'now so valueless that farmers will not remove it'.[110] To the corporation's protests of lack of powers for refuse removal the local government board pointed out that they had powers to hire contractors for refuse removal.[111]

This met with no response. In 1875 the Dublin sanitary association requested the local government board to take over the cleansing of streets and ashpits as a result of corporation negligence. In reply the corporation issued their regular public health returns listing the number of yards and privies cleansed and the local government board decided to accept this as an adequate reason for not interfering.[112] By 1876 domestic scavenging had still not been introduced and as a result, according to Dr. Grimshaw, orders for the cleansing of tenement housing proved to be useless.[113] The corporation sought to evade its responsibilities for scavenging by introducing bye-laws requiring house occupiers to clean their privies, ashpits and even the street fronting their properties at regular intervals.[114]

The *royal commission on sewerage and drainage* emphatically stated that 'the corporation must organised a proper system of refuse removal and street cleansing'.[115] Such steps were eventually taken in 1882.[116] Many households apparently continued to dump their refuse on the streets and avoided prosecution because they had no yards or ashpits.[117] From this point the question of refuse collection becomes of lesser interest. With the gradual introduction of water closets the most insanitary forms of refuse no longer had to be removed by cart. In his detailed examination of the city's health in 1906 D. Edgar Flinn chief medical officer of the local government board noted that since 1901 the corporation had levied a charge of one guinea per annum for cleaning tenement yards — previously the service had been free. As a result many yards went uncleansed.[118] The other outlets regarded as harbouring disease were slaughter houses and dairy yards. Once again corporation action was belated and ineffective. Powers to suppress objectionable slaughter houses existed from 1864 and in 1867 the corporation considered erecting a city abattoir.[111] The foundation stone was not laid however until 1880[120] and in the intervening years further slaughter houses had been licensed.[121] By 1880 there were a total of 104 registered slaughter houses, of which seventeen were concerned with bacon curing, while the remainder supplied 375 butchers.[122] Many of these were in the most densely populated and disease-ridden areas of the city; six were in Patrick St. and a further six in Bull Alley, generally recognised as among the greatest slums.[123] In addition there were 7,500 milch cows in 487 dairy yards.[124]

No steps could be taken to suppress slaughter houses until the opening of the abattoir in 1882.[125] Dublin Corporation had full legal powers to refuse to renew yearly slaughter house licences without compensating owners, according to legal opinion,[126] but in 1883 they decided to close two slaughter houses with full compensation to the owners.[127] In fact it emerged that they lacked the power to

261

compulsorily close slaughter houses, because the abattoir had been built just outside city boundaries.[128] No further steps were taken until 1890 when a clause in the corporation improvement act proposed extending the city boundaries by the fractional amount necessary to include the abattoir. This would have permitted the closure of slaughter houses without compensation and was vociferously opposed by the powerful licensed victuallers and a clause was substituted providing for compensation.[129]

There is no evidence of any resulting closures. In 1897 a local government board inspector commenting on the health problems posed by slaughter houses remarked[130]

> Fresh regulations with respect to slaughter houses will soon be submitted by the corporation; but the Local Government Board are not very sanguine, as the forces opposed to reform are particularly strong in Dublin. The dairymen and butchers are not without power both inside and outside the corporation, and a matter like this which rests on the discretion of the local authority requires time and patience and continuous representation before any impression is made.

His scepticism proved justified. When the legislation to extend the city boundaries was being drafted in 1900, one of the clauses provided that no slaughter houses were to be compulsorily closed without compensation for twenty five years, and that existing licenses would be renewed and new licenses granted. This provoked outrage in the local government board who claimed that it had been included 'at the instigation of the cowkeepers and victuallers association', perpetuating the situation brought about by the 1890 act[131]

> which has practically endowed improper slaughter houses in Dublin and made it impossible either to remove or improve them. It is from the public health point of view a most mischievous clause.

The city's butchers had the powerful support of William Field, member of the corporation and M.P. for St. Patrick's Division who was a cattle dealer and leading member of their association. When an inquiry into the city's death rate was proposed in 1900, he wrote to the Chief Secretary's office[132]

> having been requested by my fellow traders of the Victuallers Association . . . to hope that some member

of the Committee be acquainted with the Dairy Trade. The request was not acceded to, and the report noted the health risks which the city's slaughter houses posed and recommended their closure.[133]

The number of slaughter houses declined, due rather to natural wastage than to corporation policy. In 1879 there had been 104, but this had fallen to 79 by 1890.[134] By 1900 there were only 56.[135] In 1906 the overwhelming majority of the city's meat was still slaughtered in private establishments.

Table VI Animal slaughtering 1906 (average weekly killings)[136]

	Abattoir	Private slaughter houses
cattle	200	380
sheep	450	1,671
pigs	60	739
calves	6	20

A similar unwillingness to interfere with powerful vested interests characterised policy towards the dairy yards. The city's dairy yards were implicated in several outbreaks of typhoid,[137] and were almost certainly responsible for cases of scarlatina[138] and tuberculosis.[139] Prior to 1886 the Lord Lieutenant and the Privy Council had certain control over dairy yards. In 1886 this was transferred to the local government board and the sanitary authority i.e. Dublin Corporation. The authority of the local government board was limited to controlling contagious cattle diseases. Between 1886 and 1893 they worked to stamp out pleuro-pneumonia and in the process effected improvements in many yards.[13 39] General supervision rested with the corporation who had power to order the cleansing and inspection of dairy yards, even to licence new yards, if the bye-laws governing construction were in order. Even these limited controls do not seem to have been implemented. A local government board inspector noted[140]

I fear the public health committee are somewhat half hearted in administering regulations which press on struggling members of the dairy trade.

While most of the large yards were felt to be in reasonable condition this was not so in the case of the smaller yards. Corporation inspectors apparently turned a blind eye to insanitary conditions: 'some of the officers persist week after week in reporting upon yards as if they were perfect, which there was reason to suspect were not in good condition'. As a result of local government board action, three sanitary inspectors were forced to resign and new powers to restrict overcrowding and dirt were introduced.[141] It is somewhat disquieting to learn in 1904 that a speaker at the annual dinner of the Dublin cowkeepers association — an event attended by two city councillors, claimed that they had 'nothing but praise for Dublin corporation'.[142] The report on the city's health in 1906 by D. Edgar Flinn, a document not overly flattering to municipal administration, felt that dairy regulations were 'fairly well observed'.[143] Many milksellers were impoverished and lived in tenement housing where they stored milk. As a result supplies were frequently contaminated. Enthusiasm for removing dairy yards from the city had faded with the realisation that premises in the country were frequently more insanitary and beyond the control of public health regulations.[144]

Infant mortality

Concern with infant and child mortality emerged relatively slowly in Dublin and never became an issue of major concern. Sir Charles Cameron, the medical officer of health, took frequent refuge in the fact that Dublin's infantile death-rate was not above the English average.[145] While this was true in the early 1890s, Dublin failed to match the improvement shown in English cities from that time. A major measles epidemic in 1899, resulting in 568 deaths, gave rise for concern, though the resulting infant mortality was not abnormally high. Cameron noted[146]

> If the infants had not died from measles it would appear that the majority would have succumbed to some other disease.

The first lady sanitary officer was appointed by the public health committee in 1890 and by 1900, four, all holding certificates from the Royal Institute of Public Health had been appointed. They worked mainly with mothers and children, instructing them in hygiene and proper feeding methods. In 1910, the 1907 act which provided for compulsory early notification of births was adopted and this provided sanitary officers with the address of young infants. A voluntary society of ladies worked in conjunction with the sanitary officers and the public health committee.[147] In addition the Women's National Health Association under the auspices of Ishbel Countess of Aberdeen organised voluntary visitors and a limited supply of free sterilised milk.[148] It is impossible to determine the effectiveness of these measures. Evidence from England suggests that such visits were resented by the poor.[149] The main factors in high infantile mortality were held to be widespread ignorance amongst mothers as to the proper feeding of infants',[150] or want of clothing. The public health department provided a leaflet on proper infant feeding, but one questions the ability of many tenement mothers to read or understand it. The quality of the city's milk supply was a factor in high infant mortality, though by 1907 sterilising was coming into use.[151] Irish mothers in England apparently breast fed their babies to a much greater extent than their English counterparts with consequent benefits to child health. Unfortunately there is no available evidence concerning the prevalence of breast feeding among the Dublin mothers. One district medical officer of health, Dr. Strahan, noted that a major factor in infant ill-health was the inadequate food available to mothers[152] and this would suggest that breast feeding was common.

Less concern was focussed on the health of older children. Of the city's 167 national schools in 1907, 104 had no lavatory accommodation, while 21 lacked playgrounds.[153] Despite poor attendance many were seriously overcrowded. The 1900 report recommended that schools provide adequate cubic space for each pupil and that playgrounds and sanitary facilities be provided. They also proposed that adequate time be given for a midday meal.[154] Neither Dublin Corporation, nor the local government board had the means to implement these measures, had they wished to do so. The schools were totally outside all municipal control, responsible to school managers — generally clergymen and ultimately to the Commissioners for National Education.

By 1916 an increasing number of city-centre schools were providing midday meals for their pupils, while some convents also provided breakfast. These were provided by private charitable efforts rather than municipal or state funds. The public health authorities were also criticised for failing to close the schools during major epidemics. By 1906 this had not yet been implemented,[155] due perhaps to lack of authority, but one suspects to municipal indifference. A further recommendation that street trading children be restricted in their hours of work, as had been done in Liverpool[156] was not implemented until 1914.[157]

The most important determinant of children's health was social class. The differential mortality statistics were dramatic. For children aged between one and five years, mortality among the professional classes in 1905 was 0.9 per thousand. In the middle classes the figure was 2.7; for artisans and petty shopkeepers it rose to 4.8, reaching 12.7 in the case of hawkers, labourers and porters.[158]

Tuberculosis

Tuberculosis had long been a major cause of early death in Dublin but received little attention from public health authorities, presumably because both cause and cure were unknown. Koch demonstrated in 1882 that tuberculosis was an infectious disease but it took some time for this to be widely accepted. Attention was not focussed on tuberculosis as a factor in the city's high death rate until 1900[159] when its role was highlighted by the departmental committee appointed by the local government board to investigate the city's death rate. The first measures towards containment were taken in 1900 with the proposal that the disease should be notifiable on a voluntary basis as an experiment.[160] This proposal, initially rejected was put into force in January 1901[161] Dublin doctors were hostile to notification of disease, claiming that they breached patients' confidentiality.[162]

Facilities for the treatment of tuberculosis in the city were few. Many destitute patients went to the workhouse hospitals, but were discharged after a relatively short stay, shorter than in English tuberculosis institutions.[163] In 1905 a proposal to erect a TB sanitorium was raised at a meeting

266

of Dublin Corporation but was defeated.[164] In the following year it was decided to levy a rate of 1d in the £ from the urban and rural areas to finance such a project.[165] In 1907 the Dublin public health committee recommended providing separate sleeping accommodation for TB cases, but given the overcrowded state of the city's tenements this was simply impossible.[166] In 1909 tuberculosis of the lung was declared a notifiable disease and a campaign of information was launched.[167] A leading activist was Ishbel, Countess of Aberdeen who organised a travelling information service. She campaigned for better hygiene, controls on spitting in public.[168] In addition, the Women's National Health Association sought information on the addresses of tuberculosis patients and visited their homes to establish an after-care service, while the Dublin Samaritan's Committee, an offshoot organisation paid the rent of extra rooms for families of TB victims so that they would have separate sleeping accommodation, provided free milk and in general gave essential financial assistance.[169] These efforts were satirised by Sinn Fein Leader, Arthur Griffith, under the title 'Viceregal microbe'. He apparently resented the fact that the campaign[170]

> has conveyed the impression abroad that we dwell in an island reeking with TB, whose inhabitants are foredoomed to a lingering and hopeless disease, and whose products are calculated to convey the germs of the fatal scourge wherever they are distributed.

While these measures were obviously beneficial, the key factors in reducing tuberculosis were the isolation of carriers, a reduction in overcrowding and improved diet. The relationship between overcrowding and tuberculosis was documented by figures from Glasgow[171] and Finsbury[172] The Finsbury figures showed a death rate of 4.5 per thousand for inhabitants of one roomed tenements, from TB, declining to 2.8 for those in two rooms, 1.2 in three rooms and 0.6 for those living in four rooms. While overcrowding increased the risks of spreading disease, especially where healthy and sick people slept in the one room, housing conditions are also an approximate indication of overall living standards. There was a similarly strong negative correlation for a sample of London households between rent paid and infant mortality.[173] It is possible that the high mortality among those in one-roomed accommodation is only partly attributable to overcrowding and that it also reflects differences in diet. There was a strong relationship between social class and mortality from TB.

Table VII Mortality per thousand of population from TB for the year 1912[174]

Professional and independent class	0.41
Middle class	1.92
Artisan and petty shopkeeper	2.94
General service class (i.e. labourers)	3.16
Domestic servants	1.83

Tuberculosis therefore raised complex questions of income, diet and housing beyond the narrow confines of public health.

Diet
The diet of the Dublin working class was virtually ignored before Rowntree's investigations of York, published in 1900. Thereafter various publications dealing with either public health or the state of the poor included sample menus from labouring families. They record a heavy dependence on bread and tea, very limited consumption of meat — primarily bacon, occasional herrings, and vegetables limited to potatoes, onions and cabbage.[175] This diet would appear to have been established by the 1830s. The poor inquiry reported that the Dublin labourers diet consisted of 'tea and bread for breakfast; potatoes and herrings or sometimes bacon for dinner; seldom more than two meals a day; for those out of work, no meat'.[176] Tradesmen ate meat twice a day.

This diet compared unfavourably with that of the peasantry of rural Ireland in the early twentieth century. The latter ate home baked brown bread, the Dubliners white shop loaves. The Dublin labourers derived most of their protein from bread; their carbohydrates from bread and sugar. Rural diets relied more heavily on potatoes and contained a decidedly higher milk and meat content. Dubliners

268

differed from their English counterparts in consuming virtually no cheese or pulse vegetables. The dependence on shop bread and lack of pulses was partly attributable to cooking difficulties. Tenement houses were generally equipped only with open fires; coal was costly and many of the poor relied on cinders rejected by the rich for their fuel.[177]

The first scientific analysis of Dublin working class diets was carried out by Stafford in a general study of income which was closely modelled on Rowntree's work. Twenty-one families, chosen as 'typical' were subjected to detailed budgetary and dietary analysis. The very poor were deliberately excluded. Applying Atwater's scale of protein requirements he discovered that only four families showed a surplus of protein in their diet, and one of these spent more than it earned. Only five achieved a level of 3,500 calories per man — the figure which was generally regarded as necessary to perform heavy manual work. In five cases, all labourers, the deficiency was in excess of 1,000 calories.[178] This study was carried out in 1904, at a time of relatively favourable food prices. A representative working class diet drawn up in 1913-14 for the Women's National Health Association by Dr. Mabel Crawford based on bread, potatoes, sugar, a pig's head, some fish and a little beef, yielded only 2,600 calories per man.[179] High wartime prices, particularly the escalating price of the staple pig's head, from 1/- to 3/6, posed even greater dietary pressure.[180]

The role of inadequate diet in both tuberculosis and in other diseases was critical. Malnutrition was a major factor in the high mortality resulting from the 1897-99 measles epidemic. Improvements in diet related to the overall wage structure and standard of living, matters beyond the competence of a municipal public health authority.

The Dublin city death rate fell sharply in the post-war decades. By 1940 the Dublin death rate was 14.36 per thousand, compared with 20.9 in 1914. The mortality from pulmonary tuberculosis had more than halved to 1.31 per thousand, compared with 2.8 in 1914, while total tubercular mortality had fallen from 3.788 to 1.63.[181] Yet in the intervening period overcrowding in working class housing had increased[182] while there had been no major breakthroughs in treatment of TB. However the 1930s had been characterised by cheap meat, and an extended welfare system. Some supplies of free milk were available, there were widows and orphans pensions, a limited system of unemployment insurance, and a universal, if inadequate system of unemployment assistance.

Conclusions: public health administration in Dublin

Dublin's public health administration emerges as singularly ineffective. The city had a high death rate and the improvement was much less than in English cities. There were mitigating factors. Dublin city boundaries, at least until 1900 excluded most of the area's middle class population and presented figures based on a disproportionately high working class population.

This factor can be excluded by examining statistics for the Dublin registration district, which included the suburbs. This does not markedly change the general picture. In fact an examination of death rates of the Dublin registration district by social class suggests that Dublin was a markedly unhealthy place to live, even for professional families, with the professional and middle class death rates above the average for many British cities.

Table VIII Deaths per thousand of the population of the Dublin registration district by social group [183]

	1883-90	1891-1900	1901-10
Professional & independent	14.25	20.62	19.82
Middle class	26.98	20.4	16.16
Artisan and shopkeeping	22.73	23	18.1
General service and workhouse	34.71	35.2	33.38

The figures for professional mortality for the years 1883-90 are too low as they are based on the 1881 professional population, which shows a decline by 1891. Overall they give cause for disquiet. The year 1901, for example, shows a mortality rate among the professional classes amounting to 29.6 per thousand.

Sir Charles Cameron's regular defence that the city's high mortality could be attributable to its unfavourable social structure does not appear to stand up to detailed investigation. Dublin would seem to have been unhealthy for all residents. Sir Charles Cameron's own family history would bear this out. Of a family of six sons and two daughters, only one son and two daughters were alive when he wrote his autobiography. Two of the deaths were somewhat abnormal — a suicide and a drowning, but one son died of scarlet fever at the age of eight, and two died of phthisis in early adult life.[184]

If we examine the reduction achieved in the death rate the impression is one of little progress. The reduction in deaths was less than in English or Scottish cities, despite the initially high figures. Improvement would seem to have been most marked among the city's middle classes and artisans, the rich and the very poor do not appear to have benefitted.

Some of Dublin's health problems have been attributed to financial difficulties. That Dublin Corporation faced financial problems is not in doubt. A low and slowly increasing rateable valuation reduced borrowing powers and necessitated high rates. Financial constraints caused the postponement of the main drainage system for several decades.

There remains some doubt however whether sanitary policy was consistently pursued with maximum efficiency and dedication. Suspicions of lax administration, particularly where measures might have affected vested interests such as slaughter house owners or tenement landlords persist. Cleansing was not carried out as efficiently as it might have been. A city which had a similar social structure and consequently similar problems was Liverpool and the Liverpool medical officer of health was among those called to give evidence before the 1900 inquiry. He was noticeably critical concerning the detailed enforcement of health regulations in Dublin, particularly those concerning the overcrowding of dairies and the filth of tenements, particularly their waterclosets.[185] A detailed register of all tenement property existed in Liverpool and all were regularly inspected so that the authorities 'do not wait for a nuisance to arise'.[186] Similar measures in Dublin would have required a some-

271

what larger staff and greater attention to detail, but no major increase in expenditure.

It is possible that such inspection and enforcement might have interfered with allies and friends of councillors. On matters of legislation and its enforcement the impression is also one of laxity. The city was slow to appoint a medical officer of health and the appointment was still a part-time one as late as 1914. There was also a delay in adopting many other measures when they were not compulsory. The Dublin sanitary association, the city's watchdog agency concluded in 1873 that[187]

> the sanitary machine in the hands of the corporation is not only quite insufficient for the work which due care for public health renders necessary; but that which at present exists is not put in action with as much energy and discretion as might fairly be expected from the sanitary authority of a great city.

It is somewhat disconcerting in 1900 to find Sir Charles Cameron, the medical officer of health, listing among the factors giving rise to an excessive death rate: the condition of slaughter houses, lack of accommodation for fever patients, lack of a daily filth removal system and the storage of sewerage,[188] all matters which had been known and which had been within the legislative power of Dublin Corporation for decades. The 1900 inquiry made a series of recommendations concerning the city's health. Most were routine and relatively inexpensive matters such as a daily filth removal service, removal of the sewerage barge Eblana, which was used to carry refuse out to sea, to a mooring more distant from populated areas, the closure of slaughter houses etc. Several of the recommendations had been current for decades. In 1906 when the local government board's chief medical officer reported, the majority had not yet been implemented, though they required neither legislative powers nor massive expenditure. Public health in Dublin Corporation does not appear to have aroused widespread commitment, either from officials or from politicians.

One problem was the absence of strong public interest. There was apparently a Dublin sanitary association in existence in 1851,[189] but it has left few traces and would appear to have been short-lived. Concern for sanitary matters is not evidenced in the papers of the Dublin Statistical Society, subsequently the Statistical and Social Inquiry Society of Ireland, nor do sanitary matters predominate among the surviving pamphlets of the 1840s and 1850s. In 1861 Dublin Corporation's committee no. 2 which had charge of public health could report[190]

Your committee have pleasure in reporting that the city continues in a healthy state and that the registered lodging houses and the slaughter houses are reported by your officers and the police in a cleanly condition.

There is no detailed evidence as to the condition of the city at this time, but our knowledge of the position in subsequent years gives full grounds for scepticism concerning this statement. The introduction of death registration, and the reports of the medical officer of health removed much ignorance as to the true state of health but do not appear to have given rise to any immediate sense of urgency. Even the 1866 cholera epidemic failed to arouse an obvious public outcry. The first evidence of widespread interest in public health matters emerges in 1872 with the foundation of the Dublin sanitary association.[191] The initiative in establishing the association appears to have come from doctors, clergymen, an engineer, a land agent and Anthony O Neill, a leading coach builder and member of Dublin Corporation. Its objectives were similar to many English associations which had preceded it[192]

1. To create an educated public opinion with regard to sanitary matters in general.

2. To direct the attention of the authorities and the public to those points in which the existing condition of the city are either not duly exercised or are inadequate or in which the machinery at the disposal of the sanitary authorities is insufficient.

3. To watch the course of sanitary legislation on behalf of the public.

4. To form a body in which the public may have confidence and through which they may if necessary act.

The initial membership was dominated by doctors. Of 194 members, a total of 51 were doctors; there were 15 clergymen (mostly Church of Ireland), 14 barristers, 27 merchants and 12 manufacturers. There were a total of five M.P.s among the members, but only three members of Dublin Corporation. The strong presence of medical men suggests a degree of concern about the enforcement of sanitary measures, a concern motivated less by amateur benevolence than by professional knowledge. It suggests that all was not well in the city. The association commenced regular inspections and submitted lists of nuisances to the corporation. In a memorial submitted in 1873 they suggested various measures for filth removal, and control of dairies and slaughter houses, in many cases precisely the suggestions being made as late as 1900.[193] Their concern would seem to have awakened the first consciousness of the city's health problems. In a confidential report prepared by a leading physician for the Chief Secretary's Office, it was pointed out, that in 1873 Dublin had a higher death rate than London's East End, Edinburgh, Birmingham and Liverpool, though lower than Glasgow and Manchester. If the figures were corrected for burials, Dublin had the highest death rate.[194] The *Irish Times* also informed its readers that the city had a higher death rate than London, Liverpool or Edinburgh. This marks the first public awareness of this fact.[195] By 1876 Dr. Cameron was forced to issue a report explaining the city's heavy mortality level. This he did by claiming an excessive migration from the city of those under 35, and the attributing to the city of all deaths occurring in both the workhouses and the hospitals.[196] By 1878 the Dublin sanitary association applied to the Lord Lieutenant for an inquiry into the city's high death rate,[197] while Dr. Mapother, the former medical officer of health and now the consulting sanitary officer accused the Dublin sanitary association of being[198]

> self-constituted and irresponsible persons, who might possibly be actuated by such motives as greed of notoriety or of employment

Concern in Dublin Castle led to a request for a report on the health of the Dublin Metropolitan Police force: they were apparently healthier than the forces in other cities.[199] With the record death rates of 1879 the sanitary association intensified its lobbying of the Chief Secretary's office while the Chief Secretary recommended an inquiry. The tone of their communication to the Treasury is somewhat hysterical, but suggests that the city's health was being viewed with urgency[201] The matter is one of such pressing urgency and public opinion is so strongly excited in Dublin, indeed in Ireland generally in reference to the present high death rate in the Metropolis (country families being in many cases afraid to visit it) that their excellencies are quite prepared to impress on the commissioners the necessity of completing the task entrusted them as speedily as possible.

The Treasury duly sanctioned a royal commission with a budget of £1,000,[202] though Dublin Castle felt that £5,000 was necessary.[203] This marked the peak of interest in the city's health. While its report confirmed contemporary opinions concerning filth and scavenging it shifted the major responsibility for high mortality from the river Liffey, the most popular target, to the tenement houses and in the process seems to have somewhat deflated the ranks of the opposition. The Dublin sanitary association continued in existence but failed to receive a similar degree of publicity. One of its leading members, Edward Spencer devoted increasing attention to the Artisans Dwellings Co. Others may have followed the common middle-class pattern of declining interest in city affairs. Although Dublin's health improved more slowly than other cities the 1879 mortality was a peak not subsequently reached, a peak which was even more striking because it was the first year of truly accurate death registrations. With the gradual decline of zymotic disease public awareness was blunted as massive deaths from smallpox or cholera gave way to steady mortality from bronchitis, typhoid or tuberculosis.

The closing years of the century brought another bout of interest in health matters. An epidemic of scarlet fever was prevalent during the years 1897-9, and a subsequent measles epidemic increased concern.[204] On this occasion the initiative for an inquiry came from the Lord Lieutenant, rather than from public opinion.[205] The report and evidence of this inquiry with its catalogue of inadequate cleansing, persistence of slaughter houses in the city, and appalling housing conditions was duly reported in the newspapers, but provoked no specific response. By this point the committee was simply reiterating recommendations and evidence which had been well known for decades. Those critical of health policy would seem to have adopted an attitude of resignation in the face of corporation neglect, others regarded criticism as motivated by political hostility. Thus when the 1900 committee was announced the *Freeman's Journal* expressed its belief[206]

> that the sudden and furious outcry concerning the death rate is a mere political attack on the corporation.

Yet in the early twentieth century, Dublin apparently had the fifth highest death rate in the world, surpassed only by such exotic cities as Trieste, Rio de Janeiro, St. Petersburg and Moscow. Belief that all criticism, even when based on hard facts, was politically motivated would appear to have cocooned corporation members and officials.

One is left with an inescapable sense of fatalism on the part of both the public, corporation members and officials, and, to some extent the local government board and other civil servants. With the exception of some members of the Dublin sanitary association, whose interest soon waned, nobody approached the city's health with any type of crusading zeal. Many problems — those attributable to poverty and poor diet, were insurmountable, but questions of filth and scavenging were not. The city's loss of life was accepted with stoicism by so many who appear to have felt that any remedies were beyond their power.

Chapter IX

THE HOUSING OF DUBLIN'S WORKING CLASS

The question of working class housing involves virtually all aspects of the city's economic and social structure. Housing was related to income and employment, to the geographical organisation of the city, and to matters of health and sanitation. It proved to be a major preoccupation of public health authorities from the 1880s until the 1940s and it is a matter of grave concern at the present time.

Unlike other Irish or English cities, the typical Dublin working class family lived in a tenement — a large house in multi-family occupancy. This was a characteristic which they shared with Scottish and continental cities.[1] The limited evidence available would suggest that such tenements were consistently overcrowded, perhaps to a greater degree than in the later nineteenth century. In 1798 Rev. Joseph Whitelaw, rector of a city centre parish surveyed the south city Liberties[2]

> With the exception of St. James and St. Thomas St. and a few others the streets in this part of the city are generally narrow, houses crowded together in the reres of backyards of very small extent, and some without accommodation of the kind. A few streets are residences of shopkeepers and others engaged in trade but a far greater proportion of them with their numerous lanes and alleys, are occupied by working manufacturers, by petty shop-keepers, and the labouring poor and beggars crowded together to a degree distressing to humanity. A single apartment in one of these truly wretched habitations, rates from 1-2/- per week; and to lighten this rent two, three or four families

become joint tenants, hence at an early hour we may find 10-16 persons of all ages and sexes in a room of not fifteen feet square stretched on a wad of filthy

Table I Houses in Dublin city 1841-1911

	First class	Second	Third	Fourth
1841	10,171	8,289	1,494	155
1851	10,827	9,693	1,680	44
1861	10,688	10,486	1,740	21
1871	10,459	11,455	1,891	91
1881	9,067	13,061	2,064	14
1891	8,720	14,638	2,391	7
1901	8,673	18,855*	–	11
1911	8,688	26,785	–	4

* In both 1901 and 1911 the information on second and third class houses was aggregated.

Table II Accommodation of families Dublin city 1841-1911

	First class**	Second	Third	Fourth
1841	5,695	8,412	12,297	23,197
1851	5,604	9,345	14,330	28,039
1861	5,158	9,815	16,163	27,290
1871	5,033	10,523	16,819	25,952
1881	4,692	11,013	16,660	23,360
1891	4,694	13,279	14,536	19,347
1901	4,635	33,199	–	21,429
1911	4,599	37,202	–	20,564

** The classification of housing and of accommodation depended on the extent of a house, number of rooms, quality and number of windows. Fourth class houses had one room and one window; third class 2-4 rooms and windows; second class 5-9 rooms plus windows; first class was any larger house, including institutions.

First class accommodation was defined as one family per first class house; second class, one family in a second class house, or 2-3 in a first class house; third class — one family in a third class house, 2-3 in a second class house, or 4-5 in a third class house. Fourth class consisted of those living in fourth class houses plus any greater densities than listed above in the other houses.

straw and without any covering save the wretched rags that constitute their wearing apparel.

One street, Plunkett Street contained a total of 917 inhabitants in 32 houses, or an average of 28.7 per house. The average for the Liberties in 1798 was said to be 12-16 per house.

It is impossible to obtain exact knowledge of the city's housing until the 1841 Census which gave information on the quality of houses and of accommodation.

The figures confirm the impression of multi-family house occupancy as the norm. Only 8.5% of the city's housing stock in 1881 consisted of small cottages of 2-4 rooms, and only 1,876 families, or 3.4% of the total lived in such cottages on their own. In fact, only 14,334 families, 26% of the population had exclusive occupancy of a house or cottage. This figure had risen to almost 40% in 1901 as a result of the extension of city boundaries. Not all housing in multi-family occupancy can be regarded as a slum, correspondingly many third class houses were, particularly those erected in courts and yards to the rear of larger houses, which lacked air light and sanitation.

The location of slum property, according to H.J. Dyos, was determined by the supply and demand for houses: 'slums were the residue'. Slums were created by the blighting effect of docks, canals, a railway line, gasworks or dairies, 'slumness confirmed a builder's mistake'.[3] This general description is broadly applicable to Dublin. By the late 18th century the fashionable areas had been established as the north-west quadrant, including Sackville St., Dominick St. and the south-east quadrant of Merrion and Fitzwilliam Squares.[4] The south-western area, which contained the traditional city industries was almost exclusively working class, while the extreme north-eastern belt was not heavily populated, and much of it was unfashionable because it was low-lying and subject to flooding and because of its proximity to an army barracks.

The status of the north-western quadrant declined to a marked extent during the nineteenth century. Street directories trace the gradual decline of various addresses. Upper Dominick St. contained four tenements in 1861, by 1871 this had risen to ten, while the doctors and solicitors had disappeared. By 1881 much of the street had passed into the hands of the Artisans Dwelling Co. Lower Dominick St. was a more respectable address which still clung to some status. Decaying house property gradually gave way to a national school and Carmelite seminary. The number of resident lawyers had been thirty-eight in 1851; by 1861 this had fallen by ten; in 1871 a further seven had left and by 1881 they had fallen by a dramatic seventeen. One of the most dramatic social reversals took place in Henrietta St., formerly the home of judges and bishops. In 1847 although nearby Henrietta Lane contained three tenements, Henrietta St. retained much of its status. The former aristocratic residents had largely disappeared; of seven residences, three were vacant, but Lady Harriet Daly remained. Most of the remainder provided legal offices for lawyers attracted by proximity to the courts and King's Inns. By 1879 most of the street consisted of tenements and property valuations had fallen from £2,280 in 1854 to £1,040.[5] The declining status of north city streets reflects the shift of fashion towards south city residences. Tenement housing was found in the south-east quadrant, mainly in streets bounded by the railway lines and gas works.

In many cases tenements were the former homes of the upper classes, which failed to find alternative tenants. Their decline into tenement status reflects the relative absence of major rebuilding schemes in nineteenth century Dublin, a reflection of economic decline. With the exception of schools and religious institutions few alternative uses present themselves for the deserted mansions of previous generations. Yet not all tenements fell into this category. Those in the south-west quadrant of the city, such as the Coombe and High St. were simply the traditional houses of the city's tradesmen. By mid nineteenth century many were perhaps over a hundred years old and in urgent need of replacement but few private building schemes emerged. Such houses had traditionally been overcrowded and insanitary. Structural conditions had deteriorated, while contemporary standards of appropriate housing had risen to a point where these traditional houses were no longer acceptable. The final category of slum housing consisted of properties of more recent construction erected in courts and lanes at the rear of streets and houses. They were generally smaller than the older tenements, but no less overcrowded and insanitary. In 1888, G. Glorney of Kane's Court requested a change of name to Glorney's buildings, reflecting his construction of 'property for superior artisans and tenants'.[6] By 1914 Dublin Corporation could report that 589 inhabitants of Glorney's buildings had been dispossessed, the buildings demolished and a total of £39,600 spent on erecting new housing on the site.[7] The registrar-general was of the opinion that the worst housing was to be found in the courts and lanes.[8]

Most of the new housing built in the city in the late nineteenth century consisted of properties of four to six rooms suitable for lower middle class, or occasionally skilled working class occupancy. Most cheaper property, with the exception of Artisans Dwelling Co. schemes, seems to have been overcrowded and insanitary. The provision of working class housing by private companies was uncommon, reflecting the lack of large industrial concerns, the existence of a captive labour market and a general weakness in philanthropy. In 1854 the Quaker textile firm of Pim built cottages for employees at Harold's Cross.[9] The only firms to follow suit were Guinness's and Watkins' breweries and the railway and tram companies. In 1914 these amounted in total to a mere 569 dwellings, mostly built in the suburbs.[10] The absence of alternatives, and financial constraints forced the majority of the working class to live in tenements.

Housing was among the major preoccupations of public health reformers. The history of municipal public health in mid-nineteenth century England is a litany of the suppression of back-to-back housing, cellar dwellings and the introduction of water and sanitation and regular applications of white-wash. Dublin lacked any back-to-back houses and in the 1860s the small number of cellars which had been used as dwellings were closed.[11] More active intervention against tenement housing was slow to emerge. In 1862 a corporation sub-committee directed the inspector of nuisances to draw up lists of tenement houses together with names of owners, number of occupants and sanitary condition.[12] There is no evidence that this was implemented,

281

and almost fifty years later the existence of a tenement register remained in doubt. In 1866 bye-laws were introduced providing for a minimum of 300 cubic feet per person, regular inspection, water and sanitary accommodation and regular cleaning. Breaches of the regulations were to lead to fines.[13] When these measures were proposed they inevitably led to a protest from a group entitled the 'anti-political ratepayers society' who threatened to close their tenement houses rather than comply[14] and it would appear that Dublin Corporation relented.[15] Many of the 1866 regulations were still being regularly breached in 1914.

Between 1851 and 1877 only 200 houses were closed[16] while many deficiencies in tenement houses went uncontrolled. The ineffectiveness of the legal system against one landlord, a Mr. Woodroffe, is documented in detail by the Chief Secretary's Office. Mr. Woodroffe's cottages were outside the city in Kilmainham, but the legal problems were similar to those in the city. The case is documented in such detail because the officers of Islandbridge Barracks held the insanitary state of these cottages responsible for recurring epidemics of enteric fever.[17] (The fact that the Barracks drinking water came unfiltered from the river Liffey, adjoining a spot where the Barracks sewerage was discharged into the river was ignored). Mr. Woodroffe's nineteen cottages had only one privy between them and the overflow from this ran between two rows of cottages, ending in a stagnant pool.[18] The landlord was summoned a total of seventeen times between 1874 and 1876 and convicted on each occasion.[19] Convictions were not enforced and, when ultimately an order was sought to close the houses, the magistrate gave the (absent) Mr. Woodroffe time to comply.[20] When the case is last recorded the prosecutor failed to turn up in court on the appropriate day, and Mr. Woodroffe who had apparently never appeared in court escaped with a 6d fine and no evidence that the nuisance was suppressed.[21] Some of the enforcement problems would seem to reflect a measure of sympathy towards tenement owners. A divisional magistrate suggested that[22]

> Tenement owners are a large and influential class in
> Dublin both in and out of the corporation.

The case of Mr. Woodroffe would suggest that they were

282

not without influence among magistrates.

More practical problems of enforcement related to the condition of many tenements and the finances of their owners. Many tenements were built so closely together, without adequate yard space or ventilation, that provision of sanitary facilities or scavenging was impossible. Dr. Mapother, the medical officer of health described one set of buildings which exemplified this problem[23]

> Gill Square is a blind court opening by a narrow archway under one of the houses in Cole Alley, Meath St. in this city. Built on three sides of a square of about fifty feet, there are nine three-storey houses; the roofs are broken, the walls present a most unsafe and tumbledown aspect, the windows are boarded up for more than half their space; beings whose dirty ill-clad and spiritless aspect it is saddening to behold overcrowd every room to the utmost; there is but one yard for all, and in this, until last year, there was a hovel about eight feet square and ten feet high in which three adults were huddled.

The public health committee noted that of 1,648 tenements devoid of sanitary accommodation, 761 had no space where it could be supplied.[24] Many other houses, such as those described above, were so structurally unsound that efforts to install water would probably have led to their collapse.

Where space was available many owners proved either unwilling or unable to provide facilities and carry out necessary repairs. This was a reflection of financial problems and of the structure of ownership. Some tenements were said to have five levels of ownership, the average was apparently three.[25] Most houses were let by a head-landlord on long lease to a lessee, who in turn frequently let the house on a yearly lease. The second lessee in turn relet each room or group of rooms as weekly tenancies, while it was not unknown for the weekly tenant to sublet either a room, or part of a room to a lodger. This was very common in 1798.[26] Even in 1911, 17 families living in the tenement houses in Mabbot St. and Tyrone St. kept boarders. In fifteen cases, the family and lodger, frequently more than one, lived in a single room. Multiple ownership reduced the income from each house to a level where little surplus remained for investment. It also led to disputes concerning the legal responsibility for repairs. The most conspicuous landlord, the one who collected rent, was frequently only a yearly tenant and both unlikely and perhaps incapable of capital expenditure.

Tenement owners were found in every stratum of society, but while evidence is scanty, it would seem that the majority belonged to the class of small businessmen. The public health records provide some lists of delinquent landlords. In 1866, of thirty-five landlords whose houses were reported, it has proved possible to identify the occupations of twenty-two.[27] With the exception of a doctor who owned ten houses, an engineer who owned five, a cattle salesmaster who owned five and lived in suburban Blackrock, and a substantial glass and china manufacturer and retailer who owned one house, the remainder were owned by people of modest circumstances. Four owners actually lived in tenements, the remainder consisted of local grocers, publicans, a dairyman, dealer and furniture broker. The majority owned only one or two houses. Lengthier lists for the years 1884-87 confirm this picture.[28] Of 395 names, many recurring, only 97, or approximately one-third were identifiable from the directories. Of this number eighteen were grocers living either in tenements or in the neighbourhood; a further four were vintners, including our friend Mr. Woodroffe, four ran dairies, while five were victuallers or fishmongers. There was also a motley collection of tradesmen such as tanners, a slater, draper, painter and a dog fancier. Of the 97 identified, 65 belonged to this category and it seems probable that most of those unidentified were of similar, or even more modest background, too obscure to merit directory entries. The remaining 32 lived some distance from their properties, tended to own a markedly larger number of houses and belonged to a more prosperous class. The largest owner was a professor of Irish at the Catholic university who owned at least fifty houses, and probably substantially more. Other property was in his wife's name.[29] Other owners included the iron merchants Henshaw, Plunkett the maltsters, two doctors and one clergyman. A list of property owners in Bull Alley, a slum area cleared in 1899-1900 reveals a similar picture of dual types of owner. In addition to numerous local grocers and a painter, owners included a high-sheriff of Co. Down, a retired deputy surgeon general of the army, a high court registrar and a member of a Co. Limerick landed family.[30] Some of these may have held property which was sub-let on long lease and beyond their control. This was the case with John Dillon, nationalist M.P. and owner of three houses in Beresford St., by 1913 one of the worst tenement areas in the city. The houses in question, were in a very dangerous condition, but were let on long lease and beyond his control. He had merely inherited the premises, waived all compensation and did everything in his power to have them cleared so that Dublin Corporation could carry out a rebuilding scheme.[31]

A prominent representative of tenement owners, R.G. Pilkington, solicitor and chairman of the house owners protection association, stated that the more prosperous owners gradually gave way to smaller less solvent landlords.[32] Such a change, if it took place, may indicate the emergence of a different attitude towards tenement owners. In the mid nineteenth century, and for some decades thereafter, there is no evidence that tenement ownership was regarded as a disreputable activity. Tenement properties were advertised for sale, like other commercial or domestic property.[33] Ownership was for many years found among the city's most prominent businessmen. George Tickell, large furniture merchant and house agent, and Clontarf commissioner, had property rated in Clontarf at £1,421 and in Dublin at £2,097, while further property was held by his brothers and sisters.[34] His city property included a large quantity of tenement housing in Gardiner St. Even more striking is Joseph Meade, one of the city's largest builders, alderman and Lord Mayor. In 1900 he owned property in the city valued at £60,000 a considerable amount of this, tenements.[35] At his death nine tenement houses which he owned in Henrietta St. were auctioned and these alone had produced a gross rental of £1,500 per annum.[36] Yet Mr. Meade was actively involved in philanthropic housing schemes and was among the founders of the association for the housing of the very poor.[37]

This comparative lack of social stigma attached to tenement ownership, and the fact that ownership was widely diffused among the population, particularly among the shop-keeper and publican class which constituted the back-bone of Dublin Corporation, made control of tenement property more difficult. Men such as George Tickell resented corporation interference with tenement property in the same manner in which they would have resented interference in private housing investments in the suburbs. He claimed that Dublin Corporation 'served ridiculous notices'.[38] The spread of tenement ownership, even among corporation members obviously reduced the commitment to controlling such abuses.

For their part tenement landlords felt a strong sense of grievance, caught between municipal controls and tenants who flitted regularly leaving destruction and arrears of rent. One, admittedly anonymous owner, explained that 'the average tenement tenant has lax ideas about rent paying and to best the landlords is the first great object of their lives'.[39] Evicting tenants was a slow and difficult process, while windows and fixtures were regularly smashed. Piping, and gutters were sold as scrap metal, while bannisters were used as firewood. The Lord Mayor claimed in 1914, that 30,000 notices to quit were served annually on tenement occupiers, many against the same persons, a figure which makes evictions in rural Ireland, even at the peak of the land war, pale into insignificance.[40] Some tenements were beyond repair. Others, though structurally sound were filthy, overcrowded and in need of capital spending to provide sanitary facilities. Their condition could have been alleviated by adequate supervision and investment. Much overcrowding, as in the case of lodgers was the responsibility of tenants rather than landlords neglect. Cleansing and the provision of sanitary facilities required money and might have led landlords to recoup the cost in higher rents — which many tenants could not afford. Rent arrears, fragmented ownership and the comparative poverty of many landlords militated against improvements. Structural improvements rendered tenements liable to revaluation with no immediate prospect of higher income, while a deteriorating property could be revalued downwards. In 1884, Edward Spencer estimated that comparing seven city tenements at random, and seven modern, improved dwellings, each rated at £9, the rental of the tenements amounted to £322, that of the improved houses to £118. Tenement owners paid 10% of their income in rates, owners of improved houses, 27%.[41] Where the rental income was not divided among too many interests and arrears could be contained (a difficult problem) the return on investment could prove attractive. The gross rental on Mr. Meade's property in Henrietta St. amounted to £331-19-0 per annum, minus a head rent of £23-1-6. The total valuation was £131, and deducting rates and expenses left a profit of £128 for two houses, a profit almost equal to the valuation.[42]

Dublin Corporation was responsible for controlling the cleanliness overcrowding and sanitary facilities of tenement property. The 1878 public health act imposed on sanitary authorities the duty of deciding what closet accommodation was necessary and it empowered them to pass bye-laws for housing control, including provisions fixing the number of persons authorised to occupy each house. Dublin Corporation adopted bye-laws in 1880 which regulated matters such as the cubic footage available per person and required owners to provide 'sufficient sanitary accommodation'.[43] As tenements were generally only inspected during the day, when they were unlikely to be overcrowded, and 'sufficient sanitary accommodation' was not defined, these measures were ineffective. In 1890 further legislation provided for a register of tenement property, a measure introduced by this stage in many other cities, and the first measure dealing with dangerous buildings.

The register was not implemented until 1900 and even then was regarded as comparatively useless as it contained no information concerning the condition of properties, or whether they were overcrowded.[44] One contemporary claimed that there was no instance of a successful prosecution of a tenement owner for overcrowding.[45]

In 1902 a further set of bye-laws was introduced. These required the provision of one sanitary closet for every twelve people and held the landlord responsible for cleaning public areas such as stairs and passages, while tenants were responsible for individual apartments.[46] Some of these bye-laws were declared ultra vires in a 1910 court case, while Sir Charles Cameron dispensed many landlords from the closet requirements so that the 1914 housing inquiry discovered that over 20% of houses failed to meet that requirement.[47]

A provision was introduced granting rates rebates to landlords who improved tenements. This was designed to counteract the disincentive which the threat of revaluation might pose. The 1914 inquiry discovered that Sir Charles Cameron had authorised rebates to landlords whose properties had not been improved, many of which were in an insanitary, if not dangerous condition.[48]

On the introduction and enforcement of sanitary regulations the city's record is poor. Regulations controlling tenement property emerged at a considerably later date than in other British cities, even when bye-laws were passed, evidence suggests that they were not enforced. Men such as Sir Charles Cameron argued that rigid enforcement of regulations would lead to properties being closed and tenants being left homeless, and this is true in a broad sense.

This argument would suggest that the ideal was a complete absence of regulation. The 1914 housing inquiry, while admitting that any sudden enforcement of regulations would pose problems, felt that gradual enforcement would have produced results.[49]

> we cannot help coming to the conclusion that had a judicious but firm administration of the powers already already given been exercised during the last thirty-two years since the passing of the public health act 1878, it should have been possible without any undue hardship being afflicted to have produced a better state of affairs than exists at present.

A major factor in lax enforcement was the lack of political will to curb tenement landlords and to enforce improvement. The 1914 inquiry made considerable issue of the fact that sixteen members of the corporation were owners of tenement properties, or small cottages.[50] Of these the overwhelming majority owned from one to three houses, however three owners, Alderman Corrigan, Councillor Crozier and Alderman O Reilly between them owned a total of sixty-one properties, mostly tenements, the remainder small cottages. Virtually all their properties were deemed to be in poor repair, and all, plus some of the smaller owners, had received rates rebates, ostensibly for improvements

288

carried out. There are no figures available on tenement ownership among corporation members in earlier periods, but Dublin Corporation at no stage evinced any strong hostility to tenement landlords.

The strength of tenement landlords undoubtedly weakened legal enforcement. Perhaps the most appalling case concerned the collapse of a tenement house in Townsend St. in 1902, resulting in one death. This house was the property of Alderman Gerald O'Reilly a local publican and had been condemned as unsafe by the sanitary department, but the building inspector had disputed the verdict.[51] This did not prevent Alderman O Reilly being elected Lord Mayor in 1908. Corporation members obviously used their influence to prevent the enforcement of regulations against their properties. In 1908 the Sinn Fein councillor, P.T. Daly alleged that a letter came to the public health committee, bearing the endorsement of Sir Charles Cameron, medical officer of health, begging the committee not to proceed against Mr. McDowell, a corporation member, compelling him to put insanitary tenements into proper condition.[52] This, and other evidence, suggests that lax enforcement was not confined to councillors, but that officials were equally flexible. In 1909 an inquest on two men killed when a tenement house collapsed in North Cumberland St. was told by Alderman Tom Kelly, Sinn Fein member and chairman of the public health committee, and by a sub-sanitary officer, that they had issued several warning notices concerning the state of the property, but that 'senior corporation officials' had ignored these and not forced the owners to close dangerous properties.[53]

While enforcement of some regulations might have militated against the immediate interests of tenants by depriving them of housing and increasing rents, many cases of neglect appear to have been motivated by concern for landlords' rather than tenants' interests. The lack of control on dangerous houses cannot be regarded as in the interests of anybody other than landlords.

Much tenement property was incapable of improvement because of the age of the houses, or because of lack of space. In such circumstances the only option was closure and demolition. There appears to have been virtually no closures of houses by the health authorities prior to 1880.[54] After 1880 the pace quickened. By August 1881, Dr. Cameron reported that 800 houses had been closed since 1879.[55] During the month of August 1881 alone, a total of 48 houses, 22 rooms and 6 cellars were closed and an estimated 160 families or 800 persons made homeless. For the year 1881 as a whole a total of 447 houses were closed;[56] in 1882 the figure was 296, 1883, 271.[57] By 1884 it was claimed that of 2,300 houses deemed unfit for habitation in 1880, 1,875 had been closed.[58] Thereafter the fervour seems to have waned. The year 1887 saw only 79 closures; in 1892 there were 73.[59] What proportion of houses were reopened is unclear. In his 1881-82 report Cameron claimed that the majority of houses were repaired and reopened.[60] The 1886 report stated however that nearly one-third of all houses closed had not been reopened, while of the 271 houses closed in 1883, 211 remained closed at the end of the year.[61]

Local authorities were precluded from undertaking large-scale clearances of derelict property with public funds until 1875. Prior to this, such slum clearances as had occurred had been carried out by private interests such as railway companies or by local authorities building new streets.

Dublin did not experience these types of clearance to an significcanct extent, though this would not have been so if some of the ambitious central railway schemes had materialised. The 1875 artisans dwellings act provided following official representations that an area was unhealthy, the local authority could apply for a local government board inquiry and following a successful inquiry and the passing by Parliament of a provisional order, they could purchase the area, clear it, and either sell or let the land to an appropriate body who would build artisans dwellings, or themselves build such dwellings. In this latter case the houses would have to be sold by the local authority within ten years. It was envisaged that the scheme would be self-supporting with money being borrowed from the commissioners of public works, and repaid from the income generated from the sites.[62]

Following this act, Dr. Mapother and Mr. Neville, the city engineer, listed twelve unhealthy areas, all except two, south of the river Liffey.[63] Most were in the traditional working class district of the Coombe and its vicinity. Many were very small — one, Maclean's Lane contained a mere six houses, manure yards and a match factory, the largest, Boyne St. contained a total of twenty-seven houses, a coach builders yard, five stables with living rooms on top and several ruins. The areas were highly fragmented and revealed some of the problems in slum clearance. Although an area might contain derelict and unhealthy buildings it invariably contained perfectly adequate houses and business premises. Dublin Corporation faced the alternatives of clearing small areas which would make little impact on the total housing problem, or of paying considerable sums in compensation to businesses displaced by more comprehensive schemes. While some large-scale clearance schemes were carried out, many were small and fragmentary. As late as 1907 the local government board suggested that the [64]

> corporation frame some well-considered general housing scheme to be spread over a number of years rather than a number of small schemes at irregular intervals dealing with areas selected in a haphazard manner.

It is indicative of the haphazard approach to slum clearance, that one of the areas listed as unhealthy in 1876, Ormond Market, was only in the process of being cleared in 1914.

Dublin Corporation's first scheme was relatively ambitious: a four acre site in the Coombe. This proved an attractive proposition because the area was not densely populated, containing 984 persons, 320 tenancies in 110 dwellings. Much of the area was vacant, reflecting the decline of traditional industry. This was apparently not the worst area at the time. This honour was reserved for Bull Lane, an area close to St. Patrick's cathedral containing a reputed 200 prostitutes. It also contained numerous public houses so it was felt that compensation would prove expensive.[65] Even the comparatively vacant Coombe proved considerably more expensive that had originally been anticipated. In 1877 Dublin Corporation was authorised to borrow £18,386-5-9, to cover costs of acquisition, compensation, demolition, sewering and paving.[66] Compensation awards alone totalled £14,421-8-4, more than £3,000 in excess of estimates, due to the large awards made to tenement owners — of ten years net rental. Even weekly tenement keepers, those who sub-let from landlords, were given twenty-six weeks rental.[67] Among those seeking compensation was Professor Bryan O Looney, one of the most persistent violators of public health regulations. He claimed a total of £975 for four houses, all in defective condition which brought in an annual rent of £132.[68]

In Dublin's second clearance scheme, Plunkett St., acquisition was handled by a commercial firm, Messrs, Dudgeon Brothers. The claims of 105 yearly and weekly tenants — claims which had been honoured in the case of the Coombe, were ignored.[69] The fifty-two owners lodged claims totalling £39,891-3-11, but 27 of these sold out for £9,565, while the remainder settled at arbitration.[70] Messrs. Dudgeon recommended that acquiring property by private treaty was generally less expensive than arbitration.[71]

Acquisition costs again exceeded original estimates. By 1887 the total costs of the Plunkett St. site were more than double anticipated figures.[72]

The question of excessive compensation was considered by the *royal commission on the housing of the working class*. It proposed that awards be made by an official arbitrator, rather than by private valuator, and that powers be granted to compulsorily acquire vacant sites. It also proposed abolition of appeals to juries against arbitration awards. Other proposals involving extension of urban boundaries, revaluation of city property were of such broad scope that they were ignored. Dublin Castle, when asked by the Secretary of State to inform him what legislative changes in housing were required, adopted a conservative and rather confused stance.[73] In the event the only gain was the appointment of an arbitrator approved by the board of works. Part I of the 1890 *housing of the working class act* strengthened local authority powers by requiring them to condemn all premises 'unfit for habitation' and to compel their removal. This permitted demolition in many instances without compensation, except perhaps the site cost. Dublin Corporation continued to respect property rights, even in the case of virtually derelict property. The town clerk and the law agent, reporting on the proposed clearance and rebuilding of the Ormond Market area — one of the most long-standing slums remarked that the[74]

> Board wished the area dealt with under the Housing of the Working Classes Sections 30-37 — closing orders followed by demolition.

The Corporation has proceeded on the basis that utter confiscation of property is too drastic a remedy, even in the case of property owners who do not keep their property in a sanitary condition.

A 1905 Dublin housing conference attended by local MPs, the corporation and the Dublin trades council unanimously concluded that[75]

> It would be a fatal mistake to continue to put a premium on bad sanitation and improper housing by purchasing up at a ruinous price, insanitary areas and rebuilding them.

As late as 1910 Dublin Corporation was proceeding to clear Cook St., not under part I of the 1890 act, but under part II which dealt merely with unhealthy houses and entailed the payment of compensation.[76] There is some evidence that sums paid to owners of derelict property fell sharply by the early twentieth century. In 1908 the Clancy Act placed the cost of demolishing an insanitary dwelling on the owner, rather than on the rates.[77] When a Mrs. Ryan claimed compensation of £677 for cottage and tenement property in Church St. the arbitrator only awarded her a total of £43-18-0.[78] Even Mrs. Ryan did not claim compensation for nos. 66-68 Church St., her properties which had collapsed causing fatal injury some weeks previously.

The high cost of acquiring even unsafe and derelict property reflected the due respect accorded to property rights, even when the rights had obviously been misused. The falling cost of compensation also reflected some shift in attitudes, though astronomical claims were still lodged by the owners of derelict property as late as 1914. A further possible factor in some high payments was the desire of the local authority not to alienate property owners, or the wish to reward friends. On at least two occasions pubs owned by members of the corporation were acquired allegedly on favourable terms. A total of £4,200 was paid to Michael

293

O Reilly for his interest in a pub in Bride St.[79]

In this case a letter from the town clerk to the local government board claimed that there was 'no evidence that Mr. O Reilly benefitted more as a member of the corporation than he was entitled to'.[80] There is concrete evidence of misuse of funds in the case of Alderman Bergin. His pub, which had apparently been closed for two years was acquired for a sum initially proposed at £1,100. The premises were to be used as a caretakers house for the Foley St. flats. In the event a local government board refused to sanction any loan for this purpose.[81]

There is also indirect evidence that slum property may have been acquired by owners in the expectation of profiting from compensation. A motion in 1901 for an inquiry into the sums paid for property in Montgomery St., the names of the recipients, and information concerning all changes of ownership in recent years was defeated at a corporation meeting by a majority of thirty-three votes to four.[82]

Some of the areas acquired remained derelict for many years, and regular complaints were made about the extent of such property in the city centre. Some of the derelict property stemmed from the corporation's policy of acting against areas due for demolition by stringent enforcement of public health regulations which resulted in a gradual closing of houses, while others remained tenanted. This procedure was adopted to reduce costs, but it resulted in lengthy delays, particularly as the corporation, due to financial or administrative problems, tended to be slow to complete site acquisition. As early as 1903 it was stated that virtually all the properties in the Ormond Market area had been de-tenanted.[83] Not until 1913 however was arbitration undertaken, while actual building was delayed for several more years. In 1895 the ratepayers of Wood Quay ward protested about the extent of derelict space in their locality, and a delegation to the corporation alleged that the population had fallen from 28,000 to 18,000. A scheme sanctioned in 1893 had not yet been commenced.[84]

The delay in replacing derelict and demolished buildings with alternative accommodation resulted in overcrowding, and increased pressure on surviving tenement property. An article in 1900 remarked[85]

294

According as one set of tenements is cleared away another set spring up and the good work is thus counterbalanced by these fresh ramifications of the system. During the 1880s the population of the city fell. The total number of families in the city declined from 54,725 to 51,851 and those in fourth class accommodation from 23,360 to 19,342. While many of those displaced may have been forced to pay higher rents there is no evidence at this stage that housing policy increased overcrowding. The declining population of the 1880s reduced pressure on housing and gave the local authority an unparallelled opportunity to improve overall standards. In contrast the rising population of the 1890s and 1900s meant that the situation had worsened, and the number of families in fourth class accommodation rose to 21,429 in 1901, falling somewhat to 20,564 in 1911.

Families displaced by clearance schemes were faced with the necessity of finding alternative accommodation and also with the realization that they would not be rehoused in the dwellings which replaced their homes. This was the inevitable consequence of a policy which set out to provide superior accommodation without a rent subsidy, and both the philanthropic housing agencies and Dublin Corporation are equally guilty in this respect.

The philanthropic housing movement first emerged in Dublin in the 1860s, inspired, one suspects by the publicity given to London's Peabody Trust, founded in 1862. In 1865 a public meeting was held to discuss working class housing, chaired by Councillor Henry MacLean. The main emphasis was on the possible profits to be derived from such investment. The chairman reported the case of one gentleman receiving a reputed 20% return on his investment and emphasised that 'they could not carry on the project on a philanthropic principle. He was not disposed to waste money'.

Charles Geoghegan, subsequently architect to the Industrial Tenements Co. suggested renovating old houses at an average cost of £250, which he was confident would produce a return of £52 annually per house.[86] The following year Dr. Mapother the city's medical officer of health read a paper to the Royal Dublin Society on working class housing.[87] He was among the founding members of the Industrial Tenements Co. which was the first body in Dublin to build working class dwellings. With the exception of Dr. Mapother its committee was primarily composed of businessmen. It concentrated on building block tenements, four stories high, providing accommodation in the form of three room units, each costing £80.[88] This proved to be the only scheme carried out by the Industrial Tenements Co. They did not fully use the capital which they had raised and in 1914 had £800 invested in stock and paid their investors a 2% dividend.[89]

No subsequent body emerged until 1876 when the Artisans Dwellings Co. was formed. It was inspired by the reports of the Dublin sanitary association which increased public awareness of the poor state of working class housing, combined with the passing of the 1875 artisans dwellings act which provided for government loans on favourable terms to such societies. The initial subscribers represented most of the business, legal and medical elite of the city. The Earl of Pembroke subscribed £1,000, the two Guinness brothers, £5,000 each. The most notable absentees were members of Dublin Corporation. Only three current or former members were among the shareholders, though the representation of bodies such as the Dublin Chamber of Commerce was considerably stronger. Although it is impossible to discover the religious composition of the shareholders it seems that few Catholics were subscribers.[90]

The initial ventures of the company included a tenement block in Upper Buckingham St. and cottages in Upper Dominick St. while plans were drawn up for renovating existing tenements, though this was never carried out.[91] Tenement blocks were soon abandoned in favour of building cottages. By 1880 it was reported that the Buckingham St. block was proving 'difficult to fill', in contrast to the consistently excess demand for cottages. In 1880 they began building cottages in the Manor St. area on vacant land close to the city cattle market and this subsequently became one of the largest areas of Artisans Dwellings Co. investment. In December of the same year the foundation stone was laid on the Coombe housing scheme built on the slum site cleared by Dublin Corporation. A total of 210 houses, six shops and premises for two caretakers was provided.[92]

From an early stage the Artisans Dwelling Co. tended to concentrate on housing the more prosperous and more securely-employed sections of the working class. The properties generally consisted of three-roomed cottages, too expensive for the unskilled working class. The earliest cottages built in Upper Dominick St. were built at an average cost of £120 and let at a rental of 5/2 per week, which was approximately 40% of the wages of an unskilled worker. Even the *Irish Builder* criticised such rents as 'too high'.[93] A statement in an 1881 report noted that of the 56 houses in Kirwan St., all except three were let to 'respectable tenants'.[94] In 1883 the secretary of the Artisans Dwellings Co. wrote to the Under-Secretary offering accommodation in their cottages to members of the Dublin metropolitan police. The Lord Lieutenant was not prepared to make an official arrangement, though the Under-Secretary noted that 'many DMP are already tenants' and rejected any suggestion that a bargain could be made whereby rents for Artisans Dwellings Co. houses could be deducted from police pay at source.[95] Of the 202 tenants of the Coombe housing scheme, 61 were labourers, but the remainder belonged to the skilled working class with a few members of the lower middle class.[96] The labourers housed tended to be in secure employment. Further proof that many of the early tenants did not suffer severe financial pressure is provided by a survey showing that a total of 147 of the 331 families housed by 1881 had acquired more accommodation as a result of their move, while only 35 sought less. Those who had increased their accommodation paid substantially higher rents, 4/4 per week compared with a previous average of 3/-.[97] This 'trading up' took place at a time of unprecedented depression among the city's working class suggesting that the Artisans Dwellings tenants were somewhat unrepresentative.

The Artisans Dwellings Co. continued to develop a similar type of housing catering for respectable tenants. By 1914 they had built a total of 3,081 dwellings housing a total of 13,938 tenants. The peak of the company's activitiy was in the 1880s and 1890s. They built no houses after 1907 because of unfavourable costs. Most of their housing was built on virgin land on the outskirts of the city or in the suburbs. This reduced total costs but meant that their contribution towards rebuilding the decrepit housing fabric of central areas was slight. The Coombe scheme proved exceptional in this respect.

While the company consistently catered for the more prosperous members of the working class, it served an undoubted need. Its housing was consistently popular, vacancies were rare and arrears minimal, though several ejectment notices were served against tenants in the Coombe who refused to pay increased rents following the installation of water closets in 1897.[98] The company was also profitable, paying a dividend of 3% as early as its first ordinary meeting in 1878.[99] Dividends averaged 4% during the 1880s, by the 1880s they had reached 4½% and were at their maximum level of 5% from 1899.[100] By 1900 the *Freeman's Journal* raised the question whether 'there is such a thing however in such a company as being too successful'.[101] One shareholder at the company's annual general meeting wondered

> whether the objects for which the company was originally established are not being lost sight of in pursuit of a merely commercial success.

That the company had a strong commercial purpose is not in doubt. In 1897 the chairman, Sir Richard Martin in a letter to the *Irish Times* stated that the company was 'subscribed to by people who took an ordinary venture'.[102] It seems probable that a strong commercial instinct existed from the outset. In 1886 when Dublin Corporation first embarked on the building of working class housing the company issued a strong protest[103]

> Your directors regret that the corporation have determined on the further erection of classes of dwellings which cannot fail to compete unfairly with those erected by the company, as they are to be let at rents involving an annual loss to the ratepayers. The effect must be to discourage private enterprise.

Any group genuinely concerned about the provision of working class housing could only have welcomed further investment. It is somewhat ironic that the company began to pay its maximum dividend in 1899 at a time when the volume of its building activities was declining and continued to pay this amount after 1907 when all new investment

298

ceased.

Many of the criticisms levelled at the Artisans Dwellings Co. have also been made of similar bodies in London. It appears that the Dublin company showed a significantly greater tendency than its London equivalents to cater for the better-off end of the market in a city where the average standard of housing was notoriously poor. By 1914 the mean rent of their properties was 5/5, a sum substantially in excess of that paid by the majority of the working class.

The urge by philanthropic bodies to house less desirable sections of the working class emerged belatedly in Dublin. Viscount Iveagh, a notable contributor to London working class housing, founded the Guinness Trust in 1890 with a gift of £50,000. In 1899 they acquired the Bull Alley area and built a series of tenements which were subsequently managed by the Iveagh Trust. A total of 586 tenements were built, 129 with one room, 366 with two rooms and 91 with three rooms. The emphasis on smaller properties was more in tune with the needs of the city's unskilled workers. The 1914 housing inquiry claimed that rents for Iveagh Trust tenements averaged 2/-,[105] though in 1903 rents would seem to have ranged from 1/9 to 5/- with a two-roomed tenement costing from 3/3 to 4/-. However the Iveagh Trust is notable in being the philanthropic venture of one individual. Financial considerations did not predominate as they did in the Artisans Dwelling Co. However no other group of private individuals financed cheap housing on the same scale.

Table III Housing built by philanthropic agencies by number of rooms, %[104]

	1	2	3	4 rooms or more
Dublin, all	8.2%	27.1%	38.9%	25.7%
Artisans Dwelling Co	2.25%	18.3%	46.9%	33.4%
London	17.1%	45.2%	35.4%	2.3%

The only significant group initiatives for housing the poor consisted of schemes to buy and renovate existing tenements on the lines adopted by Octavia Hill. In 1897 Sir

Charles Cameron in a public letter appealed to 'benevolent men' to provide finance for housing the poorest inhabitants.[106] Although slum clearance had been driving such people from their homes for many years it seems only in the later 1890s, that public awareness of this problem emerged. In an article publicising a meeting to discuss the question the *Irish Times* noted[107]

> Many in Dublin cannot afford to pay even 2/-. They live in courts, lanes, etc. and the poorest class tenements. These are 'unhealthy' and many of them are cleared by the Corporation and on these sites new dwellings are erected but evicted people cannot afford the rent of the new. They have sought refuge in the lowest class houses in other districts and in the process of time the districts to which they have migrated will become as unhealthy as were those from which they had been evicted.

The belated awareness of this problem may reflect a lack of concern for working class interests, alternatively it may indicate that the problem was becoming more acute. The clearances of the 1880s took place at a time of falling population. At some stage during the 1890s this trend was reversed and the city's population began to grow at a relatively rapid pace. This worsened overcrowding and housing conditions for the poorest.

The Association for the Housing of the Very Poor proposed to let tenements at rents of approximately 1/- per week, catering for those earning between 5/- and 12/-, widows, casual labourers and others who lacked stable employment.[108] This body differed significantly in membership from the Artisans Dwellings Co. The founders included Charles Dawson, a prominent member of the Statistical and Social Inquiry Society, insurance agent and comptroller of Dublin corporation rates department, and Joseph Meade, prominent builder, one-time Lord Mayor of Dublin, large-scale investor in property, including tenement property. Other members of Dublin corporation were actively involved. One meeting was addressed by the Lord Mayor,[109] while a branch meeting of Arran Quay ratepayers association, chaired by J. Crozier — denounced by the 1914 housing inquiry as one of the corporation's tenement landlords' en-

300

dorsed the proposal to establish such a company. By 1914 they had provided 157 single-room tenements at rents ranging from 1/6 to 4/4. Despite a philanthropic basis, they paid a dividend of 2%.[110] A similiar, though smaller body which also engaged in renovating tenements was established by past-pupils of Alexandra College. Unlike the Association for Housing of the Very Poor this body had the avowed purpose of raising the moral tone of the tenants by teaching them cleanliness and thrift.[111] They only contributed sixty units, so that the overall improvement in the housing stock was slight.

Apart from the paternalist supervision of tenants which would alienate some families, there remains the fact that a significant proportion of the Dublin tenement stock was structurally unsound. In 1914 it was estimated that only 1,516 tenements housing 8,295 families or 27,052 persons could be classified as 'structurally sound, capable of being put in good repair'. Of the remainder a total of 1,526, housing 6,831 families were deemed 'unfit for habitation and incapable of being rendered fit', while small houses accommodating a further 1,136 families were in a similar condition. The remaining 2,288 houses inhabited by 10,696 families were so 'decayed or badly constructed' that they were 'approaching the border line of unfit for habitation'.[112] It was estimated that a massive renovation programme of existing tenements would only house a total of 13,000 families, leaving an estimated 5,991 to be rehoused elsewhere.[113] This left the burden of the housing problem, not in the realm of reconstruction, but in the building of new units. Given the economic limitations of organisations such as the Artisans Dwellings Co. the residual responsibility inevitably devolved on Dublin Corporation.

Dublin Corporation's first venture into house building took place during the 1880s in Barrack St. subsequently to be renamed Benburb St. There was the advantage that the corporation were themselves ground landlords of the area and when leases fell in, a substantial portion of the property was in immediatee need of rebuilding, but with the exception of a number of vintners few tenants seem to have been capable or willing to rebuild.[114] The evidence to the 1914 housing inquiry noted that corporation building in the

301

area was initiated 'at the request of a number of ratepayers in the district'.[115] Site clearance, assessment of valuations and other problems meant considerable delay so that the scheme was not completed until 1887. It provided a significantly more basic type of accommodation than most of the Artisans Dwellings Co. schemes, including 65 single and 65 double tenements and a mere 9 three roomed units, plus five shops. The rents charged ranged from 1/6 to 2/- for single rooms, to 3/- to 4/- for double tenements, sums that bore a reasonable relationship to normal working class rents. A contemporary survey of a slum district by Michael Davitt revealed 58 labourers paying an average of 2/4¼ rent from a total income of 12/4½, while thirteen households headed by women paid an average of 2/1¼ from a total income of 8/6.[116]

Low rents meant low standards of accommodation. By 1897 the Benburb St. tenements were deemed to be insanitary and required alterations.[117] A further low priced scheme of two and three room cottages with rents ranging from 2/- to 4/6 were erected on vacant land at Bow Lane West in 1889. The tenants were almost exclusively low earning unskilled workers: 47 labourers, 12 porters, 1 shop assistant, 2 cabdrivers, 5 draymen, 1 boatman, 2 charwoman, 1 dressmaker, 1 needlewoman, 1 nurse and five shops.[118]

These two early schemes suggest that Dublin Corporation was making a conscious effort to house the most needy section of the population in relatively basic accommodation at low rents. The next proposed scheme, that in Blackhall Place, would appear to represent a change in policy. It was proposed to erect houses at rents varying from 2/6 per week to 7/6 per week.[119] The Treasury voiced strong objections to the building of such expensive houses and suggested the substitution of smaller dwellings renting at 2/6 to 3/6 per week.[120] Sir Charles Cameron also expressed his opposition, arguing that no local authority housing should cost more than 3/6 and that tenements renting from 1/- to 1/6 were desirable.[121] The Treasury's more modest housing would have represented an income of £218-8-0 compared with £292-10-0 in the case of the more expensive housing and this presumably swung the balance. When complete the scheme contained a variety of accommodation ranging from tenements renting from 2/6 to 3/6 to the much criticised 7/6 houses.[122] Despite the effort to offset losses on the cheaper accommodation by the income from the more expensive houses, Blackhall Place showed an annual loss of approximately £29.[123] It would appear that the rise in building costs in the early 1890s was a factor in switching corporation policy towards larger and more highly-rented accommodation. The problems which this posed, and the fact that some corporation schemes differed little from those of the Artisans Dwellings Co. is evident from St. Joseph's Cottages. This was a development of eighty, three-roomed cottages built at the rear of Eccles St. in an area previously known as White's and Eccles Lane. These were rented at 4/6 per week [124] but as Sir Charles Cameron noted[125]

> the families who resided in those lanes paid 2/- to 3/- per week. Except in the case of a couple of shops not one of the families who had resided in those lanes returned to the cleared site; they took rooms in the neighbourhood at the same rents they had previously paid. I found that many of the families who took possession of the cottages had paid higher rents than 4/6 for their former dwellings.

He also remarked that

> as a rule the occupiers of dwellings let at from 4/6 or more per week occupy but little of the attention of the Sanitary Inspector. Some of them live in slum areas, but except for their environment they are not placed under insanitary conditions. If all the working classes in Dublin could afford to pay 4/6 and upwards for their dwellings there would be a very limited, if any, slum area.

When the extensive Bride's Alley scheme, erected on the derelict land between St. Patrick's and Christchurch cathedrals was initially proposed in 1896 it included some three-storey, single family shops and houses renting for £1 per week in addition to accommodation at 7/6.[126] The local government board refused to sanction loans for shops[127] and the overall accommodation became more modest, the number of tenants was increased from 128 to 198[128] and the highest rent set at 6/-. In 1914 the mean earnings of household heads in Bride's Alley was almost 27/- per week, con-

303

siderably in excess of the average among tenement dwellers.[129] Fewer tenements were ultimately built as part of the site was sold to Lord Iveagh for a swimming bath, but even the reduced development was not finally completed until 1911, eighteen years after it first received consideration.[130]

The alterations in the Bride's Alley proposals suggest growing awareness of the need to concentrate on providing basic accommodation. In 1900 it was proposed to acquire a 2½ acre site in Montgomery St. and Mabbot St. the heart of the city's 'Night-town' and to use this to house up to 2,000 of the very poor.[131] This scheme raised several interesting issues. The *Irish Times* alleged that it was being promoted with the ulterior motive of clearing out a 'loathsome locality',[132] and there is little doubt that proposals to build cottages, or three-roomed tenements on this site would have been questioned in the belief that decent families would refuse to live in the area.

The public health committee in its outline noted that dwellings were[133]

> most urgently needed for labourers, porters, small dealers, pedlars, hawkers, charwomen, rag-pickers, night watchmen, the inferior class of seamstresses, sandwich men etc.

and it proposed to house 580 families, an estimated 2,494 persons in 484 single units and 80 two-room units with rents ranging from 1/3 to 2/6 for single, and 2/3 to 3/- for double flats. Each unit was to have self-contained sanitary accommodation.

From the outset Montgomery St. was assumed to be unprofitable with an initially estimated annual loss of almost £125 on a capital expenditure of £72,000.[134] In the event even the poor shunned such an address and in 1911 it was reported that the tenements were 'almost entirely unlet' and rents were reduced by 50% in order to reduce the estimated loss which amounted to £6,000 per annum.[135] Those tenants who were attracted were apparently not of a respectable class, tending to run brothels or shebeens on the premises as the sometimes hilarious evidence given to the Dublin disturbances inquiry indicates.[136]

The extension of the city boundaries after 1900 provided the corporation with relatively cheap suburban sites and with the need to provide working class accommodation for the residents of Kilmainham, Drumcondra and Clontarf. Two to four-roomed cottages in Clontarf were provided at rents ranging from 2/6 to 4/6, while houses of three and four rooms at Inchicore cost tenants from 4/- to 7/6.[137] These had the advantage of considerably lower site costs and lower densities per acre.

Table IV Relative costs of housing scheme [138]

	Per person	Per room	Per family	No. to acre
Benburb St	£45-2-1	—	£193-17-9	1,238
Bow Lane	£27-8-1	£56-14-1	£120-1-2	254
Blackhall Pl.	£37-7-10	£66-13-8	£160-16-6	418
St. Joseph Pl.	£76-4-4	£109-4-1	£327-14-8	160
Bride's Alley	£133-5-0	£232-19-10	£573-2-3	250
Montgomery St.	£32-3-3	£114-8-10	£138-5-6	989
Elizabeth St. Drumcondra	£41-8-9	£59-3-11	£177-11-0	283
Inchicore	£32-5-3	£49-12-8	£161-6-3	138

Mass transplanting of workers to the suburbs was not feasible. Some could undoubtedly move, but the nature of the city's workforce, their dependence on casual earnings particularly from docking, and the need for many women to supplement income by charring or dealing necessitated city centre housing. The area in most immediate need of clearance in 1914, Ormond Market, was occupied almost exclusively by workers in the fish and vegetable markets, who started work at hours not served by public transport.[139]

Even suburban schemes faced financial difficulties. Official returns show that all corporation housing schemes completed by 1906 showed a loss, some as in the case of Bride's Alley, the considerable sum of £3,748. The most solvent were Bow Lane Cottages (loss £93-5-6) and Blackhall Place (loss £142-7-7). These suggest a more successful outcome from cottages than from block buildings[140] reflecting greater building costs in the case of multi-storey dwellings and the aspirations of potential tenants. Despite a long history of tenement accommodation workers aspired to live in cottages,

305

particularly those in a position to pay 4/- or more in rent. This was certainly the position among the Dublin working class in the post World War One period.[141] In 1906 a local government board inquiry was told by the city treasurer that losses on all corporation housing averaged 2% of total costs, but that in the case of block buildings the figure was 4% and for three-roomed tenements, 5%.[142] Even cottages showed increasing losses from 1904 due to increased interest rates. Schemes planned on a notional interest rate of 3½% turned into loss-making ventures faced with charges of 4%.[143] Inchicore housing was initially expected to show a profit of £121 on a total expenditure of £24,265. This included a number of five-roomed houses with bathrooms renting at 10/-[144] which the local government board refused to finance stating that[145]

> it is open to doubt whether a house to be rented at 10/- a week is of a class which ought to be provided by the corporation under the acts in view of the fact that large numbers of houses renting at 5/- to 10/- a week have been and are being erected by private enterprise in the city.

The removal of these expensive houses and the increased interest charges removed the profit and even these houses erected on cheap sites showed a loss.[146]

The frequently voiced assertions that Dublin Corporation, in common with the Artisans Dwellings Company was failing to house the most deserving of the city's working class is confirmed by a comparative analysis of Census enumerators' returns for Artisans Dwellings Co. schemes, corporation schemes and tenements. Only corporation schemes within the original city boundaries were examined, as those in the newly-annexed suburbs were built for suburban residents, while the Montgomery St. scheme was excluded because it was untypical of corporation developments. The results reveal that tenement families were more likely to be headed by women, more likely to be unskilled labourers and to have fewer working men per household. They were overwhelmingly Dublin-born, a fact which correlates with their lower socio-economic status. Tenement households contained a significant proportion of illiterates, 29.1% of such households had one or more illiterate mem-

306

Table V Comparative Household Structure 1911

	Corporation	Tenement	Artisans Dwelling
N	337	402	399
Mean Household size	5.43	3.70	4.44
% F. head	15.13%	30.84%	13.78%
Extended fam. %	12.46%	9.2%	11.52%
Boarders % Ho. Holds	10.08%	6.46%	10.77%
Incomplete %	5.34%	6.21%	4.01%
Mean Age M. Head	44.04 yrs.	41.10 yrs.	41.16 yrs.
Mean Age F. Head	53,71 yrs.	52.4 yrs.	54.7 yrs.
Occupied M per Ho.	1.48	1.16	1.37
Occupied F. per Ho.	0.53	0.46	0.3
Birthplace Head and Wife			
Dublin	52.15%	79.64%	34.95%
Ireland	41.48%	18.09%	50.06%
U.K.	5.67%	1.45%	12.87%
Elsewhere	0.68%	0.8%	2.1%
Birthplace Others			
Dublin	89.2%	95.9%	71.67%
Ireland	8.94%	3.47%	19.17%
U.K.	1.66%	0.59%	7.77%
Other	0.18%	—	1.38%
Male Occupations			
non-manual	5.25%	1.85%	19.38%
skilled manual	36.34%	21.29%	40.88%
semi-skilled	12.6%	4.62%	10.74%
unskilled	45.79%	72.22%	28.98%
of the above Brewing, Distilling	6.93%	0.92%	11.13%
'Secure' Employment	11.55%	3.0%	22.45%

bers. In both corporation and Artisans dwellings illiteracy
was virtually unknown and was generally confined to elderly
women.

The residents of the Artisans Dwellings Co. properties emerge as a genuine elite. Almost one male worker in five was engaged in non-manual activities, while one in three of the workers — many of them unskilled had secure and relatively well-paid employment in brewing, the railways or the civil service. Many were either active or former members of the army or police, which contributed to the high proportion of non-Dubliners. In one road of five-roomed houses, Oxmantown Road, almost 35% of households were Protestant. The impresssion emerges that Artisans Dwelling Co. houses were generally allocated to workers in secure and better paid employment. Further evidence of relative comfort is the small proportion of working females. Many adult daughters were unoccupied.

Dublin Corporation dwellings residents represent a group transitional between the tenement and Artisans Dwellings Co. population. They contain the highest proportion of male workers per family and the mean household size is high, as is the mean age of household head. This suggests that many unskilled families could only afford to pay the rent of a corporation property because of the earnings of sons and daughters. In other cases boarders provided a necessary supplement. Many corporation dwellings were extremely overcrowded. Families of ten in two-roomed flats were not uncommon.

Housing statistics suggest increased overcrowding in 1901 which was only slightly reduced by 1911. The gains which had been made in reducing overcrowding prior to 1891 were negatived by the emergence of a rising population combined with economic recession, unemployment and higher interest rates which made philanthropic housing schemes uneconomic. Much of the housing stock was on the point of collapse, as the series of fatal accidents indicates. Rising interest charges caused the Artisans Dwellings Co. to stop building in 1907 and the deficit on the corporation's housing fund rose from £7,335-1-3 in 1903-4 to £10,511-9-7 by 1911-12.[147]

Not surprisingly, given the precedents for solving other social problems, such as peasant proprietorship, agricultural labourers' housing, plus the fact that the state was aiding improved housing for families in the congested

308

districts, a call emerged for state intervention in Dublin housing. The *Irish Times* in a leading article in 1903 noted[148]

It is daily becoming more evident that the question of the poor, their housing and the manner their children are employed, will require to be taken in hand by the government.

The call for state involvement could be supported by unionists, sceptical of the efficiency and the ability of the city's nationalist administration. In subsequent years it was taken up by nationalist politicians.

The reorganisation and democratisation of local government after 1898 provided a new forum for discussing Irish housing problems. Conferences seem to have been in the air, with the repeated efforts to resolve the university question and the more successful outcome to the Recess committee and the land conference.[149] In 1903 the first of a series of bi-annual conferences attended by MPs from the Dublin area, members of the corporation, representatives of the county council and the Dublin trades council examined the housing question.

They were firmly of the belief that the ideal housing for the city's workers consisted of cottages built on the outskirts which could be used to rehouse city centre residents of condemned properties. By first building cottages and removing families, it was argued demolition could proceed without intensifying overcrowding. To further this proposal they recommended that the clauses of the 1890 act which permitted British local authorities to build houses outside their municipal boundaries be extended to Ireland. They also expressed the first tentative approval for town planning and the provision of open spaces and shopping facilities in new housing areas.

Concerning existing tenements they recommended speeding up the legal process, more rapid closure and demolition of houses, greater use of section I of the 1890 act which would permit demolition without compensation and an extension of the loan repayment period.[150]

In 1908 the corporation drafted a bill to obtain some of these powers. In particular they wished to compulsorily acquire sites without being required to give notice, and without an official inquiry or an appeal. The purpose of these clauses was described as 'to get rid of the intervention of the local government board'.[151] The corporation also proposed that £5m. deposited in Irish post office savings should be set aside for housing purposes and lent to local authorities at an interest rate of 2½% per annum.[152]

This bill was not introduced, as it was rejected by a citizens plebiscite.[153] Negotiations with Irish MPs bore some fruit when the 1908 *housing of the working classes (Ireland) act*, the so-called Clancy act, was passed.[154] This left the owner of an insanitary dwelling responsible for its demolition costs, permitted local authorities to build houses outside their municipal boundaries and the leasing of land acquired by a local authority to an improvement society for a nominal sum. It also removed the need for parliamentary approval for housing schemes, reducing transactions costs and delays in proceeding. The most important clause was financial; housing loans could be extended to a maximum of sixty years, while house borrowing was not included in a local authority's borrowing limit, giving heavily pressed cities such as Dublin considerable financial leeway. New housing schemes were granted a two-year moratorium on debt repayment. The act is revolutionary for its introduction of the first, admittedly tiny, subsidy. The fund of the suitors of the supreme court, amounting to £180,000 was to be invested and the interest, amounting to approximately £6,000 per annum was divided among Irish local authorities in proportion to their housing expenditure, the money to be used to defray the cost of housing schemes.[155] This measure, by admitting the possibility of a subsidy, and by distinguishing between the Irish and British housing legislation, if only to a slight extent, was invariably followed by pressure for further state assistance.

With the prospect of Home Rule, attention was focussed on the administrative competence of Dublin Corporation with the *Irish Times* demanding a vice-regal inquiry and arguing that 'the slums of Dublin will still be there whether we get Home Rule or not'[156] The appearance in Dublin of a Town Planning Exhibition sponsored by the Aberdeens and addressed by Professor Geddes added another dimension,[157] while on a more immediate plane, the collapse

310

of five tenements with one fatality gave a grim urgency to the question.[158]

In 1912 the first conference of the Association of Municipal Authorities in Ireland passed a unanimous resolution[159]

> that the State should provide financial facilities for Municipal and Urban Housing schemes not less favourable than have been provided in the rural districts under the Labourers Act.

They also proposed a deputation to the Prime Minister and the Chief Secretary. The resolution was not immediately implemented. Instead the association prepared a pamphlet, *Housing of the working classes in cities and towns in Ireland. The need for state and for municipal housing schemes* and the meeting with the Chief Secretary was delayed until the Association's second annual conference, held in Dublin in October 1913.

By this stage the housing question had acquired greater urgency with yet another fatal tenement collapse in Church St. and the Dublin lock-out. Attention was focussed on the living conditions of workers in an effort to account for labour unrest[160]

> The members of the ITWU live for the most part in slums like Church St . . . . We believe that if every unskilled labourer in Dublin were the tenant of a decent cottage of three or even two rooms, the city would not be divided into two hostile camps.

One speaker at the Municipal Authorities Conference emphasised that as a result of the Church St. disaster 'public opinion is thoroughly alive for the first time in memory'.[161] The demands of the 1912 conference for equality of treatment with the rural labourers were reiterated and the responsibility of the state received further emphasis. One paper, ostensibly an analysis of the costs of alternative types of housing, also contained the statement that the problem was[162]

> though nominally and officially a municipal one, (is) in reality both in cause and effect of national dimensions and importance.

Lorcan Sherlock, the Lord Mayor urged solidarity between urban and rural interests[163]

> When the farmers of Ireland were in a difficult position

311

over land purchases, the people of the cities and towns of Ireland made no protest against the pledging of the credit of the whole country for agricultural labourers' houses.

On the same basis he demanded that
the credit of the people of the rest of the country must now be pledged for the purpose of those in the cities and towns.

The deputation which met the Chief Secretary demanded an extension of the subsidy from the current £6,000 to £20,000, an extension of the repayment period from 60 to 80 years, as was permissable under the Clancy act, and state loans at rates of interest 'as near as possible' to those charged for the housing of agricultural labourers. Loans for rural cottages bore a charge of £2-1-7 per £100 to cover interest and sinking fund, compared with 5¾% in the case of urban authorities, though more recent Clancy loans were available at 3½%. The Chief Secretary's reply promised no immediate assistance[164]

The rural problem in Ireland was a peculiar one requiring and certainly receiving very advantageous pecuniary assistance from the State.

The problem of urban slums however was
not confined to Ireland, but involves the opening of the flood-gates of public grants to the other cities of the Kingdom.

This deputation was followed by one from the Women's National Health Association, demanding government assistance for housing and supporting the demands made by the Association of Municipal Representatives. Their potential influence was strengthened by the active involvement of Ishbel, Countess Aberdeen. Other bodies rapidly jumped on the bandwagon. A deputation some weeks later from the Housing and Town Planning Association of Ireland, demanded a vice-regal inquiry.[165] Support for this cause followed from the insurance commission of the borough of Dublin, who saw housing as the key factor in the city's high tubercular death rate, while the Irish Women's Suffrage and Local Government Association, immediately demanded representation on the commission[166] as did the Dublin citizen's association, a body which claimed to represent the ratepayers,[167] Pembroke township added their voice in favour of an inquiry.[168]

At the initial meeting with the municipal authorities, Birrell promised an inquiry and did so in relatively optimistic tones.[169]

> You won't be able to make a case which entitles you to preferential treatment but I think you can make out a case which puts you in the very front rank of those which demand assistance.

It is not clear whether this commitment envisaged a vice-regal inquiry which would represent various shades of opinion, or a departmental inquiry composed of government officials who were experts. All the popular demands were for the former type of inquiry, but there is little doubt that the composition of such a body would have posed problems given conflicting opinions of unionists, nationalists, employers, workers, ratepayers, members of Dublin Corporation and various lobbying groups such as the Women's National Health Association. Given the active involvement of the Aberdeens in housing and public health questions there is little doubt that they might have appointed an interesting team who might have favoured some radical solutions to the Dublin housing problem.

This did not happen. Once the first mention of an inquiry was made on 17 October, the Dublin Castle bureaucracy argued the need for a strictly factual investigation. In a memorandum attached to the records of the 17 October meeting it was suggested that an inquiry was needed which would examine the extent and quality of working class housing available in the city; the numbers living in the different categories of housing and the occupations of the inhabitants, their wages and rents paid; the number of vacant sites available and the cost of rehousing the numbers which the inquiry would reveal to be in need of rehousing.[170] A further memorandum also attached tended to dismiss the need for massive state finance, arguing that the money available under the Clancy act was 'more than sufficient to discharge *all* liabilities under section 5 (of the 1908 act)'. This merely demonstrated the extreme restrictions posed on the payment of this subsidy, but did not imply that further state money, available on more generous terms would not be in demand.

The attack on the concept of a vice-regal inquiry continued. A lengthy memorandum dated 31 October noted that a vice-regal commission would lack the power to summon witnesses or to examine them under oath, while it would be dependent for its facts on the evidence of witnesses who chose to come forward, frequently amateurs with causes to support. In contrast it was argued that a departmental committee could summon expert witnesses and require the production of documents. There was the added factor of time. A vice-regal commission could only meet while its members were free from their other duties, and it was argued that none had ever reported in less than a year, while a departmental inquiry, conducted by full-time experts with power to examine confidential records could issue a more speedy report. It was suggested that in order to 'elicit opinion' a 'limited number' of public sittings could be held.[171]

This report which was accepted, effectively determined the nature and limits of the investigation. There were certain merits in this approach and in the belief of the local government board that 'the question is really one of finance and administration'.[172] The resulting report provided unrivalled documentation concerning the state of the city's housing, the financial balance sheet of existing corporation schemes, the rents paid in existing tenements, the quality of such tenements, incomes of tenement inhabitants and the costs of undertaking the necessary rehousing schemes. It revealed that a total of 14,000 houses were urgently needed to relieve congestion and close tenements which were unfit for habitation.[173] To put the problem in context it should be noted that by 1913 Dublin corporation had succeeded in rehousing a total of 1,385 families in the previous thirty years.[174] Capital expenditure to 1913 had amounted to £354,215-19-0, a further £3½m. would be required.The estimated rent of new sanitary dwellings would be 5/5½, if they were not to show a loss. Only 6.95% of tenants of existing tenement residents paid rent in excess of 5/- and it is questionable whether this small group were in need of rehousing. Assuming a significant subsidy from rates, costing 1/5½ in the £, rents would still amount to 3/7. Only 28.85%

of the tenement dwellers paid rents in excess of 3/-.[175] The financial basis of the proposed rehousing scheme looked totally unfeasible, even if bodies such as the Treasury or the local government board had actually permitted Dublin Corporation to borrow £3½m.

At this point the limitations of the inquiry become evident. The report provided detailed and accurate evidence of the dimensions of the housing problem and the money needed to remedy this, it was in no position to make political suggestions for financing such a scheme. There is also a one-sided approach to the inquiry. In both evidence and report, Dublin Corporation emerges as a seriously negligent, perhaps even corrupt institution: a body which has failed to enforce existing sanitary legislation, which has granted rebates designed for improved tenements to premises which were unfit for habitation, which numbered among its members a total of sixteen tenement owners. Such criticism is undoubtedly valid and pertinent, particularly when one considers the lack of urgency shown to the housing problem. However the local government board, as the supervising agency, also played an important role and it would appear that their actions might merit scrutiny, if only the extent to which they had failed to police the activities of Dublin Corporation. Pembroke urban council, by no means a friend of Dublin Corporation, requested the Chief Secretary to establish 'a further independent inquiry unlimited in its scope' and urged that the terms of reference should include[176]

an Inquiry also of the Treasury, Board of Works and Local Government Board's failure to administer the existing housing laws with regard to loans.

Not surprisingly, these matters were not analysed. When the conclusions of the report strayed from the path of detailed financial and demographic calculations it displayed an extraordinary faith in the deterrent powers of stringent local enforcement of sanitary legislation, combined with a touching belief in the ability of private enterprise to adequately house the working population — ideas which would seem to have been thoroughly discredited by 1914.[177]

A firm administration would however, in our opinion, have deterred the rural labourers from coming into the city and the absence of such administration must therefore be held to have produced a converse result and to have had the indirect effect of keeping wages at a low level.

We suggest, also that the non-enforcement of the sanitary laws has permitted dwellings which are not fit for habitation to be inhabited by the poorer classes at rents which though in some cases low in themselves are altogether excessive for the class of accommodation provided.

Further it would seem the want of a firm administration has created a number of owners with but little sense of their responsibilities as landlords, and that it has helped much in the demoralisation of a number of the working classes, and increased the number of inefficient workers in the city.

We suggest also that the provisions of sanitary dwellings by private enterprise has been to some extent handicapped by unfair competition with insanitary dwellings which could be let at rents that would not pay for the provision of decent houses.

There is a grudging and extremely vague admission of the state's obligation to provide housing but this is qualified by the equally vague assertion that 'employers also have a moral obligation'.[178]

The overall recommendations did not commit the government to any new forms of expenditure. Such an outcome was almost inevitable given the composition of the inquiry, and it was undoubtedly something which the government consciously sought. In a House of Commons debate on the matter, Mr. Birrell noted[179]

What they wanted in Dublin was more work for the workmen.

If he were asked to apply this principle (labourers cottages financing) to great cities and for all time to build houses at rents which would involve a great loss from the very beginning, such a request required some consideration and he could not be expected to give it at this moment.

He also emphasised that it would prove impossible to give some concessions to Dublin without extending them to other Irish towns.

The outcome of the report was to maintain demands for state assistance, particularly on the part of Dublin Corporation and nationalist politicians, though the latter were becoming worried about this matter, with Home Rule pending. In January 1914 a deputation of southern Mayors met John Redmond and J.J. Clancy, who assured them that housing grants would still be available from the Imperial exchequer, despite Home Rule.[180] Presumably any move to shift this burden to a Dublin parliament would have met with an interesting response. For those of Unionist persuasion the outcome of the 1914 inquiry was to provide further evidence that Nationalists were incapable of self-government and to furnish further arguments against Home Rule.

One M.P. George Touch, in a letter to the London *Times* wrote[181]

It is the duty of the Town Council of Dublin to look after the housing of the people. Dublin has Home Rule in Municipal affairs and the town council is controlled by Nationalists. This has prevailed for fifteen years. At the end of that period Mr. Lloyd George is able to say that the housing conditions are the worst in Europe. What an object lesson in Nationalist rule. Mr. Lloyd George's policy is to extend Nationalist rule to Belfast . . . . In the circumstances Mr. Lloyd George's reference to Irish housing under the administration of his Nationalist allies is a useful reminder for which Unionists should be grateful.

This stance was also adopted by Lord Robert Cecil, who argued in the House of Lords that[182]

this particular Report does furnish a very strong and brilliant lesson of the disadvantages of Nationalist rule as compared with Unionist rule in Ireland.

While questioning the basis of such an overtly political conclusion: Belfast benefitted from being a new city, with a higher proportion of skilled workers, higher female participation rates and higher family incomes, the Home Rule issue weakened the basis of Dublin Corporation's demand

317

for state assistance. There is something incongrous in pro-
claiming their desire and fitness for Home Rule while simul-
taneously requesting special financial assistance from the
British Treasury.

We must face the task of evaluating the Dublin housing
question as a whole. The basic cause of both bad housing
and ill-health lay in the overall occupational and income
structure of the city's workers. It was simply impossible to
provide decent food, clothing and housing on an income of
approximately £1 per week: a fact which was becoming increasingly evident with the appearance of budgetary studies.
To that extent Dublin Corporation and presumably the
government stand absolved from major guilt.

Some genuine problems still remain. As already noted,
the 1914 inquiry was correct in emphasising the failure
to enforce scavenging, cleansing of stairs and toilets and other
basic services which would not have proved unduly costly.
The extent of tenement ownership by members of Dublin
Corporation and the seeming connivance of officials like
Sir Charles Cameron at breaches of the sanitary regulations
gives rise to a feeling of disquiet. It must be conceded that by
1914 Dublin Corporation had housed a total of 1,385
families, or approximately 7,500 persons, 2.5% of the population, a proportion which one corporation spokesman
claimed was greater than in any other U.K. city.[183] By the
same date London County Council had provided a total of
9,746 units, proportionately a much smaller contribution.[184]
Even Glasgow which was regarded as a pioneer in working
class housing did not achieve Dublin's level.[185] Similarly
the contribution of philanthropic agencies cannot be denied.
By 1914 the combined corporation and philanthropic efforts
had provided 5,271 dwellings, approximately 18.75% of the
city's housing stock. Yet as the statistics of the housing
inquiry reveal, this was not only insufficient to meet the
city's needs, but it seems that on the whole, those in greatest
need were not being assisted.

The final topic worthy of brief comment concerns public
opinion. Interest in organisations such as the Artisans
Dwellings Co. or the Housing of the Very Poor emerges in
response to English activities; employers were poor providers
of working class housing. Until 1913-14 there is little evi-

318

dence of urgency, either from the general public, or the corporation. The reasons for this seeming lack of concern cannot be precisely identified. Gareth Stedman-Jones traces the emergence of major concern in London to the 1880s with their threat of social unrest.[186] On this line of analysis it would not be implausible to trace a growth in interest in Dublin housing to the threat of socialism and the aftermath of the 1913 lock-out.

The lack of political commitment on the Dublin housing question is in marked contrast to the attention given to the social and economic problems of rural Ireland. This reflects the relative political weakness of Irish cities; their stagnation during the nineteenth century, and an undefined feeling that urban Ireland was somehow alien to the true Irish identity. Dublin housing lacked the powerful sympathies of the Roman Catholic clergy, in marked contrast to the land question. The Irish Parliamentary Party worked at Westminster for legislative reforms sought by Dublin Corporation, notably the Clancy act. The party was inevitably allied with the majority of the corporation and was not in a position to adopt a critical stance on urban housing. Unlike rural landlords, tenement owners tended to be nationalist sympathisers.

The lack of an effective opposition party within local politics is also of relevance. The migration of the middle classes to the suburbs removed them physically from contact with tenements and their inhabitants, blunting their awareness of the problem. Greater political urgency would not have brought an immediate solution to a problem rooted in the city's whole economic structure, but it might have alleviated some of the worst features.

CONCLUSION

The story of Dublin is a case history of the impact of nine-teenth century economic and political change in an Irish urban setting. This question has received considerable investigation in the context of rural Ireland, insofar as it has arisen in an urban context only the favourable case, that of Belfast, has been examined. The changing structure of industry, changes in market demand and in transport, combined with Ireland's proximity to the prospering British economy all served to undermine a traditional industrial structure, and, with exceptions such as brewing and biscuits, the city's industries failed to adapt. These events were by no means unique to Dublin, in fact they would appear to have been the norm for most Irish towns outside Ulster. From the declining industrial structure and the relative lack of dynamism from rural Ireland, it was inevitable that Dublin would contain a high proportion of disguised unemployment masquerading under the form of general labourers. In turn the poor wages which these labourers gained, their frequent periods of unemployment meant that problems of ill-health and congested housing — problems common to all nineteenth century cities, would be compounded.

The efforts made to resolve these social problems in Dublin illustrate the inappropriateness of transferring British legislative and administrative practices unchanged to Ireland. By the year 1870, Westminster had realised that the Irish land system differed in several important respects from its English counterpart and had made corresponding legislative adjustments. By the year 1900 rural Ireland was the beneficiary of an extensive system of land purchase —

soon to be extended — a special programme of state investment and funding to improve economic and social conditions in the west of Ireland, and a specifically Irish government department designed to assist the country's agriculture, while low-cost housing for rural labourers was being built with subsidised government loans. In contrast Irish cities received nothing until 1908 when the Clancy act provided a paltry £6,000 per annum subsidy towards the cost of urban housing schemes. The marked difference in treatment reflects differences in political muscle. The base of the Irish parliamentary party was in rural and small-town Ireland, though they were not averse to using Dublin Corporation as a political platform. Numbers counted: rural voters outnumbered the urban, while many urban voters were unionists, living either in Belfast or in south Dublin suburbs. The unity and political strength of the Irish farming community is in marked contrast to the weakness and disunity of the urban working classes. In 1896 the Recess Committee, a body which included shades of both unionist and nationalist opinion reviewed the Irish economy and concluded that 'Agriculture is now, not only the main, but over the greater portion of the country, the sole Irish industry',[1] in effect excluding cities such as Dublin from any major economic role.

Faced with a lack of special assistance Dublin had to cope with its social problems on equal terms with Manchester or Birmingham. While typical English and Scottish cities experienced a considerable rise in their rateable valuation and were able to embark on major schemes of municipal improvement, Dublin was condemned to a valuation which did not exceed its famine level until 1889. It is perhaps significant that while suburban Dublin contains Rathmines Town Hall, Kingstown Town Hall and several other municipal buildings, there is no prominent municipal building erected by the city during the nineteenth century. There were no surplus funds for municipal largesse in marked contrast to most English cities. Even main drainage had to be delayed for forty years because of financial constraints. This dependence on local taxation for virtually all social spending was perfectly satisfactory in prosperous cities, in Dublin, which was also denied access to the revenue of the expanding middle class suburbs such as Rathmines, it guaranteed that resources were totally inadequate to meet social needs. A further problem emerged from the nature of Dublin Corporation. Much British social legislation in the nineteenth century was permissive, relying for its introduction and enforcement on the disinterested concern of committed and efficient local councillors, the 'fit and proper persons' of the municipal reform act. It would seem that on the whole Irish councillors regarded local government in a different light. Membership of a council provided a platform for expressing national, not local political views. Water and sewage gave way to the Catholic university, repeal of the union and other grave issues, while council membership provided opportunities to defend the vested interests of friends, ensuring that legislation on matters such as tenement housing would not affect owners to any marked extent, or, in the case of Rathmines that the financial investments of house-owners would be protected from high taxation. Not all English councils were models of disinterested efficiency, but the problem would appear to have been greater in Ireland, while the somewhat passive role adopted by the local government board meant that interference with Dublin Corporation was limited provided that accounts were audited satisfactorily and borrowing limits not exceeded.

The exodus, both from the city and from municipal life of the Protestant middle class undoubtedly reduced the quality of municipal life. They could have provided a coherent opposition to nationalist dominance, while evidence from English cities suggests the big businessmen — who in Dublin's case were mostly Protestant — were more likely to view municipal improvement in a broader context. In addition, the considerable segregation by class and religion meant that opportunities for mutual contact and understanding were missed in virtually the only part of Ireland, excluding Ulster, where there was a sizeable Protestant population. The mutual intolerance which both groups expressed during the nineteenth century served to reduce the prospects of a more broadly-based and tolerant political climate in post-independence Ireland.

Conditions in Dublin did not improve markedly with the attainment of self-government, though the ending of the union had been a central goal for city politicians and trade unionists alike. The Cumann na nGaedhal government was forced to adopt a somewhat parsimonious approach to social spending and housing conditions actually deteriorated during the 1920s. Despite a reform of housing finance in 1930 the 1939 housing inquiry recorded a higher level of overcrowding than that existing in 1914.[2] Relations between Dublin Corporation and the new state were no more amicable than with their British predecessors. The Cumann na nGaedhal government, led by W.T. Cosgrave, a former member of Dublin Corporation, actually suspended Dublin Corporation, a matter which aroused a somewhat rueful comment from former Chief Secretary for Ireland, Augustine Birrell[3]

> Mr Cosgrave has abolished the Corporation of Dublin by a stroke of his pen. Any English Chief Secretary who had attempted to do the same piece of good work would have been compelled to resign by a combination of Unionists and Nationalists in the House of Commons. I had to be content with the abolition of the Corporation of Sligo.

Nevertheless, some advances did occur. The city boundaries were extended in 1930 to include Rathmines and Pembroke plus a considerable tract to the north of the city. The introduction of tariff protection brought about many new light industries while the introduction in the 1930s of unemployment assistance ameliorated the worst cases of destitution. A native government based in Dublin generated civil service jobs, for Irishmen rather than Englishmen, though many must have been filled by rural migrants rather than by natives. Overall mortality fell sharply, as did the death-rate for tuberculosis. Perhaps most important, the undouted psychological wound which had festered during the nineteenth century, the loss of its capital status was removed, while partition, by excluding Belfast, removed the only serious competitor for the title of Ireland's greatest city. There still remained a certain uneasy relationship between Dublin and Ireland as a whole. Despite being the cradle of the Gaelic League, centre of the 1916 Rising and a key location in the fight for political independence, Dublin was still viewed as somewhat outside mainstream Irish life. The Fianna Fail party was committed to the preservation of

323

rural lifestyle and decentralisation of industry, and while the position of Cumann na nGaedhal was less explicit, their belief that Ireland's true destiny lay in agriculture tended to exclude the city, and particularly its working class from a key role. Although Dublin's population grew in the immediate post-independence decades, it still failed to provide an effective counter-attraction for the countless emigrants from rural Ireland.

It is perhaps only in recent years, with a higher proportion of urban dwellers in Irish society, and a gradual shift from an agricultural to an industrial cum service economy that attention has come to focus on the Irish urban heritage. Growing tolerance and the cooling of nationalist passions permits the realisation that Irish history was made, not just in the countryside, but also in the towns, and that the Victorian architecture of Rathmines or Monkstown is part of the Irish heritage, as much as thatched cottages or round towers.

NOTES

Chapter I

1. Sybil Gribbon, 'An Irish city: Belfast 1911', in David Harkness and Mary O Dowd (eds), *The town in Ireland*, (Belfast 1981) pp 203-221.
2. For an excellent illustration of this attitude see C.S. Andrews, *Dublin made me* (Dublin 1979)
3. Mary Daly, 'Late nineteenth and early twentieth century Dublin', in Harkness and O Dowd, op. cit.
4. Statistics on Irish emigration, 1876-1911, published annually in parliamentary papers. County figures are not available prior to 1876.
5. David Dickson, 'Dublin in the eighteenth century Irish economy', unpublished paper read at the Scottish-Irish economic history conference 1981. Figures pre 1821 are from Dickson, the remainder from the Census.
6. *Decennial summary of births, marriages and deaths registered in Ireland.* 1871-80 1884 (c. 4153) xx, 996 Table viii, ibid., *1881-90*, 1894 (c. 7536) xxv, 325, Tab. VIII, *1891-1900*, 1904 (cd. 2089), xiv, 1085, Tab. VIII, *1900-10*, 1914 (cd. 7121), xv, Tab. VIII.
7. This area comprised the city and all the suburbs.
8. See Tables VIII and IX.
9. Sir F.R. Falkiner 'Hospitals' in G.D. Williams (ed) *Dublin charities*, Association of Charities (Dublin 1902), p. 64.
10. W.J. Reader, *Professional men* (1966) p. 135.
11. Charles Booth, 'The economic distribution of population', in W.P. Coyne (ed.), *Ireland: industrial and agricultural (Dublin 1902) p. 65.*
12. Dickson, op. cit.
13. Calculated from figures given in the *Second report of the commissioners appointed to consider and recommend a General System of Railways for Ireland.* 1837-8, xxxv, pp 813-36. These figures have recently been subjected to critical revision by Peter M. Solar, 'The agricultural trade statistics in the Irish railway commissioners' report', *Irish economic and social history*, vi, 1979, but his revision does not alter the Dublin picture to any significant degree.
14. Anthony Marmion, *The ancient and modern history of the maritime ports of Ireland* (1860) p. 243.
15. ibid., p.240.
16. Port statistics, 1868-1915, *Dublin port and docks board annual report 1915.*
17. L.M. Cullen, *Anglo-Irish trade, 1660-1800,* (Manchester 1968) pp21-22.
18. D.B. McNeill, *Irish passenger steamship services*, 2 vols. (Newtown Abbot 1969), ii, 34.

19. *Minutes Port and Docks Board*, 3 Jan. 1889. Returns made by collector of port dues.
20. *Report Dublin Chamber of Commerce for the year 1855.*
21. J.F. Bateman, 'The port of Dublin', supplement *I.T.* 7 Aug. 1867.
22. *Dublin Port and Docks Board*, minutes and annual reports.
23. In 1878 steam coasters yielded a revenue of £8-2-2 per foot of quay compared with £5-1-7 in the case of foreign steamers and £2-10-11 for deep water sailing vessels, *Minutes Dublin Port and Docks board*, 11 July 1878.
24. ibid., 6 July 1914, letter Figgis Son and Co.
25. *Vice-regal commission Irish railways, third report, evidence 1908 (cd. 4054),* xlviii paras. 31260-2.
26. ibid., para. 28939, evidence P.J. Mannion Castlebar Urban District Council.
27. *Report Commission appointed for the purpose of inquiring into various matters connected with the railways of Great Britain and Ireland.* 1867 (844-1) xxviii Pt. I para. 1175.
28. McNeill, op. cit. ii, 15.
29. ibid., ii, 23.
30. *I.T.* 1 April 1864 and *Dublin municipal council, report committee no. 1,* 14 Nov. 1866.
31. S.P.O. CSO/RP 1876/20. Report by veterinary dept. on cattle ports in the year 1875, dated 6 March 1876.
32. *I.T.* 21 Nov. 1867.
33. *Dublin Daily Mail,* 12 May 1863 and *F.J.* 21 Nov. 1863.
34. *I.T.* 15 Jan. 1872.
35. *Dublin municipal council, minutes* 27 May 1872.
36. *Irish Builder* 1 May 1872.
37. 37 & 38 Vict. cap. lxxvii, *Dublin port and city railway act.*
38. Kevin Murray, 'The Loop Line', *Railway records society journal*, no. 2, pp 50-51.
39. B.B. Storey, *On recent improvements in the port of Dublin* (Dublin 1878) and *I.T.* 19 March 1879.
40. This is a matter of almost inordinate complexity. In 1879 the High Court of Justice decided in favour of an application by the London and North Western Company to have the net tonnage of their steamer Isabella (not on the Dublin route) recalculated to make a greater allowance for machinery. This resulted in a reduction of that ship's net tonnage by approximately 15%, and not surprisingly, the remeasurement of numerous other ships followed. The loss was not just a once-off event. The transition from sail to steam meant a change from ships where the ratio of net to gross tonnage was approximately 1:2 to perhaps as little as 1:20. New ships were constructed to take maximum advantage of legal loopholes. The result was an undoubted loss of revenue to Dublin, and indeed to other ports. In 1877 steam packet companies had paid a total of £13,259 in tonnage dues, by 1889 they paid a mere £7,255. There is voluminous information on this matter in the *Minutes of the port and docks board*, throughout the 1880s, and a good resume of the matter in the *minutes* of 12 Sept. 1907.
41. ibid., 16 Aug. 1877.
42. Joseph Todhunter Pim, 'The port of Dublin', *Stat. soc. Irl. Jnl.* 1889, p. 483
44. Sources for the figures are *Thom's Directory*, except for those for the year 1875 which come from CSO/RP 1876/2).
45. *Select committee railways (Ireland)*, 1881 (374) para. 8187.
46. *Select committee railway rates*, 1882, vol. xiii, p.3.
47. *Vice-regal commission on Irish railways, second report, evidence*, 1908 (cd. 3896), xlvii, 331, para. 22165, evidence Ald. Henry Dale, Cork Chamber of Commerce.

48. ibid., *third report evidence.* 1908 (cd. 4054) xlviii, para. 31399.

49. ibid., *third report evidence* para. 29348.

50. ibid., *fourth report, second appendix volume,* 1909 (cd. 4481) xxvi, para. 44780.

51. *Select committee on railways (Ireland)* 1881 (374) para. 8248.

52. ibid., para. 8131.

53. ibid., para. 4735.

54. *Vice-regal commission Irish railways, third report, evidence.* para. 29789, evidence J.F. Nagle, South of Ireland Cattle Traders Association.

55. See footnote 45.

56. *Minutes port and docks board,* 2 May 1907.

57. *Vice-regal commission Irish railways, second report, evidence* 1908 (Cd. 3896), xlvii, 331, paras. 18688-9.

58. *Minutes port and docks board,* 2 May 1907.

59. *Vice-regal commission Irish railways, second report, evidence* paras. 18688-9.

60. *I.T.* 25 Feb. 1879.

61. *Report Dublin Chamber of Commerce for the year 1898,* p. 25.

62. *Minutes Dublin port and docks board* 1899-

63. By 1911 29.9% of the male workforce in Cardiff were employed in transport, the figure for Dublin was 15.46%. Transport employment in London in 1891 was 17.3% of the male workforce. For Cardiff see M.J. Daunton, *Coal metropolis, Cardiff 1870-1914.* p. 182. For London, Gareth Stedman-Jones, *Outcast London* (Oxford 1971), Appendix.

64. Maura Murphy, 'The economic and social structure of nineteenth century Cork', in Harkness and O Dowd, op. cit. p. 127.

65. Fergus D'Arcy, *Dublin artisan activity, opinion and organisation 1820-60,* unpublished M.A. thesis, University College Dublin, 1968.

Chapter II

1. The introduction of economic protection in 1932 generated a wave of new manufacturing units in the city.

2. See *Table II*

3. Murphy, op. cit. p. 127.

4. Thomas Brazill, *Report to the Corporation of Dublin on the proposed supply of the city and suburbs with pure water at high pressure* (Dublin 1854) p. 13.

5. Parke Neville, *Report on the capabilities of the Dodder to afford a supply of water for the use of city and suburbs* (Dublin 1854.

6. *Minutes Municipal Council,* 12 Sept. 1864. Division A comprises the south-west quarter of the city, B. south-east, C north-east and D north-west.

7. *Report Factory Inspectors 31 October 1874* P.P. 1875 (c. 1184). vol. xvi.

8. Patrick Lynch and John Vaizey, *Guinness's brewery in the Irish economy 1759-1876* (Cambridge 1967) pp. 80 and 89).
9. *Rathmines township minutes* 2 Aug. 1865 and *Dly. Exp.* 14 Dec. 1866.
10. Lynch and Vaizey, op. cit. p. 201.
11. ibid. p. 201.
12. ibid. p. 201.
13. ibid. p. 213.
14. *I.T.* 23 June 1883.
15. Alfred Barnard, *Noted breweries of Great Britain and Ireland* 3 vols. (1889), ii, 397.
16. *Minutes Municipal Council* 11 June, 1900.
17. *I.T.* 10 Sept. 1895.
18. *I.T.* 24 Feb. 1905.
19. *I.T.* 7 Dec. 1904.
20. Barnard, i, 3 and ii, 385, 297.
21. Lynch and Vaizey p. 219.
22. ibid. p. 219.
23. ibid. p. 239.
24. Barnard, i. 21.
25. Lynch and Vaizey p. 224.
26. ibid. p. 240.
27. *Report Factory Inspectors 1896*, P.P. 1897 (c. 8561) xvii, 215.
28. Barnard, i and ii.
29. *I.T.* 20 Sept. 1871.
30. Lynch and Vaizey p. 223.
31. *I.T.* 3 Aug. 1908.
32. *I.T.* 1 Sept. 1908.
33. *R.C. on the poor law*, app. vol. xi, 1910 vol. 51. App. xivii. Guinness employment conditions.
34. *Census of production 1907.* Final report 1912 (cd. 6320).
35. *Dly. Indep.* 17 Aug. 1893.
36. Lynch and Vaizey pp 237-8.
37. Barnard, i, 3.
38. *Irish Builder* 1 Aug. 1872.
39. *I.T.* 10 May 1878.
40. John Jameson and Sons, William Jameson and Co, John Power and Sons and George Roe and Co., *Truths about whiskey* (Dublin 1878) p.6.
41. Alfred Barnard, *The whiskey distilleries of the United Kingdom* (1887).
42. ibid. p. 356.
43. R.B. Weir, 'The patent still distillers and the role of competition in nineteenth century Irish economic history' in L.M. Cullen and T.C. Smout (eds), *Comparative aspects of Scottish and Irish economic and social history*, 1600-1900 (Edinburgh 1977) p.133.
44. ibid.
45. ibid. p. 134.
46. ibid. Table IV.
47. E.B. McGuire, *Irish whiskey: a history of distilling in Ireland* (Dublin 1973).
48. *Truths about Whiskey* p.11.
49. ibid. p. 66.
50. *R.C. Whiskey and other potable spirits. Final report* 1909 cd. 4797, xlix, 503.
51. Evidence· to *R.C. Whiskey and other potable spirits,* I, 1908 Cd. 4181, lviii para. 1797;
52. *Parl. Deb.* 29 April 1915, col. 864.
53. Mc Guire p. 301.

54. *Evidence to R. C. Whiskey and other potable spirits* I, 1908, Cd. 4181 lviii para. 1490.
55. *I.T.* 6 May 1889.
56. *I.T.* 5 Sept. 1902.
57. *I.T.* 5 Jan. 1905.
58. Barnard, *Whiskey*
59. Mc Guire, p. 372.
60. *I.T.* 18 Sept. 1869.
61. T.E. Fitzpatrick, *Existing manufactures of Ireland with suggestions for their development.* (Dublin 1886).
62. *F.J.* 28 May 1874.
63. *E. Tel.* 21 Nov. 1885.
64. *I.T.* 7 July 1882.
65. *Report Factory Inspectors 31 October 1888,* P.P. 1889 (c. 5697), xviii, 359 p. 149.
66. *I.T.* 7 July 1882.
67. *E.Tel.* 26 Jan. 1895.
68. *Dly. Exp.* 23 Jan. 1866.
69. *F.J.* 30 Aug. 1881.
70. *Report Factory Inspectors 31 October 1887,* P.P. 1888 (c. 5328) xxvi, 395. p.24.
71. *I.T.* 1 June 1886.
72. *I.T.* 7 Feb. 1888.
73. John Swift, *History of the Dublin bakers and others* (Dublin 1948) p. 202.
74. ibid. p. 200.
75. *Report Comm. no.2, Minutes Municipal Council,* 18 April 1864.
76. *Irish Builder* supplement, 1 Jan. 1888 and *I.T.* 29 Nov. 1889.
77. Swift pp.308-318.
78. T.A.B. Corley, *Quaker enterprise in biscuits. Huntley and Palmer's of Reading, 1822-1972* (1972) p. 143.
79. ibid. pp 171, 174.
80. *I.T.* 24 Aug. 1911.
81. *F.J.* 23 Aug. 1914.
82. *Report from the select committee on industries (Ireland): with proceedings, evidence appendix and index.* P.P. 1884-5 (288) ix, L. Sess. 1) xii, Appendix 26.
83. *I.T.* 10 June 1880.
84. *Select committee industries* (Ireland) App. 26.
85. *I.T.* 27 Sept. 1884.
86. *Irish Builder,* 1 June 1885.
87. *I.T.* 1 June 1886.
88. *Irish Builder,* 14 Nov. 1903.
89. *Irish Builder,* 6 May 1906.
90. *Minutes Municipal Council,* 4 March 1907, letter dated 7 Feb. 1907.
91. *E. Tel.* 5 Dec. 1886.
92. *Irish railway records society, journal,* vol. 1, p. 12.
93. *Minutes, Great Southern and Western Railway Co.* 6 Nov. 1857.
94. ibid. 13 Dec. 1861.
95. ibid. 21 Sept. 1866.
96. ibid. 31 March 1871.
97. ibid. 20 Feb. 1874 and 1 Dec. 1876.
98. ibid. 10 Feb. 1879.
99. *Irish Builder,* 15 Aug. 1879.
100. *I.T.* 1 Oct. 1889.
101. *Irish Builder,* 15 Feb. 1879.

102. *I.T.* 26 Dec. 1881.
103. *I.T.* 12 June 1885.
104. *I.T.* 5 June 1885.
105. *E.Tel.* 27 Nov. 1897.
106. *Minutes Great Southern and Western Railway. Co.*, 16 Oct. 1903.
107. *I.T.* 4 June 1885.
108. *I.T.* 4 June 1885.
109. *Select committee industries (Ireland)* App. II.
110. J.J. Webb, *Industrial Dublin since 1698 and the silk industry in Dublin* (Dublin 1913) p. 90.
111. ibid. p. 82.
112. *Minutes Council of the Dublin Chamber of Commerce*, 15 Dec. 1856.
113. ibid. 3 April 1857.
114. *Report Dublin Chamber of Commerce for the year 1851.*
115. *Report Dublin Chamber of Commerce for the year 1859.*
116. *I.T.* 20 Feb. 1864.
117. *I.T.* 18 July 1864.
118. *Dly. Exp.* 18 Aug. 1866.
119. *I.T.* 7 Nov. 1870.
120. *I.T.* 22 Nov. 1870.
121. *I.T.* 24 Aug. 1872.
122. *I.T.* 13 Mar. 1890.
123. *I.T.* 12 April 1895.
124. *I.T.* 3 June 1902.
125. *I.T.* 10 Sept. 1902.
125. *I.T.* 10 Sept. 1902.
126. E.J. Riordan, *Modern Irish trade and industry* (Dublin 1920) p. 99.
127. *Evening Herald*, 22 July 1901.
128. *I.T.* 26 Jan. 1869.
129. *F.J.* 18 Oct. 1872.
130. *I.T.* 18 Oct. 1881.
131. *Select committee industries* (Ireland), 1884-5 (288) ix, 1, Sess. 1) xii, evidence p. 702. Witness Mr. Strype.
132. ibid. p. 457. Witness Prof. Walter Noel Hartley.
133. *I.T.* 19 Sept. 1885.
134. *Industries of Ireland: historical statistical, biographical; an account of the leading business men, commercial interests, wealth and growth.* (London 1888).
135. Charles Wilson, *The history of Unilever*, I, (1954) p. 18.
136. ibid. pp 76-77 and 122.
137. *Boileau and Boyd: Two hundred years. Bicentenary souvenir,* (Dublin 1900).
138. *Number of cotton woollen etc factories subject to the Factories Acts in each county.* 1862 (23) LV, 629.
139. *Dly. Exp.* 12 March 1865.
140. *I.T.* 22 May 1855.
141. *Committee to inquire into the working of the factory and workshops acts. Evidence.* 1876 (C. 1443-1), xxx, q. 18373.
142. *I.T.* 31 Aug. 1871.
143. *I.T.* 20 Aug. 1870.
144. *Committee to inquire into the working of the factory and workshops acts. Evidence.* 1876 (C. 1443-1), xxx, qs. 18376 and 18386.
145. Webb, *Industrial Dublin* p.
146. I.T. 15 Oct. 1887.
147. Anne Jellicoe, 'Condition of young women employed in manufacturies in Dublin', *Transactions of national association for promotion of social science*, reprints (1862), introduction.

148. W.N. Hancock, 'Is the competition between large and small shops injurious to the community'. (Dublin 1851).
149. W.N. Hancock, 'Is distinct trading or the monster house most conducive to public interests' (Dublin).
150. Jellicoe, op. cit.
151. ibid.
152. ibid.
153. *Committee to inquire into the working of the factory and workshops acts. Evidence.* 1876 q. 19038.
154. Jellicoe, op. cit.
155. *Committee to inquire into the working of the factory and workshops acts. Evidence.* 1876 q. 18848.
156. *Report factory inspectors 31 October 1879.* P.P. 1880 (c. 2489) xiv, 93, p. 26.
157. ibid. *31 October 1888.* P.P. 1889 (c. 5697), xviii, 359, p. 148.
158. *I.T.* 21 July 1909.
159. *Select committee industries (Ireland) 1884-5.* Evidence p. 351, witness William Keating agent for a wholesaling and manufacturing company.
160. ibid. *App. 8*, evidence Mr. Winstanley and *I.T.* 26 May 1885.
161. *I.T.* 27 Dec. 1889.
162. C.S. Andrews, *Dublin made me* (Dublin 1979).
163. *I.T.* 2 July 1873.
164. Riordan, op. cit. pp 176-7.
165. *F.J.* 28 Sept. 1881.
166. *Report factory inspectors 31 October 1888.* P.P. 1889 (c. 5697) xviii, 359, p. 148.
167. ibid. *31 October 1894.*
168. *Industries of Ireland* p. 58. The remainder of information on the printing industry is also from this source.
169. *I.T.* 22 Sept. 1870.
170. *F.J.* 23 Aug. 1914.
171. *E. Tel.* 14 April 1896.
172. *I.T.* 17 Dec. 1891.

Chapter III

1. *R.C. on Poor Laws*, vol. xxxi, Statistical memoranda and Tables relating to Ireland. 1910, Cd. 5244, vol. xliv, Appendix xixb.
2. *Select committee railways (Ireland)*, 1881, (374) para. 8187.
3. *Dly. Exp.* 19 Feb. 1866.
4. W.A. Thomas, *The provincial stock exchanges*, (1973) pp. 129-30.
5. Brinley Thomas, 'Demographic determinants of British and American building

cycles, 1870-1914' in D. McCloskey (ed) *Essays on a mature economy: Britain after 1870* (1971) p. 47.
6. James Donnelly Jr. 'The Irish agricultural depression of 1859-64', *Irish economic and social history*, III, 1976 pp 33-54.
7. *Dublin Builder*, 1 May 1860.
8. *F.J.* 27 March 1862.
9. *Report of the Sick and Indigent Roomkeepers Society 1862.*
10. Larcom Ms. 7606.
11. R.C.O. Matthews, *The trade cycle* (Cambridge 1959) p. 222.
12. *Irish Builder* 1 Jan. 1869.
13. *I.T.* 31 Dec. 1870.
14. *F.J.* 16 April 1873.
15. *I.T.* 5 Dec. 1872. leading article.
16. *I.T.* 24 Dec. 1877.
17. *I.T.* 31 July 1878.
18. *I.T.* 31 Dec. 1878.
19. *I.T.* 11 Mar. 1878.
20. *Report Factory Inspectors 31 Oct. 1879.* P.P. 1880, c. 2489, xiv, 93 p. 27.
21. *F.J.* 26 Jan. 1880.
22. CSO/RP 1880/1297, meeting 15 Jan. 1880.
23. ibid. 1880/3312.
24. ibid. 1880/1297. 1962. 1963. 2030. 3312;
25. *Minutes Mun. Co.* 19 Jan. 1880.
26. ibid. 2 Feb. 1880.
27. *I.T.* 26 Aug. 1881.
28. *I.T.* 1 Mar. 1882.
29. *I.T. 13 Nov. 1883.*
30. CSO/RP 1880/1297.
31. *I.T.* 18 July 1882.
32. *I.T.* 18 Jan. 1883.
33. *I.T.* 4 Nov. 1889.
34. Maura Murphy, 'Fenianism, Parnellism and the Cork Trades, 1860-1900, *Saothar*, 5, 1979 p. 31.
35. A.C. Davies, 'The first Irish industrial exhibition, Cork 1852', *Irish economic and social history*, II, 1975 pp. 46-60.
36. *I.T.* 15 Sept. 1881.
37. *I.T.* 1 Oct. 1881.
38. *I.T.* 23 Dec. 1881.
39. *I.T.* 12 Oct. 1882.
40. *I.T.* 3 Jan. 1883.
41. *I.T.* 10 May 1883.
42. J.W. Boyle, *The rise of the Irish labour movement 1883-1907*, Ph.D. thesis, Trinity College Dublin, 1961 p. 255.
43. *Irish Builder* 15 June 1882.
44. *I.T.* 16 Aug. 1883.
45. *I.T.* 5 Jan. 1885.
46. *I.T.* 21 Jan. 1886.
47. *Even. Tel.* 22 Feb. 1886.
48. *I.T.* 12 Mar., 16 Mar. 1886.
49. *Report Dublin Chamber of Commerce for the year 1885* p. 39.
50. ibid. p. 34.
51. *I.T.* 15 July 1886.
52. *I.T.* 23 Dec. 1886.
53. *I.T.* 22 Feb. 1887.

54. *I.T.* 29 Aug. 1888.
55. *Report Factory Inspectors 31 Oct. 1887.* 1888 (c. 5328), xxvi, 395, 22.
56. ibid. *31 Oct. 1889* 1890.
57. ibid. *31 Oct. 1872.* 1873 (c. 745) xix, 41 p. 127.
58. ibid. *31 Oct. 1891.* 1892 (c. 6720) xx, 463, p. 25.
59. ibid. *31 Oct. 1892* 1893-4 (c. 6978), xvii, 65, p. 111.
60. *I.T.* 17 Sept. 1891.
61. *Irish Builder* 1 Mar. 1891.
62. *I.T.* 22 Feb. 1893.
63. *Ministry of Labour Gazette,* April 1894.
64. *Even. Tel.* 15 Feb. 1895.
65. *Even. Tel.* 14 Nov. 1896.
66. *Report Philanthropic Reform Association for the year 1906.*
67. *Irish Builder* 23 Mar. 1907.
68. ibid. 8 Jan. 1910.
69. ibid. 26 Oct. 1912.
70. *I.T.* 24 Nov. 1906.
71. *Population Census Ireland 1881. General report.* 1882 (c. 3365), lxxvi, 385, p. 19.
72. W.A. Armstrong, 'The use of information about occupation: I. As a basis for social stratification' in E.A. Wrigley, *Nineteenth century society* (Cambridge 1972) pp 191-214.
73. *Pop. Ire.* 1841 p. xviii.
74. *Returns of wages published between 1830 and 1886,* 1887 (c. 5172) lxxxix, 273.
75. *F.J.* 2 Sept. 1872.
76. A.L. Bowley, *Wages in the United Kingdom in the nineteenth century* (Cambridge 1900) p. 52.
77. *General report on the wages of the manual labour classes in United Kingdom 1893-4,* (c. 6889) lxxxiii-II, 1.
78. *Report on wages and hours of labour in the United Kingdom with statistical tables, Part III. Standard time rates,* 1894 (c. 7567) lxxxi-II, 1.
79. *Returns of wages published between 1830 and 1886. Report on changes in rates of wages and hours of labour in the U.K.* 1894 (c. 7567), ibid. 1894 (7467-II), ibid, 1896 (c. 8075), lxxx-I, etc. annually to 1905 (cd. 2674) lxxvi, 1.
80. *Mun. co. minutes,* 18 Feb. 1867. Breviate comm. no 1, July 1866.
81. ibid. 1 June 1868, Breviate comm. no. 1, Oct. 1867.
82. *Dly. Exp.* 5 Feb. 1873.
83. *F.J.* 15 May 1876.
84. *I.T.* 5 Feb. 1884.
85. *I.T.* 7 June 1886, *E.Tel.* 11 June 1886.
86. *E.Tel.* 21 May 1886.
87. ibid. 12 Jan. 1887.
88. ibid. 12 Jan. 1887.
89. *I.T.* 18 Feb. 1889.
90. *I.T.* 30 Aug. 1889.
91. *I.T.* 29 Mar. 1890.
92. CSO/RP 1890/14175.
93. *I.T.* 16 July 1891.
94. *I.T.* 18 July 1891.
95. *Report by her majesty's commissioners appointed to inquire into the financial relations between Great Britain and Ireland.* 1896 (c. 8202), xxxiii, 59, App. I, Table II.
96. *changes in wages,* 1897 (c. 8975), lxxxviii, p. 22.

97. ibid., 1901 (cd. 688) lxxii.

98. ibid., 1909 (cd. 4713), lxxx, pp 254-5.

99. *Report by commissioners of conciliation on Dublin strikes,* 1914-16, (cd. 7658), xxxvi, p. 64 Tab. viii.

100. *I.T.* 2 May 1896.

101. *I.T.* 2 May 1896.

102. *commissioners of conciliation,*

103. *I.T.* 10 Dec. 1897.

104. *E. Tel.* 4 Jan. 1896.

105. *E. Tel.* 5 Mar. 1898.

106. *I.T.* 4 Dec. 1900.

107. *changes in wages* 1904 (cd. 2199) lxxxix.

108. Bowley, op. cit. p. xiv.

109. *I.T.* 1 July 1905.

110. ibid., 3 Aug. 1908.

111. ibid., 5 Oct. 1911.

112. *Report of an enquiry by the Board of Trade into working class rents, housing, retail prices, and standard rates of wages in the U.K.* 1913 (cd. 6955), lxvi, 393.

113. *Minutes Rathmines urban district council,* 4 Sept. 1912 and 1 Oct. 1913.

114. *Departmental committee appointed to inquire into the housing conditions of the working class in Dublin, evidence and appendices.* 1914 (cd. 7273), xix, app. xxvi.

115. David A. Chart, 'Unskilled labour in Dublin: its housing and living conditions', *Stat. Soc. Ire. Jnl.* 13, part 94, 1914.

116. ibid., p. 143.

117. T. Barrington, 'A review of agricultural prices', *Stat. Soc. Ire. Jnl.* xiv, May 1926.

118. *R.C. poor law,* App. vol. x, minutes of evidence on Ireland. 1910 (cd. 5070), 1, app. IID, p. 350. T.J. Stafford, 'Note on the social conditions of certain working class families in Dublin'.

119. *Housing conditions* 1914, app. xxiii.

120. Stafford, op. cit.

Chapter IV

1. *F.J.* 27 Sept. 1884.

2. *F.J.* 30 Sept. 1884.

3. *Report of the Sick and Indigent Roomkeepers Society* 1857 p. 14.

4. Mansion House, hitherto M.H. Ch. 1/12/27.

5. *Sick and Indigent* 1866.

6. *Report Society of St. Vincent de Paul* 1895.

7. M.H. Ch. 1/13/8.

8. *Report of the inter-departmental committee on the employment of children during school-age, especially in street trading in the large centres of population in Ireland, with evidence and appendices.* 1902 (Cd. 1144), xlix, Case 53.

9. ibid. Case 26.

10. ibid. B. Division, Case 3.

11. ibid. Case 47A.

12. Hull Advertiser, *Brief notes of a short excursion to Ireland* (1853).

13. *Irish Indep.* 28 Oct. 1898.

14. CSO/RP 1898/18638.

15. M.H. Ch. 1/12/25.

16. *E.Tel.* 11 June 1886.

17. *I.T.* 13 Dec. 1864.

18. Gareth Stedman-Jones, *Outcast London* (Oxford 1971) chapter II.

19. *I.T.* 12 Jan. 1894.

20. *E.Tel.* 15 Feb. 1895.

21. *R.C. Poor Law* 1910 vol. 1.

22. E.D. Daly, 'Neglected children and neglectful parents', *Stat. Soc. Ire. Jnl*, 10, no. 78, p. 350, 1889.

23. *Thom's Directory 1912.*

24. P.R.O. I. *Sick and Indigent* 1028/4/3, Report Thomas Casey 7 Feb. 1879.

25. ibid. Assoc. relief of distressed Protestants, Jan. 1860.

26. *Sick and Indigent Report* 1856.

27. *St. Vincent de Paul Report* 1894, conference Our Lady Help of Christians.

28. ibid. 1910, Rathmines conference.

29. *Report National Society for the prevention of cruelty to children* 1889-90.

30. ibid. 1900-01.

31. ibid. 1890-91.

32. Charles Cameron, *How the poor live* (Dublin 1908).

33. *Report philanthropic reform association 1906.*

34. S. Shannon Millin, 'Slums: a sociological retrospect of Dublin', *Stat. Soc. Ire. Jnl.* 13, no. 94, p. 157, 1914.

35. M.H. Ch. 1/12/30, Letter Michael Burke, 10 Artisans Buildings, Buckingham St.

36. ibid. 1/12/6, Hubert Maguire, 38 Sth. William St.

37. Jose Harris, *Unemployment and politics. A study in English social policy, 1886-1914.* (Oxford 1972) p. 145.

38. Registers are available in P.R.O.I.

39. Laura Stephens, 'Workhouses', in Church of Ireland social service union, *Social services handbook* (Dublin 1901) p. 66.

40. *Report of the Viceregal Commission on poor law reform in Ireland* 1906 (cd. 3202), vol. li, appendix.

41. R.C. Poor Law, App. vol. xix B. *Report on the effects of employment or assistance given to the unemployed since 1886 by Mr. Cyril Jackson.* 1909 (Cd. 4890), vol. xliv, p. 6.

42. Geoffrey Best, *Mid-Victorian Britain* (1973 ed). p. 67.

43. Appendix xixB. p. 6.

44. M.H. Ch. 1/14/3.

45. *Handbook of Dublin charities, compiled by G.D. Williams.* (Dublin 1902).

46. *Irish Catholic* 1 Nov. 1913.

47. *St. Vincent de Paul Report 1897.*

48. Conference of St. Colmans, ibid. 1912.

49. ibid. 1910.

50. ibid. 1899.

51. ibid. 1902.

52. ibid. 1904.
53. ibid. 1894, Conference St. Lawrence O Toole.
54. CSO/RP 1886/5309. Poverty in Dublin.
55. *St. Vincent de Paul Report* 1901.
56. *First report NSPCC* 1889-90.
57. *Fifty-fifth annual report St. Brigid's orphanage* (Dublin 1912)
58. *St. Vincent de Paul Report* 1901.
59. ibid. 1895.
60. ibid. 1898.
61. *Sick and Indigent Report* 1874.
62. 1028/4/3. Allegations Dr. H.H. Joy at a meeting of the Association for the relief of distressed Protestants.
63. 1028/4/3. 1864.
64. 1028/4/3. 12 Feb. 1877.
65. ibid. 16 March, allegations of E. Dwyer Gray.
66. *Sick and indigent Reports*, 1863 and 1864.
67. ibid. 1880.
68. ibid. 1881.
69. Reports 1856-1907.
70. *I.T.* 19 Jan. 1867.
71. CSO/RP 1879/19932.
73. *Local Govt. Bo. report 1880* (c. 2603), vol. xxviii, para. 8.
74. 1028/4/3. Sick and Indigent, Misc. file.
75. CSO/RP 1880/1297.
76. *I.T.* 20 Jan. 1881.
77. *I.T.* 11 Mar. 1881.
78. *Mun. Co. Minutes* 17 July 1881.
79. *I.T.* 18 July 1881.
80. *Even. Tel.* 22 Feb. 1886.
81. *I.T.* 12 Mar. 1886.
82. *I.T.* 16 Mar. 1886.
83. CSO/RP 1886/5309.
84. *I.T.* 22 Feb. 1887.
85. *Mun. Co. Minutes* 8 Jan. 1894.
86. *I.T.* 14 Jan. 1895.
87. *St. Vincent de Paul* Report 1898, St. Francis Xavier Conference.
88. *Ir. Builder* 19 June 1902, and 22 Aug. 1903.
89. *Philanthropic reform association,* report 1906.
90. *I.T.* 5 July 1904.
91. *I.T.* 19 Aug. 1904.
92. *I.T.* 26 Nov. 1904.
93. *Report on committee on the relief of the Sick and Destitute poor.* Saorstat Eireann, 1927, R./27/3, para. 30.
94. *I.T.* 1 Dec. 1904.
95. *I.T.* 3 Dec. 1904.
96. *I.T.* 5 Dec. 1904.
97. *I.T.* 23 Dec. 1904.
98. *I.T.* 20 Dec. 1904 and 31 Dec. 1904.
99. *I.T.* 28 Nov. 1905.
100. *I.T.* 2 Dec. 1905.
101. *R.C. Poor Law, App.* xixB.
102. *I.T.* 14 Dec. 1905.
103. *R.C. Poor Law*, app. xixB. p. 50.
104. They had played a major role in the establishment of the enquiry into street-

trading children.
105. Harris p. 166.
106. *Philanthropic reform association*, report 1906, Appendix.
107. Harris, p.178.
108. *I.T.* 24 Nov. 1906.
109. *I.T.* Sept. 1907.
110. *Report local government board*, March 1907. 1907 Cd. 3682, xxvii p.ix.
111. *I.T.* 11 Dec. 1907, *local govt. bo.* March 1908, Cd. 4243, xxxi, pp. xii-xiii.
112. ibid. March 1911, 1911 Cd. 5847, xxxiii, p. xix.
113. ibid. March 1909, 1909 Cd. 4810, xxx, p. xv.
114. *Mun. Co. Reports*, 1908 No. 190, Estates and finance committee.
115. *I.T.* 19 Dec. 1908.
116. *I.T.* 22 Mar. 1909.
117. *I.T.* 26 June 1909.
118. *Mun. Co. Minutes*, 13 Dec. 1909.
119. *I.T.* 14 Dec. 1909.
120. Parl. Deb. 8 Feb. 1911, vol. 21 p. 407.
121. *R.C. on Poor Law. Report on Ireland.* 1909 (Cd. 4630), xxxviii, pp. 82-3.
122. Parl. Deb. 29 Mar. 1911, vol. 23, p. 1479.
123. *Mun. Co. Minutes*, 3 April 1911.
124. *Local govt. bo. March* 1912, 1912 (Cd. 6339), xxxvii.
125. *Mun. Co. Minutes* 11 April 1912, letter from South Dublin Union.
126. *I.T.* 6 April 1912.
127. *I.T.* 7 Mar. 1912.
128. *Ir. Builder* 26 Oct. 1912.
129. *I.T.* 13 Jan. 1913.
130. *Local govt. bo.* March 1913, 1913 Cd. 6978, xxxii.
131. *Mun. Co. Minutes* 2 Feb. 1914.
132. *Parl. Deb.* 8 April 1914, vol. 60 p. 1962.
133. *Local govt. bo.* March 1914, Cd. 7561, xxxix, p. xvii.
134. *I.T.* 13 April 1914.
135. W.H. Thompson, *War and the food of the Dublin labourer* (Dublin 1916).
136. Harris.
137. *I.T.* 1 Dec. 1909.
138. *Sick and Indigent Report 1857.*
139. *R.C. Poor Law*, appendix xixB.
140. *I.T.* 25 Sept. 1907.
141. *R.C. Poor Law*, app. xixB. pp 29-30.
142. Local govt. bo. 1911 Cd. 5847, xxxiii. 1912 Cd. 6339, xxxvii. 1913 Cd. 6978, xxxii. 1914 Cd. 7561, xxxix.
143. ibid. 1911 Cd. 5847, xxxiii, p. xxi.
144. *R.C. Poor Law*, app. xixB. p. 2.
145. ibid. app. vol. x, minutes of evidence on Ireland (cd. 5070), vol. 1, para. 100618.
146. ibid. paras. 10029-30.
147. Stafford, in *R.C. Poor Law*, 1910, 1.
148. B. Seebohm Rowntree, *Poverty: a study of town life* (Third ed.) 1902.
149. Maud Pember Reeves, *Round about a pound a week* (1980 ed). pp. 80-87.
150. W.H. Thompson, op. cit.
151. J.B. Hughes *Poverty in Dublin* (1914). Irish Messenger Social Action Series no. 13.
152. *Dublin housing committee 1914* app. xxiii, p. 107.
153. Harris p. 178.

337

(Pages 113-131)

154. *R.C. Poor Law. Report on Ireland* pp 82-3.
155. Thomas Kettle, *Home Rule finances* (Dublin 1911)
156. Harris pp 349-50.
157. *Philanthropic reform association*, report 1896.
158. Church of Ireland social services union, *Social services handbook* (Dublin 1901).
159. R.B. McDowell, *The Church of Ireland, 1869-1969* (1975) pp 90-2.
160. *Rerum novarum* published in 1891
161. Harris, pp 115-145.
162. Rev. P. Daly, 'The problem of the poor', *Record of the Maynooth Union 1908-9*, pp. 32-4.
163. Walter McDonald, *Some ethical aspects of the social question. Suggestions for priests* (1920) p.2.
164. *Irish Catholic* 6 Sept. 1913.
165. quoted in E. Larkin, 'Socialism and Catholicism in Ireland', *Church History*, 1964 p. 473.
166. John Robert O Connell, *The problem of the Dublin slums.*
167. J.B. Hughes, *Poverty in Dublin.*

Chapter V

1. *Thom's Directory*, 1851, 1881.
2. *F.J.* 14 Jan. 1878.
3. *R.C.* appointed to inquire into the boundaries and municipal areas of certain towns and cities in Ireland. *Evidence* 1881 (c. 2827) 1, para. 5308, Edward McMahon.
4. *R.C. on the housing of the working class. Third Report Ireland.* Evidence, 1884-5 (c. 4547-I) xxxi, paras 24594-24603.
5. For basis of dividing occupations see Armstrong op. cit. The proportions in this table relate, not just to the occupied workers but to the whole population. Calculations are derived from Census 1881, Tables 87 and 88 Summary Volume, and 1911 Tables 72 and 73.
6. Jacqueline Hill, 'The protestant response to repeal, the case of the Dublin working class', in F.S.L. Lyons and Richard Hawkins (eds), *Ireland under the union, varieties of tension* (Oxford 1980).
7. ibid. pp 45-48.
8. Available at Customs House Dublin.
9. Armstrong, 'social stratification'.
10. It is impossible from the returns to distinguish religiously mixed marriages.
11. *Reports of the Commissioners appointed by the Treasury to inquire into the conditions of the Civil Service in Ireland. Report on the Local Government*

Board andGeneral Registry Office and the Minutes. 1873 (c. 789), xxii, para. 400, Dr. Evory Kennedy).

12. E. McDowel Cosgrave, *Dublin and County Dublin in the twentieth century.* Contemporary biographies ed. W.T. Pike (Brighton 1908).

13. *Civil Service*, para. 41 John Ball solr.

14. Daire Hogan, *The legal profession in Ireland in the nineteenth century,* M.A. thesis University College Dublin 1981 chapters 10, 11 and Appendix.

15. *Civil Service* para. 444.

16. Evelyn Bolster, *The Knights of St. Columbanus* (Dublin 1979) p. 12.

17. P.R.O.I. Census enumerators returns, 1901 and 1911.

18. Andrews op. cit. pp 29, 41.

19. *Civil Service*, para. 977. James C. Colvill, Governor Bank of Ireland.

20. ibid. para. 8.

21. Bolster, op. cit. p.7.

22. Joseph Leckey, 'The recruitment of clerks to the Great Southern and Western Railway', paper read to *Irish historical society* Feb. 1980.

23. *Street-trading children.*

24. *The blind alley: some aspects of juvenile employment in Ireland.* Catholic working boys technical aid committee 1916. p. 11.

25. ibid. p. 23.

26. Andrews op. cit. p. 69.

27. *Reports Society St. Vincent de Paul.*

28. *Census Ireland 1911.* Table XXXVIII, Dublin city.

29. B. McDonnell, 'The Dublin labour movement, 1894-1907', Ph.D. thesis, University College Dublin, 1979 p. 57.

30. *Civil service Ireland. Report on Dublin Metropolitan police.* 1873 (c. 788) xxii, part II.

31. ibid. para. 103.

32. H. Llewellyn Smith, 'The influx of population', in Charles Booth, *Life and labour of the people of London*, iii, 82 (1902).

33. Andrews, op. cit. p. 55.

34. *I.T.* 5 July 1904.

35. *E. Tel.* 12 Sept. 1896.

36. *R.C. poor laws*, app. vol. xi, 1910 vol. 51 App. xivii, Guinness employment conditions.

37. David F. Crew, *Town in the Ruhr. A social history of Bochum*, 1860-1914 (New York 1979) pp 61-67.

38. H.J. Dyos, 'The slums of Victorian London', *Victorian Studies*, xi, no. 50, Sept. 1967 p. 29.

39. Andrews, op. cit. p. 15.

40. Michael Anderson, *Family structure in 19th century Lancashire* (Cambridge 1971) pp 152-160.

41. Geoffrey Crossick, *An artisan elite in Victorian society, Kentish town, 1840-1880* (1978). Tables, 6.8, 6.9, 6.10.

42. See Crossick chap. 6 for a discussion of what this signifies.

43. F.O.C. Meenan, 'The georgian squares of Dublin and the professions', *Studies*, winter 1969 p. 405.

44. *Commrs. Dublin turnpikes*, 1854 (0.1), xix, p. 764, evidence James Hickey.

45. ibid. App. 6.

46. ibid. p. 773, evidence, Robert Mallett engineer.

47. Andrews, op. cit. pp 9-10.

Chapter VI

1. *I.T.* 7 Dec. 1877.
2. *Rathmines township minutes,* Oct. 1863.
3. *I.T.* 20 June 1865.
4. *Rathmines minutes* 1 Feb. 1871.
5. *R.C. municipal boundaries,* evidence Mark Bentley para. 4151.
6. ibid. para. 6785 evidence Frederick Stokes.
7. *Rathmines minutes* 21 Dec. 1864.
8. *I.T.* 18 Feb. 1868.
9. *Rathmines minutes* 1860-
10. *I.T.* 9 June 1868.
11. *Ir. Build.* 1 Nov. 1868.
12. *Civil service Irl.* 1873 App. I.
13. *Municipal boundaries* evidence Wm. A. Mallins para. 2497, J.H. Evans, Rathmines secretary para. 6886.
14. *Rathmines minutes annual meeting,* 15 June 1870.
15. *Municipal boundaries,* evidence James T. Harricks, para. 3591.
16. *Rathmines minutes,* 21 Dec. 1864.
17. Address at opening of Rathmines water supply 23 July 1863, quoted *Rathmines minutes* 2 Aug. 1863.
18. *Municipal boundaries,* evidence Mark Bentley para. 4150.
19. ibid. paras. 1759, 3653, *report* paras. 449, 476.
20. ibid. para. 4136.
21. ibid. 5582, 5654, *report* 541-4.
22. ibid. para. 7218, evidence J.H. Evans, Rathmines secretary.
23. ibid. *report* part II, p. 22.
24. I.T. *19 June 1873,* Rathmines minutes *18 June 1873.*
25. *Rathmines minutes* 3 Jan. 1877.
26. ibid. 20 June 1877.
27. *I.T.* 10 July 1877.
28. *Rathmines minutes,* 4 July 1877.
29. *I.T.* 16 Nov. 1877.
30. *I.T.* 16 Nov. 1878.
31. *I.T.* 13 Nov. 1877.
32. *I.T.* 8 July 1880.
33. By 1888 it was costing 1/6 in the £, *Finance comm. minutes,* 11 Jan. 1888.
34. *I.T.* 17 Jan. 1899.
35. *I.T.* 31 Aug. 1907.
36. *Rathmines working class housing comm. minutes* 18 Jan. 1894.
37. *Rathmines minutes,* 13 July 1864.
38. *Rathmines minutes,* 5 Dec. 1877.
39. *Municipal boundaries, evidence* paras. 6685, 6691.
40. ibid. para. 4645, evidence John Vernon.
41. ibid. para. 4700.
42. *Pembroke estate office,* lease books.
43. David Cannadine, *Lords and landlords: the aristocracy and the towns, 1774-1967.* (Leicester 1980). preface.
44. *Select committee on town holdings,* 1886 (213-Sess. 1) xii, evidence para. 4970.
45. *I.T.* 10 June 1902.
46. *Town holdings* para. 4971.
47. ibid. para. 4913, evidence John Vernon.
48. *Ir. Build.* 23 May 1914.

49. *Dub. Build.* 1 April 1860.
50. ibid. 1 June 1860.
51. *Town holdings* para. 5191.
52. ibid. para. 5192.
53. *Pembroke estate office,* Lease dated 27 Feb. 1864 issued to John Hawkins Askins, on Newbridge Ave. Sandymount for 150 years.
54. *Municipal boundaries,* evidence paras. 4761-2.
55. 27 and 28 Vict. cap. lxxii.
56. *Municipal boundaries evidence* para. 4701.
57. *Pembroke commissioners, minutes annual meeting,* 15 June 1887.
58. *I.T.* 8 Dec. 1891.
59. *Pembroke minutes,* 26 Nov. 1900.
60. *Municipal boundaries, evidence,* paras. 4903-13, A.H. Robinson, secretary Pembroke commissioners.
62. *Pembroke minutes,* 8 Oct. 1866.
63. CSO/RP 1870/2589.
64. CSO/RP 1870/4710.
65. CSO/RP 1870/4976.
66. CSO/RP 1870/8811.
67. CSO/RP 1870/11029, 11680, 12248.
68. CSO/RP 1871/12667.
69. CSO/RP 1879/2475.
70. *R.C. housing of the working class. Third report Ireland.* Evidence paras 22794-22800.
71. *I.T.* 4 Mar. 1892.
72. *Municipal boundaries, evidence* para. 4641.
73. *Pembroke minutes,* 30 July 1894.
74. *Dublin housing* App. xxxvi, 488-9.
75. *Pembroke works and finance comm.* 21 Oct. 1887, 29 July 1895, 29 April 1892, *I.T.* 13 Jan. 1900.
76. CSO/RP 1892/13946.
77. CSO/RP 1892/14187, 1893/398.
78. *Pembroke minutes,* 3 Mar. 1902.
79. *F.J.* 26 Feb. 1901, 7 Mar. 1901.
80. *I.T. 10 June 1902.*
81. *Pembroke minutes,* 23 May 1902.
82. *I.T.* 19 Mar. 1901, the phrase is that of the local government board auditor.
83. *I.T.* 24 Jan. 1911.
84. *I.T.* 12 Mar. 1903, report of court case, Clancy v. Pembroke Co.
85. F.W.R. Knowles, *Old Clontarf* (no date, no place) pp 4, 9.
86. *Dub. Build.* 15 May 1861, 1 July 1861.
87. ibid., 15 Aug. 1861, 1 May 1862, 1 April 1863.
88. ibid., 15 April 1861, 15 May 1861.
89. ibid. 1 May 1861.
90. *I.T.* 28 June 1869.
91. *Municipal boundaries evidence* para. 6252, and 32 and 33 Vict. cap. lxxxv, *Clontarf township act* para 72.
92. *Municipal boundaries evidence,* paras. 5376-85.
93. *Dublin mun. co. minutes* 16 April 1879.
94. *Municipal boundaries evidence,* para. 5364.
95. ibid. *report* p. 2.
96. *I.T.* 17 Jan. 1899.
97. *I.T.* 20 July 1900.
98. *I.T.* 20 Mar. 1875.

99. *I.T.* 5 July 1875.
100. *I.T.* 17 Mar. 1875.
101. *I.T.* 7 Dec. 1875.
102. *I.T.* 2 Mar. 1876.
103. *F.J.* 8 Jan. 1878.
104. *Municipal boundaries, evidence* para. 5244, James Fitzgerald Lombard.
105. *Ir. Build.* 15 Oct. 1884.
106. *I.T.* 30 Dec. 1884, evidence to Local Govt. Bo. inquiry.
107. *Housing of the working class*, evidence Edward McMahon paras. 24594 and 24625.
108. ibid. para. 24603.
109. *I.T.* 20 June 1894.
110. *I.T.* 6 Nov. 1897.
111. *Ir. Build.* 19 Dec. 1914.
112. *I.T.* 25 April 1868, evidence to committee on Kilmainham township bill.
113. *I.T.* 27 April 1868.
114. *Great Southern and Western Railway Co. minutes*, 29 Mar. 1867 29 Oct. 1869.
115. *Municipal boundaries evidence*, para. 5883, Francis Moore Scott.
116. *I.T.* 25 April 1868, evidence Rev. Thomas Mills.
117. *I.T.* 10 Feb. 1871.
118. *Thom's Directory 1860,* Dublin police carriage regulations.
119. *Even Tel.* 6 Feb. 1897 and *I.T.* 12 Sept. 1871.
120. *I.T.* 13 Aug. 1868.
121. *I.T.* 12 Sept. 1871.
122. *I.T.* 27 July, 1869.
123. J.R. Kellett, *Impact of the railways on Victorian cities* (London 1969) p. 367 notes that from 75 to 90% of residents of a modern suburb are genuine residents.
124. *Dublin mun. co. minutes*, 11 April 1861.
125. ibid. 8 Nov. 1861.
126. ibid. report comm. no. 1, 1 nov. 1866.
127. ibid. 2 May 1870.
128. 34 and 35 Vict. ch. lxxxviii.
129. *I.T.* 2 Feb. 1872.
130. *I.T.* 12 Aug. 1872.
131. *I.T.* 11 Dec. 1873.
132. *I.T.* 11 Feb. 1874.
133. *I.T.* 14 Aug. 1874.
134. *I.T.* 11 Feb. 1874.
135. *I.T.* 4 Feb. 1875.
136. 38 and 39 Vict. cap. ccix. *North Dublin street tramways.*
137. *I.T.* 16 Feb. 1876.
138. 39 and 40 Vict. cap. ccxxxiii. *North Dublin street tramways.*
139. *I.T.* 23 Feb. 1877.
140. 41 and 42 Vict. cap. clviii.
141. *I.T.* 6 May 1878, 14 May, 1878.
142. *I.T.* 11 Aug. 1879.
143. *I.T.* 13 Mar. 1880.
144. *I.T.* 10 Mar. 1879.
145. *I.T.* 2 Aug. 1882.
146. *Official Irish travelling guide,* July 1879.
147. *Ir. Build.* 1 April 1894.
148. *I.T.* 17 Mar. 1898.

149. *I.T.* 6 April 1905.
150. *F.J.* 11 Mar. 1878.
151. *I.T.* 6 May 1878.
152. *I.T.* 6 Aug. 1884.
153. *Dublin United Tramway Co. Timetable*, Nov. 1886.
154. *I.T.* 3 July 1868.
155. 27 and 28 Vict. cap. cclxxxi.
156. *Rathmines minutes*, 22 Feb. 1864.
157. 28 and 29 Vict. cap. cclxv.
158. CSO/RP 1871/14634, report directors' meeting, 29 Mar. 1871.
159. *Even. Tel.* 29 May 1897.
160. *Hansard*, 16 Feb. 1911.
161. Kevin Murray, 'Dublin's first railway', *Dublin Historical Record*, I, p. 19.
162. J.J. Lee, 'Merchants and enterprise: the case of the early Irish railways', in L.M. Cullen and P. Butel (eds), *Negoce et industrie en France et en Irelande aux xviii et xix siecles*, p. 147.
163. ibid.
164. *Dub. Build.* 1 June 1860.
165. ibid. 15 May 1863.
166. ibid. 1 May 1867.
167. *Town holdings, evidence* John McEvoy, para. 6076.
168. ibid. para. 5587.
169. Lee op. cit. p. 147.
170. *Copy of report of inquiry by the Board of Trade and of correspondence relative to the present condition and high rate of charges on the Dublin and Kingston section of the Dublin Wicklow and Wexford railway.* 1878 (147) lxvi, p. 3.
171. *Dly. Exp.* 5 June 1861.
172. *I.T.* 20 May 1867.
173. *Board of Trade inquiry,* Report Major General Hutchinson pp 9-10.
174. *I.T.* 27 May 1878.
175. Kellett op. cit. p. 362.
176. ibid. p. 376.
177. *I.T.* 6 April 1865.
178. *Town holdings, evidence* James R. Stewart, agent, para. 5228.
179. ibid. 5253.
180. ibid. 5535.
181. ibid. 5221.
182. *F.J.* 12 Aug. 1898.
183. *I.T.* 29 June 1867.
184. *I.T.* 8 May 1873.
185. *Town holdings,* para. 5875, evidence John McEvoy, para. 5256 evidence James Stewart.
186. *I.T.* 3 Oct. 1884.
187. *F.J.* 16 Oct. 1884.
188. CSO/RP 1887/17750, 1888/5337, 7055 and 6925.
189. *F.J.* 16 Oct. 1884.
190. CSO/RP 1888/7269.
191. *I.T.* 16 April 1903.
192. *I.T.* 20 Mar. 1903.
193. *I.T.* 22 April 1903.
194. *I.T.* 23 April 1910.
195. CSO/RP 1863/7610.
196. Page L. Dickinson, *The Dublin of yesterday* (London 1929) p. 192.

197. CSO/RP 1865/2321.
198. CSO/RP 1865/2649.
199. ibid. 1865/3015.
200. *I.T.* 19 July 1869.
201. CSO/RP 1860/19340.
202. CSO/RP 1860/19132.
203. CSO/RP 1861/8634, 8869, 9135, 9271.
204. CSO/RP 1862/10415.
205. A Ratepayer, *Blackrock township, is it fair?* (Dublin 1863).
206. *F.J.* 29 Oct. 1884.
207. *Dub. Build.* 15 Mar. 1862.
208. *I.T.* 6 April 1865.
209. Advert. *Dly. Exp.* 18 July 1866.
210. *I.T.* 4 Feb. 1870.
211. *I.T.* 17 Mar. 1906. Local government board inquiry re sewage loan.
212. Kellett, op. cit. pp 385-6.

Chapter VII

1. *Municipal corporations (Ireland).* Appendix to the 'First report of the commissioners. Report on the city of Dublin', Part I, 1835, xxvii, paras. 33-35.
2. ibid. para. 36.
3. ibid. para. 63.
4. *I.T.* 6 Nov. 1895.
5. *Select committee on local government and taxation of towns. First report, 1876.* (7), para. 2361, evidence Joseph T. Pim.
6. This was apparently the case in Cork. Ian D'Alton, *Protestant society and politics in Cork* (Cork 1981) p. 192.
7. *List of subscriptions: Papal tribute from Diocese of Dublin.* 1860. (Dublin 1860).
8. Publius, *Letters on Dublin corporation*, p. 20. originally published in *Dly. Exp.* 1 Oct. 1860.
9. *local government and taxation of towns*, para. 23.1.
10. Joseph T. Pim, 'Municipal government and taxation', paper read at the Statistical Society, 19 Jan. 1875.
11. *local government and taxation of towns*, para. 307.
12. D'Alton, op. cit. p. 89.
13. ibid. pp 112-3
14. Sir John Gilbert, (ed), *Calendar of the ancient records of the city of Dublin*, (Henceford CARD), vol. xix, p. 349.
15. ibid. p. 359.

16. D'Alton, op. cit. p. 177.
17. David Thornley, *Isaac Butt and Home Rule* (1964) pp 15-16.
18. *Dly. Exp.* 2 July 1866.
19. D'Alton, op. cit. p. 192.
20. *Report special committee of Dublin corporation re the compact in the corporation as to the election of a Lord Mayor*, 1864. p. 17.
21. ibid. p. 16.
22. ibid. p. 17.
23. ibid. pp 18-19.
24. ibid. conclusions, I-III.
25. ibid.
26. ibid. p. 8.
27. ibid. p. 9.
28. *Address and resolutions of sympathy with His Holiness Pope Pius IX.* Meeting 9 Jan. 1860.
29. *Report of debate by Dublin corporation re granting of a charter for the Catholic University* (Dublin 1862).
30. *Report re compact as to election of Lord Mayor* pp 19-20.
31. E.R. Norman, *The catholic church and Ireland in the age of rebellion* (1965) p. 136.
32. ibid. p. 151.
33. ibid. p. 156.
34. ibid. p. 291.
35. ibid. p. 158.
36. ibid. p. 320.
37. *I.T.* 7 July 1868.
38. *I.T.* 11 Aug. 1868.
39. *I.T.* 6 July 1869.
40. *I.T.* 3 Aug. 1869.
41. David Thornley, 'Irish conservatives and Home Rule', *I.H.S.* 1958-9 p. 206.
42. Norman, op. cit. p. 418.
43. Thornley, op. cit.
44. *I.T.* 2 July, 1878.
45. T.D. Sullivan, *Troubled times in Irish politics.* (Dublin 1905) pp 224-5.
46. ibid., p. 225.
47. CARD xixi, p. 344, paragraphs 30, 31 and 32.
48. Sullivan, op. cit. p. 220.
49. ibid. p.225.
50. ibid., p. 222.
51. ibid. p. 236.
52. *I.T.* 7 July 1896.
53. B. McDonnell, *The Dublin labour movement, 1894-1907*, p. 209.
54. ibid, pp 210-11.
55. *I.T.* 6 Nov. 1896.
56. *E.Tel.* 27 July 1896.
57. *E.Tel.* 12 Aug. 1896.
58. *E.Tel.* 30 Oct. 1896.
59. McDonnell, op. cit. p. 222.
60. *I.T.* 17 Jan. 1899.
61. McDonnell, op. cit. p.208.
62. ibid. p. 212.
63. ibid. pp 228-9.
64. ibid. p. 231.
65. *E.Tel.* 7 July 1896.

66. McDonnell, op. cit. pp 236-7.
67. ibid. p. 239.
68. ibid. p. 241.
69. J.W. Boyle, *The rise of the Irish labour movement 1886-1907* Ph.D. thesis, Trinity College Dublin, 1961. p. 274.
70. McDonnell, op. cit. p. 259.
71. *Ir. Indep.* 18 Jan, 1899.
72. James Connolly, *Workers Republic* ed. Desmond Ryan (Dublin 1951) p. 46.
73. ibid. p. 103, initially published in *Irish Worker*, p. 14 Jan. 1914.
74. ibid. p. 46.
75. Patrick Cunningham, *Autobiography*, NDI Ms. N. 6205. no date.
76. See chapter IX.
77. E.P. Hennock, *Fit and proper persons*, p. 61.
78. ibid. p. 145.
79. *Minutes mun. co. 18th report waterworks committee*, dated 15 Feb. 1871, read 28 Aug. 1871.
80. Hennock, op. cit. p. 295.
81. Cornelius O Leary, 'Belfast urban government in the age of reform', in D. Harkness and M. O Dowd (eds), *The town in Ireland* (Belfast 1981) p. 201.
82. *Minutes mun. co.,* 14 Jan. 1864.
83. Asa Briggs, *Victorian cities* (Pelican ed. 1968), p. 40.
84. Ishbel Aberdeen, *We Twa*, i, 257 (1927)
85. Dickenson, op. cit. p. 14.
86. *We Twa*, ii, 178.
87. Surgeon Colonel D. Edgar Flinn, *Official report on the sanitary circumstances and administration of the city of Dublin, with special reference to the causes of the high death-rate* (Dublin, 1906, for HMSO).
88. *Report of the municipal committee to the council of the Chamber of Commerce*, 28 Aug. 1850.
89. *Chamber of Commerce*, 18 Jan. 1856.
90. ibid. 6 Jan, 1858.
91. ibid. 22 Jan. 1877.
92. ibid. 7 May 1877.
93. ibid. 21 July 1890.
94. ibid. 20 Jan. 1890.
95. *Dublin Chamber of Commerce*, annual report for the year 1885.
96. ibid. 1886.
97. *Unionist Convention for the provnices of Leinster, Munster and Connaught. (June 1892). Report of proceedings.* (Dublin 1892). p. 118.
98. *R.C. housing of the working class report on Ireland.*
99. *Minutes P and D.* 25 Jan. 1867.
100. ibid. 16 July 1874.
101. ibid. 25 April 1875.
102. ibid. 3 June 1875.
103. ibid. 22 July 1880, 12 Aug. 1880.
104. *I.T.* 1 Mar. 1897.
105. *F.J.* 16 Mar. 1898.
106. *I.T.* 12 Jan. 1899.
107. *F.J.* 14 Feb. 1901.
108. *I.T.* 27 Feb. 1908.
109. O Leary, op. cit. p. 202.
110. *Minutes mun. co.* 14 June 1860.
111. *F.J.* 2 May, 1864.
112. CSO/RP 1865/781.

113. CSO/RP 1865/998.
114. CSO/RP 1865/2043.
115. CSO/RP 1874/17604.
116. *I.T.* 9 May, 1872.
117. CSO/RP 1874/17604.
118. *Minutes mun. co.* 4 Sept. 1876.
119. ibid, report committee of the whole house, 1877 no. 211, 15 Aug. 1877.
120. *I.T.* 9 July 1878.
121. *I.T.* 29 Sept. 1881.
122. CSO/RP 1874/10666, 1874/16925.
123. 40 and 41 Vict. cap. lxxxii.
124. Letter to Dublin corporation, 28 Oct. 1875.
125. CSO/RP 1883/21011, memorial of Lord Mayor.
126. *Report select committee local government and taxation of towns* (Ireland). 1876, (362), x, 147.
127. CSO/RP 1883/21011.
128. *R.C. municipal boundaries* para. 1.
129. ibid. p. 15.
130. ibid. p. 43.
131. ibid. p. 15.
132. ibid. p. 34.
133. ibid. p. 17.
134. ibid. p. 33.
135. ibid. p. 40.
136. ibid. p. 36.
137. *I.T.* 20 May, 1879.
138. *I.T.* 1 April 1881.
139. *I.T.* 11 April 1881.
140. *I.T.* 29 Sept, 1881.
141. *Minutes mun co.* 19 Nov. 1883.
142. CSO/RP 1883/28351
143. *I.T.* 20 Nov. 1884.
144. CSO/RP 1884/291.
145. *R.C. housing of the working class* p. xi.
146. CSO/RP 1885/22404, para. 4.
147. *F.J.* 11 April 1885.
148. CSO/RP 1885/7695.
149. *I.T.* 26 May 1886.
150. *Minutes mun. co.* 4 July 1888.
151. CSO/RP 1889/109.
152. CSO/RP 1891/15735, Report John Ball Greene, re valuation of Belfast.
153. CSO/RP 1891/8189.
154. CSO/RP 1897/4992.
155. CSO/RP 189721122.
156. CSO/RP 1897/21122.
157. E. Jones, 'Late Victorian Belfast', in J.C. Beckett and R.E. Glasscock (eds), *Belfast: the origin and growth of an industrial city* (1967) p. 119.
158. *Ir. Indep.* 28 Jan. 1899.
159. *Hansard*, vol. 61 p. 1127.
160. CSO/RP 1898/18351.
161. CSO/RP 1898/19467.
162. *I.T.* 14 June 1899.
163. *I.T.* 3 Feb. 1898.
164. *I.T.* 25 July 1899.

(Pages 236-238)

165. *I.T.* 1 Nov. 1898, resolution of Pembroke commissioners.
166. *Hansard*, vol. 75, p. 1209, 3 Aug. 1899.
167. *I.T.* 4 Aug. 1899, statement Duke of Northumberland.
168. *F.J.* 20 Mar. 1900.
169. *Hansard*, vol. 86, p. 637, 20 July 1900.
170. *Report select committee on the Dublin corporation bill and the Clontarf U.D.C. bill,* 1900 vol, vi, 899 p. 5.
171. *Hansard*, vol. 87, p. 743.
172. *Mun. co. report committee of the whole house re Dublin corporation boundaries bill* 1900.
173. *I.T.* 18 May 1900.
174. *I.T.* 30 June 1900.
175. *I.T.* 3 July 1900.
176. *I.T.* 11 July 1899, evidence to select committee House of Lords.
177. *F.J.* 11 June 1901.
178. *I.T.* 13 June 1901.
179. *E.Tel.* 3 Mar. 1898.
180. 1 Edw. 7 cap. ccxix.
181. CSO/RP 1901/575.
182. CSO/RP 1901/13446 and 1901/13605.
183. *Hansard*, vol. 99 p. 250.
184. Public inquiry, 13 Dec. 1911, 26 Jan. 1912, under the *equalisation of rates act.*
185. Sect 60, 63 and 64 Vict. cap. cclxiv.
186. *I.T.* 11 Mar. 1901.
187. *I.T.* 11 May 1904.
188. CSO/RP 1906/7822.
189. *I.T.* 11 May 1904.
190. *I.T.* 6 June 1906 and CSO/RP 1906/7822.
191. *I.T.* 16 May 1904.
192. *I.T.* 9 June 1906.
193. *I.T.* 12 Sept. 1913.
194. *I.T.* 15 Jan. 1912.

Chapter VIII

1. 26 Vict. cap. 11. An act for the registration of births and deaths in Ireland.

2. *Pop. Ire. 1841. Table of deaths, V. Special report on Dublin City* p. lxviii.

ibid. 1851, Part V, i, Sect. VIII pp 479-521.

ibid. 1861, Part II, vol. iii, Sect. VII pp 52-90.

3. Royston Lambert, *Sir John Simon 1816-1904 and English social administration* (1963) pp 262-3.

4. *Census Ire. 1871*, II, ii Sect. viii.

5. 42 and 43 Vict. ch. 57. An act to amend the public health (Ireland) act, 1878.

6. Asa Briggs, *History of Birmingham* (2 vols. Oxford 1952), ii, 225, Brian D. White, *A history of the corporation of Liverpool, 1835- 1914* (Liverpool 1951) p. 92.

7. Eric Lampard, 'The urbanising world', in H.J. Dyos and Michael Wolff, *The Victorian city, image and reality* (2 vols. 1973), i, 21.

8. F.B. Smith, *The people's health, 1831-1910*, (1979) p. 288.

9. Rosen, 'Disease, debility and death', in Dyos and Wolff, op. cit. ii, pp 641-3.

10. Dublin municipal council, *Public healths reports, 1890-1914.*

11. *Report of the departmental committee appointed by the local government board of Ireland to inquire into the public health of the city of Dublin 1900* (cd. 243), xxxix, p.6.

12. *R. C. sewerage and drainage of the city of Dublin*, 1880 (c. 2605), xxx.

13. Smith op. cit. pp 196-7 for English and Scottish statistics and *Public health reports.*

14. *R. C. sewerage and drainage.*

15. *Public health reports, 1912-14,* calculations.

16. E. Finer, *Life and times of Sir Edwin Chadwick*, p. 217.

17. 11 and 12 Vict. ch. 123.

18. Charles Cameron, *A brief history of municipal public health administration in Dublin* (Dublin 1914) p. 19.

19. Cameron, op. cit. pp 21 and 23.

20. Parke Neville, *Report to the Lord Mayor etc of the city of Dublin on the sewerage of the city and proposed plans for improving the same* (Dublin 1853) pp 44-5.

21. Mun. Co. *Minutes*, 13 Aug, 1861.

22. Parke Neville, *A description of the Dublin corporation waterworks* (Dublin 1875) pp 6-7.

23. Dublin waterworks, *Report committee no. 2,* Feb. 1859.

24. Mun. Co. *Minutes of special meeting,* 28 Oct. to consider report committee of 16 May 1859.

25. Finer, op. cit. p. 298.

26. G.R. Kitson-Clark, *An expanding society, Britain, 1830-1900* (Cambridge 1967) p. 165.

27. Mun. Co. *Minutes*, 28 Oct. 1859.

28. ibid. Report waterworks comm. 21 Feb. 1860 and 27 Feb. 1860.

29. ibid. 16 April 1860.

30. ibid. 13 July 1860.

31. *Report of royal commission*, special meeting Dublin Corporation, 23 Oct. 1860.

32. Mun. Co. *Minutes*, 18th report waterworks committee, 15 Feb. 1871. read 28 Aug. 1871.

33. *Report select committee local government and taxation of towns,* 1876, para. 5601, evidence Parke Neville.

34. Mun. Co. *Minutes*, 22 June 1857.

35. G. Best, 'Another part of the island', in Dyos and Wolff op. cit. i, 391.

36. White, op. cit. pp 56-7.

37. *F.J.* 18 Feb. 1861.

38. Mun. Co. *Minutes*, 7 Oct. 1861, report waterworks comm. 2 June 1861.

39. ibid. 10 June 1861.

40. Sir John Gray, *Speech in vindication of the municipal council of Dublin* (Dublin 1864).

41. Mun. Co. *Minutes*, 28 Aug. 1871, 18th report waterworks committee, 15 Feb. 1871.

42. Finer op. cit. p. 484.

43. Neville, *sewerage*, p. 4.

44. CSO/RP 1869/14905.

45. *I.T.* 22 Nov. 1864.

46. Mun. Co. *Minutes*, 22 Dec. 1865.

47. *Dly. Exp.* 29 Nov. 1866.

48. Neville, *sewerage* p. 44.

49. Finer op. cit. p. 301.

50. *I.T.* 22 Nov. 1864.

51. J.W. Bazalgette, *Report on the Dublin sewage utilisation bill* (Dublin 1868).

52. Mun. Co. *Minutes*, 8 Dec. 1864.

53. ibid. 6 Feb. 1865.

54. *Dly. Exp.* 7 Mar. 1865.

55. Bazalgette op. cit. p. 10.

56. 34 and 35 Vict. cap. cxxviii.

57. Mun. Co. *Minutes*, 16 Mar. 1871.

58. CSO/RP 1872/19280, 1872/1539.

59. *I.T.* 18 July 1873.

60. *I.T.* 27 June 1874.

61. CSO/RP 1874/17835.

62. CSO/RP 1875/10072.

63. *I.T.* 26 Mar. 1875.

64. Mun. Co. *Minutes*, 16 Nov. 1891.

65. *I.T.* 25 Sept. 1906.

66. Mun. Co. *Minutes*, 8 July 1870.

67. CSO/RP 1874/16323,

68. CSO/RP 1875/10072.

69. *R.C. sewerage and drainage* p. iv.

70. CSO/RP 1887/10952.

71. Mun. Co. *Minutes*, 13 Mar. 1865.

72. Mun. Co. *Reports*, 1879 no. 184, report city engineer.

73. *R.C. sewerage* p. ix.

74. ibid. p. x.

75. *I.T.* 10 Jan. 1894.

76. Thomas W. Grimshaw, *Remarks on the prevalence and distribution of fever in Dublin*, (Dublin 1872).

77. Smith, op. cit. p. 244.

78. Smith, op. cit. p. 244 and *Public health reports.*

79. *Report public health committee,* 1893 no. 183.

80. ibid.

81. CSO/RP 1872/5910.

82. Mun. Co. *Minutes*, 3 Feb. 1879.

83. 1893 no. 183.

84. Flinn, op. cit. p. 22.

85. Mun. Co. *Minutes*, 6 June 1864, report comm. no. 2, 27 May 1864.
86. ibid. 3 Oct. 1862.
87. ibid. 17 Sept. 1862, letter South Dublin Union, dated 11 Sept. 1862.
88. E.D. Mapother, *Report on the health of the city of Dublin for the year 1865* (Dublin 1866).
89. E.D. Mapother 'The sanitary state of Dublin' in *Papers concerning public health* (Dublin 1864) p. 2.
90. Lambert, op. cit. p. 306.
91. CSO/RP 1865/2769, statement of E.D. Mapother.
92. 27 and 28 Vict. cap. 305.
93. Mun. Co. *Minutes*, 21 Nov. 1864, report comm. no. 2, 24 Sept. 1864.
94. ibid. 17 Jan. 1865.
95. ibid. 5 Mar. 1866.
96. ibid. 7 May 1866, report comm. no. 2. 16 Mar. 1866.
97. 29 and 30 Vict. ch. 90.
98. Mun. Co. *Minutes*, 21 Sept. 1866.
99. ibid. 8 Oct. 1866.
100. CSO/RP 1872/3857. 1872/4713.
101. CSO/RP 1872/7934.
102. 37 and 38 Vict. ch. 13.
103. CSO/RP 1874/13425.
104. 41 and 42 Vict. ch. 52.
105. ibid. part IV, section 227.
106. *Public health committee,* annual report 31 Mar. 1874.
107. *Dublin sanitary association*, report 11 July 1873.
108. CSO/RP 1873/5571, 6019 and 6676.
109. *Dublin sanitary association*, 1874 report, p. 15.
110. CSO/RP 1873/6676.
111. CSO/RP 1873/7058.
112. *I.T.* 3 April 1875.
113. *local govt. and taxation of towns*, 1876 q. 3918.
114. Mun. Co. *Reports*, 1879 no. 86.
115. *R.C. sewerage* p. xxii.
116. *Report cleansing committee*, 1882 no. 125.
117. CSO/RP 1883/3068.
118. Flinn op. cit. p. 29.
119. Mun. Co. *Report comm. no.2,* 23 April 1867.
120. *Ir. Build.* 15 Nov. 1880.
121. Mun. Co. *Minutes*, 21 July 1879.
122. *R.C. sewerage*, evidence James Boyle, Sec. public health comm. p. 170.
123. *Report public health committee,* 1879 no. 170.
124. *R.C. sewerage* evidence p. 170.
125. *Ir. Build.* 15 April 1882.
126. *Report public health committee,* 1882 no. 182.
127. ibid. 1883 no. 26.
128. Dublin corporation bill, 1890, Evidence given at Ho. of Commons, select committee, 12 May 1890, p. 423.
129. 53 and 54 Vict. cap. cxliv, clause 80.
130. CSO/RP 1897/2219. Report Dr. Stafford, 4 Feb. 1897.
131. CSO/RP 1899/20152 and 1900/4511.
132. CSO/RP 1900/1435.
133. *departmental committee public health* p. 13.
134. CSO/RP 1890/9867. memorial Dublin sanitary associaiton.
135. *departmental committee public health* p. 2.

136. Flinn, op. cit. p. 35.
137. *I.T.* 7 Oct. 1908.
138. Smith op. cit. p. 137.
139. *departmental committee public health* p. 11.
140. CSO/RP 1897/6084.
141. CSO/RP 1897/13979.
142. *I.T.* 31 Aug. 1904.
143. Flinn op. cit. p. 31.
144. Flinn op. cit. p. 33 and *departmental committee public health* evidence p. 39 q. 2685, Dr. E.W. Hope, MOH Liverpool.
145. ibid. p. 17.
146. *Report public health for the year 1899.*
147. Cameron op. cit. pp 46 and 48.
148. L. McKenna, *Handbook for Catholic social workers in Dublin* (Dublin 1918) p. 11.
149. Smith, op. cit. p. 117.
150. Flinn, op. cit. p. 22.
151. ibid. p. 49.
152. ibid. p. 50.
153. ibid. p. 47.
154. *departmental committee public health*, report recommendation no. 9.
155. Flinn op. cit. p. 12.
156. *I.T.* 14 June 1902.
157. Cameron, op. cit.
158. *Public health report 1905,* 1906 no. 157.
159. *departmental committee public health* p. 6.
160. *Report public health committee* 1900 no. 165.
161. Mun. Co. *Minutes,* 7 Jan. 1901.
162. *departmental committee public health*, evidence para. 2757.
163. Flinn, op. cit. App. information Dr. Newsholme.
164. Mun. Co. *Minutes* 19 April 1905.
165. ibid. 24 Aug. 1906.
166. *Report public health committee* 1907 no. 65.
167. Mun. Co. *Minutes* 9 Aug 1909.
168. Ishbel Aberdeen, *Ireland's crusade against TB* (Dublin 1908).
169. *Conference of municipal authorities*, 1913, pp 18-22.
170. *Sinn Fein Daily*, 8 Sept. 1909.
171. Smith, op. cit. p. 292.
172. *I.T.* 6 May 1914.
173. Maud Pember Reeves, op. cit. p.
174. *Report public health 1912.*
175. i.e. Flinn, op. cit. or Charles Cameron, *How the poor live* (Dublin 1908).
176. *Poor inquiry (Ireland), 1836(35),* Supplement to App. C. (Part II) First report commissioners. City of Dublin questionnaire, evidence.
177. W.H. Thompson, *War and the food of the Dublin poor* (Dublin 1916) p. 7.
178. Stafford, op. cit. in *r.c. poor law.*
179. Thompson, op. cit. p. 3.
180. ibid. p. 4.
181. *Report of registrar general for the year 1940* p. xv.
182. *Report of inquiry into the housing of the working classes of the city of Dublin 1939-43* R/75/1.
183. Calculated from public health reports 1883-1910.
184. Sir Charles Cameron, *Autobiography* p. 29 (Dublin 1920).
185. *departmental committee public health* paras. 2739, 2746.

186. ibid. para. 2861.
187. *Report Dublin sanitary association,* 11 June 1873.
188. *I.T.* 10 Feb. 1900.
189. Cameron, op. cit. p. 21.
190. Mun. Co. *Minutes,* 2 Sept. 1861. report comm. no. 2, 2 Aug. 1861.
191. *Ir. Build.* 1 Sept. 1872.
192. *First report Dublin sanitary association,* 11 June 1873.
193. *Dublin sanitary association, memorial,* 5 Feb. 1873.
194. CSO/RP 1874/16323.
195. *I.T.* 19 June 1874.
196. Mun. Co. *Minutes,* 13 April 1876, report 1876 no. 30.
197. *Memorial to Lord Lieutenant by Dublin sanitary association,* 1878 (148), lxv, 157.
198. *Report on death rate in Dublin,* 1878 no. 71.
199. CSO/RP 1878/4802.
200. CSO/RP 1879/9824.
201. CSO/RP 1879/10526.
202. CSO/RP 1879/10746.
203. CSO/RP 1879/12921.
204. *F.J.* 20 Sept. 1899.
205. *I.T.* 26 Sept. 1899.
206. *F.J.* 19 Jan. 1900.

Chapter IX

1. Anthony Sutcliffe (ed), *Multi-storey living: the British working class experience* (1974) introduction.
2. J. Warburton, J. Whitelaw and R. Walsh, *History of the city of Dublin,* two volumes (London 1818), i, 443.
3. H.J. Dyos, 'The slums of Victorian London, *Vict. Stud,* xi, no. 1. Sept. 1967, p. 25.
4. John H. Martin, *Aspects of the social geography of Dublin City in the Mid 19th century* M.A. thesis, U.C.D. 1973.
5. *R.C. municipal boundaries,* evidence para. 485.
6. *Report paving and lighting comm.* 1888 no. 3.
7. *Report housing committee,* 1914 no. 17.
8. Grimshaw, op. cit. p. 25.
9. Cheyne Brady, *The practicability of improving the dwellings of the labouring classes,* (London 1854) paper read to Royal Dublin Society, Jan. 1854.
10. *Report departmental committee appointed to inquire into the housing conditions of the working class in Dublin.* 1914, Cd. 7269, p. 2.

11. Cameron, op. cit. p. 67.
12. Mun. Co. *Minutes*, 24 Jan. 1862, report comm. no. 2.
13. CSO/RP 1866/22396.
14. Mun. Co. *Minutes*, 5 Mar. 1866.
15. ibid. 7 May, 1866.
16. Cameron, op. cit. p. 67.
17. CSO/RP 1874/13137.
18. CSO/RP 1874/13606.
19. CSO/RP 1876/2745 and 1876/5953.
20. CSO/RP 1876/17756 and 1876/18462.
21. CSO/RP 1877/5259.
22. CSO/RP 1872/4713.
23. E.D. Mapother, *Lectures on public health*, No. 12, 'Dwellings of the labouring classes' p. 298 (Dublin 1867).
24. Mun. Co. *Minutes*, public health breviate, Dec. 1869.
25. *housing conditions of the working class,* Evidence, 1914 cd. 7272, xviii, para. 1771.
26. Warburton Whitelaw and Walsh, op. cit. p. 443.
27. *Public health reports, 1866.*
28. ibid. 1884-87.
29. *I.T.* 14 Jan. 1879.
30. CSO/RP 1903/3462, Bull Alley book of reference.
31. *I.T.* 10 Oct. 1913.
32. *I.T.* 18 Mar. 1901.
33. *I.T.* 26 Aug. 1876. Advert.
34. *I.T.* 5 May 1899.
35. *I.T.* 26 June 1900.
36. *I.T.* 14 Nov. 1900. Advert.
37. *housing conditions of the working class,* para. 2006 evidence.
38. *I.T.* 21 July 1899.
39. *I.T.* 28 May 1892.
40. *housing conditions of the working class* evidence, para. 65.
41. Edward Spencer, 'Homes for the working class in Dublin' paper reported in *I.T.* 2 Oct. 1884.
42. Richard M. Kelly, 'The administration of sanitary law', *Medical press and circular*, 27 Feb. 1901, p.275.
43. *housing conditions of the working class,* p. 9 para. 22.
44. ibid. p. 12.
45. *Kelly, op. cit.*
46. *housing conditions of the working class,* p. 12.
47. ibid. p. 12.
48. ibid. p. 13 para. 31.
49. ibid. p. 13 para. 31.
50. ibid, evidence p. 245, paras 6269 and 6290.
51. *I.T.* 11 Oct. 1902.
52. *I.T.* 6 Oct. 1908.
53. *Sinn Fein Daily,* 23 Nov. 1909.
54. Cameron, op. cit. p. 67.
55. *Report public health,* 1881 no. 181.
56. ibid. 1882 no. 81.
57. ibid. 1883 no. 31, 1884 no. 69.
58. *R.C. housing of the working class,* 1884-5 p. vii.
59. *Reports public health,* 1887 no. 68, 1893 no. 120.
60. ibid. 1882 no. 81.

61. ibid. 1884 no. 69.
62. Artisans dwellings act, sect. 9.
63. E.D. Mapother and P. Neville, *Report on the unhealthy districts in the boro. of Dublin*, 12 June 1876.
64. CSO/RP 1907/5294.
65. *Report improvement comm. on improvement scheme of dwellings*, 26 Oct. 1876, 1876 no. 87.
66. P.O. 40 and 41 Vict. cap. cxxiii.
67. *Report of special committee*, 1879 no. 230.
68. *I.T.* 14 Jan. 1879.
69. *Report* 1882 no. 183.
70. ibid. 1884 no. 52.
71. ibid. 1882 no. 183.
72. Mun. Co. *Minutes*, 5 Jan. 1887.
73. CSO/RP 1885/20421.
74. *Report* 1905 no. 107.
75. *E.Tel.* 28 Dec. 1907.
76. *I.T.* 9 July 1910.
77. *I.T.* 8 Jan. 1909.
78. *I.T.* 22 Oct. 1913.
79. CSO/RP 1896/20645.
80. CSO/RP 1897/537.
81. *Report* 1907 no. 258, Mun. Co. *Minutes* 20 Aug. 1908 and *Sinn Fein* 20 June 1908.
82. Mun. Co. *Minutes*, 6 May 1901.
83. *Report improvement comm.* 1903 no. 145.
84. *I.T.* 28 June 1895.
85. *I.T.* 17 Jan. 1900.
86. *Dub. Build.* 1 May 1865.
87. *Dly. Exp.* 29 May 1866.
88. *I.T.* 24 May 1867.
89. *housing conditions of the working class*, p. 19 para. 43.
90. ibid., app. xxvi.
91. *Ir. Build.* 15 Jan. 1878.
92. Spencer Harty, 'Some considerations of the artisans dwelling acts as illustrated in the case of the Coombe, *Stat. Soc. Ire. Jn.* vol. 8, p. 508, 1884.
93. *Ir. Build.* 15 Aug. 1878.
94. ibid. 1 Oct. 1881.
95. CSO/RP 1883/26562 and 1883/26948.
96. Harty, op. cit.
97. Edward Spencer, *Artisans and labourers' dwellings* (Dublin 1881).
98. *I.T.* 16 Nov. 1897.
99. *Ir. Build.* 15 July 1878.
100. *Ir. Build.* 30 Jan. 1902.
101. *F.J.* 13 Feb. 1900.
102. *I.T.* 6 Nov. 1897.
103. *Ir. Build.* 1 Mar. 1886.
104. Calculated from Anthony S. Wohl, *The eternal slum* (1977), App. III and Housing conditions of the working class p. 182.
105. *housing conditions of the working class* p. 18 para. 40.
106. *E.Tel.* 8 Mar. 1897.
107. *I.T.* 7 June 1897.
108. *I.T.* 10 June 1897.
109. *I.T.* 18 Oct. 1898.

110. *housing conditions of the working class* p. 19.
111. *I.T.* 9 Nov. 1903.
112. *housing conditions of the working class* p. 3, para. 8.
113. ibid. recommendations para. 51.
114. *Oxmanstown estate committee report,* 1881 no. 38.
115. *housing conditions of the working class,* evidence para. 463.
116. *F.J.* 12 Dec. 1885.
117. *Report artisans dwellings comm.* 1897 no. 18.
118. ibid. 1890 no. 72.
119. ibid. 1891 no. 64.
120. ibid. 1893 no. 116.
121. ibid. 1891 no. 102.
122. *housing conditions of the working class* evidence para. 466.
123. *Report artisans dwellings comm.* 1894 no. 136.
124. *housing conditions of the working class,* evidence para. 465.
125. Cameron op. cit. p. 57.
126. *Report artisan dwellings comm.* 1906 no. 33.
127. *housing conditions of the working class* para. 466.
128. *Report artisans dwellings comm.* 1898 no. 129.
129. *housing conditions of the working class,* app. xxiv.
130. ibid. para. 466.
131. *Report artisans dwellings comm.* 1900 no. 179.
132. *I.T.* 7 Oct. 1902.
133. *Report public health comm.* 1902 no. 183.
134. ibid.
135. Mun. Co. *Minutes,* 13 Mar. 1911.
136. *Report of the Dublin disturbances commission* 1914 cd. 7269, evidence cd. 7272, xviii.
137. *housing conditions of the working class* para. 466. p.25.
138. ibid.
139. CSO/RP 1912/2071.
140. *Returns to 31 March 1906 under housing of the working class schemes* 1906 (337) xcvii, 843.
141. Colm Lincoln, *Working class housing in Dublin 1914-30,* M.A. Thesis, U.C.D. 1979.
142. *I.T.* 19 Dec. 1906.
143. Mun. Co. *Minutes,* 19 Dec. 1904.
144. *Report artisans dwellings comm.* 1903 no. 178.
145. Mun. Co. *Minutes* 6 Feb. 1905.
146. *Report artisans dwellings comm.* 1909 no. 22.
147. *housing conditions of the working class* app. xii.
148. *I.T.* 4 June 1903.
149. These resulted in the establishment of the Irish Dept. of Agriculture and Technical Instruction in 1899 and in the achievement of a comprehensive land purchase agreement in 1903.
150. *Report of conference on housing of the working class,* 1903 no. 176.
151. *I.T.* 4 Mar. 1908.
152. *I.T.* 21 Mar. 1908.
153. *I.T.* 5 Mar. 1908.
154. 8 Edw. ch. 81, An act to provide further facilities for the erection of houses for the working classes in cities and towns in Ireland.
155. *I.T.* 8 Jan. 1909, address of J.J. Clancy to United Irish League.
156. *I.T.* 22 May 1911.
157. *I.T.* 29 May, 30 May 1911.

158. *I.T.* 12 April 1911.
159. CSO/RP 1913/18626.
160. *I.T.* 4 Sept. 1913.
161. E.A. Aston, 'a note upon the financial aspects of urban housing schemes with special reference to the city of Dublin', *Official report municipal authorities, conference,* 1913, p. 67.
162. ibid. p. 67.
163. *Report* ibid. p. 7.
164. CSO/RP 1913/18626, 17 Oct. 1913.
165. ibid.
166. CSO/RP 1913/21008.
167. CSO/RP 1913/20339.
168. CSO/RP 1913/21470, 17 Nov. 1913.
169. CSO/RP 1913/18626.
170. ibid.
171. ibid. memo. 31 Oct. 1913.
172. ibid. 4 Nov. 1913.
173. *housing conditions of the working class,* para. 51.
174. ibid., evidence p. 453.
175. ibid, p. 7.
176. CSO/RP 1913/21470, 17 Nov. 1913.
177. *housing conditions of the working class,* p. 14, para. 38.
178. ibid., para. 51.
179. *I.T.* 17 April 1914.
180. *I.T.* 14 Jan. 1914.
181. *I.T.* 2 Dec. 1913, quoted.
182. *Hansard,* Lords, 5th Ser. 16 April vo 1914, vol. lxi, col. 379.
183. *housing conditions of the working class,* evidence p. 2.
184. Wohl. op. cit. app. iv.
185. C.M. Allen, 'The genesis of British urban redevelopment with special reference to Glasgow', Ec.H.R. xviii, (1965) espec. p. 613.
186. Stedman-Jones, op. cit. p.

Conclusion

1. *Report of the Recess Committee on the establishment of a Dept. of Agriculture and Industries for Ireland* (Dublin 1896), p.10.
2. *Report of inquiry into the housing of the working classes of the city of Dublin 1939-43* R./75/1. (Dublin 1943) para. 9.
3. Augustine Birrell, *Things past redress* (London 1937) p.219.

BIBLIOGRAPHY

Public record office of Ireland.
Census enumerators' books, Dublin 1911.
South Dublin Union, admission books, 1875, 1880, 1904.
Sick and Indigent Roomkeepers Society records, 1028/4/1-3 reports 1856-1888 and 1907 plus correspondence and a diary of a member.
Dublin Chamber of Commerce, minutes and reports, 1855-1915.

State paper office of Ireland
Chief Secretary's office, Registered Papers, countless files dealing with a wide range of matters, for individual numbers see footnotes.

City Hall
Mansion House Relief Committee, M.H. Ch. 1/12, letters and papers relating to Dublin.
Dublin municipal council, minutes and committee reports, 1855-1915.
Rathmines township minutes and reports, 1847-1898.
Rathmines urban district council minutes and reports, 1899-1915.
Pembroke township minutes and reports, 1863-1898.
Pembroke urban district council 1899-1915.

Registrar General, births, marriages and deaths, Custom House
Marriage registers, North and South Dublin Unions, 1871-1911.

Dublin port and docks board.
Minutes 1859-1915.

Records Dept. Heuston Station.
Great Southern and Western Railway Co. minutes board of directors, plus minutes Inchicore Committee and Traffic and Works Committee.

Records Dept. Guinness's Brewery.
Report on the average annual mortality and expectation of life: brewery labourers and pensioners 1896-1907.
Maps and plans of Guinness's brewery, 1840-1914.

Pembroke estate office
List of leases, giving year granted, to whom, size of plot and number of houses contained on same.
Copies of standard estate leases.

National Library of Ireland.
Larcom Ms. newspaper cuttings. 1860-78.
Walshe Ms. Cuttings, notes and pamphlets collected by Richard D. Walshe.
Walpole Ms. records of the firm of Walpole, linen merchants, Ms. 2124-29.
Patrick Cunningham Autobiography.
Ms. 191. Minutes of official inquiry, held by Thomas Henry, William Palham, Assistant Secretaries, Board of Trade, under the Merchant Shipping Act 1894 into Dublin harbour dues.

Newspapers
Irish Times
Freeman's Journal
Evening Telegraph
Daily Express
Saunder's Newsletter
Dublin Builder 1860-1869
Irish Builder 1869-1916
The Builder
The Medical Press and Circular
Sinn Fein daily
Sinn Fein Weekly
Irish Daily Independent
Dublin Gazette
Irish Catholic

Parliamentary Papers
Public and private statutes relating to Dublin and suburbs.
Municipal corporations (Ireland) App. to the first report of the commissioners. Report on the city of Dublin, part I, 1835, xxvii.
Poor inquiry (Ireland). Supplement to App. C. (Part II). First report commissioners. City of Dublin questionnaire. 1836 (35).
Second report of the commissioners appointed to consider and recommend a general system of railways for Ireland 1837-8, xxxv,
Report of commissioners appointed to inquire into the Dublin turnpikes 1854-5, xix, (0.1), 697.
Number of cotton, woollen etc. factories subject to the Factories Acts in each county 1862 (23), lv, 629.
Report commissioners appointed to inquire into various matters connected with the railways of Great Britain and Ireland 1867 (844-I), xxvii, Pt. I.
Second report of commissioners appointed to inquire into friendly and benefit building societies, Part I report of commissioners 1872 (c.514) xxvi, 1.
part II evidence, 1872 (c.514-I) xxvi, 101.
Reports of the commissioners appointed to inquire into the conditions of the civil service in Ireland. Report on the local government board and general registry office and minutes. 1873 (c.789), xxii,
ibid. *Report Dublin Metropolitan Police*, 1873 (c.788) xxii, Part II,
Return relating to valuation of tenements in the city of Dublin 1875 (425), lx, 495.
Report of the commissioners appointed to inquire into the working of the factory and workshop acts 1876 (c.1443-I) xxx, 1.
Reports select committee local government and taxation of cities and towns in Ireland 1876 (352), x, 147.
1877 (357) xii, 309.
1878 (262) xvi, 1.

Return number of reports sent in from each sanitary officer of the municipal district under the control of the public health committee of Dublin for each month from 22 Nov. 1874 to 1 May 1876 the number of houses condemned 1876 (317) lxiii, 497.

Copy of report of inquiry by the Board of Trade relative to the present condition and high rate of charges on the Dublin Wicklow and Wexford railway 1878 (147) lxvi, 511.

Memorial presented to the Lord Lieutenant by the Dublin sanitary association 1878 (148) lxv, 157.

Report of the commissioners of inquiry into the collection of rates in the city of Dublin 1878 (c.2062) xxiii, 1.

Report of the royal commission on sewerage and drainage of the city of Dublin 1880 (c.2605) xxx, 1.

Report of the select committee appointed to inquire into the charges of railway companies 1881 (374) xiii, xiv.

Report of royal commission appointed to inquire into the boundaries and municipal areas of certain cities and towns in Ireland. 1881 (c.2827), I, 1.

Report of the select committee on railway rates 1882 (317) xiii.1.

Report from the select committee on industries (Ireland) 1884-5 (288), ix, (sess. 1).

Royal commission on the housing of the working class. Third report Ireland 1884-5 (c.4547-I), xxxi.

Report of select committee on town holdings 1886 (213-Sess. 1) xii, 367.

Return of wages published between 1830 and 1886 1887 (c.5172) lxxxix, 273.

General report on the wages of the manual labour class in the United Kingdom 1893-4 (c.6886) lxxxiii-II, 1.

ibid., part III. standard time rates 1894 (c.7567) lxxxi-II, 1.

Report by commissioners appointed to inquire into the financial relations between Great Britain and Ireland. 1896 (c.8202) xxxiii, 59.

Report from the select committee on the industries (Ireland) bill 1897 (202), x, 641.

Report select committee on the Dublin corporation bill and the Clontarf U.D.C. bill. 1900 (301), vi, 895.

Report of the departmental committee appointed by the local government board to inquire into the public health of the city of Dublin 1900 (cd. 243) xxxix, 681.

Reports of commissioners on the sanitary condition and administration in cities and towns 1902 (cd. 1260) xxxvii, 429.

Report of the inter-departmental committee on the employment of children of school-age, especially in street-trading in the large centres of population in Ireland. 1902 (cd. 1144) xlix, 209.

Report on the viceregal commission on poor law reform in Ireland 1906 (cd. 3202) li, 1.

Returns to 31 March 1906 under housing of the working class schemes 1906 (337) xcvii, 843.

Vice-regal commission on Irish railways, Second report 1908 (cd. 3896) xlvii, 331.

third report (cd. 4054) xlviii, 1.

fourth report 1909 (cd. 4481) xxvi, 1.

final report 1910 (cd. 5247) xxvii.

Report of royal commission on whiskey and other portable spirits. First report 1908 (cd. 4181) xlix,

Final report 1909 (cd. 4181) lviii.

Royal commission on the poor law. Report on Ireland 1909 (cd. 4630) xxxviii, *ibid. App. vol. xix B.* Report on the effects of employment or assistance given to the unemployed since 1886 by Mr. Cyril Jackson, *1909 (cd. 4890), xliv.*

ibid., app. vol. x, *Minutes of evidence on Ireland.* T.J. Stafford 'Notes on the social conditions of certain working class families in Dublin', 1910 (cd. 5070), I, 350.

ibid. vol. xxxi, *Statistical memoranda and tables relating to Ireland* 1910 (cd. 5244) xliv.

Census of production 1907, Final report 1912 (cd. 6320).

Statistical abstract for the United Kingdom 1897-1911 1912 (cd. 6399)

Report of an enquiry by the Board of Trade into working class rents, housing, retail prices and standard rates of wages 1913 (cd. 6955) lxvi, 393.

Report of the Dublin disturbance committee 1914 (cd. 7269), evidence (cd. 7272), xviii, 513.

Report of the departmental committee appointed to inquire into the housing conditions of the working class in Dublin 1914 (cd. 7317) xix, 61. evidence (cd. 7273) xix, 107.

Report by commissioners of conciliation on Dublin strikes 1914-16 (cd. 7658) xxxvi.

Census Ireland 1821-1911.

Reports factory inspectors 1872-1899.

Reports local government board 1872-1915.

Reports on changes in rates of wages and hours of labour in the U.K. 1894-1905.

Abstracts of labour statistics in the U.K. 1906-1909.

Earnings and hours inquiry, Board of Trade, 1910-16.

Decennial summaries births marriages and deaths, 1871-1910.

Saorstat Eireann

Report of committee on the relief of the sick and destitute poor 1927 R. 27/3.

Report of registrar-general for the year 1940 T 3/20.

Report of inquiry into the housing of the working classes of the city of Dublin, R. 75/1. 1939-43.

Parliamentary debates

Hansard fourth and fifth series.

Other contemporary printed books, pamphlets and articles

Ishbel Aberdeen, *Ireland's crusade against T.B.* (Dublin 1908).

Address and resolution of sympathy with His Holiness Pope Pius IX (Dublin 1860).

A Ratepayer, *Blackrock township, is it fair?* (Dublin 1863).

E.A. Aston, 'A note upon the financial aspects of urban housing schemes with special reference to the city of Dublin'. *Official report municipal authorities conference, 1913,* (Dublin 1914).

Alfred Barnard, *The whiskey distilleries of the United Kingdom.* (London 1887).

Alfred Barnard, *Noted breweries of Great Britain and Ireland,* 3 vols. (London 1889).

J.F. Bateman, 'The port of Dublin, supplement', *Irish Times* 7 Aug. 1867.

J.W. Bazalgette, *Report on the Dublin sewage utilization bill* (Dublin 1868).

The blind alley: some aspects of juvenile employment in Ireland. Catholic working boys technical aid committee (Dublin 1916).

Boileau and Boyd: *Two hundred years. Bicentenary souvenir* (Dublin 1900).

Cheyne Brady, *The practicability of improving the dwellings of the labouring classes* (London 1854) paper read to R.D.S.

Thomas Brazill, *Report to the corporation of Dublin on the proposed supply of the city and suburbs with pure water at high pressure* (Dublin 1854).

Charles Cameron, *How the poor live* (Dublin 1908).

ibid., *A brief history of municipal public health administration in Dublin* (Dublin 1914).

David A. Chart, 'Unskilled labour in Dublin: its housing and living conditions' *Stat. soc. Irel. jnl.* 13, 1914.

ibid., *The story of Dublin* (London 1907).

Church of Ireland social service union, *Social services handbook.* (Dublin 1901).

James Connolly, *Workers republic* ed., Desmond Ryan, (Dublin 1951).

E. McDowel Cosgrave, *Dublin and Co. Dublin in the twentieth century*, contemporary biographies, ed. W.T. Pike, (Brighton 1908).

E.D. Daly, 'Neglected children and neglectful parents, *Stat. Assoc. Irl. jnl.* 10, 1898.

Rev. P. Daly, 'The problem of the poor' *Record of the Maynooth Union 1908-9.*

Dublin sanitary association, *reports*, 1873-1914.

Dublin united tramway company, *Timetables.*

Sir F.R. Falkiner, 'Hospitals', in G.D. Williams (ed) *Dublin charities*, association of charities (Dublin 1902).

T.E. Fitzpatrick, *The existing manufactures of Ireland with suggestions for their development* (Dublin 1886).

Surgeon Col. D. Edgar Flinn, *Official report on the sanitary circumstances and administration of the city of Dublin with special referenc to the causes of the high death-rate* (Dublin 1906, Thom for HMSO).

Sir John Gilbert (ed), *Calendar of the ancient records of the city of Dublin*, xix.

Sir John Gray, *Speech in vindication of the municipal council of Dublin* (Dublin 1864).

Thomas W. Grimshaw, *Remarks on the prevalence and distribution of fever in Dublin* (Dublin 1872).

W.N. Hancock, *Is the competition between large and small shops injurious to the community* (Dublin 1851).

ibid., *Is distinct trading or the monster house most conducive to public interests* (Dublin 1859).

Spencer Harty, 'Some consideration of the artisans dwelling acts as illustrated in the case of the Coombe, *Stat. soc. Irl. jnl*, 8, 1884.

J.B. Hughes, 'Poverty in Dublin', *Irish messenger social action series*, no. 13 (Dublin 1914).

Hull Advertiser, *Brief notes of a short excursion to Ireland* (1853)

Industries of Ireland: historical, statistical, biographical an account of the leading business men commercial interests, wealth and growth (London 1888).

John Jameson and Sons, William Jameson and Co., John Power and Sons and George Roe and Co., *Truths about whiskey* (Dublin 1878)

Ann Jellicoe, 'Condition of young women employed in manufactories in Dublin', *Transactions of national association for the promotion of social science*, reprints (London 1862).

Richard M. Kelly, 'The administration of sanitary law', *Medical press and circular*, 27 Feb. 1901.

List of subscriptions: Papal tribute from Diocese of Dublin (1860).

L. McKenna, *Handbook for Catholic social workers in Dublin* (Dublin 1918).

Anthony Marmion, *The ancient and modern history of the maritime ports of Ireland* (London 1860).

E.D. Mapother, 'The sanitary state of Dublin' in *Papers concerning public health* (Dublin 1864).

ibid., *Report on the health of the city of Dublin for the year 1865* (Dublin 1866).
ibid., and P. Neville, *Report on the unhealthy districts of the borough of Dublin* (12 June 1876).
S. Shannon Millin, 'Slums: a sociological retrospect of Dublin' *Stat. soc, Irl, jnl.* 13, 1914.
Conference of municipal authorities 1913, (Dublin 1914).
Report national society for the prevention of cruelty to children, 1889-90, 1914-15 inclusive.
Parke Neville, *Report to the Lord Mayor etc. of the city of Dublin on the sewerage of the city and proposed plans for improving the same* (Dublin 1853).
ibid., *Report on the capabilities of the Dodder to afford a supply of water for the use of city and suburbs* (Dublin 1854).
ibid., *A description of the Dublin corporation waterworks* (Dublin 1875).
John Robert O Connell *The problem of the Dublin slums.* (Dublin 1913), first published in *The Rosary*, October 1911.
Official Irish travelling guide 1878-1914. (London).
Philanthropic reform association, reports 1896-1914.
Joseph Todhunter Pim, 'Municipal government and taxation', paper read at *Statistical Society*, 19 Jan. 1875.
ibid., 'The port of Dublin', *Stat. soc. Irl. jnl.* 1889.
Publius, *Letters on Dublin corporation,* originally published in *Daily Express* 1860.
Maud Pember Reeves, *Round about a pound a week* (1980 ed. London).
Report of debate by Dublin corporation re granting of a charter for the Catholic university (Dublin 1862).
Report of the special committte of Dublin corporation re the compact in the corporation as to the election of a Lord Mayor. (Dublin 1864).
Report on conference on the housing of the working class (Dublin 1903).
B. Seebohm Rowntree, *Poverty: a study of town life* (3rd ed. London 1902).
Fifty-fifth annual report St. Brigid's orphanage (Dublin 1912).
H. Llewellyn Smith, 'The influx of population', in Charles Booth, *Life and labour of the people of London*, iii, (London, 1902).
Reports of the society of St. Vincent de Paul, 1893-1915.
Edward Spencer, *Artisans' and labourers' dwellings* (Dublin 1881).
ibid., 'Homes for the working class in Dublin', report *Irish Times*, 2 Oct. 1884.
Laura Stephens, 'Workhouses', in Church of Ireland social services union, *Social services handbook* (Dublin 1901).
B.B. Storey, *On recent improvements in the port of Dublin* (Dublin 1878).
T.D. Sullivan, *Troubled times in Irish politics* (Dublin 1905).
W.H. Thompson, *War and the food of the Dublin poor* (Dublin 1916).
Unionist convention for the provinces of Leinster, Munster and Connaught, *Report of proceedings June 1892* (Dublin 1892).
J. Warburton, J. Whitelaw, R. Walsh, *History of the city of Dublin* 2 vols. (London 1818).

Later books
Ishbel Aberdeen, *We Twa*, 2 vols. (London 1927).
Michael Anderson, *Family Structure in nineteenth century Lancashire* (Cambridge 1971).
C.S. Andrews, *Dublin made me* (Dublin 1979).
Geoffrey Best, *Mid-Victorian Britain* (1973 ed. London).
Evelyn Bolster, *The Knights of St. Columbanus* (Dublin 1979).
A.L. Bowley, *Wages in the United Kingdom in the nineteenth century* (Cambridge

1900).

Asa Briggs, *History of Birmingham*, 2 vols. (Oxford 1952).

ibid., *Victorian cities* (London 1968 ed).

Sir Charles Cameron, *Autobiography* (Dublin 1920).

David Cannadine, *Lords and landlords: the aristocracy and the towns, 1774-1967* (Leicester 1980).

J.C. Conroy, *A history of the railways in Ireland* (Dublin 1928).

T.A.B. Corley, *Quaker enterprise in biscuits. Huntley and Palmers of Reading, 1822-1972* (London 1972).

David F. Crew, Town in the Ruhr. *A social history of Bochum 1860-1914* (New York 1979).

Geoffrey Crossick, *An artisan elite in Victorian society, Kentish town, 1840-80* (London 1978).

Ian D'Alton, *Protestant society and politics in Cork 1812-1844* (Cork 1981).

M.J. Daunton, *Coal metropolis, Cardiff 1870-1914* (Leicester 1977).

Page L. Dickinson, *The Dublin of yesterday* (London 1926).

H.J. Dyos and Michael Wolff, *The Victorian city*, 2 vols . (London 1972).

S.E. Finer, *The life and times of Sir Edwin Chadwick* (London 1952).

R.Q. Gray, *The labour aristocracy in Victorian Edinburgh* (Oxford 1976).

David Harkness and Mary O Dowd (eds), *The town in Ireland* (Belfast 1981).

Jose Harris, *Unemployment and politics: a study in English social policy, 1886-1914* (Oxford 1972).

E.P. Hennock, *Fit and proper persons* (London 1973).

J.R. Kellett, *The impact of the railways on Victorian cities* (London 1969).

G.R. Kitson-Clark, *An expanding society, Britain 1830-1900* (Cambridge 1967).

F.W.R. Knowles, *Old Clontarf* (no date, no place).

Royston Lambert, *Sir John Simon 1816-1904 and English social administration* (London 1963).

Patrick Lynch and John Vaizey, *Guinness's brewery in the Irish economy, 1759-1886* (Cambridge 1967).

Walter McDonald, *Some ethical aspects of the social question, suggestions for priests* (London 1920).

R.B. McDowell, *The Church of Ireland, 1869-1969* (London 1975).

E.B. McGuire, *Irish whiskey: a history of distilling in Ireland* (Dublin 1973).

D.B. McNeill, *Irish passenger steamship services*, 2 vols. (Newtown Abbot 1969).

R.C.O. Matthews, *The trade cycle* (Cambridge 1959).

E.R. Norman, *The catholic church and Ireland in the age of rebellion* (London 1965).

W.J. Reader, *Professional men* (London 1966).

E.J. Riordan, *Modern Irish trade and industry* (Dublin 1920).

F.B. Smith, *The people's health 1831-1910* (London 1979).

Gareth Stedman-Jones, *Outcast London* (Oxford 1971).

Anthony Sutcliffe (ed) *Multi-storey living: the British working class experience* (London 1974).

John Swift, *History of the Dublin bakers and others* (Dublin 1948).

W.A. Thomas, *The provincial stock exchanges* (London 1973).

David Thornley, *Isaac Butt and Home Rule* (London 1964).

J.J. Webb, *Industrial Dublin since 1698 and the silk industry in Dublin* (Dublin 1913).

Brian D. White, *A history of the corporation of Liverpool, 1835-1914* (Liverpool 1951).

Charles Wilson, *The history of Unilever*, I, (London 1954).

Anthony S. Wohl, *The eternal slum* (London 1977).

Articles

C.M. Allen, 'The genesis of British urban redevelopment with special reference to Glasgow' *Economic history review*, xviii, 1965.

W.A. Armstrong, 'The use of information about occupation: I as a basis for social stratification' in E.A. Wrigley (ed) *Nineteenth century society* (Cambridge 1972).

ibid., 'The use of information about occupations: II as a basis for industrial classification', in Wrigley, op. cit.

T. Barrington, 'A review of Irish agricultural prices', *Stat. soc. Irl. jnl.* xv, 1926.

G. Best, 'Another part of the island', in Dyos and Wolff (eds). *Victorian city*, i.

Mary E. Daly, 'Late nineteenth and early twentieth century Dublin', in David Harkness and Mary O Dowd (eds), *The town in Ireland*.

David Dickson, 'Dublin in the eighteenth century Irish economy', unpublished paper read to the Scottish Irish conference on economic and social history September 1981.

A.C. Davies, 'The first Irish industrial exhibition, Cork 1852', *Irish economic and social history*, ii (1975).

James Donnelly, 'The Irish agricultural depression of 1859-64', *Irish economic history*, iii, (1976).

H.J. Dyos, 'The slums of Victorian London', *Victorian Studies*, xi, Sept. 1967.

David Fitzpatrick, 'Irish emigration in the later nineteenth century', *I.H.S.* xxii, Sept. 1980.

Jacqueline Hill, 'The protestant response to repeal, the case of the Dublin working class', in F.S. Lyons and Richard Hawkins (eds.), *Ireland under the union, varieties of tension* (Oxford 1980).

E. Jones, 'Late Victorian Belfast', in J.C. Beckett and R.E. Glasscock, (eds.) *Belfast: the origin and growth of an industrial city* (London 1967).

Eric Lampard, 'The urbanising world', in Dyos and Wolff (eds.) *The Victorian city*, i.

E. Larkin, 'Socialism and Catholicism in Ireland', *Church history* 1964.

Joseph Leckey, 'The recruitment of clerks to the Great Southern and Western Railway Co.', paper read to *Irish historical society* Feb. 1980.

J.J. Lee, 'merchants and enterprise: the case of the early Irish railways', in L.M. Cullen and P. Butel (eds.), *Negoce et industries en France et en Irlande aux xviii et xix siecles* (Paris 1979).

F.O.C. Meenan, 'The Georgian squares of Dublin and the professions' *Studies*, winter 1969.

Kevin Murray, 'Dublin's first railway', *Dublin historical record*, I

ibid., 'The loop line', *Jnl. Irish railway records society*, no. 2.

Maura Murphy, 'The economic and social structure of nineteenth century Cork', in D. Harkness and M. O Dowd (eds.), *The town in Ireland*.

ibid., 'Fenianism, Parnellism and the Cork trades, 1860-1900' *Saothar* 5, 1979.

Cormac O Grada, 'A note on nineteenth century Irish emigration statistics', *Population studies*, Mar. 1975.

Cornelius O Leary, 'Belfast urban government in the age of reform', in D. Harkness and M. O Dowd, (eds.), *The Irish City*.

George Rosen, 'Disease debility and death', in Dyos and Wolff (eds.), *The Victorian City*, ii.

Peter M. Solar, 'The agricultural trade statistics in the Irish railway commissioners' report', *Irish economic and social history*, vi, 1979.

Brinley Thomas, 'Demographic determinants of British and American building cycles, 1870-1914', in D. McCloskey (ed.), *Essays on a mature economy: Britain after 1870* (London 1971).

David Thornley 'Irish conservatism and Home Rule', *I.H.S.* 1958-9.

R.B. Weir, 'The patent still distillers and the role of competition in nineteenth century Irish economic history', in L.M. Cullen and T.C. Smout (eds.), *Comparative aspects of Scottish and Irish economic and social history 1600-1900* (Edinburgh 197?).

Unpublished theses
J.W. Boyle, *The rise of the Irish labour movement, 1883-1907* Ph.D. Dublin university 1961.
Fergus D'Arcy, *Dublin artisan activity, opinion and organisation, 1820-1860,* M.A. University college Dublin 1968.
Daire Hogan, *The legal profession in Ireland in the nineteenth century*, M.A. University college Dublin 1981.
Colm Lincoln, *Working class housing in Dublin 1914-30*, M.A. University college Dublin 1979.
Brendan McDonnell, *The Dublin labour movement 1894-1907*, Ph.D. University college Dublin 1979.
John H. Martin, *Aspects of the social geography of Dublin city in the mid nineteenth century* M.A. University college Dublin 1973.

INDEX

369